VALUE: A COOPERATIVE INQUIRY

VALUE

A COOPERATIVE INQUIRY

EDITED BY RAY LEPLEY

GREENWOOD PRESS, PUBLISHERS
WESTPORT, CONNECTICUT

❧ PREFACE

THE INCEPTION AND PROCEDURE of the present study are sketched briefly in the Introduction. It may be helpful to indicate here what the reader may properly expect to find in this book. Those familiar with the history of thought in general, and with the wide divergence of views regarding value in particular, will not be surprised to learn that the present cooperative study has not produced unanimity among the various participants—even with regard to proper methods of approach or the most elementary and basic concepts. At one stage of the inquiry it was hoped that agreement might be reached upon a common glossary of fundamental value terms. An attempt to formulate such a glossary resulted in a list of different definitions of each of several words, for example, "value," "valuing," "evaluation," "fact," "standard," "immediate value," "potential value." There were in some cases almost as many definitions of a term as there were parties to the inquiry. In consequence it was decided that each member should develop the approach and make the formulations which seem to him most justified in view of his own total perspective as affected by critical appraisals and suggestions from other participants. The aim therefore has been not so much to achieve agreement or finality as to secure and afford stimulation for the further study of value problems through an organized community of inquiry.

The propriety of the term "inquiry" as applied to this study and to the volume which has resulted from it is open to question. At many points it may appear—and in some cases perhaps correctly—that the several contributors are more interested in defending previous or merely personal conclusions than in conducting honest, open-minded, and persistent search for truth. The assertive and at times disputatious character of the writing results in part, at least, from limitations of space; also, these papers are only the end-product of many months of co-operative activity. In the first draft of the manuscript of the book all the various questions and comments formulated by the members at the outset of the study were included. These would perhaps have made more evident than does the volume as it now stands the wide range of problems and data considered and the rather empirical nature of the procedure; these materials, however, like the projected glossary and a proposed bibliography, were omitted in the final revision. But though it is true that much of the present study may not be apparent in the book itself, the contributors will, I am sure, be the first to insist that both the book and the activities which led up to it merit the term "inquiry"—when they do—only to a limited degree. This study differs from ordinary symposia—where it does—in the emphasis placed upon exchange and reconsideration in the light of criticism and upon the continuance of these processes well beyond what would have been required to contribute a group of essays for a single volume.

The reader should not, then, expect this book to report all the steps of an investigation which eventuated in one set of conclusions accepted by all or most of the participants. He may properly expect to find examples of (1) a number of different approaches and methodologies used in the study of a common set of value questions, (2) conclusions reached through use of these various methodologies, and (3) critical evaluations of these several positions by persons who hold other points of view. In short, the book—in addition to any positive contributions it may make to the solution or clarification of value problems—affords various materials which invite still further inquiry.

We gratefully acknowledge financial assistance in aid of publication from Bradley University, Harvard University, and Tulane University. We desire also to express gratitude to the editors of the *Journal of Philosophy* for permission to reprint in the Introduction the entire article which occasioned this study, and to thank other publishers or holders of copyrights for permission to quote less extensive passages as acknowledged specifically in footnotes. I feel deep personal indebtedness to the other participants in the inquiry, who have made many helpful suggestions and generously expressed appreciation for stimulation received through our cooperative endeavors. I wish also to extend thanks to my colleague Dr. David M. White for aid in correcting mechanical errors or inconsistencies at various points throughout the revised manuscript and many of the galleys, and to Mrs. Ada Morlock Emme for assistance in removing similar conditions in the galleys and page proof.

RAY LEPLEY

Peoria, Illinois
April, 1949

❦ CONTENTS

CONTENTS   ix

CRITICISMS BY MORRIS; REJOINDERS BY AYRES
AND HAHN   415

CRITICISMS BY PARKER; REJOINDERS BY JESSUP AND
MORRIS   424

CRITICISMS BY PEPPER; REJOINDER BY PARKER   440

CRITICISMS BY RICE; REJOINDERS BY GARNETT AND
HAHN   456

INDEX   471

CONTENTS   ix

VALUE: A COOPERATIVE INQUIRY

❧ INTRODUCTION

RAY LEPLEY

As THE PROBLEM OF VALUE becomes increasingly central for world community of understanding and action, it becomes increasingly central for philosophy. The present volume is the product of a co-operative study of some of the underlying issues regarding value.

The immediate stimulus to the study was an article by John Dewey that appeared in the *Journal of Philosophy* in 1944.* Here Dewey sums up four groups of questions which he feels are basic for value theory, discusses some possible answers, and challenges other interested persons to state the questions and views which they regard as fundamental.

When by the autumn of 1945 no one had responded to this challenge, it was suggested to Dewey that a cooperative study, or symposium, on value might be organized and might take his article as a starting point. He responded cordially to this proposal, and mentioned some persons he would like especially to share in the inquiry. These persons in turn suggested a number of others, and they still more. Fourteen of those most frequently nominated were then invited to participate, and to submit what they regard as at present the main issues concerning value. These questions and the comments which accompanied them were mimeographed and sent to all the participants. It was agreed that each member should make an initial draft of a paper, indicating his own answers to Dewey's questions or considering the basic issue or issues presented by them, and that the papers should be exchanged for criticism and then revised for possible publication. After the exchange and some revision of the papers it was decided that further criticisms and rejoinders should be included at the close of the volume, and that each contributor might, if he chose, limit his criticisms to one or two papers assigned to him by the editor in accordance (so far as possible) with the preferences of the several members as to which papers they should discuss.

* "Some Questions about Value," *The Journal of Philosophy*, XLI (1944), 449–455.

The revised Essays (in Part I) and the Criticisms (in Part II) are arranged alphabetically by author. Various other principles of organization were considered, but in application each was found to require arbitrary decisions which could be justified, if at all, only on the basis of some particular bias or limited perspective. The alphabetical order was finally accepted as most just to the contributors and most convenient for the reader. This order may also help to make clear the fact that the volume does not present separate phases of the value problem as discussed by persons who are specialists in those several phases, nor does it develop a single point of view leading up to a climax at the close; instead, it is the product of a somewhat representative group of students of the general theory of value who have sought—each in his own way but with regard to mutual criticisms—to consider a common set of basic issues.

The contributors exercised wide freedom in the amount of attention given to the several questions and in the organization of their papers. Accordingly, some of the essays concentrate mainly on one or two of the groups of questions in Dewey's article; others give about equal attention to each group. Some follow the order in which the questions appeared; others do not. In view of these differences, special care is taken to cite in the Index the pages upon which particular questions are discussed by each contributor.

Despite the variety of organization and emphasis in the several essays, the reader will note certain general similarities of approach, as well as numerous agreements in the conclusions reached on specific issues. It is hoped that in so far as the agreements have resulted from concert of attack on common problems, from exchange and revision of papers, or from subsequent criticism and rejoinder, they may mark significant advances in value theory; and that even the differences which have thus risen may have sharpened issues in such a way as to stimulate further inquiry.

As presentation of the central problems considered in the present study and as introduction to the chapters which follow, Dewey's article is reprinted at this point.

Some Questions about Value

When I analyze the discouragement I have experienced lately in connection with discussion of value, I find that it proceeds from the feeling that little headway is being made in determining the questions or issues fundamentally involved rather than from the fact that the views I personally hold have not received general approval. The clear-cut quality of the recent paper by Dr. Geiger [1] moves me to try to do something by way of clarifying underlying issues, with only that degree of attention to answers and solutions as may serve to make the nature of the questions stand out. I do not suppose that any formulation of questions which I can make will be uninfluenced by the answers I would give them. But if others will state the issues that seem to *them* to be basic, perhaps discussion of solutions will be more fruitful in the way of approach to agreement than has been the case.[2]

I begin with a preliminary rough listing.

I. What connection is there, if any, between an attitude that will be called prizing or holding dear and desiring, liking, interest, enjoying, etc.?

II. Irrespective of which of the above-named attitudes is taken to be primary, is it by itself a *sufficient* condition for the existence of values? Or, while it is a necessary condition, is a further condition, of the nature of *valuation* or *appraisal*, required?

III. Whatever the answer to the second question, is there anything in the nature of appraisal, evaluation, as judgment or/and proposition, that marks them off, with respect to their logical or their scientific status, from other propositions or judgments? Or are such distinctive properties as they possess wholly an affair of their subject-matter—as we might speak of astronomical and geological propositions without implying that there is any difference between them *qua* propositions?

IV. Is the scientific method of inquiry, in its broad sense,[3] applicable in determination of judgments and/or propositions in the way of valuations or appraisals? Or is there something inherent in the nature of values as subject-matter that precludes the application of such method?

[1] Can We Choose between Values?" this *Journal*, Vol. XLI, pp. 292–298.
[2] I should add that no attempt is made to list all the questions upon which division in conclusions rests. The view that gives value a *transcendent* character has been omitted, so what is said will not appeal to those who hold that view.
[3] The phrase "in its broad sense" is inserted to make it clear that "scientific" is not assumed in advance to signify reduction to physical or biological terms, but, as is the case with scientific investigations of concrete matters generally, leaves the scope of the subject-matter to be determined in the course of inquiry.

I

It can not be assumed that the meaning of the words "prizing" and "desiring" (or of any of the words of the first question) is evident on their face. To attempt to define them all is impossible and unnecessary. The word "prizing" is here used to stand for a *behavioral* transaction. If its force is reduced from overt action to an *attitude,* then the attitude or disposition in question must be understood to be taken toward things or persons, and as having no shadow of meaning if it be isolated from that which it is *towards.* Equivalent names would be nourishing, caring for, looking out after, fostering, making much of, being loyal or faithful to, clinging to, provided these words are taken in an active behavioral sense. If this meaning belongs to "prizing," then the first question concerns the connection (or lack of connection) which holds between the way of behaving that is specified and such states, acts, or processes, as "desiring," "liking," "interest," "enjoying," *no matter how the latter are defined.*

That is to say, *if* the latter words are given a behavioral description, the problem is that of the connections sustained to one another by various attitudes or dispositions which are homogeneous in dimension, since all are behavioral. It might, for example, be held that, since what is called *prizing, holding dear,* is a way of behaving tending to maintain something in factual (space-time) existence, *interest* stands for an enduring, or long-time-span, disposition of this nature, one which holds together in system a variety of acts otherwise having diverse directions. *Desire* might then be the behavioral attitude that arises when prizings are temporarily blocked or frustrated, while *enjoying* would be the name for the consummatory phase of prizing.[4] If, however, *desire, interest,* etc., are given a non-behavioral meaning, then it seems that they must stand for something "internal," "mentalistic," etc. In this case, the issue at stake would be a choice between a view which holds that *valuing* is basically a mode of behavior that serves to keep in being a thing that exists independently of being valued, and the view that some kind of a mental state or process suffices to generate value as an uniquely complete product.

[4] The word "might" is used in the text to indicate that the particular descriptions given are intended to serve as sample illustrations of homogeneous behavioral interpretation, not as finalities.

Upon the first-mentioned view, "prizing" (as here understood) has definite biological roots, such as, for example, are manifest in the behavior of a mother-bird in nourishing its young or of a mother-bear in attacking animals that threaten her young. The intensity of the "prizing" involved is then measured by the amount of energy that goes into the nourishing or the protecting behavior. Upon this view there is always an event or thing having existence independently of being prized (or valued) to which the quality or property of "value" is added under specified conditions of space-time. From the view that the desire, liking, interest, or whatever, that generates value is solely "internal" or "mental," it seems to follow that if the value in question is then attached to an event or object (something in space-time), it is because of an external more or less accidental association. For if desire or liking is an "internal" state complete in itself, then the fact that it hits upon or bears upon, say, a diamond, or a young woman, or holding an official position, is assuredly so external as to be relatively a matter of accident.

II

Another issue that seems to be basic in current literature concerns the question of the connection or lack of connection between *valuing* and *valuation* in the sense of *evaluating*. Do values come into existence (no matter how they are understood and accounted for) apart from and prior to anything whatever in the way of an evaluating condition? In case they do so arise, what is the relation of subsequent evaluations to a value having prior existence? *How* does a valuation supervene? And *why* does it supervene—that is to say, what is its function, if any?

The statements in the foregoing paragraph are based upon belief that examination of current discussions will show that some hold that nothing having the properties of value can arise save as some factor of appraisal, of measuring and comparing, enters in, while others hold that values may and do exist apart from any operation of this latter sort so that valuation is always wholly *ex post facto* as far as existence of values is concerned.

It is true, I think, that holding dear and valuing are used interchangeably. As far as usage goes, this fact might seem on its face to point to valuing being complete apart from evaluating. But the fact that valuation and valuing are also often used as synonyms is enough to give pause to such a conclusion. Appraisers in the field of taxation, for example, are said to value real estate, and there are expert appraisers in almost every field having to do with buying and selling property. And it is just as true that they *fix* value as it is that they pass upon it. The underlying issue here is whether "value" is a noun standing for something that is an entity in its own right or whether the word is adjectival, standing for a property or quality that belongs, under specifiable conditions, to a thing or person having existence independently of being valued. If the first view is adopted, then to say that a diamond, or a beloved person, or holding an official position, has or is a value, is to affirm that a connection somehow has been set up between two separate and unlike entities. If the second view is held, then it is held that a thing, in virtue of identifiable and describable events, has acquired a quality or property not previously belonging to it. As a thing previously hard becomes soft when affected by heat, so, on this view, something previously indifferent takes on the quality of value when it is actively cared for in a way that protects or contributes to its continued existence. Upon this view, a value-quality loses the quasi-mystical character often ascribed to it, and is capable of identification and description in terms of conditions of origin and consequence, as are other natural events.[5]

When it was suggested above that *appraising (evaluating)* is often used interchangeably with *valuing*, there was no intention of intimating that there is no difference between the direct behavioral operation of holding dear and such operations as valuations of real estate and other commodities. There is a decided difference. The point in calling attention to the fact of common usage is two-fold. It definitely raises the question of the relation of *valuation* and *value* to one another. Does *valuation* affect or modify things previously valued in the sense of being held dear (desired, liked, enjoyed), or does a valuation-proposition merely communicate the fact that a thing or person has in fact been held dear (liked, enjoyed, esteemed)? If the latter, what is the function of deliberation? Is it or is it not true that at times questions arise as to whether things previously highly esteemed (desired, liked, etc.) *should* be so viewed and treated? In the latter case, it would seem

[5] If this line of interpretation were carried out, it would indicate that the appearance of value-quality is genetically and functionally continuous, not only with physiological operations that protect and continue living processes, but with physical-chemical interactions that maintain stability amid change on the part of some compounds.

that reflective inquiry (deliberation) is engaged in for the sake of determining the value-status of the thing or person in question.

The other point in calling attention to occasional interchangeable use of *valuing* and *valuation* is to raise the question whether the undeniable difference between direct valuing and the indirectness of evaluation is a matter of *separation* or of *emphasis*. If there is in direct valuing an element of recognition of the properties of the thing or person valued as *ground* for prizing, esteeming, desiring, liking, etc., then the difference between it and explicit evaluation is one of emphasis and degree, not of fixed kinds. *Ap-praising* then represents a more or less systematized development of what is already present in *prizing*. If the valuing is *wholly* a-rational, if there is nothing whatever "objective" as its ground, then there is complete separation. In this case the problem is to determine whether valuation (i) is simply a "realistic" apprehension of something already completely there, or (ii) is simply a verbal communication of an established fact but not in any sense a proposition, or (iii) if it does enter at all into formation of subsequent valuings, how does it manage to do so.

III

The third problem grows quite directly out of the one just considered. It may be stated as follows: Is there anything unique or distinctive about valuation-propositions *as propositions?* (If they merely enunciate to others facts already in existence, this question does not arise, since such communications are, *ipso facto*, not *propositions*.) Outright statements that valuation-propositions *qua* propositions and not just because of their subject-matter are of a distinctive kind are not usual in the literature that discusses the subject of value. But positions are frequently taken and topics introduced that do not seem to have any meaning unless that position has been assumed without explicit statement. I give one typical example.

Articles frequently appear that discuss the relation of *fact* and *value*. If the subject discussed under this caption were the relation of value-facts to *other* facts, there would not be the assumption of uniqueness just mentioned. But anyone reading articles devoted to discussion of this issue will note that it is an issue or problem just because it is held that propositions about values are somehow of a unique sort, being *inherently* marked off from propositions about facts. I can think of nothing more likely to be clarifying in the present confused state of the subject than an explicit statement of the *grounds* upon which it is assumed that propositions about values are *not* propositions about space-time facts, together with explicit discussion of the *consequences* of that position. If a question were raised about the relation of geological propositions to astronomical propositions, or of meteor-propositions to comet-propositions, it would not occur to anyone that the "problem" was other than that of the connection between two sets of facts. It is my conviction that nothing would better clarify the present unsatisfactory state of discussion of value than definite and explicit statement of the reasons why the case is supposed to be otherwise in respect to value.

IV

Of late, there has appeared a school of theorists insisting with vigor that genuine propositions (and/or judgments) about values are impossible, because the latter have properties that render them wholly recalcitrant to cognitive treatment. In brief, this school holds that verbal expressions about values are of the nature of exclamations, expressing only the dominant emotional state of the one from whom the ejaculation issues. The ejaculation may be verbally extended into a sentence expressing a desire or liking or an interest. But, so it is said, the only question of a cognitive or intellectual nature that can be raised is whether the verbal expression in question (whether it be a shorter ejaculation or an expanded sentence) actually expresses the emotional state of the speaker or is meant to mislead others by concealing or distorting his actual state.

The practical import of this position may be inferred from the fact that according to it differences as to value can not be adjudicated or negotiated. They are just ultimate facts. In the frank words of one who has taken this position, serious cases of ultimate difference can be settled, if at all, only by "bashing in of heads." I shall not ask here how far this view carries to its logical conclusion the view that some "internal" or mentalistic state or process suffices to bring value-events into existence. I limit myself to pointing out that at the present time serious differences in valuing are in fact treated as capable of settlement only by recourse to force and in so far the view in question has empirical support. This is the case in recourse to war between nations, and in less obvious and complete ways, in domestic disputes between groups and in conflict of classes. In international relations short of war, the view is practically taken in acceptance of an ultimate difference between "justiciable" and "non-justiciable" disputes.

It can not be denied that this particular question is of immense practical import. Using the word "bias" without prejudice, I think it may be stated as follows: Are value-facts bias-facts of such intensity and exclusiveness as to be unmodifiable by any possible consideration of grounds and consequences? The question at issue is not whether some values are now actually treated as if they were of this kind. It is whether the cause of their being so treated inheres in them as value-facts or is a cultural-social phenomenon. If the latter is the case they are capable of modification by socio-cultural changes. If the former is the case, then differences in valuing which are of serious social importance can not be brought within the scope of investigation so as to be settled in a reasonable way. They may not always lead to open conflict. But if not it will be because it is believed that the latter will not be successful, or will be too costly, or that the time is not ripe, or that some more devious method will accomplish a wished-for triumph more effectively.

This fourth question is evidently connected with those previously discussed. If valuing consists *wholly* and exclusively of something inherently recalcitrant to inquiry and adjudication, then it must be admitted that it can not rise about the brute-animal level—save with respect to the *means* most likely to secure its victory over conflicting valuations and values. But if, in answer to the third question, it is decided that there is some element or aspect of valuation on "objective" grounds in every case of prizing, desiring, etc., etc., then it is possible that this element or aspect may itself become so prized, desired, and enjoyed that it will gain in force at the expense of the brute and non-rational factor.

In this connection it seems worthy of note that those writers who hold to the completely a-rational character of valuing begin by accepting the "internal" mentalistic theory of value, and then proceed to endow this quasi-gaseous stuff with powers of resistance greater than are possessed by triple-plate steel. While the four questions that have been formulated are those which seem to me to be more or less openly expressed in current discussion, the fact I have just stated leads me to raise, on my own account, another question which does not often appear in the literature on value, and which, nevertheless, may be more fundamental than those which do appear. Are values and valuations such that they can be treated on a psychological basis of an allegedly "individual" kind? Or are they so definitely and completely socio-cultural that they can be effectively dealt with only in that context? [6]

[6] Since the above text was written, I find this question explicitly raised as basic to economic theory, in Ayres, *The Theory of Economic Progress*, especially pp. 73–85, 90, 97.

PART I: ESSAYS

❦ REFLECTIONS ON DEWEY'S
❦ QUESTIONS ABOUT VALUE

HENRY DAVID AIKEN

PROFESSOR DEWEY has wisely remarked that it is not to be supposed that his formulation of questions about value is uninfluenced by the answers he would give to them.[1] The same, of course, is true of anyone. In value theory, as elsewhere, it is only possible to formulate questions in the light of presuppositions as to the kind of thing inquired about. Without such assumptions we would attach no meaning to questions which draw attention to areas of experience already provisionally separated off from the totality of things. In asking a question we already have in mind a subject matter; what presumably remain in doubt are the specific characteristics of that subject matter and their connections with other phenomena. At the same time, such preanalytic delimitations of fields of inquiry may involve us in vicious circles and defeat the purpose of inquiry, if we do not regard them as tentative, problematic, and even vague. A genuinely undogmatic approach to our problems of value demands a readiness to enlarge or diminish the scope of our questions, or even to alter radically the kind of question asked, as analysis reveals distinctions not previously noted and as the disclosure of new facts brings out unforeseen relationships even more vital to understanding than those our original questions have indicated as crucial.

It is becoming increasingly common to begin investigations of value and valuation by asking, "How do values differ from facts?" or, "How do evaluative or normative expressions differ from descriptive or factual statements?" Such questions are likely to be prejudicial if taken too seriously; if, that is to say, it is assumed beforehand that we know perfectly well what we mean by "fact" or if the distinction is assumed to be of one type rather than another. We must be careful, therefore, not to allow questions of this sort to preestablish a dualism

[1] P. 5, above.

between "fact" and "value" which at the outset will gratuitously render the latter incapable of verifiable description.[2] In short, while inquiry concerning the distinction and relations between facts and values may presuppose *some* difference, it still leaves us in doubt as to where the difference lies—whether it is a difference in kind, a specific difference, the difference between a genus and one of its species, an empirical difference, or a semantical one.

I

The first question raised by Dewey invites us to consider the relation between an attitude called "prizing" and another called "desiring." He calls attention to the fact that prizing is a transaction between the attitude itself and something which is prized. Prizing is "of" an "object." But it is also "toward" its object, implying at least a readiness to act in its behalf. In this sense, the latter is thus more than an object; it is an objective, an end-in-view, perhaps a provisional "good." Nevertheless, we must not assume that every prizing issues forth, or, indeed, that it should issue forth, into overt action. It would be fatal to the integrity and economy of the moral life if every prizing demanded an immediate or continuous striving to realize its object or to preserve it in being. A person may quite properly be said to prize a certain work of art, for example, even though for long periods of time, interest remains wholly quiescent. Prizing, in short, is a dispositional property, a potency, an affective-conative habit or power. Were "value" to be defined in terms of it, it would have to be defined in terms of a contrary-to-fact conditional.

If "prizing" or "holding dear" are thought of as dispositional properties, then "desire," as Dewey suggests, might be reserved for the emergence of such properties into overt action when they are "blocked or frustrated." It seems to me, however, that although we do wish to draw some such distinction, and that "desire" might be as good a name as any to designate the latter term, it might perhaps be more fruitful to draw it in a broader way so that the behavioral attitude arising from blockage or frustration would be only a subspecies of "desire." The point is simply that the active arousal of a disposition need not presuppose conflict. Many attitudes normally called "desiring" are re-

[2] One is reminded here of the dualisms of the seventeenth century philosophers, which followed essentially from analogous preconceptions.

sponses of dispositions to a stimulus which invited its appropriation or enjoyment without prior frustration of any sort. If the connection between "prizing" and "desiring" is to be construed as the distinction between a disposition and its active arousal, still we need not presuppose that its arousal indicates the presence of frustration or blockage, but merely the presence in the environment of some stimulus to which it is called upon to respond. But this response may be nothing more than "approval" or "disapproval." No assumption should be made that an object is not "really" liked unless something overt is done about it.

Whether prizing and liking have as their purpose, in any given instance, the preservation of something already existent (as a value?) or, rather, the creation of something which as yet does not exist, depends upon the situation in which prizing or liking is aroused. As R. B. Perry has reminded us, the greater part of desiring is for what does not exist at all. Many of our most serious problems of conduct involve precisely the bringing into being of valued objects. We must not assume, then, that "value," if it is to be predicated of prizings and desires, should be reserved for those objects whose present existence is already assured. The contrast between what exists and what is hoped for is in fact the principal source of that ideality which is traditionally ascribed to the "good."

If value is regarded as a function of prizing and desiring, it cannot be limited to existing states of affairs because (a) prizing, as a dispositional property, is itself latent during most of its "existence," and (b) the objects which would satisfy desires are often nonexistent. It is for these reasons that most value-judgments, perhaps, must be conceived as contrary-to-fact conditionals: that is, statements about what would be the case under such and such conditions, even though those conditions may not at the moment exist.[3]

Now I should not wish to deny that desires and enjoyments have biological roots, or that there are always organic behavioral correlates and conditions of their occurrence. At the same time it seems quite obvious that desire implies something more, although perfectly palpable, than its bodily correlates or biological roots. But whether or not we are to define "value" *exclusively* in terms of this "mentalistic" some-

---

[3] This remark, which I have no space to elaborate further here, must be borne in mind throughout the remainder of my discussion. It would also apply, I think, to definitions which conceive value in terms of "satisfaction."

thing more, depends upon us, upon the *use* to which we wish to put the term to be defined. If we seek an objective, behavioral criterion of value —if, for example, we wish to measure the intensity of value in terms of the amount of energy expended in nourishing and protecting behavior—we would have to define value not in terms of the mentalistic factor alone, but also in terms of its behavioral relations. Dewey has elsewhere denied emphatically "that causal conditions of the occurrence of an event are *ipso facto* qualities or traits of the event."[4] This is true of any useful definition of "event." We want to distinguish things from their causes, so that we can significantly ask what the latter in fact are. But how broadly we construe "event"—whether, in short, we will allow "event" itself to be so broadly construed as to include a causal relation within it—depends upon us. Thus, for example, we may ask what the causes of desire are, but still leave open the question whether desire itself is to be conceived in terms of a causal relation. We can, if we please, so define desire that it refers not merely to its "mental" factor, but also to certain of its accompanying behavioral conditions. But since it is desirable to define value in such a way as to make possible public verifications of value-judgments, we must include more in our definitions than the subjective attitudes themselves.

Notice, here, that our common desire to keep valuation within the bounds of scientific method gives, for most naturalists, a persuasive influence to definitions of value in which the terms of the definiens are capable of intersubjective designation: such terms, for example, as "motor-affective," "adjustment," "equilibrium." Our interest, however, is not in directing attitudes of approval and disapproval, commonly "associated" with the term "value," to behavior rather than to mental states, although this might, fortunately or unfortunately, be a consequence of such a definition.[5] Our interest is, rather, in laying down, through our definitions, rules for the "scientific" use of value-expressions and value-judgments, a use which has an analogue in common usage, and which relates our "clarified" scientific meanings to those of ordinary speech.

This point is of some importance because of the undeniable fact that "definitions" of value-expressions are likely to be implicitly per-

[4] *Problems of Men*, New York, 1946, p. 264.
[5] It is precisely such a mistaken assumption as this which has led many thinkers to speak disparagingly of the degrading "materialistic" consequences of ethical naturalism.

suasive, as C. L. Stevenson has shown.[6] But whereas, according to Stevenson, the purpose of persuasive definitions of ethical terms is to inculcate favorable attitudes toward the things specified in the definiens, the purpose of what I shall call "scientific" definitions of value is (a) to give value-terms meanings which are publicly verifiable in terms of overt behavior, and (b) to give value-judgments an intelligible status as "factual" or "descriptive," in some acceptable sense of these terms. We are, then, pleading a cause, but it is not simply because of our desire to redirect attitudes toward the satisfaction of needs. The cause we plead is the cause of a science of valuation, which is possible only if our value-terms are given a definite descriptive meaning.[7]

These considerations suggest that the questions which a theory of value seeks to answer fall somewhere between two other types of question: (a) what are the conventional usages of expressions involving such words as "good," "right," "value," and (b) what do we want these terms to mean? There is a pre-existing system of usages and meanings which roughly (but only roughly) determines the contexts in which such expressions are appropriately employed. These usages and meanings will determine the field with all or part of which value theory will be concerned. But the uses and meanings of value-expressions are many, and it is unlikely that all of them will be of interest to the student of value theory. Thus, for example, there is that sense of "good" which refers only to questions of conformity to a given standard. There is also the sense which refers primarily to questions

[6] See *Ethics and Language* (New Haven, 1944), pp. 206–226.
[7] In this connection it is worth remarking that Jeremy Bentham's utilitarian definition of value and his felicific calculus were explicitly motivated, not by a desire to redirect men's attitudes toward pleasure, nor by a desire to inculcate democratic ideals (which may or may not be supported by such a definition) but rather by a desire to render valuation amenable to definite scientific methods. His purpose was not simply to clarify ordinary usage, but, admitting the customary vagueness of the term, to give it greater precision, so that a science of morals would be possible. If, inadvertently, acceptance of his definition actually changed people's attitudes toward their ideals, so much the better. But it was their attitude toward the process of valuation itself that interested him, not the particular quality, "pleasure," which eighteenth century writers generally considered synonymous with "good." The purpose of Bentham in equating "good" with "pleasure" was thus quite different from that of the Epicureans, who were actively preaching a sermon in the guise of defining a term. In an indifferent and hostile world, the latter seemed to say, nothing can be "good" or valuable but pleasure. But Bentham, whatever his faults, was not interested primarily in education. His purpose was that of extending the methods of science to problems of morals and legislation. I take it that contributors to this symposium are disciples of Jeremy Bentham in this sense if, perhaps unfortunately, in no other.

of instrumentality or utility. Finally, there is that sense which refers to questions of desirability or satisfaction. Now whether the theory of value has to do with some or all of these meanings of "value" depends, I think, primarily on how broadly the theory of value is to be conceived. In any case, such terms as "value" or "ethical" are not sufficiently stable or sufficiently clear for us to "analyze" their conventional meanings and have done. Our problem is also one involving a decision, or perhaps a series of decisions. In the first place, there is, as I have said, the question as to which of these various meanings or uses we, as value theorists, desire to investigate; which we choose to regard as primary, and which as secondary or irrelevant. In the second place, there is the question not merely of selecting the sense or use to which we wish to devote attention, but of assigning to it a more precise and explicit signification than is normally present in common speech.

If, for example, I define "value" as "satisfaction," I am trying to assign a meaning to "value" which is roughly in accord with at least one of the principal uses of this term in common speech. But I am at the same time selecting this use as primary because I regard this meaning as central for those who are interested in giving verifiable answers to the question: "What are the causes or objects of human well-being?" And I am also specifying and giving explicitness and determinateness to a problem which in ordinary discourse lacks this characteristic. "Analysis" is not, then, solely a matter of *discovering* meanings which are already "there" implicitly. It is also a matter of *giving* determinateness and specificity to terms which were hitherto both confused and vague.

II

As for the second question concerning the relations between "valuing" and "evaluating," I should be inclined to regard this as the relation between the institution of a value and the judgment as to the comparative worth of what is so instituted. The main purpose of evaluation and appraisal is to assess the degree or amount of value a thing possesses as compared to other things. But this evidently presupposes that values are logically prior to appraisal. Suppose I am called upon to appraise a piece of real estate. Now in one sense it may perhaps be said that the appraisal "determines" what its value will be, what value is *to be put* upon it. But even granted that this is so, and that as a *result of appraisal* values are changed or rendered more determinate, does this imply that value has no meaning apart from or prior to the act of appraisal? I think not. The appraiser of a piece of real estate "fixes" its value only in the sense of determining what price is to be asked for it.[8] But this presupposes a prior agreement to set the price according to the appraiser's decision. Prices are not "fixed" in thin air. They are fixed in the light of a whole system of interests and conventions established to adjudicate between and direct those interests. If individuals did not want (value) real estate, "fixing" of prices would have no meaning. Appraisal, in short, is an estimate of what human beings will be willing to "pay" for a commodity; and what they are willing to pay depends upon the urgency of their needs.

Again, there is no guarantee, apart from the supposition that people's values will remain about what they were before the act of appraisal, that the "fixing" of a price will stay fixed. If I have no interest in selling, the object has no actual price; or if I choose to sell for less than the "value" set by the appraiser, the price set by him is rendered null and void. There is no such thing, in short, as the "fixing" of a value, *unless* there are individuals who are willing to allow the appraisal to stand. Granted that interests may change in the light of appraisals, it remains for the interests themselves to give force to the latter.

Is it not the case, then, that the "establishment" of a price is simply a prediction as to what human beings are likely to do under certain circumstances? I think it is. Similarly, I suggest that appraisals and evaluations are essentially estimates and predictions (which are merely probable) concerning certain types of human behavior which we call "values" or "valuings." Whether they turn out to be valid or not depends, not on anything which the appraisal or evaluation itself can fix or determine in advance, but rather upon the preferences and interests which are the springs of conduct.

Dewey suggests that the "underlying issue" concerning the relation of valuing to evaluation is whether "value" stands for something "that is an entity in its own right" or whether it is adjectival, standing for "a property or quality that belongs under specifiable conditions, to a thing

[8] It should be pointed out, here, that "price" may be regarded as one way of measuring value, but is not identical with it. Price presupposes value, but obviously value does not presuppose price.

or person having existence independently of being valued." [9] Now I suppose we must agree that every distinguishable "thing" is an entity of some sort "in its own right." A color or sound is an event, having a certain temporal and spatial location. Yet we usually regard colors, if not sounds, as properties or qualities belonging, under certain conditions, to something else which may well continue to exist without them. The distinction between "thing" and "property," in short, is unclear and, I suspect, is largely verbal.

I should say, then, that value is a property or relation of persons or situations which may well continue to exist without it. It is in this sense "adjectival." But I fail to see how this fact, if it be such, is affected by the question whether "values" exist apart from evaluations. For if value is construed to mean "object of interest" or "satisfaction," it is just as clearly the property of a person as any act of evaluation.[10]

As to the question whether the distinction between "valuing" and "valuation" is a matter of "separation" or of "emphasis," I have already suggested an answer. It is a question of separation, although only in the *logical* sense. We are not to suppose that there is no interaction or mediation between the two, simply because we recognize the difference.

Granted that common speech sometimes blurs the distinction, it can usually be determined from the context whether a *judgment* of value or an *act* of direct valuing is meant. In any case, the distinction is a crucial one, and it seems desirable, since we have the two words, to restrict "value" to the act of desiring or being satisfied (I do not here decide which) and "evaluation" and "appraisal" to judgments about values.

If the distinction is blurred, then (and this point cannot be too greatly emphasized) value-judgments lose their status as genuine judgments. If the difference between appraising and valuing is merely a difference of emphasis, then appraisals become mere *acts* of valuing, decisions, interests, attitudes, even though they are "mediated" by genuine judgments. A value, as such, is, I suggest, arational, in the sense that it *may* exist apart from evaluation and deliberation. What we mean by a "rational" value is one which is selected in the light of a deliberation concerning its probable consequences or comparative worth, one which retains its status, its desirability, after it has been appraised. But even then we must distinguish it from the *trial* to which it is subjected, from the gauntlet which it has been made to run. No doubt it comes out chas-

[9] *Problems of Men*, pp. 276–277.   [10] *Ibid.*

tened by the ordeal. But it remains as a value only in so far as it continues to be an object of satisfaction or desire.

It follows from this that we may properly speak of "pre-rational values"—those which are not mediated by appraisals, and of "post-rational values"—those which *are* mediated by appraisals. It may be true that our post-rational values will be different to some extent from our pre-rational ones. It is to be hoped so. But even then, it is confusing to speak of valuing itself as a rational act, since this implies that it is *in itself* a judgment. Strictly speaking, a "rational" ethics would be one in which values are not merely discovered, compared, or mediated by reason, but *instated* by it. But naturalistic ethicists since Aristotle have continually insisted that values and ends cannot be *defined* in purely cognitive or judgmental terms.

Let us agree to distinguish valuation from value, and the value-judgment as a statement of fact from the value which it is "about," while still admitting that such judgments may modify desire or what is "held dear." To this extent they may change or even indirectly institute values—if by these we mean objects-of-desire, ends-in-view, or "holding dear." But we must point out at once the danger of defining "good" exclusively in conative terms, or, at any rate, of failing to recognize that the sense of "good" or "value" which connotes "object-of-desire" is not the sense which connotes "satisfaction," enjoyment, or happiness. There is no necessary connection, logical or psychological, between the genuinely satisfactory (which I wish to regard as the root meaning of "good" in at least a rough sense) and the actual desires of persons. At the same time, we *usually* do desire what we believe, on the basis of our own experience and that of other persons whom we trust, will give satisfaction. It is largely for this reason that the communication of value-judgments or an evaluation may often, although not always, be expected to arouse desire and modify behavior.

What must be avoided if a "scientific" and yet "practical" theory of value and evaluation is to be achieved are (a) the erection of an unbridgeable dualism between "fact" and "value," (b) a confusion of the property or relation "value" with the judgment which ascribes this property or relation to an object, and (c) a definition of value which sheds no light upon the behavioral changes (the factor of "magnetism") which are normally expected to accompany the communication of a judgment of value or evaluation. I believe that a definition of "value" (roughly) in terms of satisfaction,[11] rather than interest, accomplishes these results: for it brings "value" within the realm of "fact"; it enables us to render intelligible the function of deliberation and the fact that deliberation alters what we prize without confusing the judgments which lead to such change with the act of "valuing" itself; and finally, it enables us to account for the habitual though not necessary emotive effect of value-judgments without denying to them the status of genuinely "descriptive" propositions.[12]

III

My answer to the third question raised by Dewey, "Is there anything unique or distinctive about valuation-propositions as propositions?" has already been suggested. We must at all events avoid prejudging our answer by the use of the word "merely." This word, like "as such," is commonly employed to deny the presence of relation, or to conceive the entity in question wholly apart from its context. But in conduct relation, context, and interaction are of the essence. Valuation-propositions are, I believe, "outright propositions," and they *may* be used to convey information concerning entities already in existence; nevertheless they also often occur in contexts in which something is to be or may be brought into existence, and they often themselves play an important role in bringing about this result. This indeed seems obvious if what they communicate has to do with what human beings want and care for. This being so, there is no more reason to be surprised that they tend to modify behavior than there is reason for wonder that the utterance of the word "fire," in certain circumstances, modifies behavior.

But let us examine some of the grounds which seem to underlie the assumption that judgments of value are somehow inherently different from judgments of fact.

In the following discussion I will try to show that what is really in question here is whether value-judgments are propositions *at all* (this will be considered at length in subsequent parts of the paper), *not*

---

[11] This, however, does not imply that "satisfaction" itself is not in need of careful analysis.

[12] If to some, the term "value" seems to be usefully applied to ends-in-view or objects of interest as distinct from satisfaction, I propose that the expressions "ostensible value" or "prima-facie value" would indicate in what sense they are values, and also their connection with value or satisfaction. I will return to this point below.

whether value-judgments have a "peculiar" subject matter.[13] In this and the following section my concern will be to show that (1) no distinction can be drawn between "value-judgment" and "factual-judgments" simply on the ground that the former are not judgments about actual space-time existences, since the latter are not limited to "facts" in this sense; [14] (2) the paradoxes commonly supposed to result either from the denial or from the assertion that judgments of value are judgments of fact are due in part to a failure to observe that "fact" and "value" belong to different logical types and in part to naturalistic theories which define value in purely volitional terms; (3) the distinction between "values" and "facts," on the ground that the former are decisions and the latter are cognitions, is not one of mutual exclusion, but that elements of attitude and perception are involved both in value-expressions and in factual-statements; (4) since this is so, agreements in attitude underlie all "knowledge," so that a sharp distinction can be drawn between "arguments over" values and "arguments about" facts simply on the ground that arguments over values usually or often involve attitudinal agreements and disagreements, whereas arguments about facts do not; and (5) just as it is true that once science has *agreed* on its criteria of meaning and truth it can then proceed impartially to examine statements from the standpoint of these criteria (regardless of the fact that other criteria might logically have been employed if someone had chosen to do so) so it is true that once we agree on a criterion, such as satisfaction, for value, we can also proceed impartially to examine activities from the standpoint of that criterion, regardless of the fact that other criteria *might* have been chosen. Indeed, it may be desirable to have a series of criteria or definitions of value, corresponding to different uses to which valuations are to be put. So long, however, as we are clear about the meaning of these criteria, and are in agreement as to which one, in a given situation, is to be employed, no difficulty need arise. We may still insist that no one can "force" one definition or criterion of value rather than another into use, and that agreement concerning a criterion of valuation must be based upon a decision as to the meaning which shall be assigned to value. But the same privilege which is open

[13] By "peculiar," here, I mean a nonempirical subject matter.
[14] I have already discussed the question whether value can be understood in behavioral terms without denying the "mentalistic" factor which might, for some, be regarded as a chief reason for regarding value and judgments as "peculiar."

to the epistemologist who wishes to establish a scientific criterion of meaning or knowledge is also open to the value-theorist desirous of establishing a scientific theory of valuation.[15]

At the same time, it should be noted at once that there is a sharp difference between the inevitable relativism as to the meanings or criteria of "value" and the relativism which holds, on a given criterion, with respect to *values*. Ineradicable differences in attitude do not necessarily imply differences in basic theories of values any more than they imply differences in theories of meaning. *This depends upon what "value" is taken to mean.* From the standpoint of an interest theory, for example, a difference in attitude necessarily indicates a difference in *value;* though this does not imply a difference as to the meaning of "value." Again, if we were to *assume* that different decisions as to the meaning of "value" were themselves indications of different *values,* in some sense, we would still need to be clear as to the difference between the meaning of value which is the result of a decision to use this term in a certain way, and that preanalytic meaning according to which the identity of value and decision is taken for granted.

1. Regarding the question of existence, I contend that there is no reason why, in order that valuation propositions, as propositions, should be regarded as factual, they must be "about" something already in existence. Only a small part of what are regarded as "factual" propositions are judgments that something exists. I do not pretend to have solved this question, but I believe, for example, that "contrary to fact conditionals," upon which so much discourse, scientific and otherwise, depends, are properly spoken of as "factual." "If I opened the window, the temperature in the room would fall" is, I believe, a statement of fact at the moment that I write. Yet it does not "enunciate a fact already in existence." If "description" is the term used to refer to all "scientific" or "true" propositions, and by this we mean to exclude all propositions not describing existing states of affairs, then not merely most value-judgments, but most judgments, will not be "scientific," even though science and the ordinary business of life cannot dispense with them.

2. The traditional problem of the relation between judgments of "fact" and judgments of "value" has sometimes been stated in the form of a paradox: if judgments of value *are not* distinct from judgments of fact, then (a) the all-important distinction between what is and

[15] The elaboration of (4) and (5) will be presented in the following section.

what ought to be is blurred, and (b) valuation is reduced to a mere description of what already exists, hence negating the ideality or normative character which is regarded as essential to value.[16] But if judgments of value *are* distinct from judgments of fact, then it seems impossible to regard them as verifiable by scientific means, and a science of value or morals is an illusion. In short, either value-judgments are not factual, in which case they cannot be regarded as scientific, or they are factual, in which case the distinction between what is and what ought to be is lost.

In trying to resolve this paradox, if such it be, we must begin by pointing out that the terms "fact" and "value" clearly do not belong to the same logical type, and that they designate not coordinate but independent realms of being. Bearing in mind the danger of all analogical reasoning, especially in matters of meaning, let us compare the preceding "paradox" with another: If judgments of "men" are not distinct in some sense from judgments of "fact," then the distinction between "man" and "fact" is lost; whereas, if they are distinct, then a judgment of men can never be regarded as verifiable by scientific means. This is absurd, you will say. Granted; but it is no more absurd than the other "paradox." Again, why do we not make a "problem" of the distinction between "fact" and "red"? Because, first of all, we immediately recognize that the distinction, although it can be drawn, is a distinction between entities belonging to entirely different levels of discourse. "Red" is presumably a term in the language of objects, whereas "fact" is not. "Fact" is a word in the meta-language which refers perhaps to the class of true or verifiable propositions. To say that "red" is not a "fact" is, then, simply to say that red is not a proposition which is true or verifiable. This is true but wholly unilluminating as to the specific nature of red. Similarly, *if* "fact" refers to the class of true or verifiable propositions, then a value is not a fact. But this neither sheds light on the nature of values nor precludes the possibility that value-judgments are "factual."

Let us rephrase the paradox in a different way; we will see, perhaps, that stated in this way the third and fourth questions come to much the same thing: If value-judgments are verifiable, we lose the distinction

[16] This way of formulating the problem was suggested to me by a speech given by F. S. C. Northrop before the Harvard Law Forum, January 10, 1947. He is responsible neither for my way of formulating the dilemma or paradox nor for my solution; in fact I believe he would reject my solution.

between what is and what ought to be; whereas if they are not verifiable, they lose their status as genuine judgments. So conceived, however, the paradox loses most of its force. There is no a priori reason why statements about what ought to be should be incapable of verification. The first half of the paradox is analogous to the argument that the distinction between what is and what was is lost if historical statements are regarded as inherently verifiable. But this seems to me hardly to need discussion. The criterion of verifiability does not mean that the state of affairs described by each verifiable statement must now be present in experience, or, indeed, that it ever will be. All that is essential is that its deducible consequences could be observed. Hence, even if value-judgments never in fact referred to what exists, this would in no way preclude the possibility of their being regarded as verifiable or factual in any workable sense of these terms. We may, then, insist as strongly as we please on the distinction between what is and what ought to be, without *implying* thereby that value-judgments are not "factual" in a sense which is perfectly in accord with viable scientific conceptions of meaningfulness and factuality. As for the second side of the paradox, it is a tautology, and may, therefore, be admitted with impunity. Since for the naturalist or empiricist every proposition is theoretically verifiable by the procedures of science, the *only* question is whether so-called value-judgments are propositions at all.

3. It is commonly held that value-judgments, in contradistinction to judgments of fact, are essentially "expressions" of decisions. This view is held at the present time by most of the logical positivists. At the outset, let me say that there is no logical necessity that this should be so. The positivistic theories of meaning and testability are perfectly general. They cannot, therefore, determine a priori whether a certain class of judgments meets the requirements of significant statement. But this is not, perhaps, the crucial point, since the positivists have not merely held the negative view that value-judgments are descriptively meaningless; they have also put forward the positive view that value-judgments are volitions. Our problem, then, is to examine the justification for the radical separation between statements and decisions.

In the first place, those who have emphasized the disparity between facts and values on the ground that the latter are decisions have usually chosen to ignore, for the nonce, the element of decision which goes into any judgment of fact that passes beyond what is given in experience. Nor have they taken into account the evident cognitive factors which are present in most if not all attitudes and decisions. It is often alleged that "This object is good" merely expresses an attitude of approval or a favorable volition with respect to the object. Observe, however, that the direction of an attitude is *toward* an object, and that the expression is, therefore, not *merely of* an affective-conative state. If this state is itself regarded as essentially noncognitive (otherwise there would be no point in speaking of attitudes, decisions, and volitions as sharply distinct from judging and believing), then the only way of accounting for the direction of the attitude, its fixation upon an object, is to acknowledge the presence of a cognitive factor which mediates between the attitude and its object. But this cognitive factor is itself, for the most part, a judgment to the effect that the object in question is harmful or dangerous or friendly or useful, etc. It is this latter judgment, in fact, which is largely responsible for the kind of attitude aroused, and for the way in which the organism responds to its environment. In short, there is present in any conative or affective situation which is more than that of blind drive or all-consuming passion, a belief or expectation which is an appraisal of the object as a possible source of good or evil.

Let us fully acknowledge the necessity of distinguishing the affective-conative from the cognitive factor. Still, even if we take the view that value-judgments are expressions of decisions or attitudes, they are *by virtue of that very fact* also expressions of judgments. If "This object is good" is an expression and hence a potential sign of a favorable disposition on the part of the speaker toward an object, it is also, and quite as legitimately, the expression and sign of a judgment, which, to the extent that it is an appraisal of the harmful or beneficial qualities of the object, is itself quite properly spoken of as a *value-judgment*. If, as some writers wish, the first "expression" is itself thought of as a "value-judgment" in the "primary" or "characteristic" sense, then we may at least fairly claim that there is another judgment, itself explicitly cognitive, that is a necessary though not sufficient condition of the so-called "primary" judgment. It is this mediating judgment or appraisal which functions as a condition of the attitude and hence its "expression," which has been the main concern of value theory in the past. Let it be called, since names are merely names, the "secondary" or "non-

characteristic" value-judgment. Let the proponents of the emotive
theory then concern themselves, if they wish, with the "primary" judgment of value. Let them have the "advantage," if they wish it, of treat-
ing the "basic" or "characteristic" value-judgment as "fundamental."
Very well—there is still room for a scientific ethics and theory of
valuation.[17]

But let us now turn to the normative factor, the element of decision
involved in judgments of fact. The question arises as to what precisely
is involved in a "judgment of fact." In the first place, no "judgment of
fact" and no conjunction of "judgments of fact" will give us scientific
statements as these are commonly understood, if "judgment of fact"
is taken to mean a judgment limited to a characterization of the given,
that is, to what is indubitably present in sense-experience. A scientific
statement is a theory which goes beyond anything that can be deduced
from the "facts" themselves. As F. S. C. Northrop has pointed out:
"One cannot deduce the theories of science from the facts. Instead,
the logic of deduction in scientific method runs in the opposite direction. One deduces the facts from the theory; retaining the theory if its
deductive consequences are confirmed by fact, rejecting it if they are
not." [18] The act of postulation, as Northrop goes on to say, is itself the
free act or decision of the scientist. No one can force me by logic to
believe in a world beyond what is immediately given in experience.
No one can force me, by logic and sense-experience, to accept as "fact"
the existence of the physical world as science "describes" it. But if
I choose to believe in such a world, then, as Northrop says, "it follows
by logic from this conception that the observed and experimentally
determined data should be what they are. In other words, our theories

---

[17] But we may discover in this analysis another reason why the interest theory of
value must be given up. On Perry's analysis the judgment which mediates interest
is not as a rule a judgment of value, since it is not a judgment *about* objects of interest. It is what he calls an "interest judgment." But this very interest judgment is,
in nine cases out of ten, an appraisal of the harmful or beneficial, the agreeable or
disagreeable, traits of the object in question. Interest is aroused, not simply by the
judgment that this is an apple, but by the further qualification that apples are "good,"
that is, pleasant, satisfactory, agreeable, and so forth. On Perry's view, judgments of
value are usually supererogatory, and of interest primarily to the curious. The practical function of evaluation and its influence upon our attitudes are not clearly understood so long as value is *identified* with volition or interest. The practical and emotive
effects of appraisals are, I think, explainable only when we view them as concerned
with satisfactions and the instrumentalities whereby the latter are realized.
[18] *The Meeting of East and West* (New York, 1946), pp. 204–205; by permission of
The Macmillan Company, publishers.

imply the facts which we observe, but the facts do not imply the theories." [19]

It would seem, then, that if the verifiable propositions of science are to be regarded as "facts," an element of choice or decision goes into the constitution of any fact which is more than a judgment of immediate experience—if, indeed, there is such a thing. This volitional factor is the pragmatic element present in all knowledge. But if so, then the sharp bifurcation of decision and fact, norm and actuality, breaks down, and we are left with a theory of knowledge, as well as a theory of decisions and attitudes, in which both factors are present.

IV

In the light of the preceding discussion let us consider a recent statement of the view which would deny to valuational and ethical judgments any cognitive status, on the ground that they are decisions, and that as such they are, from the standpoint of logic, "arbitrary." I have chosen this statement partly because of its succinctness and partly because its author does not hedge with respect to its consequences. It may be said, however, that essentially the same view has been recently propounded by Karl Popper [20] and earlier by Ayer, Carnap, and others. I do not include Stevenson in this group, because his analysis of the "language of ethics" is so qualified and so keenly aware of the flexibilities of language that one hesitates to say whether he would agree, in essence, with the position about to be discussed. [21]

In the article in question, entitled "Philosophy: Speculation or Science," [22] Professor Hans Reichenbach, in the course of some remarks upon the methodological difficulties which beset the social sciences generally, makes the following statements:

Another reason [why the social sciences are not so highly developed as the natural sciences] is derived from the confusion of cognitive statements and volitional aims. . . . Social organization is a means to an end; but to what end it is to be adjusted cannot be found out by scientific methods because

[19] *Ibid.*, p. 204.
[20] Cf. *The Open Society and Its Enemies* (London, 1945), Vol. I.
[21] I should like to say here that whatever differences may exist between my views and those of Stevenson, I regard his work as of great importance. It is by far the most sensitive, as well as the most comprehensive, statement of the emotive theory in existence.
[22] *The Nation*, CLXIV (1947), 19–22; by permission of the editors of *The Nation*.

the question of the end is not of a cognitive nature. Purpose is man-made and is not derivable from the structure of the universe. We human beings set up the aims of our society; what we call a better world is a matter of volitional decision. If we stand for our decision, if we are willing to take upon us the trouble of the fight for a better world, we do so because we trust in human will. There is no such thing as "the good" in the sense of an object of knowledge. The distinction between good and bad is volitional; and to follow our decisions requires confidence in our set of values but does not presuppose an adherence to cognitive truths.[23]

"Only the *relation* between ends and means is of a cognitive nature," Reichenbach goes on to say. Thus

not all political controversies . . . can be settled by cognitive means. The proponents of the existence of a master race, for instance, cannot be shown by cognitive means to be wrong; they stand for a different aim. We do not wish to say that such aims should be tolerated, but we should know that we cannot convince our adversaries by something like logic. The different aims are represented by different social groups; which group will be victorious is a matter of social power. Our hope that the social struggle can be settled without resort to bombs and bullets is based on the fact that the majority of men prefer peaceful aims to the valuational system of the superman.[24]

These statements are, I think, fairly representative of the "school of theorists" to whom Dewey alludes in the article which is the occasion for this symposium, and who insist "with vigor that genuine propositions . . . about values are impossible, because the latter have properties that render them wholly recalcitrant to cognitive statement." What shall we make of them?

Nowhere in his article does Reichenbach acknowledge that his own view of cognition involves acts of a volitional nature which cannot be derived from logic or an analysis of the data of experience. Both knowledge and meaning, as he himself understands them, are to be construed in terms of probabilities. But the concept of probability which, according to him, is "indispensable" to a solution of the problem of inductive inference itself involves an element of "wagering" which is volitional: "It turns out that the procedure of inductive knowledge is more closely related to the betting of the gambler than to the rationalized conception of knowledge which so far has been the basis of

[23] *Ibid.*, p. 21.   [24] *Ibid.*, p. 22.

philosophic investigation." [25] I shall make no comment here upon the accuracy of Reichenbach's scholarship in the history of philosophy. Suffice it to say that it is an act of will which alone makes gamblers of us all. We don't have to "know" the facts of science, even though it is unquestionably true that we won't "know" them unless we are willing to make the bets which, according to Reichenbach himself, knowledge presupposes.

It is simply not true, then, that cognitive statements are utterly divorced from volitional aims, even on Reichenbach's own theory of knowledge. Moreover, it is necessary to remind him that the statements "A question is meaningful only if it is so asked that before we can give the true answer we at least can tell how a possible answer would look. . . . [But] to ask for the origin of the universe is an unreasonable question; it is meaningless because we cannot say how a possible answer would look" [26] are themselves the consequences of a "theory" of meaning which is itself an act of volition. It thus ill behooves Reichenbach and others of his school to cast stones at "knowledge of the good" on the ground that the distinction between good and bad is volitional. So is the distinction between the "meaningful" and the "meaningless," and the "factual" and the "non-factual," the "warranted assertion" and the "unwarranted assertion."

However, let us agree that we may distinguish between those distinctively "cognitive" aims which result in "knowledge" and those aims which do not. Let us also agree that the good is not knowledge, and that the distinction between good and evil is not a cognitive distinction; that is, a distinction which can be defined in epistemic or logical terms.[27] Does it follow from this that there can be no knowledge of good and evil? I think not.

The point is that Reichenbach is guilty of a series of non sequiturs when he argues that because our ends-in-view (he calls them simply ends) are, in part, the product of (although, as we have seen, only in part, since they are mediated by judgments or appraisals) man-made

[25] *Ibid.*, p. 20. Anyone interested in the explicitly normative character of epistemology as opposed to psychology, as Reichenbach conceives them, should consult his *Experience and Prediction* (Chicago, 1938).
[26] *The Nation,* CLXIV (1947), p. 20.
[27] Cf. Hume's *Treatise of Human Nature,* ed. by L. A. Selby-Bigge, 1896, Bk. 3, Pt. 1, Sec. 1, pp. 455–470.

volitions, there is no such thing as knowledge of values. (I am assuming, by the way, that when he says that the distinction between good and evil is "volitional" he is not merely asserting that our use of the terms "good" and "evil" is a matter of preference, because this is no more and no less true of these terms than of any other. Reichenbach, unfortunately, does not make this clear.)

Several considerations which are relevant to this point may be mentioned. In the first place, nothing follows directly as to the nature of values, or the status of judgments about them, from the fact that ends-in-view are volitional. Why this should imply that we cannot make rational assertions about, and comparisons of, ends-in-view with respect to their worth is not made clear. Granted that ends are not wholly cognitive, this does not render them incapable of analysis and understanding, any more than the fact that a tree is not cognitive renders it incapable of being known by cognitive means or incapable of comparison with "standard trees." The setting up of a standard of comparison involves an act of will, to be sure. But we may distinguish the act of will which sets it up from the meaning of the criterion which is thereby established. Nothing but an act of will can impose "rational animal" as our standard conception of a "man." But "rational animal" presumably means something independently of that act. This being so, we can compare ends-in-view according to some standard of valuation which we agree to regard as primary and, if the standard is intelligible, our comparisons will be capable of verification.

In the second place, ends-in-view are not unchangeable or irrevocable. The relationship between cognition and interest, between belief and decision, is very close. Our ends are altered or even removed by our knowledge of them and their consequences. Interests are or may be guided to their ends by reason; they may in turn be modified when reason discloses their undesirable consequences; and interests may be adjusted to one another through appraisals of their mutual requirements. This does not, of course, eliminate the noncognitive element in our decisions; but it shows the reciprocal relationship between will or desire and cognition or belief. And it indicates the fact that if valuation is conceived in cognitive terms, disagreements in attitude may be removed through valuation and appraisal as well as by force or rhetoric. If both evaluations and ends are thought of as wholly irrational, this very fact will tend to render cognitive methods unacceptable as procedures for resolving differences in purpose. The acceptance of a scientific theory of valuation is one important step, therefore, toward the removal of war and propaganda as "ethical methods." One acceptance carries in its train another and another. One commitment is followed in the "logic of events" by further commitments. To accept, as a point of departure, an objective standard by which values can be compared and appraised, is thus likely to be followed by an acceptance of goals which are appraised in the light of this standard, as "good" or "better." If, however, valuation is thought of as wholly volitional and noncognitive, then, I say, it is likely to be followed by contempt for or indifference to "valuations" which express attitudes unlike our own.

The point is that however vague and confused the garden variety of value-expressions may be, these expressions, in many instances, are commonly intended and understood as descriptions, and "assertions" involving them are regarded as true or false. In the light of this, it is highly dangerous to stipulate, as Reichenbach and others would, that they *should* be considered as wholly emotive and volitional. This will be taken everywhere, not as an attempt to classify the terms of discourse, but as a discrediting of rational procedures as ways of adjudicating differences of attitude. This is why I am compelled to say that those theorists who seek to remove all value-judgments from the sphere of rational discourse are doing a serious disservice to the very humane ends they themselves accept. I have previously contended that analysts *make* meanings as well as uncover them. I believe this is true in all spheres of discourse. There are remote common-sense ancestors of most of the concepts of physical science; but the latter are also in very large part the inventions of the laboratory. Now, if this is so elsewhere, it is also true in the field of values. We do not, however, wish to construct definitions of value-expressions which, when placed in the hands of those who do not understand the qualifications and conditions that properly circumscribe such analyses and stipulations of meaning, will in fact widen the areas in which irrational procedures prevail through an uncritical transference to the already *existing* cognitive and descriptive uses of value-expressions and terms, the associations of arbitrariness and irrationality which appertain to "emotive meaning," "non-cognitive aims," "meaningless" standards, and "volitional decisions."

In the third place, we simply do not, in ordinary discourse, *identify* "value" with volition. There are many things which are regarded as good which have nothing to do with choice or desire. The friendly smile of a pretty girl, a sunny day in June, the sense of contentment that suddenly "comes" we know not how or why—these things are in fact regarded as good by the ordinary. But they have nothing to do with "ends" or "decisions," nor do statements which appraise them as valuable have anything to do with the distinction between volitional aims and cognition.

I conclude that there are appraisals which are descriptive and which may, with no distortion of accepted usage of value-terms, be regarded as characteristic valuation propositions. Moreover, such judgments may be about ends as well as means. At the same time, it may be granted that they usually have a magnetic effect upon attitudes and volitions, due, as I have said, primarily to the nature of their subject matter.

In the following section I will introduce further considerations in order to show the importance of distinguishing between ends-in-view, which I shall call "ostensible" or "trial values," and genuine satisfactions and consummations, which I shall call "real values." Any adequate theory of value, as I see it, must avoid regarding the former as constitutive of intrinsic value. If the practical purpose of appraisal and evaluation is to be understood, and the essentially tentative and instrumental character of ends-in-view as directives for conduct is to be appreciated, *no mere interest theory of value will suffice.* On the latter view, value-judgments are largely ex post facto, and serve, on the whole, merely the purpose of curiosity. But if valuations are regarded as having "real values" as their primary concern, the dynamic effect of such judgments, as well as their function as guides to conduct, may be understood without difficulty.

V

Let me say in passing that I have come to closer agreement with Rice as to the desirability of distinguishing (and retaining *after* they are distinguished) several senses of the term "value." Thus, I would distinguish between "ostensible value," which I would ascribe to objects-of-desire, and "real value," which I would reserve for consummatory activities, satisfactions, and enjoyments. I would retain the distinction between "instrumental" and "intrinsic" value, not as an invidious distinction, but, among other things, as a way of indicating an important relationship between "ostensible values" and "real values." The following pages will summarize my main reasons for these distinctions.

The instrumentalist school, of which Dewey is the most distinguished representative, has properly insisted that human conduct cannot be understood in terms of fixed goals whose intrinsic goodness is absolute and eternal. The "ends" which govern behavior are ends-in-view that are tentative and modifiable. This school has also emphasized the importance of viewing the means-end relationship as a continuum involving a constant and reciprocal readjustment of aims in accordance with an emerging clarification of instrumentalities or means. As Stevenson has pointed out, "One who, ignorant of means, proceeds to recommend intrinsically valuable ends, may recommend ends which are impracticable because unobtainable." [28] In practice, means and ends are relative to one another, and what is thought of at the outset as a mere means may itself become an end, as interest is directed toward the problems of realizing it and as experience shows it to be enjoyable or satisfying. Likewise, increased awareness of the consequences of ends discloses that they also are means to further objectives. Put in another way, expectation and aim are dynamically and mutually interactive. The present direction of most conative activity is the resultant of both and is subject to change according to variations of either.

Emphasis has also shifted from the idea of a goal as something which when realized will terminate activity, to the idea of a goal as a modifiable objective from which present activity proceeds. Aims or purposes are thus means whereby present action is transformed from blind or random groping into controlled adaptation. It is argued on this basis that it is not the end as a fixed *terminus ad quem* which confers value on present activity, but the action itself which gives value to any goal. From this standpoint, indeed, all values become instruments of action, and the notion of intrinsic value tends to lose its meaning.

It is interesting and somewhat puzzling to observe that it has been a cardinal point of the instrumentalists to insist that it is they who restore to life a savor and significance which is lost when values are identified with fixed, immutable termini, and everything else is reduced to the level of bare meaningless instrumentality. What the instrumen-

[28] *Ethics and Language,* p. 177.

talists reject is the view that goods are to be understood as something always deferred, something reached for but never possessed, something which exists around a corner which it is never given to us to turn. In place of such a conception we are invited to consider present goal-directed activity as the valuable thing. If a distinction is still retained regarding means and ends, extrinsic and intrinsic values, this distinction is regarded as a matter of emphasis. The distinction is now construed as a distinction between predominant and subordinate aims, between governing propensities and intermediate interests, between the total process and its parts. But each is dependent upon the other: the means, the subordinate goal, transforms the dominant end-in-view from the status of an idle wish into purposive behavior, whereas the governing propensity in turn gives order and direction to what would otherwise be an unconnected sequence of activities.

It may be questioned, however, whether the shift in emphasis from ends to means and from the eventual outcome to the present struggle toward it has not gone too far. The dominant value theories of our time have been primarily volitional and conative theories for which the point of departure in conduct is *also* the locus of value. This is true of both Perry and Dewey. It is less true of Prall, who suggested significantly that all intrinsic values are "aesthetic"; it is also less true of Santayana, who is not, however, consistent in his usage. It should be possible, nevertheless, to acknowledge the importance of instrumentalities and the role of objects-of-interest or ends-in-view as instrumental mechanisms necessary to the intelligent realization of values without *defining* "value" itself in terms of them. It is certainly desirable to avoid the tendency of the older eudaemonistic ethics to conceive of the good in terms of rigid and fixed ends of action, without regard to their means. But it is equally desirable to avoid the voluntaristic alternative which would limit "value" solely to the struggle by which our ends are realized. Theories which, like Perry's, define "value" in the generic sense, in terms of objects-of-interest, in terms of prospective goals, and those which like Dewey's are concerned solely with the appraisal of present ends-in-view, tend to ignore the fact that objects-of-interest and ends-in-view themselves would be regarded as vain, apart from the genuine consummatory satisfactions and enjoyments which they envisage and to which they may lead. Ends-in-view or objects of desire are provisional *objectives for* desire. Their worth consists in the direction they give to activity which would otherwise be merely random action and blind urgency. An object of desire is thus, properly speaking, a "trial value," and it should retain this status until its realization brings the satisfaction which transforms it into an actual good. *All* objects of desire should thus be regarded with qualified approval as *merely* trial values.

The notion of end as fulfillment and not merely as terminus is, then, an indispensable term for the analysis of values. What is to be hoped for is a theory of value which will emphasize the experimental and instrumental function of valuation and conation, without reducing value itself to these alone. As Dewey insists, objects of desire and choice are and should remain provisional and tentative, not a final basis for reckoning value. Precisely because objects of desire are often initially vague and fluctuating, because they often begin merely as wishes, because it takes time and effort to know just what we want, intrinsic value cannot be defined in terms of them. But this, again, does not impugn the notion of intrinsic value, but only the attempt to define it in merely conative terms.

Dewey has, almost unwittingly, shown the futility of a purely conative definition of value through his own acute analysis of the instrumental function of *aims*. But his sound emphasis on (a) the dependence of choice upon a knowledge of means, (b) the failure of many moralists to recognize the illusoriness of fixed goals, and (c) their failure to take into account the tendency of means themselves to become valuable on their own account, does not in the least obviate the necessity for an idea of intrinsic value, nor the necessity for determining how intrinsic values may in principle be compared.

With these considerations in mind let us attempt to establish a provisional definition of "value" in terms of satisfaction.

We must first of all insist that satisfaction is to be regarded as not *merely* a terminal result of conduct. We may distinguish as sharply as we please between consummatory enjoyments and those which attend and reinforce the conative process. The important point is that value, as satisfaction, is present in most phases of conative behavior, and not merely in its concluding phase. We must, however, emphasize the distinction, which is obscured by any purely conative or volitional theory of value, between what I have called "real" and "ostensible" or "trial" values. Granting the importance of conceiving "values-in-view"

as objectives-to-be-realized, and not as fixed ends of action, still we must
not forget that only some "values-in-view" result in and are attended by
satisfaction and well-being; others are accompanied by or lead to
misery, frustration, and disillusionment. Not just any *"prima-facie
value"* is therefore worth realizing; not just any end-in-view is an unqualified good. When we shift our emphasis from ends-in-view to the
want itself which the latter serves, we see that the function of an end-
in-view or object of desire is to guide the organism to a bona fide satisfaction of a want; but apart from the possibility of such satisfaction it
has no real value, and hence no moral claim to justice or good will.[29]
An "ostensible" value coincides with a "real" value, then, when its
realization removes privation, restores the individual to a state of equilibrium, and results in a state of enjoyment or satisfaction.[30] There is no
guarantee, let me repeat, that an ostensible value will not lead to dissatisfaction and conflict rather than enjoyment and reintegration. A failure to bear this point constantly in mind has led to those conative theories of value which define value or goodness exclusively in terms of
objects of interest or ends-in-view—that is, in terms of what I call ostensible values. But the "real value" of a thing is not a mere point of origin
or a direction of present activity, any more than it is an end of action
in the literal sense. It is, in fact, what lies between the arousal of interest and quiescence that is significant, and not the extremes themselves.
This is why I would regard as valuable and hence as the real good of
human conduct, enjoyable experience rather than end-in-view or object
of interest.

Now satisfaction, I believe, is a quality of activity more readily perceived than defined, and while I should not wish to preclude the possibility of its definition, I have not succeeded in providing one. Certain
of its characteristic attributes and conditions may, however, be described. It is activity which is generally free from irreconcilable conflict, free from frustration, free from want in the merely privative sense,
though certainly not free from interest. In it, interest is continuously

[29] These terms are of course not precise. It is questionable, in the present state of
value theory and psychology, whether greater precision is either possible or desirable. The clarification of the definition of value must attend the progress of the
psychology of affective experience. What should be avoided is a specious appearance
of clarity which conceals lack of specific understanding of the behavioral processes
which determine affective experience. Cf. P. T. Young, *Motivation of Behavior*
(New York, 1936), pp. 337 ff.
[30] See my "Definitions of Value and the Moral Ideal," *The Journal of Philosophy*,
XLII (1945), 337–352.

and progressively renewed without being sated, and each moment of satisfaction provides a fresh stimulus to further interest.

One last word concerning the relation of the present view of value to other contemporary theories.

1. It accepts with Perry the distinction between the volitional and cognitive components of activity. It stresses the importance of cognition as a mediator between interest and its object and between interest and interest. It considers, however, that Perry's definition of value as "any object of any interest" is deficient on three scores: (a) there are wants or needs which do not have "objects," but whose satisfaction counts for something from the standpoint of what we would regard as a good or happy life; (b) it regards value as *wholly* prospective and active,[31] whereas value is often retrospective, passive, and, conceived as satisfaction, prior to desire; (c) it misses the point, which Dewey has emphasized again and again, that ends-in-view are themselves tentative and instrumental. There are other differences, but these are fundamental.

2. The present theory accepts Dewey's emphasis on the relativity of means and ends to one another, and his insistence on the possibility of a scientific and yet practical theory of valuation. I should also like to acknowledge that it was partly through a study of his work on the theory of valuation that I have been able to clarify my own criticisms of the interest theory of value. Still, like Parker, I cannot dispense with the conception of a scale of values. Granted that means and ends are functionally interdependent, still this does not obviate the necessity for distinguishing between intrinsic and extrinsic value, or for standards of comparison by means of which the former may be evaluated. As Parker says, "if all means are actually ends, the problem remains the same, the only change being that the field of the problem has been extended."[32] Instrumental values are, properly speaking, instruments *of* value. This does not, of course, preclude the possibility of their being valued "for their own sake" as well. It only requires us to recognize that the value *of* a means is distinguishable from its value *as a*

[31] Cf. William Savery, "A Defense of Hedonism," *The International Journal of Ethics*, XLV (1934), 13. ("Jam tomorrow, jam yesterday, but never jam today.") Savery's amusing allusion to the perplexity of Alice is very much to the point.
[32] D. H. Parker, "Reflections on the Crisis in Theory of Value, I: Mostly Critical," *Ethics*, LVI (1946), 198. I am much indebted to this, as well as to Parker's other writings, on the philosophy of values. My general viewpoint seems to me to be closer to his, perhaps, than to that of any other contemporary theorist.

means. This seems to me so obvious that I hesitate to labor it further.[33] Finally, I do not find in Dewey any clear-cut idea of value as distinct from valuation. At times, he too seems to think that the hoped-for and aspired-to result of all evaluation, the effect of equilibrium and the resolution of conflict, is "value" as I have conceived it. But he also seems at times to hold that "value" is dependent upon judgment, and that there can be no values which have not been subjected to critical appraisal. With this I cannot agree.

3. With Parker I should at least wish to amend Perry's definition to read, "the satisfaction of any interest in any object." But even this seems to me too narrow, since there are satisfactions which seem prior to any interest in an object. His view of value still remains too voluntaristic for me.[34] The late William Savery, in a notable and unfortunately neglected article, makes the point succinctly: ". . . all realizations [of desire] are satisfactions, and there seem to be additional pleasures which are not satisfactions of previous desires." [35]

In conclusion I should like to emphasize that the "crisis" in the theory of value, which is the source of so much discomfiture to Parker, Dewey, and others, is also indicative of a period of renewed interest in moral philosophy, an interest which is already cutting beneath the dominant formulations of the first third of the present century. The demand for greater analytical precision, greater awareness of recent developments in the psychology of motivation,[36] and greater sensitivity to the enormous semantical problems which attend the theory of norms is already beginning to bear fruit. One word of caution: new beginnings are likely to be attended by wholesale renunciation of what has gone before; but intellectual progress is dependent upon a sense of continuity with the past, which we may hope to correct and implement, but which we renounce or ignore at our peril.[37]

[33] It goes without saying, at this late stage, that in adhering to the *idea* of "intrinsic value," I *in no way* accept the view that these are fixed or immutable *values*. The fact that X is now regarded as "intrinsically good" in no way commits us to the view that it will be so eternally.

[34] Parker, *op. cit.*, p. 197.   [35] Savery, *op. cit.*, p. 10.

[36] Here let me record my belief that insufficient use has been made in most previous theories of value of the important and often revolutionary discoveries of psychoanalysis and dynamic psychiatry. The present theory is, on its motivational side, oriented toward the assimilation of this material to the theory of value. In particular, it represents a reaction against the unduly intellectualistic psychologies of motivation on which most previous ethical and value theories depended.

[37] For the Criticisms and Rejoinders which relate especially to this paper see pp. 350–355, 360–362, 366–371, and 375–377, below.

❧ THE VALUE ECONOMY

C. E. AYRES

THE TIME WILL COME, I think, when the present hubbub over value will be hard even for students of the history of ideas to understand. For if scientific enlightenment continues to spread, as I think it will in spite of contrary forces, the world will eventually come to realize that from the scientific point of view there is no difficulty at all. "Value" is of course a relational word like "truth" and "cause," to which, indeed, it is closely related. All these words refer to the interconnectedness of things in the universe and to the continuity of human experience which is itself a part of the universe. We speak of causality when we are thinking of the unity of the universe; we speak of truth when we are thinking of the coincident unity of our discourse; and we speak of value when we are thinking of the likewise coincident unity and continuity of our own life process.

The Life Process.—The unity of the life process of mankind is of course a natural phenomenon, in this respect identical with the motions of the planets and the metabolism of all living things. This does not mean in any of these cases that any given outcome is foreordained or fated. The earth may collide with an asteroid, as it came near doing only a few years ago; and in that event both its planetary motion and its human habitation might be seriously affected. But the regularity of planetary motion is a fact nevertheless, and so is the continuity and developmental regularity of human life.

When I was an undergraduate just beginning to take an interest in such things a book appeared by a young Harvard professor, Ralph Barton Perry, bearing the title, *The Moral Economy*.[1] The candid empiricism of that phrase appealed to me very strongly in those days, and it does so still. During the intervening years I have used it many times to point out the meaning of what we call "value" in any context,

[1] New York, 1909.

and I can still think of no better phrase to identify the subject of the present inquiry.

Whenever we discuss values it seems to me that what we have reference to is the existence of some sort of pattern in human behavior or whatever segment of it is under discussion at the time. Certainly this was true of the social philosophers who made the word "economy" one of the most important in the language. Theirs was a great discovery, one of the greatest of all time; for they perceived a sort of pattern in the hurly-burly of early modern commercial and industrial life. It was a pattern not altogether unlike that of the ordinary household. But its scale was comparable only to that of national communities, which it seemed to regulate by laws no less binding than those of governments; and so they called it the "political" economy. Recent usage has dispensed with the qualifying adjective, so that when we speak of "the economy" everybody understands that we refer to the commercial-industrial economy. But nobody has ever supposed this pattern to be wholly separate. Analysis of human behavior (or of society) reveals distinguishable foci of interests and activities which are therefore quite properly distinguished; but these special patterns are parts of a more general pattern which is coextensive with human experience itself. It is to this over-all pattern that we refer when we discuss values without any special qualification.

What is the nature of that pattern? What is the value economy? In trying to find answers to such questions it has been our inveterate habit to probe the individual organism, mind, or soul. We have done this for compelling (if not valid) reasons, to which therefore I shall revert presently. But we have reaped nothing but confusion, as the present joint inquiry virtually attests. In recent years, however, inquiry has taken another direction. Instead of seeking to explain organized behavior in terms of the virtues presumed to be inherent (or intrinsic) in supposedly elemental acts or experiences, recent inquiry has recognized organized behavior as a universe of discourse in which the material under examination is the organizational process.

Viewed in this manner the organizational process can be dissected with almost disconcerting ease. Obviously all organized behavior is a system of relationships. One type of relationship, which might be conveniently identified as chronological, is that in which every act or experience is related to every other act or experience in a continuum

of antecedents and consequents. This is the continuum of means and
ends. As Dewey has exhibited most clearly, every act or experience
is an end in relation to some antecedent means and a means to some
consequent end-in-view. This is true on whatever scale one views the
pattern. The momentary acts and experiences of individuals are so
related to earlier and later acts, and so are the experience of whole
communities and generations.

Another type of relationship, which might be identified as a sort of
cross section of behavior, has to do with the coincidence or contrariety
of all the various possible experiences at any given moment. In the
effort to make our means comport with our ends-in-view along the
chronological continuum we are obliged to "choose," and this necessity
has given rise to the presumption that objects of choice are in some
absolute and final sense, by their intrinsic character, mutually exclusive.
This presumption is further strengthened by observed fact. Health
and disease, for example, are mutually exclusive. Indeed, this may
well be true of certain types or aspects of human behavior itself; and
I shall therefore return to this problem shortly. But it is certainly not
true that all our experiences are aligned against all others in such
contrariety.

For a very considerable area of human behavior—indeed, for one
whole type or aspect of behavior—the opposite is true. Although at
any given moment of the chronological continuum we may have to
"choose" between eating and listening to music, food and music are
not contraries. Eating does not paralyze the ears, nor does music kill
the appetite or upset digestion. A lot of nonsense has been talked along
these lines. Darwin evidently thought he had sacrificed some aesthetic
sensibilities by subjecting himself to scientific discipline, and many
people talk as though closed plumbing or the use of automotive vehi-
cles were somehow inhibitory of what they call "the life of the spirit."
But the evidence is overwhelming that Darwin was wrong on this point,
and we have only his word for the sensibilities he thought he lost.
Some people detest contemporary music, literature, painting, sculpture, and even architecture. But that is a very different matter from
saying that no such thing exists.

What organized behavior in fact reveals is a very general mutuality
of human experiences, or values. This principle might be called the
concert of values, or experience. Though it is true in a sense that any

one of us can only have one experience at a time, it is not true that health, knowledge, technical skill, artistic sensibility, and the like are mutually exclusive and inhibitory. The exact opposite is true. If this were not so, organized behavior would be impossible, and we would still be apes. I have sometimes put this proposition in terms of the organization of a social microcosm such as a university. If chemistry and physics, or mathematics and archeology, were mutually inhibitory, making up the university budget would involve "choices" beyond the powers of any administrator. What makes a "university" possible, as the word itself suggests, is the certainty that all knowledge and discovery contribute to and facilitate all other knowledge and discovery. What makes civilization possible is the fact that "useful" arts and "fine" arts, "pure" science and "applied" science—and so on all down the line—do not inhibit and nullify each other but on the contrary stimulate and fructify each other.

So considered, all values arise in and have reference to the pattern of organized behavior. What we mean by value is the bearing of any act, experience, thing or condition experienced, upon other such acts, experiences, or things in the continuum and concert of social life. To say this is not to deny that values are related to desires and their satisfaction. It does mean that desires and their satisfaction are significant and meaningful—which is to say valuable—according to their relation to the continuum and concert of experience, or civilization.

This sounds formidable. To go through life continually exercising one's judgment with regard to the relation of every act to the continuum and concert of experience does indeed seem to be a dreary prospect. Many people hesitate to subject their admittedly feeble judgment to such a burden. Their hesitation is due in part to a becoming modesty, but it is also due in part to misconception.

Twenty years ago R. H. Wilensky pointed out that people who say, "I don't know much about Art, but I know what I like," are discussing, not the painting in question, but themselves. Such a remark, he argued, is autobiographical, not aesthetic. This might seem to suggest that it is a product of conceit, but in fact it is the precise opposite. Critics like Wilensky himself, Roger Fry, John Ruskin, and the rest, never hesitate to tell us what is and is not art. But most of us hesitate to bandy judgments with such authorities. Indeed, most of us do not even know what their judgments are. The disavowal, "I don't know much about Art," is a literal confession of ignorance.

In the same sense the statement, "I know what I like," contains a judgment. We often talk, and perhaps "feel," as though such judgments were isolated fragments of experience and did not involve any calculation of the relation of the immediate experience to the continuum and concert of experience in the whole life process of mankind; but that is a misconception. The fact is that many simple experiences have been so generally assessed by the community, and were assimilated so early by the individual in question, that his present experience is one of simple recognition involving no recapitulation of the labors of assessment and judgment.

We all have some capacity for innocent enjoyment. We all love to hear the little brook agurgling, and listen to the merry village chime We "like" the pictures which we now (correctly) identify, without any effort of judgment, as like those to which we were solicitously exposed in childhood by our respected parents and teachers. But somebody judged those pictures, somebody whose judgment we have judged worthy of endorsement. The innocence of the merry village chime is not established by the listener's instantaneous pleasure. Indeed, neither the pleasure nor the innocence of such a sound is wholly unaffected by the fact that it is made by a church bell. If for a hundred generations such bells had been used solely to identify bordellos—if no greater sacrilege could be imagined than the ringing of such a bell on ecclesiastical premises—our feelings would be somewhat different.

The truth is there is a sort of James-Lange relationship between feeling and judgment. Certainly feelings do not continually wait upon judgment. In that sense they are indeed quite spontaneous. But neither does judgment wait upon feelings. If it did, we would spend most of our lives abasking in the sun—and still be apes. Neither feeling nor judgment is spontaneous in the sense of being unaffected by previous experience. On the contrary, each is in its own way an accurate register of previous conditioning. Our feelings are, as we often say, "clear" and therefore instantaneous with regard to matters on which our experience has been consistent and uniform. But we have not achieved uniformity and consistency merely by following our feelings, nor is it sufficient that we should "feel" that our lives are consistent and uniform. No one ever feels more certain of himself than a lunatic. What is most important about feelings no less than about judgment is that they should be correct, and they are correct precisely to the extent to which they register our achievement of some degree of consistency and uniformity in the life process itself.

Feelings and judgments, truth and beauty, and all values whatsoever are matters of degree. All of us recognize this in all the ordinary affairs of life. Nobody denies that the feelings and judgment of the man who knows what he likes are correct in some sense or other. At the same time we all know that such feelings and judgment may be "correct" in a very special and limited sense. To say that one man's feelings, or judgment, have the same validity as those of anybody else is arrant nonsense. The man who declares that he knows only what he likes in effect admits that others probably know more than he and that their knowledge gives significance to their judgment which his judgment lacks.

Such judgment, based on such knowledge, does not tell us what values are "best." Why should it? Does such a question make sense? Does it make sense to inquire which is best, music or poetry; or, for that matter, music or food? Does it make sense to inquire what is the best poem ever written? Then does it make any more sense to ask what is the best "value"? Questions such as these are nonsensical precisely because they do not arise in actual life. That is, they do not arise in any of the affairs either of common citizens or of scientists or artists.

What is "best" in all our affairs is the continuity and consistency of values in the social pattern, and this is a growing, changing thing, never finished and never completely known. If truth is "a body of knowledge infinite in content and perfect in form"—a definition which I learned as a college sophomore from the greatest teacher I have ever known, Alexander Meiklejohn—then the *summum bonum* is likewise a body of experience similarly infinite and perfect. In neither case does any such body exist to be the "standard" by which particular truths and values may be measured. In both cases the definition is a sort of mathematical projection of the process of knowing and living, just as mathematical infinity is a projection of the process of counting. The life process in which we are all engaged is the continuous and universal effort to get things straight and set them straight, meaning by "straight" just what we mean in science and technology; and the fact of civilization, and its amazing continuity throughout the ages, give evidence of the genuineness of that effort. The real problem of value is that of the fuller apprehension, or appreciation, of the significance of anything for everything else; and that in truth is problem enough.

Nevertheless, other questions do persist. Why they persist, and what they mean, are therefore inescapable parts of our inquiry.

The Persistence of Credulity.—One of the strangest puzzles future students of the history of ideas in the twentieth century will have to solve is the resurgence of emotionalism in what would otherwise seem to be an age of science and technology. It is this phenomenon, I judge, which has prompted the present joint inquiry. At all events this is the problem in which the questions Dewey has set us do seem to culminate. "Of late" he writes, "there has appeared a school of theorists insisting with vigor that genuine propositions (and/or judgments) about values are impossible because the latter have properties that render them wholly recalcitrant to cognitive treatment. In brief, this school holds that verbal expressions about values are of the nature of exclamations, expressing only the dominant emotional state of the one from whom the ejaculation issues. . . . They are just ultimate facts. In the frank words of one who has taken this position, serious cases of ultimate difference can be settled, if at all, only by 'bashing in of heads.' " Hence the question upon which all the other present ones converge is directed at this supposition. What is the ground on which this notion of value stands? Is it solid and compelling? Or is it illusory; and if so, how can such an illusion be dispelled?

Dewey has not left us in any doubt about his answer to the basic question. Clearly this movement is a twentieth century manifestation of "the quest for certainty." The only puzzle is why there should have been such a resurgence of the age-old quest in an age of science, and why it should have taken this peculiar form. Dewey himself may be partly responsible for this enigma. In his anxiety to do full justice to a way of thinking he abhors, he has long conceived the quest for certainty itself as "a method of dealing with the serious perils of life," one which has the same object as the "mastery of nature's energies and laws" (as he puts it in the opening paragraphs of *The Quest for Certainty*), and thus differs only in the procedure by which mastery is sought. Fortunately, Dewey does not adhere to this conception throughout his analysis, for I believe it is quite wrong.

On this point, indeed, I think Veblen was much closer to the truth. It was from the first the perils of civil disobedience, not those of nature, which men sought to overcome by magic rite and mystic ecstasy. All ecclesiasticism is hierarchical and was so from the outset. In regarding this sort of thing in all its manifestations as a late development of "the barbarian stage" which he thought of as following a much older "savage stage" in which men labored matter-of-factly with their simple tools, undismayed by totem and taboo, Veblen was caught in the backwash of Rousseau's noble savage and of the "primitive communism" of the early evolutionists. It now seems very unlikely that even the earliest human beings were matter-of-fact communists. In all probability horrendous rites go as far back in human experience as any tools; and as far back as intelligence and speech extend, doubtless men were trying to get the better of each other by hook or crook and most especially by hocus-pocus. Life has always held two sorts of perils for the sons of Adam: those implicit in the forces of nature, and those implicit in the coercions of social power systems.

It is these latter perils, surely, from which mankind has always sought surcease in the quest for certainty. That is why emotionality has always played a predominant part in that particular quest. What we now call the supreme coercive power of the state has always been physical enough. But over and above and behind the physical coercion of organized society there has always loomed the much vaster force of emotional coercion. All government, indeed all the institutional foci of the whole social power system, rest on the consent of the governed —that is, on emotional conditioning. This is true because emotional conviction has always seemed more certain, more devastatingly obsessive, than any mere fact of work-a-day experience. People have believed the legends which condemned them to sacrifice their first-born on the altar of Moloch not because of any direct physical compulsion— nothing is more difficult than to change another human being's way of thinking by direct assault!—but rather because under the influence of soul-shaking magic rites they "felt in their hearts" that Moloch would strike them down if they did otherwise.

Such myths have disappeared. In recent times enlightened peoples have dispensed with the divinities that once hedged priests and kings and patriarchs. But emotion still remains to plague us. No doubt the uniquely vivid and, as we say, "moving" quality of emotional experience contributes to our difficulty. But it is doubtful nevertheless whether that inherent quality of emotional seizure would be sufficient to upset our thinking if we had completely outgrown our past conditioning. We know a great deal now about the psychology and even the physiology of emotion. There is no type of emotional experience that has not been subjected to detailed analysis. We know quite enough about the "evidence" of dreams and similar hallucinations to be fairly safe from their imaginary promptings—if only we could rid ourselves of our presentiments, carried over from the age of myths, that in spite of everything emotional seizures do still possess evidential authority.

Obviously what prevents our making a fresh start emotionally is the dead hand of the past. There are certain areas of experience in which it is still heavy upon us. Aesthetic experience is such an area. Literate people—the very ones who are most fully cognizant of the accomplishments of science—are therefore more fully aware than others of the glory and grandeur of human achievement in the Fine Arts. They honor the Arts with capital letters. Indeed, it is a matter of pride with them to do so. But nobody can understand everything; and consequently such people frequently find themselves in the embarrassing position of having to pay honor to something they take in only dimly and, as it were, emotionally or even "intuitively."

As everybody knows, this situation is further complicated by an element of status. I certainly do not mean to suggest that there is "nothing to" the arts but their leisure-class associations, any more than I would suggest that financial control of industry means that there is nothing to engineering. But it does mean that the arts are cursed with humbug and that the awe and veneration in which works of art are held is no simple, direct, and certain evidence of anything. It may express an enthusiasm born of genuine understanding, but it may also express sheer snobbery unrelieved by any glimmer of intelligence; and since the snobbery is successful only if it passes for genuine appreciation, a great many people who "don't know anything about Art but know what they like" insist with passionate intensity on the validity of the emotions which in many cases they sincerely attribute to the intuitions they are sure they have by reason of being "persons of refined sensibilities."

Thus people who would ridicule the notion that a serf's emotions are valid evidence of authentic kingship or a mother's intuitions a valid

guide to infant care nevertheless insist on the superior validity of emotional experience as such. Even scientists, who of all people ought to
know better, still do so. The following paragraph culled from one of
the papers presented in celebration of the fiftieth anniversary of the
University of Chicago is an extreme example, perhaps, but an example
nonetheless. At the conclusion of his "Basic Comparisons of Human
and Insect Societies," Alfred E. Emerson has this to say.

Although I am here advocating a great comprehension of social phenomena
through scientific method applied to comparative sociology and to borderline
fields between the biological and social sciences, I do not wish to leave the
impression that intellectual understanding is the complete solution. We all
inherit and develop emotional responses that are an important aspect of our
lives and, like intellect, may be modified by experience and trained toward
richer and more harmonious expression. It seems fairly obvious that "emotional discoveries and principles" often precede ratiocination. It has been
said that thinking is hard work while prejudice is a pleasure. Scientists seem
to get much pleasure from their prejudice in favor of logical thought, but they
should not overlook the place of emotional force and harmony even in science.[2]

It may well be that this zoologist did not mean what he said, but it
seems to me significant even in that case that his unintended meaning
should be an assertion of the validity of emotional experience as something lying beyond science and independent of ratiocination.

What could he have meant by suggesting that "intellectual understanding" is not "the complete solution"? Complete solution of what?
The task in which he has been engaged is one of analysis. Are we to
understand that there may be some other solution of analytical problems than analytical ones? Is there some other kind of understanding
than intellectual? This passage suggests that emotion has been ignored
and overlooked, but that is certainly not the case. Neither mankind
at large nor scientific analysis has overlooked emotion. Science has
learned a great deal about emotions, as I have already remarked. We
know that emotion is neither a substitute for judgment nor a kind of
judgment; and since Professor Emerson makes no reference to any new
discoveries in this field, it seems fair to assume that his proposal that
science defer to emotion does not originate in any new conception of

[2] *Biological Symposia,* ed. by R. Redfield (Lancaster, Pa., 1942), VIII, 175–176; reprinted by permission of The Ronald Press Company.

the role of emotion in human life. Consequently, I am forced to the conclusion that it does originate in a very old conception.

No contemporary writer has been more candid than Mortimer J. Adler in saying exactly what this old conception is. According to Adler, science in general and John Dewey in particular have committed a dreadful intellectual crime: "the 'nothing-but' fallacy." This, so he wrote a few years ago, is what has been wrong with Dewey, modern education, and the modern world.

At its very center [he thinks], exercising centrifugal force, was a hard core of negations and exclusions. The denial of metaphysics and theology as independent of empirical science, the denial of stability in the universe and certainty in human knowledge, the denial of moral values transcending adaptation to environment and escaping relativity to time and place, the denial of intellectual discipline in education and of the light shed by an abiding tradition of learning, the denial of a personal God, self-revealed, and of a Divine Providence concerned with man's supernatural salvation—these kept the ball rolling, and gave it its terrific impact on American life.[3]

Now it certainly is not true that what gave science its terrific impact on American life is these denials. The truth is just the reverse of this. These denials (whatever they are) derive their force from the terrific technological impact of science on America and the world. Science does indeed have its negative aspect; and the scale on which it has impacted upon modern life does indeed give this negation tremendous importance, which in turn lends importance to Adler's identification. In large part this also is false and misleading. Science certainly does not deny the certainty of knowledge or the stability of the universe. Indeed, if it did, Adler would have no cause for complaint, for it would then not be committing his "nothing-but" fallacy. Neither science nor the instrumentalist philosophy denies the importance of intellectual discipline or the existence and importance of cultural traditions. Neither denies that moral values transcend the narrow limits of a particular time and place. But they do deny the supernatural, and consequently they do deny that moral values transcend the natural universe. That is the issue; and it is, as Professor Adler says, "the crucial issue of our day: *whether science is enough, theoretically or practically.*"

Science denies the supernatural. But the sons of Adam—even those

[3] M. J. Adler, "The Chicago School," *Harper's Magazine,* CLXXXIII (1941), 382; reprinted by permission of the editors.

who have spent much of their lives in laboratories—feel the greatest reluctance to doing so. That is what they mean when they talk about the importance of man's emotional nature. Unlike Adler, they hesitate to speak up for supernaturalism; but what they cherish is not the importance of being angry or afraid, or even of falling in love. It is rather the importance which immemorial tradition has imputed to those ecstasies in which "higher truths" are presumed to be, as Adler says, "self-revealed." That is why Aldous Huxley assumes as a matter of course that the arts, or as he prefers to say, "Art," is a realm of being quite distinct from that of science. As such it is a step towards higher truths. The miracle of direct apperception is presumed to be established by the ecstasy we feel upon hearing Beethoven's last quartets; and since the quartets do in fact exist, it is but a step to the presumption that any ecstasy is similarly evidential.

Our emotions are indeed evidential, but what they are evidential of is past conditioning. The same volume which contains Emerson's article also contains a magnificent study of "Modern Society" by Robert E. Park, in the course of which he quotes Walter Lippmann as remarking that "modern man has ceased to believe without ceasing to be credulous." This, surely, is the crux of the matter—the explanation of the upsurge of emotionalism to which Dewey calls attention, and the explanation of the "factitious plausibility" which, as Aiken remarks,[4] "is likely to make the emotive theory attractive to many philosophers in coming years." When revelation fails, we have recourse to "intuition"; and when intuition fails, we have "no other recourse than to adopt the emotive theory," that last infirmity of noble mind!

The Technological Imperative.—The problem of value is the problem of human life and civilization. The present generation is greatly preoccupied with it because we are passing through a revolution. This is the post-Copernican revolution of which Immanuel Kant warned his posterity. It is perhaps the most fundamental transformation to which our way of life has been subjected since our forefathers came down out of the trees. Throughout the intervening period we have been doing two sorts of things which have been in conflict with each other. We have been engaged in tool-using, and we have been engaged in mystery-making. At all times the mystery-making has checked, thwarted, and

[4] H. D. Aiken, "Emotive 'Meanings' and Ethical Terms," *The Journal of Philosophy*, XLI (1944), 470.

generally interfered with the tool-using. A sort of race between enlightenment and superstition has been going on. In the vast majority of particular cultural instances superstition has prevailed. But the expansive pressure, as it might be called, of tool-using and instrumental knowledge has likewise been constant; and, in those few instances in which it has prevailed, its triumph has been on such a gigantic scale that the net result has been that science and technology have taken possession not only of the whole world but of virtually the whole of human life. The momentousness of the present revolution derives from the fact, that after all these ages, superstition seems about to pass completely out of the picture.

This transition is of course extremely painful. The cripple loves his crutches. We are still strongly moved to "trust our feelings," and this impulse is strengthened by our knowledge of the antiquity of ceremonialism and the extreme novelty of science and technology as we know them today. It was only the other day, so to speak, that natural philosophers made bold to urge us not to be content with "nothing but" theology; so that when mystics like Aldous Huxley and theologians like Adler now urge us not to be satisfied with "nothing but" science, their plea seems altogether reasonable, being an echo of the one science was making just the other day.

Moreover, science itself has always counseled open-mindedness. It is in this spirit, I think, that many scientists, like Emerson, are prepared to respect a boundary beyond which science presumably cannot go, and to place all "values"—those of economics and politics along with those of beauty and goodness—beyond that pale. Even social scientists recognize this barrier. The notion prevails very widely today that social analysis can deal only with the institutional procedures by which (purportedly) values are attained, while values themselves, being matters of "direct human experience," lie beyond the scrutiny of science.

This is thought to be true whether value is conceived as the inner experience of metaphysically unique spiritual being, or whether it is the tribal dictum of whatever community may happen to cherish it. Thus contemporary social science has impaled itself on the horns of a dilemma. According to immemorial tradition, values are directly self-revealed spiritual experience. But the "sociology of knowledge" shows these experiences to be mutually contradictory, relative in each case to the "mores" of some community, and having no other meaning or sanction. This would seem to mean that all values are utterly relative and without any general meaning. But since all have a common emotional quality and a common social determination, many social scientists propose to assume these qualities as the determinants of value and to "respect the feelings" of any and every community without further inquiry. Thus social anthropologists propose to respect the feelings of every community, however "primitive," for their ancestral culture, and to make the preservation of that culture a sort of categorical imperative. Sociologists do the same with the (conspicuously emotional) "adjustments" they consequently undertake to promote; and economists likewise propose to treat "wants" as "primary data," rejoicing in the realization that it makes no difference to such an assumption whether such "data" are taken as "given" because they have the neo-Cartesian authority of the "human spirit" or because they are the dictates of the community whose dictates they are.

Whether as a community we shall succeed in resolving this dilemma, and whether industrial society will emerge intact from the trans-Copernican revolution, I do not know. But all that we do know seems to me to mean that we can do so, if at all, only by further understanding; that is, by extending such understanding as we have already achieved. It seems to me that such an extension of our present understanding will involve three sets of problems.

The first is that posed by the present situation. As we come to understand this situation better, we will, I think, be bound to realize that deference to feelings, such as we have seen so much of in recent years, does not originate in any new increment of understanding of the emotional aspect of experience. The sanction to which appeal is made is not that of emotive apperception at all. More or less unwittingly, but quite unmistakably in every case, the real appeal is to the myths, magic, and mysticism generally, by which our sentiments have been conditioned from time immemorial. The only reason anybody attaches any importance to emotional "judgments" is the immemorial belief, fostered by all the superstitions of our legendary past that emotions are profoundly and mysteriously significant. If this is a fact, as I think it is, further analysis is bound to bring it in plainer view. I am not saying, as people sometimes charge, that such facts will come into view of their own accord. Obviously further understanding will result only from an effort of understanding. But if that effort is made, facts that are already evident to some will become evident to all.

Such a development will inevitably bring a second problem into view. Taken at face value and without further reflection, the appeal to something that lies beyond science seems to have reason on its side. "Why should we close ourselves in," it seems to say, "by recognizing nothing but science?" But further reflection and analysis will bring to light another compelling fact. The trouble with the appeal to sentiment, which is really an appeal to superstition, is that metaphysical judgments not only go beyond our scientific knowledge; they flatly contradict it. If it is true, as Emerson suggests, that scientists "favor" logical thought only because of a "prejudice" from which they derive "much pleasure," this can only mean that pleasure and prejudice, and not logical consistency, are the determinants of human action and even of scientific analysis. This is as much as to say that the only guarantee we have of the validity of such analysis is the pleasure we get from conducting, and doubtless—as in the case of "Art"—from contemplating it. But this is directly contradictory of all the principles of science.

Moreover, any such allegation inevitably commits the Cretan fallacy. Is Emerson writing as he does only because it pleases him to do so, or does he draw his conclusions with regard to pleasure and prejudice from his scientific knowledge? If the former, then it may equally well please somebody else to think otherwise and there is nothing Emerson can do to say him nay; if the latter, then his own claim to knowledge contradicts his deference to prejudice. This is the dilemma on which many present-day social scientists have impaled themselves by their eagerness to recognize extra-scientific sanctions. If science is only the climate of opinion in which we now happen to live, and if it derives its sanction only from the credulity with which modern man has come to regard it, then that is true of the sociology of knowledge, which certainly purports to be a part of the corpus of modern science. But if the truths of science have no force over people whose inclinations to credulity are different, that is true also of the sociology of knowledge, and the truths of science may be valid after all.

Thus we are confronted by a third problem, that of extricating ourselves from the dilemma of mores nihilism. In suggesting that further understanding may enable us to solve the problem I am not merely evincing a blindly sentimental faith in ratiocination. The gap in our analysis is already apparent. Art worshipers do not deny that artists use tools and materials. They do not even deny that they solve problems, or that the solution of problems such as the history of any art reveals is a cumulative process. Indeed, they do not even deny that their own enthusiasm for great works of art is in some fashion related to their understanding of the problems to which the artist has addressed himself and the effectiveness of his solutions. They simply ignore all that sort of thing as being the "mere means" to the transcendent "end" which is their own ecstasy.

And social scientists do the same. No economist denies that wants are affected by what goes on in the community. Indeed, the indefinite expansibility of wants is an economic axiom, and all economists recognize that one of the principal forces to which wants respond is that of an advancing technology. Sociologists all know that emotional adjustments are affected by the empirical facts of social life, and that among those facts none is more significant than advancing technology and institutional "lag." And anthropologists are likewise well aware of the material culture. They know well enough that it manifests a clear continuity of development, for they use that very line of development to classify the cultures with which they deal. They know also that the world diffusion of industrial technology is a fact with which every people now has to reckon, whatever their sentiments may be.

Since we have got into trouble by ignoring and depreciating science and technology, the material culture, and the whole tool-using aspect of human life, it is not unreasonable to suppose that we may get out of it by repairing that deficiency. This does not mean that we must ignore or depreciate the emotional character of man. Emotion as such is neither infirm nor ignoble. Nobody, so far as I know, has ever denied that it plays a big part in human life. We do indeed experience wants, desires, and interests; and values are indeed proportional to their satisfaction. But what we have to understand is the relation of these emotional experiences to the life process.

In particular, what we have to understand is that all such experiences derive from and must be judged in relation to the life process, not the other way around. To do so is a categorical imperative from which there is no escape, for it arises from the life process itself.

This means that we must be prepared to declare, without fear and without scorn, that nothing but science is true or meaningful. We must do so because it is a fact. The uniformity of nature and the consistency of science are obverse and reverse of the same fact, and the consistency of science is a function of the continuity of instrumental procedure— that is to say, of that tool-using activity which is the life process of mankind.

Most scientists are reluctant to dogmatize. As I have already noted, this reluctance is in part humane. After all, denouncing follies which have been shared by virtually the entire human race throughout the whole of history and are still shared by many who are near and dear to each of us—follies so persistent that none of us can be quite sure of his own complete immunity—is a uniquely ungracious performance. Furthermore, scientists are habituated to open-mindedness and consequently "feel" great reluctance to excluding anything from the universe of possible truths.

But whatever scientists may do or fail to do, science is quite peremptory. The scientific universe extends to the entire universe of discourse which is defined by the use of tools and instruments, and by the same token it stops at the limits of that universe. Any proposition which is incapable of statement in scientific terms, any phenomenon which is incapable of investigation by scientific methods, is meaningless and worthless as meaning and value are conceived in that universe of discourse.

This is the universe of discourse of human life and action. Expressions such as "universe of discourse," and especially such words as "phenomenon," necessarily imply the possibility of other "realms of being" or universes; but that implication is no ground for embarrassment, intellectual or emotional. In the past philosophers have indeed made much of it; but, as we should know by now, their concern has been prompted not by any failure or limitation of scientific-technological procedure but only by the stubborn persistence of primeval legends which continue to live in our emotions even after our minds have been emancipated.

As well as we know anything, we know that neither emotion nor mind nor any other aspect of experience including even the creation of legend is an exception to the uniformity of nature. For that uniformity itself is a function of the use of tools. "I cannot but think," said Thomas Huxley in one of his most luminous passages,

that the foundations of all natural knowledge were laid when the reason of
man first came face to face with the facts of Nature; when the savage first
learned that the fingers of one hand are fewer than those of both; that it is
shorter to cross a stream than to head it; that a stone stops where it is unless
it be moved; and that it drops from the hand which lets it go; that light and
heat come and go with the sun; and sticks burn away in a fire; that plants and
animals grow and die; that if he struck his fellow savage a blow he would
make him angry, and perhaps get a blow in return, while if he offered him
a fruit he would please him, and perhaps receive a fish in exchange. When
men had acquired this much knowledge, the outlines, rude though they were,
of mathematics, of physics, of chemistry, of biology, of moral, economical,
and political science were sketched.[5]

Does man impose this uniformity upon nature, or does nature impose
it upon man? With Dewey's help we are beginning to see that sentences
such as this are meaningless. They are sentences by virtue of grammatical structure, interrogatory in form but substantively meaningless.
For such a question begins by dividing man from the universe of which
all that we know shows him to be a part and ends by imputing to nature-
other-than-man a characteristically human act, that of "imposing."

It makes no difference whether we identify our universe as that of
nature or that of man. It is the same universe in either case. The uniformity of nature and the continuity of human experience are twin
characterizations of a single universe of discourse. I am tempted to say
that it is our universe "whether we like it or not," and that we therefore "have to make the best of it." But again, expressions such as these
derive from subdivisions of experience in which alternatives exist,
whereas the whole meaning of the scientific and technological imperative is that we have no choice.

In that sense the technological imperative is no imperative at all
but a fact of nature and of human life. We think like men because we
are men, using tools—manually and conceptually—and thereby getting
consistent results which coincide with the continuities of previous experience and the uniformities of nature. This is what we mean by
truth, since anything else is meaningless. Even when we invent legends
we continue the same process, putting an imaginary hammer in the
fictitious hand of a legendary Thor, or providing the Heavenly Throng

[5] T. H. Huxley, "On the Advisableness of Improving Natural Knowledge" (1866),
Essays (Modern Readers Series, New York, 1929), p. 222; by permission of The
Macmillan Company, publishers.

with zithers of distinctively human artisanship and endowing them with characteristically human skills. We know these legends to be in the literal sense untrue, since we know that only men wield hammers and play zithers; and we know further that whatever truth such imaginings may have they have acquired by virtue of reflecting the life process of mankind.

In like manner whatever has value for us does so because of its bearing on the life process. This does not mean that some metaphysical abstraction, "Life," is the ultimate value from which all others flow. The supposed sacredness of human life derives from the life process, and not the other way around. We all recognize this to be so in our own personal experience. What motivates for each one of us the elaborate maneuvers we adopt in order to keep going is not any mere animal instinct to survive, much less any belief in our own legendary sanctity. It is of course the realization that each of us had made commitments and assumed responsibilities. The man who desisted from committing suicide because he heard the factory whistle blow was thereby recognizing a profound truth, namely, that his existence is so intertwined with those of other people that his death must inevitably send forth waves of disturbance and interruption, affecting most those who are closest to him but also prejudicing, to however tiny an extent, the whole effort of mankind.

Nor does any one deny that all values are more or less keenly felt. We all rejoice in the satisfaction of our desires, and we fear and dread their disappointment. But what this means is intelligible only in terms of the life process, and is so judged by all of us. To think of an aesthetic experience—say that afforded by some poem or picture or piece of music—so ecstatic that all who had this experience died of it is to imagine nonsense. As we all know and have always known, what we desire is stimulation and refreshment, or as we often say enrichment or even re-creation, always measured by our continued participation in the life process of the race. When our feelings at such a moment of ecstasy are verified by our subsequent performance, we judge those values accordingly; and when the ecstasy—induced perhaps by opium—results in the unmistakable disorganization of our working lives, we pass the opposite judgment. Clearly our feelings are trustworthy or not according to the outcome of the judgments they invariably represent.

Like the whole life process, these judgments are always capable of analysis and subject to the outcome of such analysis. For the life process itself is one of analysis. It is the tool-using way of life. All that we have achieved or can hope to achieve has resulted and will result from this activity. This is the basic fact and therefore the primary imperative of human life. Consequently its discovery is the greatest discovery we have made since men first discovered tools and thereby acquired the character of men, a discovery far too momentous and extensive to be attributed to any individual man or single generation, one toward which men have been moving ever since men first began to talk and pound and weave and handle fire. It involves nothing less than the whole of life, and we therefore rightly call it the problem of value, meaning the problem of the nature of the life process.

Can we adjust ourselves to the realization that all values arise in the tool-organized pattern, or economy, of human life? That remains to be seen. We have passed through the Copernican revolution, in effect accepting the natural universe. We have passed through the Darwinian revolution, accepting our identification as an animal species organically like any other. But since human life is very different from that of any other animal species, we have still had ground for maintaining that we are not "nothing but" a species of animals inhabiting one of the lesser planets. The problem of value is the issue of that "nothing but;" for if man differs from other animals only by virtue of his use of tools and the patterns of organized activity which the use of tools makes not only possible but inevitable, then nothing is left to be a mystery and a source of authority to those who interpret mysteries.

In this crisis the clear imperative of science and technology and all the fine and useful arts is to go forward: to identify the value economy as the tool-and-instrument life process of mankind. But we differ from the other animals not only by virtue of our tools but also as regards the fantasies with which we have always titillated and tortured our emotions. We no longer believe the fantasies, but we still feel their force. That is why we still think of science and technology as "mere means" to the "end" of "direct" experience of value in emotional consummation. As they have always done, these suppositions directly contradict all that we have learned by using tools and instruments. Wherever they prevail, the technological life process is interrupted and disorganized, as it has always been. Nevertheless it still remains to be seen whether they may not ultimately prevail in the final disorganization of the life process. We have come a long way, but not too far to lose our way and even perhaps to return to the racial womb from which we came. There are some even now who are explicitly calling for a return to medievalism, and some who are practicing what most people recognize as savagery. They may yet prevail. Unless we go forward, they will prevail.[6]

[6] For the Criticisms and Rejoinders which relate especially to this paper see pp. 331–333, 415–417, and 419–421, below.

❦ THE FIELD OF "VALUE"

JOHN DEWEY

IN THE PRESENT STATE of the subject of value, the decisive issue is methodological: From what standpoint shall the subject matter of valuings and evaluations be approached? What postulates shall determine selection and treatment of this subject matter? The reference made above to "the present state of the subject" is important. It is not meant that the methodological question can be separated from that of subject matter, nor that the former should remain paramount indefinitely. On the contrary, if and when it is cleared up we shall be able to go ahead and use it, testing and developing it as we proceed, without need for special discussion of it. But a glance at the controverted present state of inquiry shows that no question is more pertinent or more penetrating than the one asked by Pepper: "How guarantee that different writers on 'value' are discussing the same subject?" [1] And I find the phrase (in his previous sentence) "subject or field of value" equally significant. For the confused controversial state of the subject seems to arise from the fact that there is no agreement about the *field* in which events having value-qualifications are located. Till this field is reasonably settled, discussion is a good deal like firing bird-shot in the dark at something believed to exist somewhere, the "where" being of the vaguest sort. In such a state of affairs, it would be pretentious to do more than put the methodological issue first or do other than offer an hypothesis.

I

I begin then by saying the hypothesis that gives direction to the following pages is that the field in which value-facts belong is *behavioral*, so that the facts must be treated in and by methods appropriate to behavioral subject matter. The words "behavior and behavioral"

[1] Contained in the questions and comments preliminary to the present cooperative inquiry.

are, however, far from self-explanatory. A few preliminary remarks are called for. As here employed, the words refer exclusively to events of the nature of *life-processes* in general and animal life-processes in particular. Objections and criticisms that are made from the stand-point of the assumption that the words apply only to what is stated in *physical* terms—those of strictly physical knowledge—are, accord-ingly, aside from the point. Life-processes have a physical aspect, and no account of them is adequate that does not draw from available physical knowledge. But this is a radically different matter from *reduction* to physical terms. Furthermore, while *human* behavior has, without doubt, an animal, as well as a physical, aspect, it has such distinctive features and properties that it cannot be reduced to ex-clusively physiological terms. It suffices here to cite the fact of *language,* that cannot occur without physical conditions nor without physio-logical processes, but that cannot be reduced to them without mak-ing nonsense of all its characteristic traits.

Reference to life-processes takes us only a little way in locating the field of value-events. The qualifications to be added are (1) limita-tion of life-processes to those of selection-rejection, and (2) specifica-tion of the fact that such processes serve, from the amoeba to the highest form of primate, to maintain all life-processes as a going con-cern. That is, all have an *end,* not in the metaphysical or quasi-metaphysical (often called "mental") sense of that word, but in the sense in which *end* is equivalent to result, outcome, consequence—in short, is a strictly *descriptive* term.

These qualifications, in connection with the primary statement about life-processes, indicate that the field in which value-facts are located is *behavioral* in a way that renders the facts open to observation and test in the usual sense of those words. Since the tendency of life-processes of selection-and-rejection is to sustain and continue life-processes in general (not merely those then and there engaged in), the word "field" is particularly applicable whenever the names *valuings* and *values* are used. For the hypothesis stated rules out any view that treats them as independent and self-contained and as momentary or short-span "acts." It rules out any view that assigns them to some peculiar agency or agent. The selections in question not only themselves extend over a considerable stretch of space and time but they cover, in their results or outcomes, the whole course of life, including, through the processes that effect reproduction, the life of the species.[2] Processes of rejection take in long-term functions of elimination, of protective defense, and of aggression directed against destructive elements.

There is no implication that the facts mentioned do more than locate the field in which value-events are located; it is not implied that they cover, without further qualification, these events. But even without further qualifications, certain *methodological* conclusions directly follow.

1. Since the field is one of observable space-time facts, appeal to *introspection* when that word is used to designate observation of events that by definition are wholly *private* is ruled out. While the exclusion follows from the hypothesis presented, it is not arbitrary. On the ground of *any* theory, appeal to mere introspection is wholly inadmissible in *discussion*. That which is wholly private has to be left where it occurs and belongs—in private seclusion. Appeal to it in arguments directed to others is one of the Irish bulls of philosophy. The idea that the introspection of another person can be assumed to note the *same* fact repeats the bull; it doesn't escape it.

2. It follows that since selection-rejection as life-processes always take in something—some *thing*—which is selected or rejected, the answer to the preliminary question raised by Lee "Is there any such thing as value which is not the value of some particular thing, event or situation?" is definitely negative.[3]

3. Another methodological conclusion, given the hypothesis, is that there is no peculiar class of things (much less of "entities") to which value-qualifications can or should be attributed. The previous point indicates that "value" is an *adjectival* word, naming that which is a trait, property, qualification of some thing—in the broad sense of *thing* mentioned. It is like, say, the words good, fine, excellent. What is now added is, in effect, that when *value* is used to designate any special class or category of things, it is used as an abstract noun. If language had provided us with a special abstract noun (such as *goodness* in connection with *good*), say *valuity* or valueness, a good deal

[2] It is not meant that observations extending over much narrower fields are not legitimate in certain inquiries, but that observation of life-processes of selection *in respect to the issue in hand* must take into account their full reach.

[3] The word "thing," as in the words *anything* (as in the phrase "any such thing" above), *something*, is to be taken idiomatically, not as denoting a substance, physical or mental. It covers events, situations, persons, groups, causes, movements, occupations, pursuits, of all kinds.

of ambiguous discussion resulting in incoherent conclusions might have been avoided. Anything under the sun may come into possession of what is named by "value" as its adjective. And cultural anthropology would seem to indicate that at some time and some place almost everything has in fact been assigned that qualification.[4]

4. It is almost a restatement of the point just made to say that "intrinsic" as applied to "value" is so ambivalent as to be more than question-begging. It so effectually conceals the genuine question as to close discussion in advance. For, in one sense, the word is innocent; it only means that the trait in question *actually* belongs to a specified something *at the time and place:*—as snow is "intrinsically" white *if and when it is* white. But as a plus question-begging epithet, it is used to take the thing and its property out of all space-time connections, rendering them absolute. In this usage it is a belated survival of that "essence" which once was used in all branches of "science" to account for properties of things, making the latter *what* they "really" are. In every progressive branch of knowledge "essences" have long since given way to consideration of space-time connections. Progress of inquiry in the value-field waits upon a similar methodological change.

II

Discussion now arrives at consideration of the specific qualifications that accrue to life-processes of selection-rejection when they come into possession of value-qualifications proper. Introduction of the term "caring-for" to designate a particular kind of selections-rejections may suggest the point to be made. *Carings-for* occur in the case of some sub-human animals, and are not of themselves equivalents of valuing. But they point in the direction of the latter. Caring-for mates and young is characteristic of the behavior of some animals. A robin, for example, manifests care in sitting upon eggs till they hatch; feeding and otherwise nurturing the young; keeping them warm, protecting them from enemies, helping them learn to fly, and so on.

If one additional condition were added, we should be obliged, I believe, to identify these carings-for with valuings. But as far as we can tell, these carings-for, although systematized and extending across particular places and times, do not include express recognition of their

---

[4] It is this fact that renders the preliminary question raised by Jessup especially searching—the question, namely, as to the relation between occurrent values and standard values.

result as the ground or reason for their being engaged in. *If* the animals in question have an anticipation or foresight of the outcome and if they perform the caring-for behaviors so that they are colored and directed by the foresight, *then,* on the basis of the hypothesis advanced, they fall within the value-field proper. In an illustration used by James, eggs in the case of a broody hen are "never-too-much-to-be-sat-upon." If the hen observed the outcome on account of which they are to be sat upon, we should be obliged, I believe, to say that she "values" the sitting, and the eggs, and the chicks, as integral in and to the sitting.

The above is hypothetically stated. In the case of humans we know that the condition of foresight and use of what is foreseen as ground or reason is fulfilled. Since many varieties of things furnish grounds for various kinds of carings-for, we find, as might be expected, that carings-for, valuings, take many forms. In consequence, the word breaks up into a set of words including such behaviors as "Prizing, holding-dear, cherishing, esteeming, admiring, honoring, approving, reverencing, supporting, standing-up-for and/or by; being faithful, loyal, devoted to; concerned, occupied, with." And the phrase "interested in" has to be used, if at all, in the specifically behavioral sense in which a partner has an "interest in" a business, or as in cases in which an "interest" is subject to legal determination. Idiomatically, the word is still generally used, I believe, in this sense; but subjectivistic psychology has colored the word in its own direction and the result has so seeped over into discussions nominally philosophical that use of it is hardly safe.

Whichever one of the above words is used, it is evident that the *facts* involved extend widely across times, places, "objects," and agents-patients. There is a systematized interconnection of various special acts and "things" such are given, in the case of digestion and circulation, the name of *function.* Whether this word is used or not in the case of prizings, esteemings, cherishings, and so on, the observed facts emphasize a point previously made: "Valuing" is *not* a special isolated type of act performed by a peculiar or unique agent, under conditions so unique that valuings and values can be understood in isolation from orders of fact not themselves of the "value" kind.

Accordingly, this is as appropriate a place as any to call attention to the ambiguity of the phrase "relational theory" as applied to theories about valuing. The hypothesis here advanced is "relational" as opposed to the "absolutistic" nature of some presentations of the "intrinsic" theory. But this highly general consideration leaves the nature of the "relation" in question open to a variety of interpretations. The idea that *value* is a relation between "mind," "consciousness," a "subject" and an "object"; or between an organism and an "object"; or between some special act variously named liking, enjoying, desiring, being interested-in (viewed as "mentalistic processes") are some of the current types of "relational" theory. All are radically different from the hypothesis here advanced. Indeed, I believe the attitude of taking valuing (when the absolutistic version is repudiated) as some kind or other of unique direct relation between two separate things accounts for more of the confused state of the subject than does any other one thing. Only if the "relation" in question is understood to be plural (since involving a variety of space-time connections of different things) not singular, and it is also definitely observed that the connections in question are *across* spaces, times, things, and persons, will "relational" theory lead to any commonly agreed-upon conclusions.[5] In that case the "relations" will be seen to be the connections constituting a *transaction,* and "transactional" will displace "relational."

III

So-called relational theories often retain an attenuated relic of absolutistic theories in the use of the term "intrinsic." This retention is manifested when "intrinsic" is placed in opposition to "extrinsic" and the latter is identified with a "value" belonging to things as mere means ("means-in-themselves"), and the former with the "value" belonging to things as "ends-in-themselves." In fact, the necessity of employing the phrase "in-themselves" shows that the absolutistic retention in question is *more* than attenuated. "In-themselves" is always a sure sign of denial of *connections,* and hence is proof of an affirmation of an absolute. As long as this continues, discussion of valuings-values will remain in its present backward state as compared with the subjects

[5] More specifically, until "liking," "desiring," "enjoying," and so forth are identified in terms of some inclusive behavioral transaction, as long as they are taken to name separate acts, mental or organic, complete, ready-made in themselves, I doubt if there is much point in introducing reference to them. When they are identified as aspects of a behavioral transaction, the case is, of course, quite different.

in which "scientific" advance has taken place only because inquiry has abandoned search for anything "in itself," and has devoted itself instead to search for observable connections.

If observation, not conceptual (actually verbal) abstractions be resorted to in this matter of "instrumental" and "final" values, it will be noted that things used as means (whether material or procedural means) are in fact prized, cherished, made subject matters of loving care and devotion, in every art and pursuit that has attained any desirable development. The notion that *value* is "instrumental" because "instruments-means" are what are prized hardly attains the dignity of a pun. Is there a special type of value, deserving a name of its own, in the case, say, of dogs or jewels being prized? If values are of an instrumental type when things as *means* are cherished, why not a *type* of dog-value or diamond-value in these other instances?

The idea that things as ends can be valued, cherished, held dear apart from equally serious valuing of the things that are the means of attaining them is more than a fallacy in theory.[6] The man who says he deeply or intensely values some "end" and then shows himself indifferent to, neglectful of, the things upon which the "end" depends is either a liar intent upon deceiving others or is badly self-deceived. In spite of the currency of *theory* as to the difference, with respect to "intrinsic" value, between things that are means and things that are ends, the conduct of decent and competent people is better than their professed theoretical beliefs. They manifest their devotion to "ends" by the patient and constant care given to "means."

The practical consequences of theories which separate means and ends with respect to the value they possess are two-edged. On one side, their import is to render so-called "ends," in the degree of their ultimacy, "ideal" in the most utopian, sentimental, empty and impotent sense of that word. They are not only so "ultimate" as to be unattainable, but they lack directive power. I have yet to see an answer even proposed to the question: "Of what good is a 'final' value unless it *also* has 'instrumental' value?" The other edge concerns the implication that things which are means have no value of their own; no "intrinsic" value in the intelligible sense of that word. This implication is best shown

---

[6] Repetition of the phrase *"things as means-ends"* may seem finicky. But in the present state of discussion I do not believe too much care can be taken to obtain protection against the notion that there are such matters as means and ends in themselves; a notion of the same nature as that *value* is a "concrete" noun in and of itself.

when we take an extreme case. *Fanaticism* is the legitimate practical outcome of sharp separation of means and ends as to value. When it is assumed as a matter of course that certain "ends" are ends in and of themselves (and hence are ultimate), and therefore are not themselves capable of being subjected to inquiry and to measure of worth, attention properly (on the ground, that is, of the assumption) goes wholly to the means for attaining them. All the evils that result from acceptance of the theory that the "end justifies the means" are the outcome. Since whatever is set up as end is fixed and unquestionable, being such in and of itself, there is no need for examination of the *consequences* that in fact result from the use of certain things as means. Sadistic cruelties, brutal persecutions, only *seem* to be such. In reality, according to the logic, theoretical and practical, of the view, they are means of attaining values of such supreme worth that those who use means which seem to be inhuman are in "reality" humble servants of ultimate overruling good. Escape from utopian unattainable "ideals" consists in fanatical devotion to whatever is arbitrarily set up as means. The latter view is the complementary aspect of the former. Any view which in the name of inherent difference in "type" between final and instrumental values sets up values per se, no matter what consequences or "ends" they *are* "instrumental" to, tends in practical logic to promote fanaticism.

IV

Some of the material found in the questions and comments preliminary to the present study gives evidence of a misapprehension that distorts the meaning of caring-for (valuing) in the sense of behavior which maintains in existence the things prized or cherished, the things in question being said to have existence prior to the prizing in virtue of which value-qualification accrues to them. No one, I suppose, would question that a pearl, say, takes on color-qualification when it comes into specified connections with light, optical apparatus, and so on, and I hope it may also be assumed by this time that such connections as these, not a "relation" to mind, consciousness or whatever, is what counts. The hypothesis here offered is that a pearl takes on value-qualification under conditions of the same type—though not circumstantially the same. The following passage is, then, worth quoting because correction of the misapprehension it evinces should bring the position held into clearer relief.

It seems to me that in some experiences ordinarily held to be valuable we are concerned with preserving the existence of an independently existing object that we prize, in other cases we are not so concerned. In the aesthetic field, the former is the attitude of the curator of a museum, the latter the attitude of the visitor who merely wants to look at the pictures and who leaves their maintenance to the museum staff. Each type of prizing is legitimate and may be valuable, and they are distinct. So a complete theory of value must allow for both attitudes, and each must be assigned its distinctive kind of value.[7]

While I have difficulty in seeing how a reader of my original text could understand the relevant passage in such a way as to make this criticism seem pertinent, I welcome it, now that it has taken place, since it affords an occasion for fuller statement.

1. There is a shift, occurring twice in the passage quoted, from that which is prized as that which is valuable over to the "experience" of prizing as that which is valuable. Presumably, the shift occurred because the latter expression states the view held by the author. But it is not mine nor relevant to mine. Aside from the ambiguity of the word "experience" (since it is often given "mentalistic" meaning but may be used as a generalized equivalent of behavior), it is definitely implied that prizing is what is prized, and hence that which has "value." I do not doubt that *after* acts of prizing have taken place they are often submitted to judgment to see whether *they* should be prized, and hence "maintained" in future conduct. But such reflective inquiry and its judgmental conclusion is assuredly no part of an original prizing "experience." If I dwell upon this aspect of the passage, it is because it seems to me to afford a fine illustration of the vagueness in which the subject of value-field is at present wrapped.

2. The words "maintenance in existence" are given, as in the curator illustration, an exclusively *physical* import. It is possible that there are some curators whose care does not extend beyond that point. How such care can be said to be in the "*aesthetic* field" escapes me. If the acts of caring-for or prizing that are involved *are* aesthetic (as I hope is the case with curators), then care for the physical preservation of a painting is surely but one aspect of a much more inclusive prizing.

[7] Statement by Rice in the preliminary questions and comments.

3. The "looking" of a visitor is a *behavioral* act on the hypothesis I have advanced. If the behavior in question is in the aesthetic field, it is anything but a manifestation of "merely" wanting to look at pictures. The behavioral act of looking does not became aesthetic merely because paintings are the *things* looked at. "Looking" may be a casual glance; it may be intended to identify the painter, or the probable commercial value of the picture, or to identify the scene represented, and so on and so on.

4. If the act of looking *is* in the aesthetic field, then (a) a non-aesthetic seeing or looking comes first, and in that sense has prior and independent "existence," and (b) the act *becomes* aesthetic in qualification when the seeing is cherished or prized as something worth sustaining and developing. No looking that is momentary is aesthetic; the maintaining in question is explorative across spatial parts of the picture, and it takes time to be genuinely aesthetic. A measure of aesthetic worth is whether "seeing" is soon exhausted or one finds something new to appreciate at each seeing. The visitor who goes into raptures the very moment his eyes light on the painting is indulging in gush, not in aesthetic envisagement. Aesthetic perceptions are *trans*-actional more emphatically perhaps than any other kind of observation.

The present also seems a fit occasion to say something about so-called different types of value. I do not doubt that after the groundwork has been laid in a general theory of valuings-values and of critical judgments (evaluations), it is needful in discussing problems of genuine importance to discriminate various aspects of value-qualification. Some specifiable aspects and phases are proper to aesthetic theory; others to ethical theory; others to economic theory; others still to logical theory as methodology. But I believe (1) that reification of aspects into separate types is a weighty factor in producing the lack of agreement that now marks discussion in these subjects; and (2) that until a groundwork has been laid in a tenable general theory of valuings-values, forays into these subjects are so far from being helpful as to add to the present state of confusion in any attempt to arrive at a sound theory of "value."

V

I now come to consideration of *judgments* about valuings-values; namely to the topic of e-valuations. In the first place, with due respect to those holding the opposite opinion, I would say that there *are* such events as e-valuating inquiries terminating in judgments; and that, like judgments in all other fields, the latter are more or less well-grounded at given times. In short, propositions about values may be genuine propositions and not *mere* reports that a given thing is or has been valued. It seems to be generally admitted that genuine inquiry, resulting in genuine judgments, is possible and desirable in the case of so-called instrumental values. But it is often held that in the case of so-called final or ultimate values all that is possible is communication of a particular item of information, namely, that they are or have been valued, plus, strangely enough, in some cases, the assertion that they *ought* to be universally valued, although no reason can be given beyond the assertion that they are "ends in themselves." As against this view, which is bound to play "logically" and practically into the hands of external "authorities," formulation of a comprehensive theory of the connection of evaluations with *de facto* occurrent valuings is indispensable.

Discussion begins with the fact that carings-for, cherishings, as *de facto* valuings have what in psychological language is called a *motor* aspect. Observation of the fact that animal selections-rejections are attended frequently with rage, fear, sexual affection and attachment, shows they also have an *emotive* aspect. The question of whether there is also an "intellectual" aspect determines the answer to be given the question whether direct prizings (and so on) as valuings have genuine or "intrinsic" connection with evaluative judgments (and the latter with the former), or whether they constitute two separate kinds of events. The hypothesis presented answers this question in the sense of the first of these alternatives. Anticipation, foresight, of the outcome, of a caring-for as *ground* for a behavioral caring-for, supplies the link of intrinsic connection.

For ground *when it is itself inquired into* is identical with *reason*. Given carings-for may have conditions of the kind often called "causal." If they are investigated to find out whether they are *sufficient* to warrant the particular outcome, whose anticipation is the ground of a given valuing, then prizing enters explicitly into the class of events that are judgmental. There is no normal human being who does not have at times to raise the question whether some prizing he has more or less habitually indulged in should or should not be itself maintained in existence. If he more or less habitually raises that sort of question, he becomes aware that the "causal" conditions of some valuings are irrelevant and even perverting in respect to the result or consequence that has been prized. It is seen that class membership, irrational prejudice, dicta proceeding for those in possession of special prestige and/or superior power, and the like, have operated to determine a given valuing (which as transactional includes that which is valued). From the inquiry and its conclusion (judgment) a changed prizing and thing prized necessarily proceeds. Judgment of values, in short, is the deliberate development of an aspectual constituent of the more direct prizings and cherishings that human beings as living creatures must and do continually engage in, and under such conditions that *at first* they are relatively "thoughtless." [8]

As far as *de facto* prizings rest upon current mores, plus the manipulations of those in positions of superior economic, political, and/or ecclesiastical power, they are so perverting in effect as to provide whatever color of plausibility is possessed by the view that rational valuations are impossible. It is doubtful whether, at least for a long time to come, their operation can be wholly eliminated from the most reasonable evaluative judgments that can now be framed. But that is no reason for shutting out the attempt in advance and thereby maintaining the evils to which attention is called. Moreover, it is most decidedly to be noted that not many centuries ago conclusions in astronomy and physics were vitiated by the predominant influence of conditions of the kind mentioned; that less than a century ago biological inquiries were subjected to great distortion from the same source. The liberating movement that has taken place in these other fields of inquiry is sufficient ground for the attempt to emancipate valuings and evaluations from similar influences. The notion that there are such affairs as exclusively "final" values is now the chief obstacle to making the trial. It is hardly less than a moral tragedy to find those who profess "liberal" tenets actively aiding and abetting dogmatic absolutists.

[8] The answer to the question I raised in my original list of "Questions" as to whether the distinction between direct valuings and evaluations as judgments is one of separate kinds or one of emphasis is, accordingly, answered in the latter sense. I am the more bound to make this statement because in some still earlier writings I tended to go too far in the direction of separation. I still think the reason that actuated me is sound. In current discussion, traits distinctive of valuing are frequently indiscriminately transferred to valuation. But the resulting confusion can be escaped by noting the distinction to be one of phase in development.

Since my hypothesis is that the methods of inquiry in observation, formation and test of theories that have proved effective and fertile in other fields, be employed in the value-field, there is no reason for going into detail here as to the inquiries that will progressively yield sound judgments in the field of "value." It should, however, be pointed out that such inquiry will be systematically directed (1) to the *conditions* that at a given time determine the valuings that take place; and (2) to the consequences that actually follow from valuings determined by that sort of conditions. In inquiries of this sort the "valuings" may be temporarily left out of account and attention go to the consequences produced by the uncriticized customs, prejudices, class interests, and exercise of superior power (including particular claim to the power to settle penalties and rewards, temporal and "eternal") that determine the valuings. The idea that judgments about valuings-values must themselves be made in terms of values is on a par with such views as that judgments of color must be settled in terms of colors, not of conditions set by vibratory processes or corpuscular shocks. It is exactly the kind of methodological view that kept all the "sciences," or knowledge generally, in a retarded state for uncounted millions of years.

The question has been raised whether all value-judgments do not have the function, and implicitly the intent, to which the name "persuasion" can and should be given; and whether this fact does not confer upon them a property so peculiar as to mark them off from all other kinds of judgment. Upon the ground of the hypothesis here proposed, the answer to the first part of this compound question is affirmative (under a qualification to be mentioned), while the answer to the second part is negative. That the office of *moral* evaluations is to influence the behavior of others through forming in them an intellectual disposition favoring a certain kind of conduct does not seem to me open to question. The view is not so easily applicable to aesthetic judgments. But I believe that adequate discussion would show that it holds. For the present occasion,[9] I limit myself to saying that wherever *standard* values figure in any way, the function of *should* or *ought* comes in, so that the office and intent of influencing, directing, subsequent behavior is clearly in evidence. The qualification mentioned above is that "persuasion" be

[9] For more detailed discussion of this point, I refer to my article, "Ethical Subject-Matter and Language," *The Journal of Philosophy*, XLII (1945), 701–712. "Persuasion" takes effect in selecting and ordering factual subject matter, but is not itself any part of that subject matter.

limited to the *intent and office* of evaluative judgments, and not be treated as one constituent along with factual evidential constituents in the *subject matter* of the judgment.

That the use or "function" in question does not render evaluative judgments in any way unique in kind may be clearly seen by examining the case of judgments recognized to be of the "scientific" kind. Competent judgments (conclusions) in the field of astronomical, physical, physiological subject matters are, by the very definition of "scientific," the outcome of scrupulous and systematic care in selection of genuinely evidential material, with equal care in rejection of all subject matter whose presence can be traced to bias, prior commitment to a particular theory, professional prestige, popular repute, and so on. Both the morale and the technique of effective valuing are more highly developed at present in "scientific" subjects than in those conventionally allotted to the field of "value." The function of persuasion and of producing conviction is so far from being peculiar to judgments conventionally recognized to be in the value-field that it is now better exemplified in "scientific" inquiry and the propositions that result from it.

It follows from what has been said that there is nothing whatever that methodologically (*qua* judgment) marks off "value-judgments" from conclusions reached in astronomical, chemical, or biological inquiries. Specifically, it follows that the problem of "the relation of value to fact" is wholly factitious, since it rests upon and proceeds from assumptions that have no factual foundation. The connection of value-*facts* with other facts forms a problem that is legitimate-plus. It is indispensable. Evaluative judgments cannot be arrived at so as to be warranted without going outside the "value field" into matters physical, physiological, anthropological, historical, socio-psychological, and so on. Only by taking facts ascertained in these subjects into account can we determine the conditions and consequences of given valuings, and without such determination "judgment" occurs only as pure myth. I can hardly better conclude this statement of the theory I hold as to valuings and evaluations than by expressing my agreement with words of Dr. Stevenson when he said that moral evaluations should "draw from the whole of a man's knowledge"—extending the statement to apply to evaluations anywhere and everywhere.[10]

[10] For the Criticisms which relate especially to this paper see pp. 312–318, below.

INTRINSIC GOOD: ITS
DEFINITION AND REFERENT

A. CAMPBELL GARNETT

PROBABLY THE GREATEST CONTRIBUTION YET MADE to philosophy by the modern discipline of Semantics is its insistence that the philosopher should find the referents of the terms he uses. It is a rediscovery and restatement in modern terms of David Hume's first principle of philosophical method—to ask concerning every idea "From what impression does it come?" Nowhere is this approach of more importance than in questions concerning the theory of value. If philosophers could point with certainty to the referents of such terms as "good" and "ought" most of the remaining questions could, I believe, be handed over to the psychologists, physiologists, social scientists, and educators.

The importance of this question of *what* it is that we are talking about when we speak of value may be illustrated by reference to the discussions preliminary to this symposium. Dewey raised the question as to whether the attitude of prizing or desiring (whichever may be primary) is itself a sufficient condition for the existence of values, or merely one necessary condition, requiring to be supplemented by a further act of appraisal or evaluation. He inclined to the view that it is both necessary and sufficient. Frankena,[1] on the other hand, raised the question whether it is either necessary or sufficient. In the former view, apparently, value is regarded as a character a thing possesses by reason of its being an object of prizing or desire, or, in R. B. Perry's terms, the character of being an object of interest. In the latter view, suggested by Frankena's question, value is something quite independent of these attitudes on the part of related minds. It might be a unique quality, such as pleasure; it might be the character of being instrumental to promotion of life, whether prized or desired or not, as vitamins may be said to have had value even before they were discovered;

[1] William Frankena, University of Michigan, who contributed some of the questions and comments preliminary to the present cooperative inquiry.

or it may be some unique character of form in will or other mental process, as Kant maintained in the dictum that nothing is good in itself save a good will.

This situation indicates the necessity of a preliminary definition of terms before attempting to answer the questions raised in Dewey's article. But definition, if it is to serve as a means of communication concerning the facts of experience, cannot be arbitrary. It must give a recognizable description of the fact referred to. So we must begin by finding the referents of our terms.

The confusion found in the usage of such terms as "good," "value," "right," and "ought" strongly suggests that they are used to refer to a variety of different referents. When terms are used with different referents communication is unsuccessful. But when communication concerning facts is successful, the terms used (if the success is not merely accidental) must have the same referents. And it is certain that human beings do succeed in communicating with each other (to a degree which cannot be merely accidental) concerning features of experience referred to by such terms as "good," and "right." Evidently, then, these terms must have a certain common range of referents even though they are not always used strictly, each referring to its own unique kind of referent. Our first problem, therefore, is to search for the referents in cases of successful communication concerning values.

Let us take first the adjectival use of the term "good"—a good knife, a good car, a good idea, a good man, a good deed, a good time. In the first three instances "good" is, plainly, a synonym of "useful." The value referred to is instrumental value, or utility value. The thing is said to be good because it is "good for" some end. "Useful" always means instrumental to the fulfillment of the needs, desires and interests of living things; and the term "good" can always be substituted for it without loss of this meaning. The only reason why "useful" cannot always be substituted for "good" (used in this instrumental sense) is that custom tends to confine the term "useful" to instruments for fulfillment of our less honorific needs and interests. We speak of a useful piece of furniture if it merely serves our creature comforts, but to describe the picture on the wall as useful is to damn it with faint praise. If the picture serves our aesthetic needs it is not merely "useful" but "good." Yet, in a broader sense of the term, this capacity to satisfy higher needs is also utility; and every utility is, in the instrumental sense, a good. Utility is instrumental value; and instrumental value is, in the broad sense, utility.

When we speak of a "good man" and a "good deed," however, another element of connotation enters in. Part of the meaning is probably that the good man and the good deed are socially useful, at least in intention. But the term is used to refer also to something in the character of the man or the deed that does not seem, at first sight, to be necessarily connected with service to the needs or desires of living creatures. This is still more definitely the case with a "good time." When we say we have had a good time we do not mean that the time has had utility, that it serves as an instrument to fulfillment of the needs, desires, and so on, of some living thing. We mean that, apart from any reference to consequences, the experience had within that time was good in itself, considered apart from its consequences. It is probably true that all experiences we call good involve a progressive or complete fulfillment of needs, or consummation of desires, interests, and so forth. But this is to explain the causal antecedents of the sort of experience that feels good. It does not define what we mean by saying it is, or was, good. To say that the feeling, or lived experience, of the present moment is good is to say something of its character here and now, not something about its relation to its causal antecedents or consequents.

In these latter three cases the terms indicating value are used to refer to something in the *intrinsic* [2] character of the man, deed, or experience. In the former three cases the value terms are used to refer to a *relation* between the thing said to have value and something else—the need, desire, and so forth, of some living thing. In cases where value terms are used to refer to an intrinsic character of something the referent is much more elusive than in those where they refer to a relational character (that is, instrumentality). We must give attention to this problem. But first there are some further questions concerning instrumental values.

When the distinction is made between instrumental and intrinsic values it is often assumed that this must imply the existence, now or

[2] No particular metaphysical conception is intended by this term. It is used simply to indicate the practical distinction between the structural features and qualities that enter into the constitution of a distinguishable thing (as perceived or conceived) and the relations of that thing to other things, whether antecedent, consequent or contemporary. In this sense, intrinsic properties are constitutive of it; extrinsic properties are its relations to other things.

in the future, of some ultimate end, or ends, which have intrinsic value and constitute the final answer to the problem of the nature of the good. However, the attempt to make a sharp distinction between means and ends breaks down. Food, as an instrumental good, serves the end of bodily function, which serves a variety of other ends, and so *ad infinitum*. Even when we insist, as I think we should, that there is intrinsic value in the immediate experience of progressive satisfaction of eating, and in the somewhat different progressive satisfaction of reading to which the eating is instrumental, it does not follow that we must be able to find in these experiences some static quality of intrinsic value, production of which can be regarded as an end, distinct from the things and processes which are mere means. Instrumental values serve the ongoing and expanding processes of life, of which our specific interests, desires and prizings are a part, and it may be (as so many have claimed, and as I agree) that there is no end beyond this ongoing, expanding process itself—that the goal of all living is the more abundant life.

This last statement, however, raises another question. Are there any instrumental values which are such because they serve to produce or maintain something other than sentient or conscious life? Would an inanimate or vegetable world, which contained no possibility of producing or affecting any sentient or conscious life, contain any value? It will be sufficient if we answer this question concerning instrumental values, because, if it could contain no instrumental values, then it would contain nothing whereby we could do anything to affect any other possible kind of value for better or worse.

In answer to this question I can only say that anything which is not good for any form of sentient or conscious life seems to me (and, I believe, to almost all other people) to be useless, good for nothing, in the sense in which we commonly use the value terms. Any claim that something is instrumentally good and yet has no effect upon sentience or consciousness seems, therefore, to be a contradiction in terms, meaningless words. Such words fail in communication and thus lose their principal claim to have a referent. Value terms are usually intelligible when they are used to refer to things having consequences for sentient or conscious life. But when used to refer to something that neither is, nor has any consequences for, such life, they become meaningless to me—and, I suspect, to all others who have not constructed, in their imagination, some special theory to give the terms meaning.

This is one important consideration bearing upon another question: Can values be discussed in purely behavioristic terms? The view that they can is often held by those who regard all values as instrumental. Its possibility is seriously considered by Dewey in the essay taken as the starting point of the present symposium. He regards the terms "holding dear," "prizing," and "valuing" as interchangeable and asserts that this attitude (or that of desiring, liking, interest or enjoying, whichever is primary) is a *necessary*, and perhaps a *sufficient*, condition of the existence of values. But he thinks it sufficient if these terms are understood to stand for a behavioral transaction. "Prizing," for example, is said to refer to "a way of behaving tending to maintain something in factual (space-time) existence. . . . *Desire* might then be the behavioral attitude that arises when prizings are temporarily blocked or frustrated."

Now, ordinarily, these attitudes and ways of behaving are taken as indicative of sentience and usually of consciousness. But the choice of behavioral referents for these terms is specially designed to fix their meanings without reference to these subjective processes. This, however, makes the terms irrelevant to questions of value, for, as we have seen above, to say that something has instrumental value is to say that it in some way serves the needs and desires of sentient or conscious life. That which neither is, nor can in any way affect, such life has no value in any sense commonly intelligible. Therefore terms which contain no necessary reference to such life (that is, terms which refer only to physical existents and their changes) can have no reference to values.

If any further objection to the effort to define value terms by use of purely behavioral referents is needed it is to be found in the resulting ambiguities. Every person who speaks English knows what is the psychological mental state (with its tendencies to action) designated by the term "holding dear." But the behavioral transactions which manifest this state are so various as to beggar description. Further, they are not all peculiar to the attitude of holding dear. The behavioral transactions normally expressive of this attitude can be simulated by a good actor who does not experience the subjective states and processes

—and who therefore does not really hold dear, however well he may deceive the observer.

It is impossible, therefore, to discuss values—even instrumental values—without direct or indirect reference to subjective states and processes. This, however, does not render the connection of value with objectively observable facts merely "external" and "more or less accidental," as Dewey contends.[3] The inference from behavior to subjective mental process introduces an additional possibility of error (as when we are deceived by a good actor) but only the solipsist would deny that it is reasonably secure.

If instrumental values, therefore, are defined as things and processes (physical and mental) which serve the needs of the lives of sentient or conscious beings, then the study of such values can proceed by objective scientific methods, utilizing as required the results of all the sciences. Such life is a growing process, essentially conative and cognitive, at the very least a feeling-striving process integrated with physical processes. It is limited in certain definite ways, but replete with unrealized potentialities. It is a process, not a static thing; and its very nature is to expand its cognitive grasp and conative control of its environment. It is the conditions of this expansion that constitute its needs and shape the development of the active life in specific desires, interests, prizings, and so on. Specific values are therefore to be found in the things and processes that serve these specific tendencies, but such things have only an illusory appearance of value unless they also really serve the needs of the expanding life as a whole.

The concept of personality may be taken as summing up the idea of such living beings in their most fully developed forms. But there are degrees of development of personality, that is, in the scope and use of intelligence and other capacities, in the cultivation of varied and special functions, and in that integration with the physical and social world which makes possible the living of a full life. The criterion of the degrees of value, in instrumental things and processes, may therefore be taken to be that of their contribution to the development of personality.

Instrumental value, then, which is the commonest referent of the term "good," can thus far be studied by the methods of the empirical

[3] P. 7, above.

sciences, so long as the descriptive terms used in those sciences are not arbitrarily confined within the limits of a behavioristic interpretation.

We cannot, however, stop here. An adequate theory of value must enquire into other uses of the value terms, to discover their referent, if any, and to relate it to that of instrumental value. It must also take up the problem of the relation of value and obligation—of what is *right,* of what we *ought* to do. For in many, though not all, uses of such terms as "good" something more is intended than a reference to instrumentality to human or animal needs. There is a reference to something in the nature of demand, of obligation. This must be clarified in order that we may understand the nature of moral values—for any theory of value that failed to give an intelligible account of what people mean when they speak of moral values would be woefully inadequate. Of these two questions we shall first take up that of intrinsic value.

What, then, is the referent—or what are the referents—when people successfully communicate ideas concerning intrinsic value? In attempting to answer this question we must not overlook the possibilities of error in regard to referents even in cases of successful communication. But if there are such errors, then appearances must be such as to suggest them to both parties to the communication, so that both make the same error. The child who points to the moon and says "Look at the big lamp" is perfectly understood by the adult who knows better, because the moon to him also has the appearance of a lamp. Similarly people may, because of certain appearances, refer to certain objects as having intrinsic value (value in themselves, apart from their consequences) and many others may understand and accept the reference, while a few more careful observers understand, but detect the error.

What then are the things commonly believed to have intrinsic value? Prominent among them are pleasure and feelings of satisfaction; interested and successful activity, both mental and physical; moral actions and moral character; aesthetic objects, food and other things that are immediate means of fulfilling needs and giving satisfaction. In regard to aesthetic objects, physical activity, and such things as food, however, a little reflection shows that these are really instrumental values, mistakenly assumed to have value in themselves because something called "value" is felt as an intrinsic character of the experience they produce when appropriately contemplated or acted upon. The fact that this element of "value" in the experience does not arise unless the *action* of the living agent is *appropriate* shows that such "value" is not a character possessed by the object independently of its effects upon living agents—and therefore not intrinsic. The aesthetic properties of a primrose, for example, have no value for a Peter Bell, nor the food properties of an apple for the boy who has already eaten too much.

Physical objects, then, can have no intrinsic value. All intrinsic values, if there really are any, must be found in the actual, lived experience of living agents. But experience is bi-polar. It contains subject and object, activity and content, experienc*ing* and that which is experienc*ed*. On which side, if either, does intrinsic value lie? Can we say of any of the contents of experience, in their function as content, that they have intrinsic value, that is, that they are in themselves, apart from their effects, good, in some commonly understood sense of the term?

The strongest claim for the intrinsic goodness of any content of experience has been made for pleasure. But against this there seems to me to be one argument which is decisive. Let us imagine a moment of the most intense pleasure we have ever known. There is certainly a commonly accepted sense of the term "good" in which that moment of experience contains in itself, apart from its effects, a very great good; that is, it is intrinsically very good. Now imagine that moment of experience continued without change and without further activity for the whole span of a normal lifetime. If it is pleasure and pleasure alone that gives to experience its character of intrinsic goodness, then such a life span should, as a whole, have the greatest intrinsic good imaginable in any life span. But, I think, few of us will agree that it has. We would gladly exchange some of the pleasure content for a little variety, for an opportunity for genuine activity.

Pleasure then, as content of experience, cannot either *be* what is called intrinsic value, nor can it be that alone which has intrinsic value, or the principal source of it. Yet the persistent tendency to say that pleasure is good in itself shows that it is closely connected with whatever it is that is referred to as being or having intrinsic value and tends, in general, to vary concomitantly with it, or even to form part of it.

Let us look, then, at the rest of the content of experience, apart from pleasure-pain. It consists of sensory qualities, spatio-temporal forms, and subjective activity; for subjective activities, the *ings* of experience, are also experienc*ed* in the after part of the specious present, and so form part of the content. But none of the sensory qualities or spatio-temporal forms can be said to be good in themselves, nor can this be said of any special combination of their form and quality. For the same sensory quality, or spatio-temporal form, or combination of these, appears sometimes as good and sometimes as evil. Its relation to other elements of content (present or before or after it), and this relation as affecting the subjective reaction to it, is what determines whether the experience appears as intrinsically good or bad.

This leaves us with the subjective activity itself as the sole remaining claimant to possession of intrinsic value. And sometimes it appears as good and sometimes as bad. Can we then find any general characteristics of subjectivity that vary concomitantly with what is generally spoken of as the intrinsic value of the experience?

We are not yet ready to discuss moral value but, to avoid confusion, it should be pointed out that intrinsic value should not be identified with moral value. Ordinary speech quite intelligibly refers to experiences recognized as non-moral, or even immoral, as good in themselves, considered apart from their consequences.

Our question then is, What is it, in the character of our subjective activity, that makes it sometimes good, sometimes bad, in this communicable sense of good and bad which considers experience in its present character, apart from its consequences? I think we must concede this much to the Hedonist, that no experience devoid of pleasure would commonly be recognized as good in this sense. Indeed, we may go further and agree that the intrinsic goodness and badness of experience *tends* to vary concomitantly with the degrees of pleasure and pain. Yet, as we have seen, there is also another factor that enters in. The value of subjective activity depends also upon the degree and form of that activity. It requires change in its object and opportunity for growth.

Mental activity—in the broad sense which includes even the simplest kind of feeling-striving process—may be either positive or negative. It is either a striving towards or a striving away from, a seeking to know or experience something more fully or to know or experience less of it. And I think it will be generally agreed that, if we analyze any moment of experience in abstraction from its antecedents and consequents, then a moment of experience wherein the active tendency is purely positive is of the sort commonly called "good" in the sense of "good-in-itself," "intrinsically good," and experience with a purely negative active tendency is called "bad" in the sense of "intrinsically bad." Also any such isolated moment of experience is commonly pronounced intrinsically good or bad "on the whole" according as it is predominantly positive or negative—for, in our complex mental activity, positive and negative elements are commonly mingled.

This would suggest that to call a mental activity intrinsically good is simply to say that it is positive in form. But the matter is hardly as simple as that. We have already noted and agreed to the Hedonist's insistence that no moment of experience would commonly be called good in itself (in isolation, in abstraction from antecedents and consequents) unless it were predominantly pleasant in quality. It must be admitted, therefore, that the reference, in this usage of the term "good," is to *both* form and quality, to both the *direction* of the striving and the *tone* of the feeling. Activities that are positive in form are positive in quality. When our striving-toward is unsuccessful or inhibited it gives place, in its immediately active tendency, to a striving-against the opposition. Difficulty in achieving that toward which we are striving does not make the striving unpleasant until the sense of frustration enters in. Then we must strive against the source of frustration and the experience of doing so is unpleasant until it begins to be successful. Then the progress achieved changes the mental outlook. The striving-against becomes to us a part of a longer-range striving-for and so tinged with pleasure. By maintaining the long view a great many difficulties and frustrations can be overcome while the total striving experience remains pleasant on the whole.

Positive quality (or pleasantness) and positive form (appetition rather than aversion) thus go together; and so do negative form and quality. We commonly call a moment of experience good in itself when it is predominantly positive in form and quality, and bad when it is predominantly negative in both. This togetherness of form and quality constitutes the value character of the experience of any moment. It is the referent of the terms "intrinsically good" and "intrinsically bad." But the only things that can be intrinsically good or bad are mental activities—in the broad sense of "mental" which includes every phase of sentience or consciousness.

Mental acts, and mental acts alone, can be intrinsically good or bad. But they vary in their degrees of value. What is the nature, then of the

variations that can occur among mental acts, considered "in themselves," that is, as isolated moments of experience? Each such mental
act involves both feeling and striving—a cognitive and a conative
element. But they can vary in both complexity and intensity. The more
intense the striving process the more intense the feeling-tone, whether
pleasant or painful—for example, an intense interest or intense sensing. The more intense act, if good, is generally recognized as a greater
good than a similar act of less intensity; and so also for evils. But we
also recognize that the more complex modes of activity—our higher
interest processes—may be greater goods or greater evils than the
simpler. This is as our analysis shows it should be. That which is intrinsically good is the mental activity; its goodness is its positive form
and quality. There is therefore more of the sort of thing that is intrinsically good in a moment of complex and purely positive mental
activity than in a moment of simpler mental activity. There is therefore
a perfectly intelligible sense in which there is more of that which is
intrinsically good in a moment's activity of our higher (for example,
intellectual and aesthetic) interest processes, if purely positive, than in
a moment's simple sensing, even though the latter may, by reason of
its intensity, contain the more intense pleasure. Hedonism, seeking to
measure intrinsic values by estimating quantities of pleasure, is apt to
support the facile judgment that the intensely pleasant sensation is a
greater good than the mildly pleasant higher-interest process. Our
analysis supports, instead, the judgment usually endorsed by deeper
reflection, that there is more intrinsic good in the higher and more
complex process (if purely positive) than in the lower and simpler.
Act for act (assuming both to be purely good), the intenser activity
is a greater good than the less intense. But the complexity of the higher
mental processes is an increase in the fullness of life and contains greater
potentialities for both good and evil.

In the higher mental activities (and even in a moment of mere sensing) there is, of course, usually a mixture of positive and negative activity. Also, every moment of mental activity has not only intrinsic
but instrumental value. Value-judgment must take into consideration
this mixture of good and evil, and of intrinsic and instrumental. This
raises the question whether the two kinds of value, intrinsic and instrumental, are commensurate. However, it is quite clear that they are.
Intrinsic good consists of unobstructed sentient and conscious life, the

fuller, the richer, and the more free the better. Instrumental values consist of those things and processes, mental and physical, which minister to the needs, provide the conditions, of such life. That which has intrinsic value or disvalue is animal life, and especially human personality, and most especially the higher development and expression of personal activity—life and life more abundant. That which has instrumental value, as we have already seen, is that which ministers to the more abundant life.

Intrinsic and instrumental values, taken together, can therefore be studied by the ordinary methods of scientific investigation, and can be expressed in terms of psychology and the other sciences, providing these terms are not given a merely behavioristic interpretation. We are aware of intrinsic goods in our own experience (the mental activities that are positive in form and quality) and can fairly accurately judge when these good activities occur in the lives of others. We also know a great deal, and can learn more, of the conditions of the occurrence of such goods. This brings the whole sphere of values, intrinsic and instrumental, within the scope of scientific investigation.

We have shown the connection between intrinsic and instrumental values and pointed to their referents. Our next task is to distinguish the special place of moral values in this value system. It is obvious that a mental action may have intrinsic value in the sense above defined (may be positive in form and quality) and yet be generally recognized as morally wrong, for example, an expression of selfish greed or foolish prejudice. This raises fundamental questions of ethics which here can only be lightly touched upon.

I have argued in a recent article [4] and in a forthcoming one [5] that to do right is to do one's best to produce the best possible conditions for all concerned, that is, for all those affected by our actions. Here, "to do one's best" means to put forth one's most efficient efforts in investigation and performance; "the best conditions" are those of greatest value in the sense defined above—broadly, the conditions of personal development. This moral ideal, I have claimed, is endorsed by a growing general consensus of competent (intelligent and earnest) opinion throughout the history of man's moral development. Departures in

[4] "Relativism and Absolutism in Ethics," *Ethics*, LIV (1944), 186–199.
[5] "Naturalism and the Concept of Obligation" (to appear in *The Review of Metaphysics*).

theory from this consensus, once it has been clearly formed, are due to special psychological conditions (such as those giving birth to the Nazi reaction) creating moral blindness. Departures in practice from the admitted ideal are due to the fact that other factors, besides rational discernment of value and obligation, enter into the determination of conduct. But the fact of the growth (through critical reflection) of the consensus of ethical opinion indicates the presence in common experience of a referent called "obligation" (with its variants called "ought" and "right") which, though obscure, has been gradually elucidated by thoughtful attention and discussion.

The obligation thus discovered is a demand, rooted somewhere in common human experience, that the individual should concern himself, not with his own welfare alone, but also with that of any others affected by his actions. We say "I feel that I ought," and the statement expresses awareness of a unique constraint. It is a constraint to which we can only be blind or disobedient at the cost of some stultification or distortion in the development of our own personalities. Attention to this constraint has issued in its elucidation as a demand that each concern himself equally with the good of all.

Space forbids further discussion here of the source and nature of this sense of obligation. But it is clear, and generally recognized, that value and obligation are very closely connected in our experience—so much so that some attempts to define the good fail to make any distinction between them, including the demand of the "ought" within the concept of the good. This, however, is a mistake. Every recognized value can be seen to present a claim, a demand, an obligation, somewhere. But value and obligation are differently related to the same persons. The present and potential values of one human life place obligations upon that person and various other persons in different ways. The fact that X is good for A does not necessarily mean that I am under obligation to administer X to A. The proof of the existence of the general principle of obligation stated above cannot be simply deduced from the definition of value. It is clear, however, if we accept the definition of instrumental value and the general principle of obligation stated above, that there is a sense in which the action of greatest *instrumental* value is also *right*. It is right in the sense that it is the goal at which right conduct must aim. Right conduct consists in *aiming*, as intelligently and effectively as possible, at the production of the greatest possible instrumental values, as conditions which give the opportunity for those concerned to produce the greatest possible intrinsic values. For we cannot directly produce intrinsic values in the lives of others; each produces his own mental activity, good or bad.

This may be termed the objective sense of the term "right." It applies to that one, of all possible actions, which is of greatest instrumental value in the circumstances. The question of which action has this greatest value can, as shown above, be determined by the methods of the sciences—providing we accept both the definitions of value given above. And the question of which action is objectively right can be settled in the same way, provided we also accept the general principle of obligation. It is only *after* acceptance of the moral principle and value definitions that the non-value sciences (psychology, physiology, and so on) perform their function. But, when "right" and "good" are understood in the senses here defined the decision of *what* is right in each particular case is purely a question for these sciences. There is nearly always some one line of conduct which alone is right, because it is best; the only exception is where consequences of equal value follow from different actions, and then the choice is morally indifferent.

Thus, in each particular case, the right is absolute. Yet it changes from one situation to another, because the good is always relative to changing conditions. The general abstract principle of obligation—to produce the greatest possible good of all concerned—is also absolute. But principles of secondary generality (such as prohibitions against lying and stealing) are justified only as useful guides as to the sort of conduct that is, in general, productive of the greatest good.

The action that is objectively right is not, however, always right in the deeper, subjective sense. We never know for certain what is objectively right. It is our obligation to make our best efforts to discover what is right (objectively) and to do it. Such effort is always subjectively right, for a person can have no other obligation than to use his best intelligence and to do what that best use of his intelligence convinces him is right. Moral and immoral behavior, as distinct from nonmoral, is behavior of a person who has grasped the idea of obligation (more or less accurately) and is aware of his conduct as more or less in accord with the standard his idea sets for him. Mental activity directed toward the maintenance of such a standard is both moral and good, that is, morally good. Mental activity that is aware of such a standard and yet directed to the avoidance of it is both moral (in the sense of not merely non-moral) and bad, that is, morally bad or immoral. Morally bad activity may be predominantly (not purely) intrinsically good, though it will be instrumentally bad in nearly every instance—the only exception being where an objectively false moral standard is held which it is instrumentally good to break. Morally good activity may be predominantly (not purely) intrinsically bad for example, involving suffering, but it will (to the extent that the standard and conditions are accurately grasped and the execution intelligent and efficient) be instrumentally good.

However, in genuine moral activity there is always high intrinsic value, rarely offset to any great extent by negative (bad) elements. In cases of great moral effort the whole personality is keyed to its highest pitch and integrated at a high level of activity in a supremely living whole. Such moments of high decision and moral effort are universally admired, if understood, as moments of great intrinsic value. We rightly try to produce personalities capable of such effort when the need arises, yet we also, and rightly, try to avoid producing situations where such effort is needed—cases where it requires great effort to do right. When we understand the nature of our obligation, as outlined above, and strive to perform it, we seek to produce the conditions (instrumental values) wherein we and others can produce the greatest intrinsic values (the life activity that is full and free). In thus taking care of the instrumental and intrinsic values of a non-moral character, guided by the consciousness that this is what we ought to do, the moral values take care of themselves. Moral value is a by-product of the pursuit of the general run of values, when we pursue them vigorously and intelligently, and with an eye to the equal good of all.[6]

[6] For the Criticisms and Rejoinders which relate especially to this paper see pp. 325–326 and 464–469, below.

❧ VALUES AND INQUIRY

GEORGE R. GEIGER

DISCUSSION ABOUT VALUE can be pointed in one of several directions. There is the familiar direction—familiar, at least, in an academic orientation—of professionalized and highly technical exposition, exposition which is more frequently argument. Here the aim is apparently to convince one's colleagues, although "convince" is hardly the word, since in the regions where value discussion flourishes—philosophy and economics, in particular—confession of a change of mind is rare enough to be disregarded. The aim, then, sometimes turns into a demonstration of professional competence.

Another direction leads "downward" to a level where, say, an intelligent layman can be found. This layman in philosophy may be a president, a foreign secretary, a nuclear physicist, an international journalist. He probably does not read the philosophy trade periodicals. Yet at the moment he appears to have an almost cataleptic concern with "values." In these first years of an Atomic Age he has become convinced, in a frightened way, that questions of value are about to determine the continued existence of man and his culture; and if he is a layman with political power he may even be aware that his own value decision may play an enormous role in such a determination.

It is this level of discussion that any symposium on value must take into account. Not that the discussion must confine itself to what an intelligent layman can be expected to understand. (That would be too much to count on.) Nor does it have to be limited to a realization that "modern man is obsolete," and that his obsolescence is in some way tied up with what Veblen and now Ayres calls the "ceremonial" anachronisms. For that obsolescence is only an illustration, theatrical and journalistic as it may be, of a long-time predicament upon which the atomic bomb has focused. The predicament is nothing less than the Hogarthian story of the dualist's progress. The dichotomies of mind-body, reason-"experience," religious-secular, that-world-this-world, morals-technology—all are etched into it, too. In less rhetorical terms, this is only to say that the issue of value is an issue of basic human importance; it is more than a theme in professional dialectic.

All of this has become so evident that it is now a matter of journalism, popular editorials and best-selling books, and radio news bulletins. Is it also a matter for technical philosophy? The basic assumption of this paper is that it is. One justification for that assumption is, however, so hackneyed that even a bare statement of it may seem gratuitous: The cooperative efforts of all forms of human intelligence—philosophy included—must be enlisted to preserve man from socially irresponsible scientific thinking, for that is what the threat of the atom reveals. Banal and threadbare as this now must sound to all literate men, the danger hanging over us cannot be dissipated by sophisticated shrugs or bored smiles—or by a retreat into fashionable neo-mysticisms. This justification will have little to recommend it in a symposium on value. It will seem too quotidian, too much like a series of clichés à la Frank Sullivan. Other supports have to be found for the assumption—the assumption that value discussion must face squarely the discrepancy between morals and technology, an age-old discrepancy become dramatically relevant. To call the problem commonplace is not to lessen the tragedy of it.

One of those "other supports" might be the blunt statement that millenniums of value discussion haven't seemed to advance us very far. If this is too blunt or too naive, it might be reworded to the effect that, as the present panel fully demonstrates, the cardinal premises, and even the purpose or proper status, of value theory are still in question after literally thousands of years of philosophic scrutiny. The impasse becomes more pronounced rather than less. Bertrand Russell, for instance (and he is a good illustration since his recalcitrance has no traffic with idealistic or theological notions), can assert more vigorously than ever as time goes by that values involve nothing more than taste-plus-power. Several writers in the present book are of a similar opinion. When there is yet no basic decision about handing values over to power politics or to scientific method—and this is but one of many dualisms in the field—the feeling that value discussion has been singularly inoperative is not merely mischievous.

Disagreements as fundamental as those found in discussions about value are not simply matters of language or of definition or of "reasoning." Symbols and syntax are undoubtedly important, as a number of essays in this volume make clear; but ascribing the failure to achieve some kind of value synthesis to matters of language alone, or even of logic, is a prime example of philosophic shortsightedness. For whatever it is called, the discrepancy between human achievements in ethics and in the natural sciences involves institutional, historical, and cultural factors; it is not the result simply of inadequate demonstration or of the lack of analytical rigor. Thus, the assumption that philosophy must take into account the gap between morals and technology is at the same time a demand that philosophy also pay attention to the social, economic, and political backgrounds of human interests and choices.

I

Many things can be considered basic in a discussion of value, and it may be arbitrary, although inevitable, to insist on making one more fundamental than another. But one thing that certainly is *not* basic is the definition of value. Bizarre as this may sound, it is no more than the simple observation that definitions are customarily *ex post facto*. (This would not necessarily be so if values were regarded as undefined elements or as indefinable—a way out of trouble that has proved increasingly popular in some philosophic and economic circles.) Definitions are rationalizations of a point of view, of an attitude, a temper of mind; they illustrate what is indeed fundamental, a kind of philosophic or cultural pattern. They illustrate it, but they do not establish it. It is not the way in which, say, John Dewey and Bertrand Russell define value that is important; what is important is that their definitions reveal genuinely basic contrasts in approach. These contrasts are not merely matters of taste, about which there is no arguing. If that were so, then the Russell approach—that the choice between values is a question of sentiment rather than of logic—would be unchallengeable. Although the personal equation must be reckoned with (for example, Russell's "mischievousness" *versus* Dewey's earnestness), the contrasting value patterns and attitudes have been etched into our culture with an acid more penetrating than that of human temperament alone.

Even if definitions are not fundamental, it will be necessary nonetheless to put down what the word means in the context of the present discussion. That it is a directional definition, and that others will object

to it, will not be denied. *Values are the products of human choices.*
In ethics, the choices are usually long-time ones, but this is not a necessary part of the definition. Furthermore, "choice" is not exclusively
a mentalistic term; actually, human choices are determined in great
part by the mores. Nevertheless, choices will determine values even
if they run counter to the mores. Why they may run counter to the
mores, and whether the choices are "good" or "bad," are not essential
parts of the definition of value. Such factors are essential when we have
to choose between values. In other words, choices can produce values,
"any old" values, but there is a further problem of discriminating between values themselves.

The grounds for proposing (at least hypothetically) a definition as
broad as this are frankly experimental. If definition is no more than
a sort of semantical stop-gap, the attitude or point of view rationalized
by definition is what must claim the major share of attention. The function of definition may be to illuminate sharply the great divide in points
of view. That divide separates those who assert and those who deny
there is a peculiar class of things to which value applies, that judgments about value can be determined without reference to "outside"
factors such as those presented by anthropology and cultural history.
The divide (if the metaphor can be changed) becomes a veritable
chasm when values are set up as unique, as different from anything
else in the world, when judgments about good and bad, beautiful and
ugly, precious and vulgar, are regarded as *sui generis,* cut off from
all other human experience.

To be more specific, in the alternatives presented by Dewey in his
original questions [1] there emerge a pattern and a counter-pattern. For
example, by choosing the "correct" alternatives in each of the question
groups, the follower of Dewey will block out a familiar outline. Those
"correct" choices will indicate that the dimension of value (a) is determined by factors that are behavioral, biological—"objective"; (b)
is the result of a process, that of interest, judgment, and choice; (c)
is not sharply cut off as something unique from the realm of fact; and
(d) is therefore not exempt from scientific handling or from "socio-
cultural" influences. In similar manner, the contrary alternatives would
sketch out a counter-pattern: values are "subjective"—that is, mentalistic or introverted; substantive rather than adjectival; and therefore

[1] Pp. 5–12, above.

unique, exclusive, and generally impervious to any process of scientific engineering. Or in Dewey's words—words which seem to be the central point of his essay and (I should venture to add) of this inquiry:

Are value-facts bias-facts of such intensity and exclusiveness as to be un-modifiable by any possible consideration of grounds and consequences? The question at issue is not whether some values are now actually treated as if they were of this kind. It is whether the cause of their being so treated inheres in them as value-facts or is a cultural-social phenomenon. If the latter is the case they are capable of modification by socio-cultural changes. If the former is the case, then differences in valuing which are of serious social importance can not be brought within the scope of investigation so as to be settled in a reasonable way.[2]

This challenge seems so important and so closely connected with the basic assumptions of the present paper that it will be given the major attention here. Not that the specific questions Dewey raises will be passed over, but they may perhaps be more appropriately considered as contextual parts of a general pattern. The pattern is the crucial thing.

Equally crucial are the origins of the counter-pattern. The point of view—and it is all but universal—which regards value-facts as exclusive and unmodifiable bias-facts must have antecedents; it did not spring completely equipped from any philosopher's head. To trace those antecedents would be an interesting although formidable task, but the items to be looked for might include something like the following.

In his early attempts to "escape from peril," the human animal must have found it comforting to fall back upon a world that would compensate for the frustrations and fears promoted in him by a crude and resisting "factual" realm. He must have developed—he did develop, if our cultural anthropologists are to be trusted—a notorious inferiority complex. Bewildered by things that so exceeded his capacity, man turned first to animism and then to metaphysics (if Dewey's analysis is at all plausible) to escape from a suffocating feeling of helplessness. The game did not always fall to the arrow; so there must be a happy hunting-ground where no arrow missed its mark. Similarly, "facts" were recalcitrant and uncompromising: something else was needed. There is nothing preposterous in the hypothesis that a unique realm of "values" came to satisfy that need. Here was a dimension clean, classic, and

2 P. 11.

amenable. Here was the ultimate hunting-ground of the Good, the True, and the Beautiful, so superior to the crass, untrustworthy, and sordid appearances of the everyday flux.

The ceremonial compulsions would carry on from this point: they might be primitive taboo, Greek metaphysics, or Christian theology. Prestige and permanence come to be bestowed upon what originally were the cries for compensation and relief. Certainty has been found, and the quest ended. A separate world of human wishes has been apotheosized, separate because anything so dear must be disinfected from facts and their contingencies.

This outline of the dualist's progress is a familiar one and has been traced many times. However, the anthropological and sociological details have yet to be organized and interpreted on a scale sufficient to convince the doubtful. There is a natural history of value still to be written. Such a history might include the quest for social as well as for cosmic certainty, since a refusal to insulate values from their social setting is also a refusal to recognize dogmatism and totalitarianism in man's affairs. When human decisions are tied up empirically with perspicuous cultural changes, less opportunity is provided for moral absolutism, and more for a consistent relativism. This history would also go beyond the genetic approach to the isolation of values. It would examine the privileged position claimed by obscurantism. Unless and until values are divorced from the naturalistic realm and immunized from scientific infection, no clear place is left for supernaturalism. The contextual interpretation of values is a powerful prophylactic against mumbo-jumbo. Indeed, the whole counter-pattern of ethical isolation-ism would be a persistent theme in any natural history of value. These suggestions are but bare samples, no more than minimal cues; yet they intimate that a non-behavioral conception of value is not something simply to be taken for granted. It has roots. The roots indicate the kind of growth that might have been expected.

II

The pattern that places values (and mind and reason and religion) in the context of socio-cultural processes, that does not consider them amputated from "objective" and "scientific" procedure, is clearly the one that has always claimed Dewey's attention. It must also claim the attention, if not the allegiance, of all thinking men if there is to be any hope of reducing the discontinuities in human experience which are now breaking under us in so ugly and portentous a fashion.

But "objective and scientific procedure" are words the meaning of which cannot always be assumed. Particularly is this the case when they are alleged to apply to values. For there is a fake science and a fake objectivity: the "science" which is found on a movie set gaudy with colorful alembics and high-lighted test tubes and sprinkled with surgical coats, the science that never gets beyond laboratory routine; and the "objectivity" implying that nothing makes any difference, that it is better not to give a damn.

Instead of anything as absurdly artificial as this, scientific and objective procedure refers to what is primarily an attitude of mind, a temper of approach, a general way of handling problems. This is not to minimize techniques. But it is an insistence that some disenchantment with gadgetry is necessary when discussion like this centers on values. The attitudes and temper that characterize scientific method are hardly matters of mystery. Whatever philosophy of science is invoked, items like these cannot very well be omitted: Willingness to observe and unwillingness to take for granted—thus, a genuinely "objective" and critical spirit. Insistence on the use of hypothesis and deprecation of the use of fixed, unalterable dogma—a feeling, then, for tentativeness. Discrimination between hypotheses on the basis, among other things, of their operational possibilities and their general predictableness and verifiability—so, the instrumentalistic position.

Is there anything intrinsic in these attitudes that excludes them automatically from certain areas of human experience? At one time, even stars and bodies and minds were outside the ambit of intelligent inquiry. It is an historical commonplace that scientific method is young. Its revolution was a contemporary of other revolutions that ushered in the modern world. What we call science is the product of recent historical processes and technological developments; the privileged position it now occupies had to be fought for and won. The extension of its orbit has been the end result of social decisions. There was nothing innate in atoms, motion, and inertia that made them the property of "science."

Nor is there anything innate in human decisions that excludes them irrevocably from intelligent control, free inquiry, and self-correcting instruments and attitudes. What does exclude such choices from science is custom and historical accident. The traditional (not to say neolithic) dualism in European culture (in all culture, for that matter) could not allow the Scientific Revolution anything like free rein. There was resistance at every stage; it must not be forgotten that insanity and disease were once regarded as precious and untouchable. They are now respectable subjects for scientific analysis. Other things are not. Human decisions involving taste, the price market, right and wrong, and political affiliation would be among those things. It seems outrageous to some that these decisions can ever be amenable to observation-hypothesis-discrimination. It is just as plausible to suggest that this feeling of outrageousness is no more than a cultural hang-over.

After all, what is there about value which puts it beyond the pale? Is there any question, for example, that we can make "objective" and "scientific" reports about human choices? Do not—or at least cannot —those reports enter into the fabric of further human choices? Are value-decisions never to be approached tentatively? True, they have not been so approached ordinarily. Instead of considering value-decisions as a kind of hypothesis, as amendable reflections of the conditions under which men live, we have, with a fatal persistence, put them outside the area of intelligence by making them eternal and unconditional. Therefore the only way to manipulate them is through power alone. But this is no more than a prescientific absolutism, once practiced on everything not understood. To regard anything in human experience as fixed and immutable is not simply to avoid scientific method: it is to testify that nothing has been learned. Finally, is the realm of human choice non-instrumental? This is perhaps the most difficult point. Yet the very minimum that can be noted here is that a proposition is meaningless for science unless in some way it can be implemented. It must be actionable. This can apply to ethics and economics as it does to chemistry, even though the precise operations need have little if anything in common—litmus paper has minor relevance for politics. The operations may be as unlike those of a laboratory as winning a fight against deliquency, or carrying on a new experiment in child training, or changing the listening habits of a nation, or extending the influence of a cooperative. They may be incredibly long-range, or even appear like desperate fumbling or improvisation; yet some action must be foreshadowed, some specific difference must be made somewhere if hypotheses in value—as in anything else—are to be regarded as meaningful. The question becomes then: is the realm of human choice meaningful?

No hereditary allergy prevents human choices from associating with scientific method. The act of choosing, especially the causal agencies responsible for choice, can clearly become a matter of specific investigation. So can the degree of approval or disapproval choices provoke, as well as the variety of choices and the possibility of discovering common elements between them. These empirical phenomena are not simply matters of casual introspection; they furnish the ground for much of social psychology, anthropology, and history.

It goes without saying that there is nothing facile in this contention that the scientific spirit be applied to all phases of human experience, to ethics and religion as well as to physics. The argument is simply that those phases *can* be so treated, and *must* be, at least if man is ever going to bridge the chasm between his desires and his practices. That there are enormous practical difficulties to be overcome is transparently evident; but those obstacles are not theoretical obstacles. That is to say, there is nothing in the intrinsic nature of human choice that condemns it from the start to remain forever the plaything of wishful thinking, pious exhortation, or brute force. It is not because values are values and not star clusters that their processes must be regarded as non-scientific. Such a notion is magnified, deliberately or unconsciously, every time we are told that choices cannot be stained for the microscope or be dissected. The staining of cross-sections is not a synonym for intelligent inquiry.

If this is still unconvincing, as it well may be, what are the alternatives? If the phenomenon of value is not accessible to some kind of scientific approach, what then? What is the substitute for free, intelligent inquiry? If such inquiry be renounced must not some sort of psychologically suspect introversion be given a free field? And is not rampant emotion, backed by force, its logical outcome? Does not a repudiation of "science" widen irretrievably the gulf between wishes and action, a gulf which will be crossed, if in no other way, by totalitarian bridges? It is no accident that every variety of supernaturalism starts by repudiating the jurisdiction of science over human motives. In all soberness, what other jurisdiction is to take its place?

III

To regard values as part of a cultural process that can be scrutinized scientifically is not, however, to decide which values are to be preferred. Human choice may be susceptible to objective and intelligent inquiry, but, it will be argued, that is simply descriptive. It does not help in deciding that some human choices are *better* than others. Nor does it indicate the grounds on which such decision can rest. A distinction must be made between ethics and psychology: choices must be normative as well as historic. But is this the case? Are there not, as Abraham Edel has said, first and second order choices? Choices themselves can be criticized. They can rest in part upon the choices of others as well as of ourselves. Above all, cannot the very process of free inquiry itself be used as a determiner and criterion of human choice? Is there not a continuity of scientific decision to which we can appeal?

Clearly enough, such questions must first consider the existence of other continuities besides the scientific. There is, for example, the continuum of the biological wants that drive man's energies. This is undoubtedly the starting-place for any discussion of value. The straight physiological demands for food, shelter, sexual expression, health, and growth; the psychical urge for meaning, self-expression, satisfaction of curiosity, and a widened and heightened sensitivity; the gregarious needs that force the individual to stretch out for others—all these form a pattern of survival which alone can give coherence to any discussion of value. The choices that men make begin at the level of survival. Not that they remain there. Even in a strictly biological continuum, men choose early to play as well as to survive. But no hierarchy of choice can be established with any pretense to relevance or permanence unless a foundation has been laid; the building blocks of that foundation can be nothing else but the elemental human wants.

There is, in addition, the continuum of the social conditioning of these wants. For wants are not primary data except in the vague sense that *something* is wanting or lacking. *What* is wanted—that is, the kind of food, shelter, or sexual expression—is a cultural artifact. Even if we employ familiar naturalistic criteria such as that men must live as well as is possible with full all-round development and maximum realization of potentialities, the specific capacity of these criteria is set by what society regards as living well and by the potentialities which are permitted to develop. The content of still more familiar standards—such as happiness or pleasure or "hedonic tone"—is no less a matter of cultural conditioning. Pleasure-providing activities vary as do sociological activities; and if pleasure or some similar goal is thought of as an identity unaffected by the ways through which it is reached, then the old atomistic psychology of insulated mental substances has been resurrected.

The satisfaction of food, shelter, and sex wants is, however, a high order abstraction on either the biological or the social level: specific itemizing, on the one hand, of tissue changes, and, on the other, of the culture patterns human wants have fallen into is what must give content to primer-like statements about "the satisfaction of basic physical needs" or "pleasure is the end of all human desire." Even the brute datum of biological survival is itself but a kind of diffuse potential depending for its motivation as well as its direction upon social activators. Like the space-time continuum there is a bio-social one.

A scientific continuity, therefore, is not a substitute for others. Gadgets are not intended to replace art, nor technology love. These other dimensions—the biological and social, for instance—are taken for granted. They are what any theory of value must reckon with. The emphasis on scientific method and on human intelligence is a contribution to discrimination, not to coercion. Above all, it is addressed to what Ayres has called "mores nihilism" or the "absolute relativism" of value; such relativism has been in large measure the result of the work of science (of sociology and anthropology), and it is therefore fitting for scientific method itself to challenge the "meretriciousness" of the mores. For moral nihilism provides a vacuum into which rush the winds of authoritarianism; moral relativity paralyzes nerve, and the failure of nerve is a fatal disease.

But moral relativity cannot be avoided by an appeal to some abstract standard which, however noble, stands outside the system it is expected to judge. Such a criterion would require either a super-culture —and, glorious as that would be, it has not yet appeared; or some intuition or revelation of the *right* values. This does not mean that efforts of synthesis such as those of Northrop are not of the highest importance. Any attempt to discover the common components in diverse cultures and to draw them together is noteworthy and fruitful. Yet even these common components must be located within a going "technology," within a set of functioning social institutions. Of course, the words "going" and "functioning" are question-begging ones, for what makes a system "go" or "function?" The following assumptions, all of them closely interrelated, would attempt to suggest a possible answer. They would also seem to afford a clue to the location of an intramural and genuinely intrinsic standard of value, individual as well as social.

1. A culture may be judged by its ability to survive and to develop along a given technological line.

2. That line of technological progress is determined by the degree in which men understand their surroundings—surroundings (or environment) *being interpreted in the broadest possible sense as a culture matrix involving biological and psychic factors as well as social and physical.*

3. Understanding or knowledge is a matter of doing—of control and change—not simply of contemplation. Conversely, among man's most potent tools are his conceptual tools.

4. The scientific enterprise is the symbol of this particular line of technological development.

It may sound impudent to propose that assumptions like these add up to a test for human values, that qualities like "right," "dynamic," "evolutionary," and so on are to be discovered in the direction in which a culture is moving. Equally bald may seem the suggestion that the direction in which a culture moves is determined in large part by the continuum of science and technology [3] and its competition with ceremonial anachronisms. Impudent or bald as these may be, the one social force that cannot be disregarded without peril is the Promethean process, the intelligent understanding and control of all elements of human experience. There has been resistance to that force, and whole areas have been by-passed. Dualisms of all kinds have been set up, and anti-technological nerve failures have spread. Cultural integration is still only a goal. Nevertheless, the locus of human preference cannot

[3] What is intended by "continuum" used in this way? And why "technology?" The latter should call attention to the significance of tools and technics (conceptual as well as motor) in man's expanding comprehension and control of his surroundings. Technology seems to assert that philosophy and "reason" are not alone the weapons for such comprehension and control. "Continuum" suggests the steady cultural development, even "progress," which is found in the history of human tools, and therefore in the history of human control. There is a cumulative power here that can neither be ignored nor put outside the area of human choice and its determiners.

possibly be appraised, or even surveyed, without the orientation provided by the process of intelligent inquiry. Is that process, then, an "ultimate" value which is to be preferred over all others? Or, on the other hand, are not science and technology themselves simply amoral means until they are used to effect some "good" end? What about the strictly individualistic and possibly aberrant choices that men make —how do they gear in with a cultural process?

IV

Terms like "ultimate," "intrinsic," "final" are commonplaces at almost any point in a discussion of values. But they start to proliferate when, as in the paragraphs above, certain human choices come to be regarded as decisive. It is at such time also that the "end-means" motif (the Yogi-Commissar motif) comes to be heard, first thinly in the strings, then ponderously in the brass. To what do these terms refer? Above all, is there not something misleading and factitious about them?

That some choices are to be preferred to others can be denied by no one. Moral nihilism or authoritarianism are the only alternatives to moral choice. It is naive and slightly preposterous to indict, say, instrumentalism (or some other subversive philosophy) on the grounds that it continues to take the next step without knowing where it is going. Every moral theory has direction. But direction does not necessarily imply some arbitrary stopping place, some "final" goal which eventually is to be reached. The word "intrinsic" itself testifies to this confusion. For the allegedly intrinsic values that ethical theorists have talked about are actually "extrinsic" for the most part. They are imposed from without, often tending to become rigid to the degree they are resisted. The ascetic ends of certain philosophies and religions, or the "genteel tradition" in education, might be cases in point. A genuinely intrinsic value is one within and part of a valuation process; it functions in a context. This point would appear to be crucial in any discussion of value.

A final end must be as suspect as a final cause, for nothing comes to a stop in the history of human choice. Just as effects are also causes, so ends are in turn means. There is a continuum here just as in so much other human experience, a logical continuum (if-then) and a chronological (antecedent-consequent). To arrest the logical or chronological process is to do no more than seize upon some apparently spectacular

element and hypostatize it, or at least divorce it from a context. It is
like jumping naked into the snow to quench a fever. What happens
next is not taken into account. The blindness is pathological (or comic,
as with Lamb's roast pig). Dewey—who has called attention to this
roast-pig element in final values—has constantly insisted upon ends
being regarded as ends-in-view, as "ultimate" only in a temporal, not
a teleological, sense. He writes, for example, that

A thing may be ultimate in the sense of coming last in a given temporal
series, so that it is ultimate *for that series*. There are things that come last
in reflective valuations and, as terminal, they are ultimate. Now [one] is
quite right in saying that for me the method of intelligent action is precisely
such an ultimate value. It is the last, the final or closing, thing we come upon
in inquiry into inquiry. But the place it occupies in the *temporal* manifestation
of inquiry is what makes it such a value, not some property it possesses in
and of itself, in the isolation of non-relatedness.[4]

This does not interdict the use of generalized directions. Nor does
it gainsay our earlier point that human decision must take into account
fundamental continuities such as the biological and the social. No
matter in what way it may be regarded as "ultimate," the process of
intelligent inquiry is still addressed to the resolution of problems; that
is true in the field of value as in all other fields. It will be remembered
that values (according to the present interpretation) are being looked
upon as the products of human choice. Now, choice arises when there
is "conflict," when there are incompatible alternatives between which
decision must be made. Man is a complex creature; some of his wants
inevitably clash with others, and a kind of federation of wants must
result. This conflict-situation is the characteristic background for all
inquiry. Therefore, if one continues to insist that there must be some
"final end," he might be comforted by the suggestion that the resolution of conflict is such an end. At least, it is an end which has contextual
relevance. But it probably would not satisfy. For problems are unique,
and the only "goal" is a common method of handling them. This elevates
method above conclusion and (the teleologist would argue) brings
us back full circle to the complaint that only ends can justify means
—Koestler's commissar morality.

[4] From *The Philosophy of John Dewey* in The Library of Living Philosophers, ed.
by P. A. Schilpp, Evanston and Chicago, 1939, I, 594; by permission of the editor.

The point here is not to swing the pendulum to the other extreme (that of Koestler's Yogi) where means alone count, for both extremes point to fanaticism. Yet it is imperative to understand that the technological continuum, the continuum that determines the degree to which men understand and control their surroundings, is one of method. It is within this continuity that the criterion for human choice must be found. Which does not mean that experimentalism is a technique that must be applied everywhere and at all times. As Horace Fries points out, many problems have to be handled on an emergency basis: decision may need to be made abruptly on whatever grounds are available. But non-experimentalistic decisions can be reviewed; they can be reconsidered in the light of the general context of scientific method, and better preparations can be laid for future urgent situations. In no way does this contradict the basic contention that the test of human value-decisions is *the degree in which they manifest and preserve free intelligent inquiry.*

But suppose all this is unacceptable. Suppose there is a clash between two continuities or between two technologies (if that is really possible), or between two value-systems within the same culture? What then? What internal or external criteria can be invoked to support free intelligent inquiry? Why is one context to be preferred to another? Cannot technology itself become ceremonial? These are critical questions, and no guarantee can be given that they are answerable in terms of the present analysis. Yet at least a sketch of the direction in which such "answers" may be sought should be suggested.

That direction would point to some kind of identity of facts and values. It would turn away from the notion that values are private matters of taste, or matters of sociological conformity alone. The way to answer questions like those above, the "technologist" finds in a continuity of knowledge. To be valid, value decisions must resemble other valid decisions—they must rest on knowledge. The choices to be known as values are reached through a process of confirmation similar to any other *process* of confirmation. Particular techniques and routines will vary, but the general procedures of predictability, instrumental appropriateness, and empirical verification can never be absent even when judgments like "true," "right," "correct," and the like are involved. Such judgments have literally no meaning unless some kind of "scientific" continuity is involved. "Every choice," as Ayres has said, "has as its prototype the mechanic's choice of the right tool."

It is at this point that the continuities paralleling that of intelligent inquiry make their appearance again—that is, the biological and the social continuities. For the questions raised above are not simply teasers. If they assumed that "intelligent inquiry" alone is a test of value, they might be. But men have to live, and they have to live in some sort of social community. If these continuities are unrecognized, value discussion becomes no more than a philosophic exercise. The clash between "technologies" must first be resolved on the level of whether men can live, and live well. "Technologies" which are oblivious to such prosaic questions are irrelevant and cannot satisfy any of the basic assumptions of a going culture.

"Free intelligent inquiry" is not something outside of a culture. It is not extrinsic. If there is anything genuinely intrinsic in the arena of human decision, anything which ties in with all levels of significant choice, it is the critical, self-correcting enterprise that challenges the welter of folkway systems and disinfects itself from ceremonialism. For folkways are not a matter of choice but only of conformity; and "technological" and "ceremonial" are antithetic, since the latter opposes ritual to instruments, tradition to verifiability, and myth to theory. There is nothing necessarily sinister about ritual, tradition, or myth. There is something necessarily backward about them, of the nature of a "pseudomorph." They cannot be truly intrinsic, since they change little and slowly. As a criterion of value, they must show a lag, they cannot be self-corrective, they are inevitably foisted upon a culture from "without"—that is, from the past; they are atavistic reminders (internal as well as external) still haunting a continually developing tool-using animal.

It would seem, therefore, that choice among values cannot be confined to acts of introspection or of social conformity, however much those acts may be organized into the general pattern of human decision. Introversion or folkways cannot themselves be ultimate, at least not as "ultimate" is being understood here—as, in Dewey's earlier words, "the last, the final or closing, thing we come upon in inquiry into inquiry. . . . The method of intelligent action is precisely such an ultimate value." Like knowledge, values are contextual. They are part of a process, the most typically human of all processes—free intelligent inquiry.

V

That free intelligent inquiry has lost its magic is, however, undeniable. That men are losing their nerve is just as undeniable. Failure of nerve is illustrated not by the spread of Hollywood mysticism alone, nor by the Niebuhrian gloom inside of which latter-day Christianity hopes to gather its forces. It is not simply the disaffected liberals—the Sorokins, Druckers, and Mumfords—and the middle-aged novelists who have given up. For the antics of the intelligentsia may be no sure clue to a general loss of vigor. More disheartening is the facility with which totalitarianism, left now as well as right, exercises its appeal and makes its converts. No index, for example, is more chilling than that which points to the desertion of civil liberties by their erstwhile left-of-center defenders. These observations are banal, but no less frightening for that.

The point here is not to contribute to a jeremiad. Neither is it to attack or defend an over-all philosophy of history. It is rather to emphasize the velleity resulting from mere lip service to intelligence, and the schizoid character of the resulting dilemma. Intelligence applies to every aspect of experience, or it does not; if it does not—say, if it is amputated from the body of human choices and values—then something else applies to these precious areas. What is that "something else?" In anti-naturalistic and totalitarian grotesqueries we see the familiar answer. The dualism between morals and technology is no longer an academic matter of logic. It has become the most vital of issues. It is what must be given the very highest priority in any discussion of value.

The word "must" is perhaps out of place, for this priority has been all but universally established. However, it has been established often with malice prepense, as when "power politics" is deliberately divorced from "scientific man"—the theme of a recent book by Hans Morgenthau. His approach is mentioned as typical of an entire school of modern thought, a school convinced that scientific man is through, that rationalism, positivism, liberalism, and all the sorry brood they have spawned are the warped effects of man's attempts to solve social and political problems by means of intelligent inquiry, that science can never handle anything but the natural world—certainly not values. (It might be interesting to note the political alternative Professor Morgenthau presents: instead of "scientific man" we must be reconciled to the "statesman," the power engineer. Some of the names? Alexander, Caesar, Brutus, Napoleon, Lenin, and Hitler.)

Collapse of faith in man may be traced to many things. But one of the things to which it certainly cannot be traced is "scientific man." That is to say, the basic assumption of all arguments of the Morgenthau-Mumford type is nothing less than that modern culture is indeed dominated by the genuine practice of scientific method and by an emotional commitment to that method; that scientific method *has* been applied consistently to problems of value and that there has been opportunity to judge of its impact. To detect these assumptions is to refute them; yet without them the position of any kind of anti-rationalism becomes pathetically meaningless. It would be an amazing optimist who could see the rule of scientific thinking prevailing in men's lives now or at any time in the past—even though a Goddess of Reason was once crowned on the Parisian boulevards. Just the categorical opposite of what "anti-scientists" profess to believe, we have failed precisely where scientific and positivistic methods have *not* been tried—in value discussion, for example. That the bankruptcy of value discussion is to be blamed on the failure of the scientific spirit is fantastic. If ever cart were put before horse this is it. "Scientific man" has been striving to penetrate the area of human choice; to say that he has succeeded in penetrating and then has failed to make good is a monstrous perversion of intellectual history.

History cannot be appealed to as proof of the failure of intelligence. It *can* be appealed to as a record of power politics. No literate man needs to be convinced of that. What the anti-rationalists are doing is celebrating that record. They may use honorific and gaudy language, but the upshot is surrender of the most indefensible sort. Surrender and nerve paralysis are not new. But they can no longer be regarded as merely interesting symptoms of a charming decadence. There is a crisis in contemporary atomic culture that is journalistic only in the sense of being timely and pressing—so pressing that even professional philosophers cannot ignore it. This crisis, however technological its present form, is no more than an up-to-date version of the perennial dualism which has plagued man forever—the split between intelligence and conduct. That dichotomy can be accepted as inevitable and ineradicable, and morals can, in theory, be permanently divorced from technology. Yet such an acceptance in these days is not simply constipated or Pickwickian: it is as grossly unrealistic as the exorcism of devils out of the atomic nucleus. For the gap between mores and science *is* going to be closed—the only question being, how? The closing of the gap can be the close of human culture. Without being pontifical, one may therefore insist that the aim of value theory, of philosophy, of science, or of any aspect of human intelligence must be to draw together the now-separated regions of technical competence and moral fumbling. Free intelligent inquiry seems alone capable of performing that task. It is therefore of supreme consideration in the area of human choice.[5]

[5] For the Criticisms and Rejoinders which relate especially to this paper see pp. 306–307, and 312–320, below.

❧ A CONTEXTUALIST
❧ LOOKS AT VALUES

LEWIS E. HAHN

IF WE TAKE as a rough common-sense starting point the kinds of things philosophers, economists, and others interested in theory of value have been writing about for the past fifty years, it is soon apparent that not all of this material seems equally significant for an understanding of value problems. Though all or most of those writing on the subject may say that they are simply interested in the plain facts or evidence concerning value—and I have no doubt that they are all interested in the relevant facts—it seems reasonably clear that such men as R. B. Perry, Prall, Parker, Santayana, Bosanquet, Dewey, Geiger, and Lepley do not have the same basic approach. They cite different areas of fact as the significant ones; and even when they agree to include what seems to some of the others to be fundamental facts or evidence, they include it in such fashion as to disturb those who gave these facts preferential treatment. Dewey and Parker, for example, are clearly marshaling different lines of evidence for their views on values, and what one of them may regard as fundamental the other may barely mention.

If all concerned were to draw up postulations regarding their observations or experiences with (or of) values, I should be very much surprised if Parker's postulations, say, turned out to be the same as those of, say, Dewey and Bentley. I should rather expect, moreover, that one set of these postulations would fit in pretty clearly with a given world view, or metaphysics, and that the other would not fit in very well with that reasoned view of the nature of things but would fit in with another. Where these views are systematized as a set of postulations, we may be able to see in what direction they take us. Where they are not recognized at all, only confusion is likely to result; and much value discussion and disagreement may depend upon metaphysical theories not explicitly recognized.

If we go back into the history of philosophy and value theory, it will be readily apparent that certain views of value are the outgrowth of particular world views. Even now, when discussion may turn around subjective, "inner" values as over against objective, "outer" facts, the problems which look fundamental to many in the field are ones generated by these historical metaphysical theories, and one reason why it is difficult to get a reformulation of problems is perhaps because so many writing on them feel that the problems as stated in terms of these historical views are the only genuine ones in the field of value. Others, however, declare that we must leave out metaphysical questions, because they are convinced that following out the leads suggested by certain of these historical views will add little to the development of value theory. Their own basic metaphysics they may call by some other name.

Some thinkers in this field hold that the facts or data of value are incomparably clearer and more certain than any metaphysical theory could possibly be. These individuals accordingly advise concentrating upon extending the realm of value-facts instead of worrying about metaphysics. Even they, however, are likely to find that not all of the facts are equally clear or equally helpful in developing a fruitful account of the field. Some data, properly interpreted, seem to afford keys to the understanding of other more troublesome facts. This is not to say, of course, that gathering facts is not important or that metaphysics is a substitute for them; but it is to suggest that if we are to get maximum returns from additional data, we need to see how these data or facts are interpreted by different metaphysical views. It takes only a cursory survey of the papers in this volume to show that there are facts and facts in the field of values but that, for one reason or another, some of them seem much more basic to one group of writers than to another. Where this is the case with men of good will equally interested in doing justice to the facts, is it not worth inquiring whether or not these differences in emphasis have some connection with fundamental differences in metaphysical outlook?

Many apparently think, however, that bringing metaphysical considerations into value discussion is to go backwards rather than forwards; but methodologically, there are at least two advantages to bringing them in. First, there is the matter of clarity. If, as I think likely, metaphysical assumptions are involved, it will aid in clearing up value problems and issues to recognize them; for this will make possible seeing how they function in this connection. Whereas it is possible to recognize and allow for an acknowledged metaphysical bias, an unrecognized one may be smuggled in under the guise of neutrality to work havoc with our discussion. If metaphysical assumptions are not involved, a statement of why they are not and how what is offered differs from what is sometimes called metaphysical pronouncements might be equally helpful. In the second place, as perhaps a development of the first point, if one of the aims of discussion of values is to develop as large a body of metaphysically neutral data as possible, this end may be furthered more readily by explicit recognition of the role that metaphysical theories have played and now play in value debates than by setting out simply to gather and interpret facts on the (erroneous, I should think) assumption that all these facts are metaphysically neutral.

When I examine the kinds of things philosophers and others interested in value theory have been concerned with, I find that what impresses me most favorably—what appears to be most adequate in explaining value situations—seems to grow out of a contextualistic, or pragmatic, approach. That this should be the case for one who regards the contextualistic metaphysics as one of the most adequate, if not the most adequate, of metaphysical or world views is not strange. Others, with different metaphysical presuppositions, may very well find another interpretation of value facts and problems more helpful; but even they may be aided methodologically, by seeing what the relation, if any, is between their views on value and their metaphysics. I am accordingly serving notice that to the extent that I am consciously operating under the influence of a metaphysical bias, it is that of contextualism, or pragmatism, which I have attempted to characterize elsewhere.[1]

---

[1] See *A Contextualistic Theory of Perception,* Berkeley, Calif., 1942, pp. 6–19. Contextualism I think of as a form of pragmatic naturalism which takes as its basic fact patterned events, things in process, or historical events. The main traits of such events constitute the fundamental categories of the view and may be used to characterize or explain any set of problematic facts. Though there are various alternative statements of these categorical features (see, for example, S. C. Pepper's "The Conceptual Framework of Tolman's Purposive Behaviorism," *Psychological Review,* XLI (1934), 108–133, especially, 111, or his chapter on "Contextualism" in *World Hypotheses,* Berkeley, Calif., 1942), one convenient grouping divides them into (1) a set of filling or textural traits which indicate the nature or "stuff" of an event, and (2) a group of contextual or environmental traits which serve to denote the place of the event in relation to other events. The textural categories include *texture, strand, quality, fusion,* and *reference* (distance-direction values), whereas the most important contextual ones are perhaps *environment, initiations, means* (or *instruments*), *consummations,* and *frustrations* (blocking).

Dewey's discussion of his first question—"What connection is there, if any, between an attitude that will be called prizing or holding dear and desiring, liking, interest, enjoying, etc?"—indicates that what he is primarily concerned with is the choice between a behavioristic (or "behavioral") and an "internal," "mentalistic" approach to these attitudes; and in studying values from the point of view of a contextualist, the choice between these two is readily made in favor of the behavioral approach if it is not interpreted in too narrow terms. A behaviorism of the Watsonian variety is too narrow. A behaviorism which reduces behavior to physical or physiological terms is inadequate. It must be a behaviorism broad enough to include all that is observable in human activities on whatever level. Indeed, it may be said that the essential thing about this type of behavioral approach—some would question whether it should be called behavioral—is that whatever experience reveals in any sense, whether it be my attitude toward behaviorism, my introspections concerning values, the folkways of a particular section of the country, or a thing such as an automobile, has specific traceable relations to other events; and by tracing out these relations (strands), or certain of them, we can "locate" or characterize the event. But if we define value or anything else in terms of inaccessible areas of feelings, ones which make no difference in what we observe, we make explanation extremely difficult, if not impossible. Contextualistically speaking, moreover, I do not find any "inner" realm of satisfactions and desires of a radically different kind from "outer" facts. Whatever else, then, we may say about the specific relations between the various attitudes mentioned by Dewey, they are all behavioral transactions, things open to investigation and study.

In the main, some such approach as that of E. C. Tolman's *Purposive Behavior in Animals and Men* [2] seems to me to be in the right direction. His molar, or purposive, behaviorism does not limit behavior to muscular, glandular, or neural processes. It is rather concerned with behavior qua molar, and such behavior Tolman assures us, has its own identifying properties. Before specifying these properties, however, I should like to make clear that in using such a framework I have no intention of denying the importance of social and cultural considerations. Though the psychologist may naturally enough emphasize the individual, purposive behaviorism allows for the contextualist's con-

[2] New York, 1932.

tention that individuals are not insulated centers of desire but are rather of a piece with their social environment.

But what are the identifying properties of molar behavior? Tolman suggests that "the complete descriptive identification of any behavior-act per se requires descriptive statements relative to (a) the goal-object or objects, being got to or from; (b) the specific pattern of commerces with means-objects involved in this getting to or from; and (c) the facts exhibited relative to the selective identification of routes and means-objects as involving short (easy) commerces with means-objects for thus getting to or from." [3] These descriptive statements are made in terms of two sets of identifying properties: (1) initiating causes, namely, (a) environmental stimuli and (b) initiating physiological states; and (2) behavior determinants, namely, (a) purposive and cognitive immanent determinants (which should include behavior adjustments, Tolman's substitute for the conscious awareness and ideas of the mentalist), and (b) purposive and cognitive capacities.

As I have pointed out elsewhere,[4] the outstanding feature of such molar behavior is its purposive character, the fact that it is motivated by some drive. Certain results or ends are aimed at and achieved. Other results or states of affairs are to be avoided. Such behavior is carried out for the sake of satisfying various demands,[5] overcoming problems in connection with food, water, or any of the multiplicity of wants and needs of the acting organism. It is an attempt of the organism to maintain the relations necessary or, if need be, to change or modify its environment or itself to bring about the fulfillment of these demands. The very preservation of the organism or the species depends upon the degree of success achieved in fulfilling certain of them. Though fundamental physiological drives provide their core, demands of any adult human being are far richer and more varied than this central core might indicate. Demands for social approval, for aiding children and the weak, for wealth or power, for taking in as fully as possible a given perceptual pattern, or for any one of an indefinitely large number of other things may loom large in such an individual's behavior.

---

[3] *Purposive Behavior,* pp. 7–8; by permission of D. Appleton–Century Company, publishers.
[4] *A Contextualistic Theory of Perception,* pp. 28–29.
[5] Tolman defines a demand as "an innate or acquired urge to get to or from some given instance or type of environmental presence or of physiological quiescence (q.v.) or disturbance (q.v.)."—*Purposive Behavior,* p. 441.

Perhaps the two crucial aspects of behavior for our purposes, then, are these two: (1) its demand character, and (2) its cognitive aspect, what Tolman speaks of as an attached more or less vague sign-gestalt readiness as to the appropriate sorts of means object to be selected for commerce with in order to fulfill these demands.[6] The demand character I take to refer to the kind of thing Dewey calls "prizing." Those objects or situations "demanded" are ones he would say are "prized." Some prefer to state the demands in terms of *needs*: instead of demands made upon the environment, one may speak of the needs of the organism. Or, with Otis Lee,[7] one might state the whole question in terms of demands or requirements of the situation. In any event, however, wherever needs can be established, they are relevant in evaluating the prizing.

Let us examine briefly the behavior of children playing ball. Let us suppose that the ball lodges in the fork of a tree above the reach of the tallest child. The game is interrupted. A demand is set up for its continuance which necessitates getting the ball. Their behavior, or that of any one of them, may be patterned in terms of the steps necessary to recover the ball, for the most important means object to continuing the game is its recovery. Let us suppose that attempts to climb the tree fail and that in the absence of readily available ladders or boxes someone of them suggests that two of them could hold a third up high enough to reach the ball and that they act on this basis and recover it. The immediate goal is continuance of the ball game, not indefinitely but within limits set by other activites of the children. The superordinate means object to this goal is recovering the ball. Various other means objects, such as cooperative activity of at least three children, may be involved in getting this superordinate means object. Cognitively, certain expectations are set up, and these anticipations are fulfilled. The continuance of the ball game marks the completion of both the cognitive and the conative phases of this particular act.

For this act the final goal is continuance of the game. Instrumental to this are various other activities or means objects. Among these means objects is the cognitive phase—the plan of action which resulted in the continuance of the interrupted activity. Means objects I have dis-

[6] *Purposive Behavior*, p. 443. See also R. B. Perry's governing propensity (*General Theory of Value*, New York, 1926, ch. vii and elsewhere), which includes both the demand aspect and an anticipatory cognitive aspect.
[7] See "Value and the Situation," *The Journal of Philosophy*, XLI (1944), 337–360.

cussed elsewhere [8] under the heading of utilitanda (a term taken over from Tolman); and, as I attempted to show there, objects may have utilitanda with respect to any state of affairs viewed as an end. Thus so far as means-end relationships are concerned, we find that those involved in human value situations are continuous with sub-human or even sub-organic levels.

What about the final goal of this particular act? Continuance of the game is related in various ways to numerous other important factors in the activities of these children; but so far as this particular incident is concerned, it is the terminating state of affairs. It is that which is demanded through these means. The other things demanded, positively or negatively, are for its sake. This is not to say that certain things are in some fixed or absolute sense always means, others always ends; for what is goal in one situation may be means in another. It is simply to note that any given situation sets up some order among the activities involved. If a goal is demanded, the means necessary to achieve that goal are also demanded. Though not just any means will fit into a demanded pattern, certain alternatives are usually possible. And within this total situation we may note certain striking differences in quality between the goal as anticipated and the goal as achieved.[9] The strongest conative activity is prior to the continuance of the game. Its continuance is demanded most strongly before it is achieved. Throwing the ball back on the playing field relieves the tension, for what had been sought is had. Activity turns largely in other directions, is no longer focused on this particular point. The ball playing activity, however, sets up a certain pattern which resists change, a pattern held sufficiently dear to possess drive for its continuance. Indeed, it was the interruption of this pattern, or the blockage of it, which set up a strong demand for the ball as a means to continuing this pattern. What we are noting now is that, though continuance of the game is demanded in both instances, there is a difference in attitude between the situation in which the break existed and that which marks the closing of the break.

Some apparently prefer to say that we have conative value only in the latter instance, only where the goal is being enjoyed. Resumption

---

[8] A Contextualistic Theory of Perception, for example, pp. 55–61, 63–70.
[9] As molar behaviorists it does not seem to me that we are excluded from noting the felt quality of the experience involved. See Pepper, op. cit., pp. 108–133, especially pp. 122–126.

of the game, prior to its actual taking place, they might say, is merely a potential object and hence a potential object of value, since resumption of the game is not yet and may never be. It is quite true that the goal object, as viewed from some early stage, is not yet and may, indeed, be impossible of attainment. Such risks are part of living and the value situation. Without them reflection on values would probably never arise. Nonetheless the conative activity turns about this demanded goal object and is likely to be more intense before it is achieved than at the moment in which the organism is having commerce with it. Even though analysis reveals the demanded object to be largely a system of symbols or plans of action so utterly at cross-purposes as to be impossible of achievement, still it is around anticipation of that object that conative activity turns; and the enjoyment of these anticipations may constitute a major portion of the conative value of a given situation such as playing ball. It may be held, of course, that in such cases the enjoyment of these very anticipations constitutes the goal or a significant portion of it.

Certain qualities, or qualitative complexes, then, may be demanded positively or negatively, with varying degrees of intensity. They may be prized or held dear, or they may be avoided or held remote if possible. Enjoyment or commerce with these qualities may be liked or disliked. Desire for any one of them may be evoked or intensified by temporary blockage of the drive for their attainment. Interest may well be, as Dewey suggests, an enduring or long-time span disposition to prize, positively or negatively. The achievement of any goal depends upon the available utilitanda. And the explanation of no one of these terms requires abandonment of a behavioral approach.

"II. Irrespective of which of the above-named attitudes is taken to be primary, is it by itself a sufficient condition for the existence of values? Or, while it is a necessary condition, is a further condition, of the nature of *valuation* or *appraisal,* required?" In part, this is a verbal question of what we shall call value. In part, it is a factual question of the extent to which reflective or critical factors enter into our demands or prizings. That anything which is demanded, prized, held dear, or cared for is or becomes what H. N. Lee would perhaps call a putative object of value or a candidate for value in the standard sense would perhaps be admitted by almost everyone; and some would call this *immediate value* or *value in a primary sense.* That there is another sense of value in which only those candidates which have met (or could meet) the tests of critical appraisal are included might also be admitted. This second class may be called *standard values,* or perhaps reasoned values. Another group of values concerning which something should be said is the utilitanda, or means-end values.

With reference to these utilitanda, we have already noted that their range is wider than that of human prizings. Whether they should be spoken of as a fundamental ground for values or as values may be debated; but if they be admitted as values, we shall have to say that, though the values with which we are primarily concerned are ones in which human experience is a generating factor, there are extensions of this realm which may be significant. Being instrumental to a given result is not limited to things human or organic. Hence certain instrumental values do not depend upon being prized.

If the utilitanda point in the direction of a broader realm than human demands or prizings, they also call attention to a significant use of reflection in human value situations; for wherever there is concern for utilitanda, there reflection enters. Wherever an organism works for a goal, there is concern for short or long, direct or circuitous, paths to that goal. When we speak of demands apart from cognitive concerns, apart from means of satisfying them, so far as the contextualist is concerned this is an abstraction, or we mean to indicate, not that reflection is absent but rather that relatively little reflection enters into the situation in question. Available paths to the goal also help determine even which goal will be sought. Ends are not sought, demanded, or prized in abstraction from the means of attaining them; and the demand for a particular goal may be strong enough to overcome resistance to the available paths to it. Extremely rare in normal adults, moreover, if, indeed, it ever occurs, is the situation in which only one goal object makes demands on the behavior of the organism. Ordinarily the organism is faced with a choice of goals or with situations in which the pursuit of one goal is modified by the demands of others, situations in which one prizing is modified by other prizings; and such situations provide the framework for appraisal. Considerations of the nature and amount of value afforded by a given end, then, are intrinsic to the value situation; and the fundamental question with reference to a given situation of this kind is not whether judgment or appraisal enters, but rather to what extent or how adequately.

One further observation which might be made concerning utilitanda is what happens in connection with competing goals. Wherever we are forced to choose between goals or ends and attempt to decide this reflectively, we must determine a further end and then evaluate these prior goals or ends as utilitanda, as means, to this further end. This, I think, is at least one of the reasons why views which stress the possibility of verification in values are likely to give important places to such ends as growth or freedom, for these are of special value in evaluating less comprehensive competing ends or goals. The disparagement or neglect of instrumental values in much value discussion is accordingly particularly unfortunate.

Though the question of critical appraisal or reflection is raised with special force in connection with utilitanda, it can also be approached with reference to the distinction between immediate and standard value. Immediate value, I take it, refers to prizing or enjoyment; and I have already indicated that the former seems to me to contain some measure of reflection, which is developed more fully in the standard value situations. Enjoyment of qualities without some reference, anticipatory or retrospective, does not seem to me to involve value. If the qualities (or the enjoyment) are not prized, they surely do not possess *immediate* value, though it might be argued that they possess standard value of some sort.

I should be willing to say that a necessary condition for inclusion as a goal or end object is being demanded or prized by some one. That which is prized or demanded by no one may be the end or outcome of a particular line of action, but it is not an object of final value. Prizing or demanding, however, does not seem to me sufficient to constitute standard value. A thing may be demanded without being valuable, as is suggested by the fact that some things initially accepted as valuable, some candidates for standard value, turn out upon examination of conditions and consequences to be other than we originally accepted them as being. Upon examination, we may decide that our initial prizing was not warranted. We may find that it was based upon a propaganda appeal or a narrow prejudice, say, rather than upon the requirements of the situation. After hearing a nutrition expert, for example, we may find that the white bread we prized for various reasons does not have the food values of another type of bread and change our value estimates. To possess value in the full sense, then, an end or goal must be prized or demanded in the light of careful consideration of conditions and consequences.

Certain objections to the conclusion that value (other than certain extensions of utilitanda) involves an element of appraisal or criticism may be noted. In the first place, it is pointed out that we frequently enjoy or care for things which occur without our having anticipated or planned for them. To say that value involves reflection, they declare, rules out such undoubted goods; but this is true, it seems to me, only if we narrow reflection more than the facts justify. If qualities or experiences are recognized as good or valuable, does not this involve appraisal, reference to standards? The mere fact of enjoyment is not enough to constitute value, for we enjoy various things we do not prize, demand, or care for. If prizing is added to enjoyment, however little foresight of the qualities we had, a critical element comes in. The qualitative complex is recognized as possessing marks of some sort which make it prizeworthy; for not everything is prized or demanded on any particular occasion. And this is to say that reflection enters in here not merely in the sense of a report on what has already been prized but rather as a significant aspect of the prizing. In short, we find, it seems to me, that value experiences involve reflection or critical appraisal in varying degrees, ranging from this perhaps minimum participation on up to ones in which critical appraisal functions as a means of instituting or modifying the demands or prizing.

As a second objection to the conclusion that value experiences involve an element of appraisal or criticism, it is urged that in retrospect we decide that a particular experience we had was a value even though at the time we did not recognize it as such. We did not prize it, but we now prize it or things of its kind. It seems fairly clear that this was not an instance of immediate value, the thing not being experienced as valuable at the time. Hence one or the other of two possibilities seems likely in this case. Either such value as it possessed is instrumental in character, and I should admit that reflection may show that various means are valuable for certain ends, even though we may have failed originally to notice this; or though it was not experienced as value, *as a result of reflection* it has been recognized as worth prizing henceforth and a demand set up for things so characterized—a rather curious result in an argument intended to show that reflection has no place in such value experiences.

Perhaps another reason why some are hesitant to hold that "nothing having the properties of value can arise save as some factor of appraisal, of measuring and comparing, enters in," is that this seems to make an already dark picture dismal indeed. So long as these things are believed to be matters of irrational preference or prejudice, it may be hoped that when reason or reflection enters there will be some improvement in the chaotic value situation; but if reason or reflection is already there, if this sorry situation already has within it something of what intelligence can bring, then, to some perhaps, it seems that only pessimism remains. However, one might grant, it seems to me, that the situation is bad and still hold that from this germ of reason or critical evaluation, not miracles, but better things may be expected. In this case, it is not a matter of bringing critical evaluation into a field where it is alien but rather an affair of developing critical inquiry and giving it the larger place we think it deserves.

My answer to the question of whether value-judgments are different as judgments or propositions from other judgments and propositions is in the negative, if by the assertion of a difference is intended either a denial of cognitive import to value-judgments or a statement of the impossibility of confirming them.

My answer to the question as to whether scientific method in the broad sense is applicable to value-judgments or evaluations, as has perhaps been made clear in the above discussion, is in the affirmative.

My answer to Dewey's perhaps more fundamental fifth question, thrown in as a kind of postscript, of whether values and valuations can be treated on the basis of individual psychology or whether they are so definitely socio-cultural that they can be treated only in this context is at least suggested in the earlier discussion. Certainly no atomic individual has any place in contextualism; and the social environment of human values and evaluations is, of course, a basic concern. Individuals of the sort contextualism finds are not isolated, independent centers of desire or introspection. A large part of what they are is due to their environment. The culture of an area or epoch is a very significant factor in the prizings of an individual. In general, what he prizes will bear the stamp of his culture. When this has been granted, however, the fact remains that the activities of men differ a great deal as to their social or individual quality, and we may find in the life of any normal being a wide range extending from relatively individual, private concerns to ones of an almost exclusively social character. Accordingly, I should not wish to treat the alternatives offered by the questions as mutually exclusive.

There are important considerations to be developed in connection with individual psychology if we remember what the character of an individual is for the contextualist, but certainly more than the individual side must be filled in. Any discussion which neglected the socio-cultural context would be inadequate. Values are not purely private individual concerns. We must consider both the individual psychology and the socio-cultural context. In fact, I hardly see how either could be treated adequately without drawing in the other.[10]

[10] For the Criticisms and Rejoinders which relate especially to this paper see pp. 417–419, 421–423, 456–464, and 469–470, below.

❧ ON VALUE

BERTRAM E. JESSUP

THE BEGINNING OF DISCUSSION OF VALUE, I agree with Pepper, is the question of value data. We need to ask, says he, "How is a definition of the subject or field of value obtainable that will not be arbitrary? How guarantee that different writers on 'value' are discussing the same thing?" [1]

I

Need for agreement is axiomatic: Between persons there can be no rational disagreement, that is, disagreement of the kind that leads to discussion rather than contention, unless there is first agreement. And likewise an individual can examine and correct his beliefs only in terms of his more basic beliefs. The pre-discussional agreement which is required is of two kinds: first, agreement concerning the nature of the data which are to be investigated, and, second, agreement as to the nature of the questions to be asked concerning those data. The task of this symposium, as set by Dewey and as accepted by its other members, seems to me to be primarily that of clarification of agreements of the second sort—agreements, in Dewey's words, concerning the "questions or issues fundamentally involved" in "discussion of value." [2] Clarification of agreement concerning data is a further step back in the proposed task of attempting to find assured ground for subsequent discussion. [3]

Demand for agreement on data, is not, of course, demand for certainty or finality. Agreement may be tentative and that which is agreed upon, vague and indefinite. On some points we may even be confused

[1] Quoted from the questions and comments preliminary to the present inquiry.
[2] P. 5, above.
[3] Dewey in "Some Questions about Value" does not take this further step back, but assumes agreement on the "what" of the data. His questions invite inquiry concerning the connections between certain denominated data, namely, attitudes, prizing, holding dear, desiring, liking, interest, enjoying, valuation, appraisal, evaluation.

and mistaken in thinking that we do agree or that we do know our data. But appeal to agreement is still the way of finding this out and amending it. If there is any possibility of *coming* to agreement or of *reaching* reasonable assurance about particular uncertainties or differences which turn up, it must lie in appeal to remaining agreements. Retreat from questionable data is retreat to less questionable data, and the limits of retreat, if investigation is to go forward, are the limits which finally mark the field of data.

The problem of data is thus real and basic; however, I think its difficulties may be exaggerated. My reading of the literature of value leads to the conclusion that relatively few disputes in value theory stem from original disagreements as to data, but rather from the fact that special positions have a way of theorizing themselves out of the initially agreed field. Thus most value philosophers (at least empiricists) agree that, whatever else, the data of value include desires and enjoyments, and desired and enjoyed objects. But it is not hard to find developed theories in which each one of these data is in turn theorized away or out of recognition. In what follows I shall, accordingly, attempt to indicate not only how the field of value data is found, but also to set down certain principles which must be followed in order to keep within this field.

Though it proceeds rather more gropingly than do the special sciences, being initially somewhat more in the dark as to the nature and the disposition of its data, empirical value theory does not start blindly. True, the value theorist is in peculiar perplexity at his first step in not knowing observationally what his center or core of data is, whether it is thing, quality, state or act of subject, relation, or something else still. Nonetheless, he is from the beginning on familiar ground and concerned with familiar features of an already known field, a field neither virgin nor uncharted. The life of value has been and is being lived, and it is the life of value which is his range. There are value problems at all because there are value facts. Experience says "good" to some states of factual affairs, "bad" to others, and simply "so it is" to still others. When these facts are observed in some regularity or order of recurrence, value data are recognized. The value theorist thus knows in the main what it is he is dealing with and where he can expect to find it.

II

Value theory then starts with observational data, but these data are not a collection of specimen-like values in pre-definitional clarity; they form, rather, a vague "value-complex" in which are knotted together various "things" in descriptively uncertain and probably inconstant relations. Among writers on value there seems to be fair agreement that these things include: (1) value-feelings (pleasures and pains and affective dispositions); (2) volitional activity (based on felt tensions), setting up ends or purposes, the drive toward which is not simply additive of the moments or points of felt-pleasures along the way; (3) value-judgment (appraisal or evaluation), which may reject, censure or approve both feeling and will; (4) the value object, which may be any thing, quality or situation, actual or ideal, and of any degree of intricacy.

To get under way, value theory must accept as data some such complex as this. There is no empirical way of beginning discussion of value except that of laying hold boldly on everything that looks value-like or seems to pertain to value, of taking data for granted at the start, just as in piscine theory it is sensible to start by taking for granted everything that looks fish-like, even though further investigation makes necessary the dropping of whales.

This value-complex, then, in which everything that looks like value is taken initially for granted marks the observational and probable field of value. It is a field of fact, a real field, and not merely a verbal one. The relationships to be studied are within the observed factual complex and not merely in names and words; that is, they are in behavior other than or more than linguistic.

That the field of the value-complex does exist, and that certain of its ingredients are given is not open to reasonable question. That it is given, and is already indeed partially digested for the philosopher of value, is seen by analogy in the special field of aesthetic fact. Aesthetic facts are largely given in the histories of art and literature, in the contents of museums and libraries, and in the preserves and collections of archaeological remains. Existing and historically described works of art together with the facts of their production and of their appreciation are the data of aesthetic theory. Collectively and in the main they must stand, otherwise the theory which starts out to explain them ends by disowning its reason for being and becomes a theory of nothing.

This is not to say that aesthetic theory, or any other, cannot question facts as data. Theory does check facts, but not *in externo* nor *en masse*. It can detect intruders or pretenders, but only by appeal to the remaining majority facts themselves. In other words, theory addressing itself to the given field of facts can eliminate some and perhaps add others—but not too many either way. What is true of the way of finding aesthetic data and staying with them is true similarly of the way of finding general value data.

Two further observations in connection with the field of value may be made: (1) Theory of value is not history. (2) Theory of value is not a special science or social science. History as descriptive record of value lived (including all special histories and imagined histories in the arts) furnishes the material (raw data) of value; the special sciences and social sciences its (ideally) precise data. The material of value is gathered in history and biography; it is embodied in works and social institutions; it is sifted and formulated into data by the sciences and social sciences. Theory of value is not biography, history, or anthropology; neither is it psychology, sociology, biology or neurology. Conversely, none of the special sciences or social sciences is theory of value; nor do they conjointly produce theory of value. Many specialized investigations produce value data; none except philosophy of value itself is capable of producing value theory. It is not unimportant to be clear that it is *their* function and competence to supply data and not the function of theory of value, and equally to be clear that it is the function and competence of theory of value and not of the special sciences to theorize these data. Theory of value needlessly perplexes itself in assuming that more and more facts or items of value are what it needs, and it can well dissipate its labors in going in endless search for them. Likewise theory of value renders itself impertinent if it undertakes to produce data in the way of the special scientist. As the metaphysician is not a super-physicist or a synthetic scientist compounded of all the other scientists, so is the philosopher of value not a superpsychologist nor a psychologist, a neurologist and a sociologist all rolled together. What the value theorist needs is not more and more fact—especially not of his own endless seeking—but more precise data;

for example, a more precise psychological clarification of such concepts as "enjoyment" and "desire." He will look for them in the sciences. And what the value theorist has to do is not to usurp a place in any one of the special sciences, but rather to strive to understand the relations among the various data of all the relevant sciences. If the philosopher arrogates to himself a false scientific function, he will merely invite from the scientist a counter-arrogation of philosophical function. The scientist will be encouraged to believe that the special data which he alone competently has to offer will of its own accord produce a general theory of value. So-called "scientific" or biological theories of ethics and psychological theories of aesthetics come to mind as prevalent examples of the resulting error.[4]

To argue that theory of value is properly more interested in securing precise data from competent sources than in the multiplication of the quantity and variety of supporting material does not mean that it should or can go its way safely unacquainted with its material. On the contrary, it should know all the material of value possible, in order to check and corroborate both its data and its conclusions. It should not confuse material with data. It should not be so impressed by the multiplicity and particularity of its material that it will get lost in it or betrayed by it into principles of mere material occurrence. What theory of value is interested in is the nature of value, that is, the recurrent pattern of value, of the constant constituents of value. It is interested in *value* and not in values. In being too much impressed with the quantity and variety of its material it may actually miss what it is looking for. For example, if the value theorist takes too narrowly the, in some degree, materially correct observation that "every moral situation is unique,"[5] he may pass to the questionable formal conclusion that the only true value judgment is "The singular judgment"[6]—questionable because if true it would make impossible the comparative judgment, and therefore of *any* value-judgment except the purely descriptive.

What theory of value produces in its first operation on its data is not an increase of data nor addition of material, but, rather, an inspectional definition of value on the basis of data given. If the gathered materials in

[4] Thus, strictly, there can be no psychological theory of aesthetics, but at the same time there is much important psychological *data* for aesthetics.
[5] P. B. Rice, "'Objectivity' in Value Judgments," *The Journal of Philosophy*, XL (1943), 8.   [6] *Ibid.*, p. 12.

the history of morals, for instance, shows a recurrent pattern of "radical changes in values," [7] the pursuit of theory needs only to take note that among the inspectional features of the data is this fact of radical change in the material of value.

To proceed so as to keep within the field made up of observed data is to proceed empirically and naturalistically. In general theory of value this means (1) that nothing from outside can be introduced *as fact* to challenge what actually appears or goes on in the field, and (2) that no single element in the field can "explain" out of existence any other observed element in it.

From (1) it follows that data offered as in the field must not be anything in the way of a prescriptive absolute (for example, an unobservable quality or entity) in either a metaphysical or a verbal sense. Neither speculative "data" nor merely intended "data" are admissible. Either to prescribe or to stipulate data is to proceed with undue arbitrariness. This means simply, (a) that the whole field of value is not itself a value, that it is not itself subject to value determination; and (b) that a part of the field cannot by fiat or intention be made the whole field. As such it is subject neither to addition or subtraction in kind, it remaining true, of course, that *observation* of the field may be corrected by being either extended or contracted.

From (2) it follows, for example, that a simple "desire theory" is suspect, that so too is a simple "pleasure theory," and that so also is an "evaluational theory," one, namely, in which felt values have to be "evaluated" in order to be values genuinely.

The field of value having been established, and the principles of keeping it in view having been indicated, the next step in the pursuit of theory of value is to gather together or arrange in their fairly obvious relationships the features which stand out in the field. These features are, of course, the data already come upon in discovery of the field. The result will be an "inspectional definition" of value. The philosopher of value today does not, however, need to begin at the bottom to produce such a definition; indeed, it would be a waste of labor to do so. A broad reading of the literature of value theory shows a sufficient measure of agreement as to what the basic features of value are; and unless genuinely new data are turned up, the task of definition begins simply with a summary statement concerning the area of agreement; that is, of the

[7] Quoted from Mitchell's preliminary questions and comments.

discriminations which are allowed to be categorically in the field. Disputes as to their precise nature and as to how exactly they are in the field (which are many) will in this methodology occur at a further stage of investigation, sufficiently more close in detail to be called "analysis" rather than simple inspection.

Formulation of the inspectional definition marks some advance beyond the discovery and enumeration of data; it gathers them together in a restatement which brings out something of the nature of the value-complex which they form and which is the basis of the subsequent analysis.

The basic or controlling agreement concerning the inspectional field of value is that which discriminates the field as such, which marks its boundary within the whole field of reality or experience—in other words, which recognizes that there *is* a field of value. That "value" stands for *some* discrimination in reality or in experience is implied in undertaking a theory of value. If it is agreed that value does stand for some discrimination and also that all reality is factual, then it is implied further: (1) that not everything is value, that is, that fact per se is not value, (2) that if fact is as fact knowable, then knowability is not value, and that knowing (cognizing) is not valuing.

Value is a post-factual discrimination, that is, a discrimination within the field of fact, not one between fact and non-fact. Some fact is value and some fact is not.[8] For this reason the traditional terminology of "fact" and "value" is not good. It belies the post-factual nature of the value discrimination. A more nearly though still not entirely adequate terminology is that which distinguishes "descriptive-fact" and "value-fact." Descriptive-fact is coextensive with reality (factuality); value-fact is a division within reality (valuity). That is, value-facts are always also descriptive-facts, but the converse is not true. Whatever the terminology, and whatever the subsequent disagreements or refinements, it is implied in the meaningfulness of value theory that there is a distinction in reality and experience between facts which are (in context) complete as being known and facts which have a further character—for example, that of being favored or disfavored after being known or in addition to being known or, in one manner of speaking, in being "known" in a special way.[9]

[8] Not invincibly, but actually.
[9] Cf. R. Demos, "Moral Value," *Philosophy and Phenomenological Research,* VI (1945–46), 172, "values are cognized by feelings."

"Fact and value" is a false, that is, an overlapping opposition, and, therefore, a confusing one. It is not correct to speak of fact *and* value (or fact versus value), but rather of fact and *its* value, or its lack of value. The latter terminology keeps in view the discrimination between value existent and non-value existent which is the beginning of value theory. At the same time it preserves in value the factuality which it must have if it is to be an object of natural and rational investigation rather than of absolutistic or mystical acceptance. It is recognized that value is not fact (factuality), but that any value is *a* fact.

All fact is and must remain or be succeeded by fact. Given value-fact need not remain value-fact (except historically), nor be succeeded by value-fact. On an ocean beach, for example, the observed removal or addition of a teaspoonful of sand must either way be a fact as positive in character as any other fact, but it need not be a value-fact at all. On the other hand, the removal of trees from a beachside or the littering of broken glass or other debris on the strand, while marking no diminution in the factuality of the scene, will very probably alter the sum and nature of its value. Value-fact will have been changed from positive to negative, but fact will have remained positive. It cannot be otherwise. A littered beach is as completely and as positively understandable as a clean beach.

The factual object as such is not the value object, and factuality is not valuity.[10] A given factual object may not enter into a value state of affairs at all. It may be noticed and left to itself, not in the sense of being weighed and rejected, but in the sense of being accounted indifferent, neither accepted nor rejected, as the teaspoonful of sand in the foregoing example. In value experience there are actually encountered many things which make no difference either in value-feeling or in value-judgment.

It may be objected that what has just been said of value is equally true of factual pursuit. In cognitive experience there are also many things which make no difference in knowing the fact. The same example may be cited. We don't have to count teaspoonfuls of sand to *understand* an ocean beach. It is granted, to a given cognitive interest or purpose some facts too may be negligible. If we want to understand a beach

[10] Cf. Dewey, "The significance of being, though not its existence, is the emotion it stirs, the thought it sustains."—*Intelligence in the Modern World*, ed. by J. Ratner, New York, 1939, p. 248.

as a geographical or topographical configuration we don't have to count teaspoonfuls of sand. But this means only that a certain given thing need not be known in order to know another given thing, and that we are interested in knowing the first. By the introduction of interest the factual pursuit becomes a value pursuit; the cognitive experience is then also a value experience. However, long standing tradition to the contrary, it is seriously questionable that knowledge per se implies value, or that truth as such is value. Truth is, of course, pursued and thus valued, and rational value, that is, a system of value, is impossible without truth in the sense of acquaintance with fact. But the converse does not hold. To know fact and to take an interest in it is not the same thing. Truth as verifiable belief about fact is a wider experience than value as felt satisfaction in fact. Common experience supports the distinction. Much factual information comes unsought, passes idly through attention, and is indifferently surveyed, or floats inconsequentially along the course of awareness. Also, knowledge (truth) may be pursued experimentally. We may value the pursuit in the sense that we judge that it has interesting possibilities, but find in the outcome that these possibilities are not realized, in which event the knowledge pursued and attained will not have value. Nothing interesting or satisfying will have turned up. We may, of course, arbitrarily call knowledge only those factual occurrences which we do linger over or take into account. But it is an arbitrary exclusion of much other awareness of fact. The daily occurrence of such unvalued awareness is sufficient evidence for maintaining the distinction between knowledge-fact and value-fact, between truth and value. Value is a post-factual determination.

To maintain the post-factuality of value (in the sense not of nonfactuality, but of further determination of factuality) is to avoid the equally unsatisfactory consequences of standing on either one of the extremes of objectivity and subjectivity in regard to value. It is to assert that value is an object-subject determination, or that, if value is to be ascribed to an object, it is to be ascribed as referential to a subject, or, conversely, if value is to be denoted as from a subject, it is to be denoted as respective of the factual object.

A description of an object (though it may do so on the basis of implicit value assumptions) never strictly denotes value. If we take the predicate "good" loosely as the value predicate, we may say that "good" predicated of something is neither a summary description of it nor an addition to the description of it. "It is so and so" means that it is true that it is so and so, but specifically "so and so" does not mean "true" and generally it does not mean "good."

What is true of the generalized value predicate "good" is true also of all particular value predicates such as "interesting," "right," "lovely," and so on. If, for example, we give an accurate description of, say, a gingko tree as belonging to the genus of gymnospermous trees, native to China and Japan, having fan-shaped leaves and yellow drupelike fruit, said to be the oldest extant tree, and having certain habits of growth; and if we then add: "It is a very interesting tree," we have not added a descriptive detail. We have made a value predication. The value predication does not denote an attribute or circumstance of the same order as the set of factual predications do. At the same time, in the other direction, the value predication is a predication about the facts previously described. It is the facts of the tree which are interesting, but being interesting is not *one* of the facts; it is all of them together standing in a certain relation to a subject who regards them. Or it is a fact about the tree *and* the person who feels interest. And so with all value. The discrimination which finds value as such is a discrimination between fact noted and fact noted with a purpose or attitude. The purpose may itself be that of fact seeking, and the value is then cognitive, but this, to repeat, does not destroy the discrimination between fact and value-fact.

The inspectional definition of value follows upon this discrimination of value as post-factual. In minimum form it is: Value occurs in a state of affairs between object and subject of such a nature that rejection or acceptance or approval or disapproval of the former by the latter takes place. All the terms, "object," "subject," "acceptance," and "rejection," are preanalytical. An enlarged definition may include an enumeration of typical data observed in the value-complex, the general "shape" of which is stated in the minimum definition. It may be noted that it includes value-feelings or moments, value-tensions or volitions, and value-judgments or appraisals. Analysis proceeds upon them.

III

Assuming essential correctness and completeness in the inspectional definition of value offered, it should make no difference to the outcome of analysis of the value-complex where or upon what term the analysis begins. Analytical pursuit of any one of them will uncover the others, and, what is more important, any beginning pushed through will lead to the crux of the whole value problem, namely, that of the relation of value-feeling to value-judgment, or of primary value to standard value. This is Dewey's Question II: Is the primary attitude of "prizing or holding dear" or of "desiring, liking, interest, enjoying, etc." (I should say "primary value," but Dewey does not) "a *sufficient* condition for the existence of values? Or . . . is a further condition, of the nature of *valuation* or *appraisal* required?" [11]

I begin at hazard, then, with the question, what is the nature of "the state of affairs" in which value occurs? In my *Relational Value Meanings* [12] I named it a "relational" state of affairs and specified the relation as one of feeling-conation of a subject for an object ("object" being understood to be not exclusively a "thing" but a situation or set of circumstances as well, and as either actual or ideal).

Dewey's term for the state of affairs is "transactional" or "behavioral," and in this usage he finds agreement from other members of the symposium; for example, I think, from Rice and Lepley. My own agreement will be qualified. I wish to ask: Is behavior purely operational and judgmental, or does it include contemplation and a felt state of consciousness towards something given or consummated? Are feelings and felt-tensions themselves behavior, or are they merely part of the material upon which behavior (for example, judgment) is directed, or are they, at most, signs of behavior?

I believe the term "behavioral" or "transactional" bears the extensive meaning. If it cannot, I should reject it as too narrow to cover the data. Without sufficient range to include "mentalistic" data, behavioral terms cannot "perform all the functions needed or desirable in everyday 'practical' communication and living." [13]

The mentalistic facts in question are those of feeling and felt-tension (liking, enjoyment, desire, and so on) admittedly subjective and, therefore, private in occurrence. They are introspective. From the present point of view, the question concerning their status in respect to behavior may be put in asking, Is introspection (inside inspection) inspectional? Or in terms of value-judgment, is value-feeling a part of the

[11] P. 5, above.   [12] Eugene, Ore., 1943.
[13] Quoted from Lepley's preliminary questions and comments.

value state of affairs such that it can be offered as evidence in judgment of value? Or most simply, is feeling datum? My answer to each
question is "Yes." My reasons are these:

1. Feeling is observed. It is, like sensation, a *de facto* element of
awareness. It appears directly in the awareness of the consciousness
of one person. If it be objected that in this it could be at most merely
a *mode* of awareness, it may be further advanced (i) that feeling may
be accompanied by awareness of *it*. Feeling does not, or need not wholly
occupy the awareness of the person having it. It can be attended to
while occurring. And (ii) feeling has or can have extension in time.
It may be remembered and reflected upon.

2. Feeling is verifiable. Both its occurrence and its quality can be
checked, (i) directly, by repeated experience of the one person having
the feeling. For example, the experience of a given person that a certain
vintage of muscatel wine tastes "good" (that is, the tasting is agreeably
toned) under specified conditions, may be verified by repeating the
experience. Feeling is verifiable(ii) indirectly by other persons, in the
reports and other observable (public) effects concerning it coming
from the persons having it, part of the conditions of verification being
the observed or inferred absence of motives for deception. That is, feeling is verifiable in language and other overt behavior.

In general, verification of feeling or agreement concerning it is
established in common language report and exhibited in common behavior. It is not, it should be noted, the overt behavior (language or
other) which is verified; *they* verify the feeling.

3. In "everyday 'practical' communication and living," feeling *is*
taken successfully as evidence for judgment and action. In medical
practice, for example, diagnosis and treatment take reported feeling
very much into account. The physician, besides making urinalyses, recording cardiographs, and taking X-rays, or perhaps before doing these
things, asks the patient, "How do you feel? do you have a pain? where
is it? and how exactly *does* it feel?" The answers count. And it may
be assumed that the subsequent objective examination and the treatment are not of the language of the feeling and the inferred conditions
of the feeling reported. What the doctor wants mainly to do is to make
the patient feel well. In this pursuit, unless on other good grounds he
suspects malingering, the physician believes the patient's report of pain,

that is, takes the pain itself as evidence; he initiates a search for causes and attempts to remove them. Even if the feelings or pains be wrongly reported by the patient (that is, fail to correlate with the factual conditions of the organs normally involved) the wise physician or dentist will still believe the patient in *some* appropriate (that is, probable) way. If X-ray reveals no cavity in the reportedly aching tooth, the dentist may send his patient to a neurologist. If physical examination shows no probable grounds for reported physical collapse, the physician may refer his patient to a psychiatrist. In any case, in therapy, as in much else in daily living, report of feeling is taken as referential to fact as are reports of sensation. And they—not only the reports, but the feelings themselves—are as truly a part of the evidential structure as are sensations and reports of sensation.

It may be objected that this conclusion is true only in so far as there is no difference between feeling and sensation, and, specifically, that in the case cited there is no difference. Pain is sensation. It is indifferently called a feeling or a pain. It may be asked with the same meaning, do you have a feeling of pain? or, do you have a sensation of pain? Likewise, the two questions, does it hurt? and, does it feel hot? call for the same kind of answer.

The identity of cognitive reference in such cases is admitted. However, it is maintained that in value reference they are not the same. The pain besides being painful is unpleasant, and the value reference is finally to the unpleasantness. Furthermore, there are experiences in which feeling (affective-state) is quite unambiguously the value datum —in which the feeling is in no wise the sensation, but is about the sensation. For example, a person may be perturbed or in a state of anxiety over observed physiological changes in his body—changes not physically painful at all. He may seek medical advice and receive as "treatment" an explanation that the perturbing changes are really normal alterations due to age or some other innocent cause. Clearly, the feeling in such a case is evidence or fact and the treatment is basically of the feeling. The physician or counselor accepts as evidence what he cannot observe or examine, what is private to someone else.

All future-reference affective states, such as anxiety, feelings of dread, or of joyful anticipation are of this status. They cannot be reduced to (are not the same as) a set of sensations, nor to an objective factual state of affairs. Such feelings are about sensations or a factual state of affairs. A joyful anticipation is not a joyful sensation or perception of something present; it is joy in expectation.

It may be still objected that nothing in the foregoing argument establishes feeling as *veridical*, that is, as evidential in the required sense. It may be said that feeling does not provide objective reference, which is a condition of evidence for judgment, nor possibility of value error, which is a condition of value-judgment. If, for example, I feel something to be pleasant, and you feel the same thing to be pleasant, your feeling, it may be alleged, cannot verify my feeling—does not make mine right, nor the judgment affirming rightness true. Likewise, if I feel something to be pleasant and you feel the same thing to be unpleasant, your feeling cannot be urged as evidence for the judgment that my feeling is wrong. Each feeling is a simple fact, merely additional to every other feeling as well as to the object which occasions it. The same may be held of successive feelings of one person, feelings either the same or opposite in quality; one feeling succeeds another and is either similar or different in quality from it, but can neither confirm nor refute the other. If, accordingly, a *judgment* is once made—for example, that the object in question is "good," it will have to be verified in terms other than that of "felt-pleasure" (or any other subjective effect) taken as complete in itself, that is, as without consequences or implications.

Against the position that feeling and feeling-complexes are strictly private and non-veridical, while sensations and sensation-constructs are public and verifiable, it must be answered simply that it is not so. Both are private and both public in exactly the same way. Feeling has as much and the same kind of status in experience (behavior) as sensation. Both are in occurrence mentalistic and both enter into practical affairs (in judgment and in action) without limit. Neither as a single, isolated moment of experience, that is, as a simple here-now occurrence, is capable of verifying any other here-now experience. One sensation or one feeling cannot prove rightness in another sensation or another feeling—if the sensations or feelings in question are detached or insulated one from the other. My completely isolated here-now sensation of yellow can be neither proved nor disproved by your completely isolated there-now sensation of yellow. And the same is true of felt-value, but nothing more is. Felt-value or feeling is on a par with sensation. Somehow, judgments of fact come out of sensations; and equally, somehow value-judgments come out of felt-values. Value-judgments proceed in the same way upon feeling as judgment of fact proceeds upon sensation.

It is agreed that what is required of value-judgment is that it be capable of verification, of having objective reference, of being true or false. The question then is, what is the nature of the evidence which can verify value-judgment? The answer may be put in the form of a basic principle: *Judgment of value can be verified only by value, not by fact-simple.* Apparently against this principle, it is maintained by Dewey and others that the judgment of value, like any judgment, is verified by the consequences of the thing or situation judged. It may be agreed, consequences, yes. But a second principle needs to be added: *For value-judgment, the relevant consequences of value are values.* The consequences of feeling for evaluation are, in final reference, further feelings.

This does not mean that factual consequences are irrelevant, but merely that they are not enough. In the phraseology of current slang it is always possible in the face of merely factual consequences to answer with factual finality, "So what?" And the only appropriate answer to that answer is a value predication, "You won't like it," or, "You'll be sorry!" or something similar.

The alternative to these principles, whatever the language used, involves a clear abandonment of the empirical field as described in an earlier section of this essay. It is, in other words, to lapse back into some form of absolute objectivity, holding "good" or "value" to be a quality of the object in detachment from the subject, or of the merely factual consequences as such. The value attitude, that of "prizing," Dewey says rightly has "no shadow of meaning if it be isolated from that which it is towards." [14] Must it not also be remembered that the value attitude has no shadow of meaning if it be isolated from that which it is *from?* This is not remembered in any view which denies felt-values as final evidence for the value-judgment.

What, then, is value-judgment? "Value-judgment" in current usage means two things: (1) descriptive value-judgment; (2) operational value-judgment. In the first meaning it is an existence judgment about values *factually.* In the second it is a constitutive act of valuing. It is

⁴ P. 6, above.

evaluation understood to mean *en*-valuation or *de*-valuation. In this meaning "judgment of value" is an operation upon given values such that it modifies or qualifies their further character.

In the first sense, I agree that value-judgment is of exactly the same formal nature as any other judgment of fact, that it is peculiar only in its subject matter. The descriptive value-judgment *is* a value-judgment. It can say, with possibilities of error, what a value-factual state of affairs is; and it can make predictions as to what a future value state of affairs will be, in terms, that is, of probability of facts plus probability of attitudes towards facts.

But this is not the operational value-judgment. To have an operational value-judgment it is necessary to have a judgment of fact (either fact-simple or value-fact) which is *charged*—charged with feeling-tone or tension. There must be attendant upon or concomitant with the merely factual judgment a feeling about the facts described as existing or predicted as probable. My answer to Dewey's Question III is, accordingly, that value-judgments in the sense of operational judgments *are* different from other judgments. I will not add that they are logically distinct from other judgments. The preferable language, I think, is to say that the operational value act, of "evaluation," or "value-judgment" is not purely an affair of logical judgment of fact. It is, rather, a complex act which includes a feeling or tension-set about the facts judged to exist or to be probable or possible. In my *Relational Value Meanings* [15] I called this attendant feeling a "felt preference." This seems to me still to be a correct denotation of the fact that there is in value-judgment (sense 2) a necessary element of feeling or attitude, and that it may be feeling about feeling as well as about fact—or, if it be better to say it that way, a feeling about feeling about fact. In a recent moving picture [16] the heroine says, "I feel that whatever I feel about Robert I should go back to him." This, I think, is accurate language to report what goes on in the operational value-judgment. The obligation in the face of a contrary feeling is itself feeling, a feeling of obligation.

How, or on what grounds, it may still be asked, does the evaluational act proceed so as to produce propositions which can be verified? What is the "somehow" alleged on the foregoing page [17] in which out of "here-now" felt-value there is obtained the necessary objectivity? The

[15] Ch. vi.   [16] "Vacation from Marriage."   [17] P. 139.

answer is not new. Recent and current literature of value theory is replete with it—in statement and restatement, in amplification and in seemingly all possible verbal variation. Essentially it is that value-judgment, the act by which some felt-values are accepted and some are rejected, depends upon the facts of dimensionality and interconnectedness of values. As Dewey rightly insists, values have consequences. In rejecting a genuine given value, that is, one which is felt as such, we do not strictly deny its value character; more accurately, we sacrifice it because its consequences are felt in anticipation or judged in factual prospect to be contrary to maximum occurrence of further felt-values.

The term "felt-value" is simple, but the fact to which it applies need not be, and normally is not. The life of value—the life of the valuing individual and of the social community of individuals—is a system of value, comprising individual and collective affective states directed upon long-range purposes and often giving rise to vastly mixed and profoundly conflicting feelings. To attempt to discredit felt-value by forcing an artificial simplicity upon it is to do impossible violence upon the facts of felt-value. Any system of felt-value is certainly as complex as any factual system and therefore as capable of its own rationality.

A system of felt-values determines all that needs to be determined in value. It explains the remembering and foreseeing individual, as something more than an addition of occurring and satisfied impulses. It explains the social community bound together by interconnections of sympathies and common felt purposes among individuals. It allows an individual to have a life to lead as well as moments to spend, and it sanctions a society with meanings in traditions and institutions not built for today only, but for time beyond. In brief, felt-value is retrospective and prospective; it has past and future as well as present reference. It is so because it is causal—has consequences and antecedents. In naturalistic view, dimensionality and connectedness in occurrent value are all that is needed and all that can be demanded in order that t have the objectivity and verifiability required to make value-judgment meaningful.

Another way of answering the question, On what grounds does the valuational judgment produce propositions which can be verified? is, in one word, that of *agreement*. Verification in value, in other words, proceeds in the same way that any other verification does. Feelings, like sensations, can stand in the relation of agreement. Consider, as the simplest imaginable, a case of two sensations or two feelings: I see yellow in object X, and you see yellow in object X; or I taste object X as "good," and you taste object X as "good." Is it strictly correct to say that my seeing yellow in agreement with your seeing yellow is not evidence for the judgment "X is yellow?" Or, similarly, to say that my tasting X as "good" in agreement with your tasting X as "good" is not evidence for the judgment "X tastes good," or, elliptically, "X is good?" I think not. The more exact statement, with a view to the countless other possible correlations of sensations and feelings and their consequences, is that it goes only a little way as evidence towards proving the judgment in question. But a little way it does go—and equally in matters of sensation and of value.

Agreement of data with data is the very nature of evidence. Two "here-now" facts, either of sensations or of felt-value, are in their degree evidence—positive if in agreement, negative if in disagreement—evidence of something in the object or in the subject upon which they are directed or from which they derive. The simplest imaginable occurrent value *situation* has, then, dimensionality—in the case just offered, for example, social dimension. Two "here-nows" of the same order are comparable—can therefore agree or disagree. What more than agreement either in fact or in value can be asked in the demand for verification—agreement either in the simple form here instanced or in the more intricate form called "integration" or "corroboration?"

The method of agreement admits no other. If given agreements be questioned as inconclusive, they must be questioned in reference to further agreements, or predicted. If an individual's agreements with himself (I "like," or I "prize" these things) are challenged, it must be by group agreements—these things are not liked or prized generally. If group agreements are appealed, it must be to a larger or wiser group, and so on, and so on. The declension of felt-value on the principle of agreement runs from mere impulse through integrated individual, to social group, to national, to international agreements—the terminal agreement within the naturalistic or empirical frame being the basic conditions or ideals of humanity itself. But the principle of agreement does operate from the lowest and simplest to the highest and most complicated situation in which verification is possible. And the principle of order in value is the same as the principle of order in fact. That actual agreement is harder and less frequent in value does not mean that we have to seek harder principles to make it seem easier. It means, rather, that greater variability in value is a fact about value.[18]

The summary statement of the principle of agreement in terms of hierarchical ascent from mere impulse to the perspectives of continuing humanity is, of course, oversimplified. It is meant simply to indicate the principle of agreement as that which can finally make a value system, that is, provide for rational value-judgment. It does not preclude disagreements of an individual with the agreements of a group, or of disagreements of a smaller group with agreements of a larger, from being right. Just as historically, an individual or a few individuals who disagreed with the agreement of the many that the world is flat were right, so in matters of value the minority voice may be the right one. But what this means can itself be understood only in terms of agreement. If it is an individual case of one against the world, it is still implied, if the case be rational, that the individual stand is taken on the conviction that the world is in disagreement with him, and that it would be better if it were not. That is to say, an individual disagreement may be right against an opposed agreement of any proportion. But the possibility of a disagreement being right is finally always the possibility of agreement. Between invincible or radical disagreement, no value-judgment is possible.

IV

The foregoing discussion has throughout posited "feeling" as directed upon an object as primary in the value situation. It has not so far stopped on the question which Dewey sets first in his list; namely: "What connection is there, if any, between an attitude that will be called prizing or holding dear and desiring, liking, interest, enjoying, etc?" [19] To this question I now turn.

I agree that the distinction indicated is real, that there is a difference between an attitude of "concern for," "devotion to," on the one hand, and "liking," "enjoying," "desiring," on the other. I do not agree, however, that the distinction is *categorical* in primary or felt-value, that the choice lies between resting in an unresolvable dualism in primary value, or rejecting the one or the other attitude as primary—the latter

Cf. Dewey, "values are as unstable as the forms of clouds."
P. 5, above.

being Dewey's course. The primary value-fact is that of feeling, of which the two attitudes are equally expressive. The categorical consanguinity of the two can be denoted in calling them attitudes of "feeling of" and "feeling for." Each is an expression of feeling and subject to innumerable specifications and mutations. A "feeling for" in the form of "devotion to" may, for example, demand all manner and degree of self-denial and sacrifice, the surrender not only of many pleasures and desires, but of life itself. But somewhere the surrender must have a term in feeling. A specific feeling may be deferred, sublimated, or sacrificed, but only always in the interest of another or other specific feelings. The extreme case, the surrender of life (that is, for positive value cause) is no exception. Surrender of life is not a denial of felt-value, but, rather, the distillation or concentration of it in one supreme moment. And likewise, at the other end from "nobility," the reckless squandering of future value for present "cash value" in the attitude "I burn my candle at both ends" or "let Rome in Tiber melt!" *may* be embraced with equal rationality. Felt-values may compete, but feeling itself cannot be surrendered. The alternative is, again, to desert the field of value, to forget that the value is *from* as well as *towards*, and to rest in the fact unqualified.

The two attitudes in question may be interpreted as two ends of the value relationship or transaction, the one emphasizing the *from* and the other the *towards*. To say "I prize something" is to emphasize the thing and the consequences of it upon which my feeling of or predicted feeling of (enjoying, liking, interest) is directed; it is not to rule out the latter as determinant. Conversely, to say "I enjoy" something is to attend to my felt state in the presence or prospect of the object it is not to rule out the object and my concern for it as also determinant

The analogy of the two ends may seem to break down when it i further observed that one end may in a specific course of value actio take precedence over the other; or, in other words, when it is observe that the two ends may compete. It is possible at the extreme to lea either a life of devotion and self-sacrifice or one of self-indulgence an pleasure. Or it is possible to waver between them, as did Antony. Suc conflict is, however, material and must always be materially resolve not in kind. It is not possible to argue merely formally that a life of act of pleasure is unworthy and a life or act of sacrifice noble. It depenc upon the material circumstances. Choice, when it must be made, between two felt-values and not between felt-value and something els

Conflict, moreover, is not merely between the two ends; it may occur in any combination: feeling of versus feeling of; feeling of versus feeling for; or feeling for versus feeling for. And any attitude of any combination may be wrong. Specifically, a "feeling for" can be wrong in conflict with a "feeling of" or a course of such feelings, as it is, for example, in innumerable cases of sentimentality in which devotion to the dead is permitted to afflict the living.

What the right attitude is in a given situation depends upon what the situation materially is. The right attitude, for example, in respect to a child's safety is not one of "liking" its safety and doing nothing, but, rather, one of being concerned practically by providing appropriate safeguards and guidance. The right attitude, i. e., the meaningful one, towards a Prokofieff sonata is not one of concern for but, rather, one of enjoyment of it. To suppose that one attitude is basically or primarily right and the other wrong is to suppose that life as a whole is the value situation. This is error. Life is not value; values occur in life.

My final question is Dewey's Question II: "Irrespective of which of the above-named attitudes prizing or liking is taken to be primary, is it by itself a *sufficient* condition for the existence of values? Or, while it is a necessary condition, is a further condition of the nature of *valuation* or *appraisal*, required?" [20]

My answer follows from what I have maintained concerning value-judgment and feeling. Except in sense 1, in which value-judgment is merely descriptive judgment, judgment of value is also a feeling of value. The question, accordingly, becomes for me: Is feeling a condition of feeling? Or more accurately, is perspective feeling a condition of immediate feeling? (Perspective feeling is itself conditioned by attendant judgment of fact or of factual consequences.) My answer is that the judgment-feeling act (feeling-judgment) is a determinant of some values but not of others. Some values are so conditioned. On the other hand, many values are, practically speaking,[21] complete as face-values. There are, namely, many undisturbing, problemless "enjoyeds" of daily living, especially those of aesthetic awareness:

P. 5, above.

Theoretically or ultimately it may be assumed that feeling is always a condition of feeling in the same sense that fact is always a condition of fact. But just as we can safely take many daily facts without justifying them in antecedents or consequences, so we can safely take many values in an immediate way. If there is any judgment it is the "judgment" of successful habit.

> Such the sun, the moon,
> Trees old and young,
>
> the grandeur of the dooms
> We have imagined for the mighty dead.

Such too are the consummations found in "transactions" that are finished, the completed task, the accomplished deed, which though they be beginnings are firstly ends.

However, many important alterations in felt-values do occur as the result of appraisal or judgment—that is, feeling-judgment. We judge the factual consequences of a proposed act and at the same time feel the consequences in apprehension or pleasurable anticipation. Depending on what the consequences are materially judged to be, they may take precedence over the feelings of merely present reference. For example, an individual may be advised that continued smoking (a recurrent enjoyment) will bring consequences of ill-health—pain and disturbances of many desired functions. Acting on the advice, he may resolve to give up the habit. The judgment (advice), accepted and acted out, may eventually change the original felt-value in all its immediacy. Smoking may become not an enjoyment given up, but an aversion. Smoking to the reformed smoker may become distasteful.

Though value is finally always a matter of what is liked or what satisfies, no specific liking or satisfaction is absolute. It can be reviewed and challenged, that is judged, not in its character of being a liking or a satisfaction, but in its consequentially favorable or unfavorable position in the whole system of satisfactions which describes the valuing individual or social community. If it be incorrigible, fails to fall in, it can perhaps be eradicated. We can will or psychologically and physiologically condition ourselves out of such inimical likings. But the force which alone can do it, can will it to be done, is that of further liking. Judgment in the purely descriptive sense, judgment which states, "these are the consequences," is powerless. It remains true, of course, that without that judgment, no ground or occasion for liking arises. And in that important sense and measure, descriptive judgment is a necessary condition of value. Evaluation or appraisal—that is, feeling-judgment—is also a condition of many values. But evaluation is itself conditioned by felt-value. In the end only value begets value.[22]

---

[22] For the Criticisms and Rejoinders which relate especially to this paper see pp. 424–428 and 435–437, below.

METHODOLOGY OF
VALUE THEORY

HAROLD N. LEE

MAN KNOWS THINGS. He also cares about them. Things happen, and sometimes he cares what happens: he feels that it is of some importance—it matters. Presumably it is not necessary either to the existence of the state of affairs or to his knowledge about it that he should care, and pathological conditions have been reported in which the person did not care. It is in the contrast between these two aspects of man's experience that the fundamental questions of value theory lie. That aspect of things whereby they are cared about is their value. My caring for something and the value of that something are the obverse and reverse of the same state of affairs. The thing that is cared about is valued. That which is valued is valuable; that is, it has value.

It is by means of the foregoing considerations that I would answer the questions "How is a definition of the subject or field of value obtainable that will not be arbitrary? How guarantee that different writers on 'value' are discussing the same subject?" [1] The field of investigation is given in "common sense experience." All men recognize the distinction pointed out in a common sense manner and in common sense language in the foregoing paragraph. The term "care about" is purposefully vague. I have not specified whether it is primarily conative or affective in meaning. It is not, however, primarily cognitive: this is the point of its contrast with "knowing." As long as it is common sense and vague, it does not matter much what term is used: "things are important" may be just as good as "things are cared about." I am confident that every member of this inquiry (much as we differ about some things) will get the import of the preceding sentence. If he does, he is making the distinction brought out in the first paragraph, and so understands what I propose to take as the field of experience in which the data of value theory lie. He may not agree with the sentiment ex-

Question raised by Pepper at the beginning of the present cooperative inquiry.

pressed by the sentence, but again, that is a different matter. He does not have to agree with it to get its import. He could not disagree unless he got its import.

The philosophic task of value theory is to clarify these vague, indefinite data, and to understand their relationships both to each other and to other fields of experience. This task can be accomplished only by logical analysis and by the development of categories that put order into the field. The study cannot take its departure from precise definitions, for definitions themselves are products of the categorial activity and of understanding. It is true that complete understanding can be achieved only in terms of precise definitions, but this fact indicates that the processes of definition and understanding are interactive and undergo successive development. By logical analysis I mean the discovery of the meanings that are involved or implied by our grasp of the data that are being analyzed.

I

The most important question of methodology in this inquiry is the one brought up in the first group of questions in Dewey's article [2] and made the basic hypothesis of his present paper, namely, that of behaviorism in value theory. Lepley, in the preliminary discussion, has indicated a suspicion that "introspective analysis" is a dangerous or unreliable operation, and suggests that the way to avoid the danger is by a constant awareness of the behavioral character of experience. I do not think that he considers logical analysis to be introspective. Logical analysis can be equally applied to data that are derived from any portion of our experience, whether it be experience of feelings or of behavioral transactions. Dewey's unequivocal emphasis is that only those data derived from behavioral transactions are legitimate subject matter for scientific or philosophical inquiry, whether or not the method be primarily analytical.

The reason for excluding feeling (or anything else that Dewey or Lepley call internal or mentalistic or subjectivistic) [3] from our analysis lies in an extreme reaction against Cartesian dualism. Dewey points

[2] Pp. 6–7, above.
[3] Dewey does not equate mental and subjective as does Lepley. I shall treat of Dewey's meaning for the term subjective below. The use of the suffix "istic" is to be deplored, for it serves no purpose except to emphasize that the terms are pejorative.

LEE

this out in the course of a discussion carried on with Rice in the pages
of *The Journal of Philosophy.* "Denial of the primacy and ultimacy of
this relation [between subject and object] . . . is the basic feature of
my general theory of knowledge, of judgment and verification, my
theory of value-judgments being but a special case of this general
theory." [4] He adversely criticizes Rice for introducing an element of
"subjectivity" that is "defined in terms of a special order of Being, viz.,
one that is directly open to observation only by one person, and by a
special kind of knowing called 'introspection' or 'self-knowledge'—an
order of Being which accordingly is 'inner' and 'private.'" [5]

In spite of these rejections of Cartesian dualism, I have a feeling
that the appeal of behaviorism, both in psychology and philosophy,
rests upon implicit Cartesian assumptions: its plausibility depends
upon assumptions that are part of the framework within which the
dualism is erected. Even I will admit, however, that this feeling is not
evidence unless it gives rise to the behavior involved in certain peck-
ing reactions I make at my typewriter, and if the evidential character
of that behavior depends on its success in convincing Dewey, I am
probably doomed to frustration.

Let me give some of the reasons that lead me to think that the rejection of the Cartesian framework is not complete. Behaviorism deals
with a world in which what is publicly accessible is distinguished from
what is wholly private.[6] This distinction may not be a distinction in
orders of being, that is, a metaphysical distinction, but is potent enough
to determine in every case what is relevant evidence in a scientific
inquiry and what is not. The public domain is identified with space-
time facts and expenditure of energy. This is the field of behavior. It
is true that the assertion is explicit that the words behavior and behavioral do not apply only to what is stated in terms of strictly physical
knowledge. They must not be reduced to physical or (in the case of
human behavior) to exclusively physiological terms.[7] When Dewey
says this, however, he seems to be talking about the bodies of knowledge to be found in the natural sciences of physics or physiology. The

"Valuation Judgments and Immediate Quality," *The Journal of Philosophy,* XL
1943), 315; reprinted by permission of the editors.
Ibid., p. 309.
See Dewey's present essay, p. 66, above; and his "Theory of Valuation," in *Inter-
national Encyclopedia of Unified Science,* Chicago, 1939, Vol. II, No. 4, pp. 14–16.
See Dewey's present paper, p. 65, above.

passage does not deny that behavior takes place in what is ordinarily called the physical realm.[8]

What is not in the public domain is internal and mentalistic. Here again, the distinction is stated to be not metaphysical, but is concerned only with what is good evidence for scientific and philosophic knowledge. He finds no "satisfactory evidence for holding that situations with respect to their qualitative immediacy, are 'subjective' instead of being prior to, neutral to, and inclusive of, any distinction and relation that can be legitimately instituted between subject and object."[9] In other words, the "situation," being in the nature of things, cannot be said to be either public or private, but nevertheless, the private aspect of it or analyzed out of it must "be left where it occurs and belongs—in private seclusion."[10] This is the Cartesian bifurcation even if it is not applied to nature. Behaviorism accepts the public and rejects the private. This extreme position makes no sense except within the framework of the bifurcation.

I have no adverse criticism of the analysis of experience into the subjective and the objective (to use the well-established terms instead of "public" and "private"). What I do criticize is the assumption that *just because* behavior is objective while feelings are subjective, behavior is respectable subject matter for scientific knowledge but feelings are not. If there is a *difference in nature* between the subjective and the objective, this assumption may be warranted. I see no prima facie reason why it is warranted if the difference is only an analytical difference.

Dewey does not define the terms subjective and objective according to the Cartesian bifurcation. He defines them according to sufficiency of evidence: "Propositions (judgments, beliefs, or whatever) are *subjective* when they are produced by causal conditions which fail

[8] There is similarity of statement if not of spirit between Dewey's position and the short manifesto of "Physicalism" by Otto Neurath in the *Monist*, XLI (1931), 618. I hasten to add, however, that Neurath does not develop the position expressed by some of the more extreme followers of the Viennese Circle, which Dewey feels, in Section 4 of the article that originated this inquiry, leads to moral nihilism. Neurath takes the position in regard to ethics developed by Moritz Schlick in *Fragen der Ethik* (translated under the title *Problems of Ethics*, New York, 1939) that ethics is the science that makes "it possible for man to attain happiness by definite arrangements or definite methods of conduct (behavior)."—"Physicalism," *loc. cit.*, p. 622.
[9] "Valuation Judgments and Immediate Quality," *loc. cit.*, p. 315.
[10] Dewey's paper, p. 66, above.

to possess genuine evidential capacity and verifying power." [11] He indicates that, contrariwise, propositions are objective if produced by conditions having genuine evidential capacity.

Notice here, however, that he is defining subjective *propositions* or *judgments*. This procedure seems to stem from the use of the terms in such a context as "a scientist must have an objective rather than a subjective attitude," meaning a fair, open-minded attitude that relies on the facts instead of one that is influenced by prejudice, bias, or feelings. These are derived meanings of "objective" and "subjective," which have come into vogue only comparatively recently. They hark back to the need in the seventeenth century of clarifying the field of the physical sciences, which deal with energy transformations in material bodies. Feelings, traditional beliefs, and final ends are irrelevant to the physical sciences, and Descartes got rid of them by putting them into mind, which he defined as another kind of reality. In Cartesian terminology, the material bodies and their behavior are objective. Evidence in the *physical sciences*, then, is relevant because it is objective. Dewey reverses the order and makes it into a definition. He says that objective *means* having relevant evidence. It still remains, however, that it is relevant evidence because it is (in the Cartesian framework) objective. In addition, this principle applies only to the physical sciences. Scientific method should not be defined in terms of these alone. [12]

If scientific method can deal only with behavior—that which is composed of space-time facts or energy transformations—then mathematics is not a science. It is true that one cannot do mathematics except in terms of symbols (space-time facts) and without the expenditure of energy, but mathematics is not about the symbols or the energy. Neither are the symbols (as space-time facts) nor the energy the evidence that distinguishes between true and false propositions in mathematics.

Dewey's new definitions of subjective and objective introduce semantic confusion into the course of the investigation. They have specious plausibility because we are accustomed to thinking that relevant evidence in the natural sciences must be objective in the Cartesian

---

[11] "Valuation Judgments and Immediate Quality," *loc. cit.*, p. 310.
[12] See my article, "Scientific Method and Knowledge" in *Philosophy of Science*, X (1943), for a more complete analysis of this point of view.

sense of the word. The strict dichotomy between subjective and objective (or between what is private and what is public in knowledge) developed out of Cartesian dualism and depends upon it. Furthermore, the assumption that what is objective is the proper subject matter for scientific inquiry also developed out of the dualism and depends on it, no matter whether it is made by a contemporary behaviorist or by an eighteenth century physicist. It *is* the proper subject matter for the *natural* sciences, and in so far as psychology aspires to be a natural science, perhaps behaviorism is warranted. Philosophy is not a natural science even though it aspires to the scientific method, and theory of value is not a natural science.

I am going to adopt the analysis of experience into objective and subjective for the purposes of understanding the conditions of that fact of human experience that I called in the first paragraph of this paper "caring about." [13] I do not assume that this analysis necessarily reflects anything in the nature of reality. Though it may not, it may nevertheless be a distinction that proves useful in understanding experience and in dealing successfully with it. There is nothing whatever in our experience that can be displayed by itself as purely subjective or as purely objective. These are categories built up by our experience and within it. If it is recognized that they are analytic categories there can be no objection to their use. If, on the other hand, they represent different kinds of reality, then it may well be that one kind is proper subject matter and evidence for scientific inquiry while the other is not. It is because behaviorism takes this latter position that I think it to be connected with a not wholly complete rejection of the Cartesian ontology. It is exactly because I reject the ontology and hold that subjective and objective do not refer to different and disparate kinds of reality that I do not accept behaviorism in philosophy.

Several papers in the present symposium take the position that Dewey's concept of behavior must be broadened to include reference to states of feeling. That Dewey himself does not think so is evidenced on page 14 of his *Theory of Valuation* where, in explaining the term affective-motor, he says, "care must be taken not to permit the 'affective' quality to be interpreted in terms of private 'feelings.'" I do not think that the concept of behavior should be broadened to include the

---

[13] See my article "A Precise Meaning for Objective and Subjective in Value Theory," *The Journal of Philosophy*, XXXVII (1940), 626.

feelings. To do so would be to confuse the terms of the analysis.

Dewey does not deny the existence of mental states and feelings. He says, "I do not deny the existence of the kind of *subject-matter* which is called private and inner." [14] Of what use is it, however, to admit their existence when any reference to them as evidence "is wholly inadmissible in *discussion*"? [15] I propose to admit them to my discussion whenever to do so will further the purposes for which the discussion is carried on. I propose also to admit the evidence of sensations, although sensations are just as subjective as are feelings. Whether either the subjective or the objective in my analysis of experience is to be credited or discredited depends in each individual case upon the evidence, and I do not think that the evidence requires any sweeping general discrediting of the internal or mental or subjective. The evidence is to be found in the realms of psychology and epistemology. It is unnecessary for me to go over it here because much of it is presented by Parker, Rice, and Jessup in their papers in this volume.[16]

In spite of the fact that I do not agree with the denials implicit in the behavioral approach to philosophy, I admit that the positive emphasis on behavior is all to the good if it makes us more critical both of the acceptance and of the accreditation and verification of the kind of phenomena we classify as subjective. The nature and existence of value and the appreciation of value is neither explained by calling it subjective and letting it go at that, nor is it explained away.

II

At the beginning of this paper, I characterized the experience of valuing as "caring," or "thinking it important," or "feeling that it matters." I called attention to the fact that for the purposes of a preliminary delineation of the field, these terms were deliberately vague. Now that I have confessed that I have no phobia concerning the subjective,[17] I might as well go on with my heresy and say that the evidence seems to me incontrovertible that there is something subjective about "car-

---

[14] "Further as to Valuation as Judgment," in *The Journal of Philosophy*, XL (1943), 549. (Italics his.)

[15] Dewey's present paper, p. 66, above. (Italics his.)

[16] An interesting presentation of evidence on this point is to be found in the dialogue entitled "The Ontological Status of Value" by K. Koffka, *American Philosophy Today and Tomorrow*, ed. by H. M. Kallen and S. Hook, New York, 1935, p. 275.

[17] Even fifty years ago, G. Santayana found it advisable to deny such a phobia. See the fourth paragraph of the "Introduction" to *The Sense of Beauty*, New York, 1896.

ing about." The caring about is an attitude of mind. It is both conative
and affective. It is both because it is the kind of concrete experience
out of which we analyze the distinction between conation and affection.
The attitude is taken toward an object. The attitude is subjective, the
object is objective. There may be other "mental states" making up
whatever it is I call my mind; [18] and there may be aspects of the object
other than that by virtue of which I care for it. Evidence would indicate
that both statements are true.

The object, in this case, may be called a *real* object. I am not using
the word "real" here in any foreordained metaphysical sense. I am
applying reality as a category of the understanding. I mean that the
attitude of caring is taken toward an *object*, and that the object is not
created by the attitude. It is a real object for the caring: it is independent of the caring. The caring is exercised *toward it.* On the other hand,
it may be that the aspect of the object by virtue of which I care for
it is not independent of my caring and is not a real object or even a
real quality of the object. I am not using the word object here only in
the sense of a physical entity, but in the sense of anything toward
which attention can be directed. The object of my caring may be a
physical entity, as for example a picture, or a dwelling house; or it may
be an event or a set of conditions, such as a just act or a sunset; or it
may be another mental state, as when a lover cares that his loved one
loves him. The lover is not satisfied that his loved one displays toward
him all the behavior of affection: he really cares that the loved one
feels the affection. The object of a person's caring may be a mental
state even of the person himself, as when I morally value my own
feelings toward others. [19]

That aspect of an object by virtue of which I care for it is its value.
This may be called an aspect or a quality or a characteristic or what
not. The point is that its relation to the object is adjectival. Value is
adjectival. Thus it is evident that I would answer my own question
in the same way that Dewey answers it: no, there is no such thing
as value that is not the value of some particular thing, event or situation. [20] Parker's objection to this position [21] seems to be due either to

[18] The language is substantive. The theory of what mind is need not necessarily be
substantive to yield meaning to the above sentence. It may be functional.
[19] Pepper, p. 256, below, points out that cognitive states and anticipatory sets may
be objects of evaluative judgments.
[20] See p. 66, above.   [21] See p. 226, below.

the fact that he uses language differently than does the common run of mortals, or to an incomplete analysis of the situation. Rice, who takes a somewhat similar position, candidly admits that the ordinary use of language in ascribing value to an object is only a figure of speech.[22] When I look at a sunset, however, I *do not* think that, if speaking literally, I should say "My feelings are beautiful when I look at the sunset." When I approve of a morally good deed, I do not mean that my feelings are good when I contemplate the deed. If the ascription of value to an object is a figure of speech, this is what I should say if I dropped the figure and spoke literally. Beauty is the common name for positive aesthetic value. Goodness (in the specifically moral sense) is the common name for positive moral value. If values are feelings, or characterize feelings, then beauty and goodness are feelings or characterize feelings.

I do not propose that the ordinary use of language proves that value is adjectival, or even that value is not subjective. I do not propose that one can prove anything about it except that his conclusions are bound up with his premises. I have emphasized the view that we are here dealing with the analysis of a situation. I submit that this is the analysis closest in accord with the use of language, and if the language did not serve to categorize experience with reasonable accuracy, it would not have developed in the way it did. It is a philosophic task to criticize the categories found in the ordinary use of language, and it is inevitable that as a result of the criticism they should be clarified and modified. If they were not, there would be no such thing as intellectual advancement. They should not be rejected altogether, however, unless a cogent reason is found for the rejection. This reason would lie either in the discovery of covert inconsistency or ambiguity, or in the discovery of a more adequate analysis. I do not think that the analysis in the present case requires that we cease ascribing beauty to the sunset or goodness to the deed or economic value to the commodity.

The problem here is accentuated by the somewhat confusing ways in which different members of this symposium either distinguish or fail to distinguish between the expressions "such and such *is* a value" and "such and such *has* a value." When I call anything "valuable," I

[22] See footnote 24, p. 281, below. See also his article "Quality and Value," *The Journal of Philosophy*, XL (1943), 337.

mean that it *has* value. I may be naive, but it seems to me that this is what most people mean by it. Parker cannot mean this by it, however, for he emphasizes that only satisfactions *are* values, and thus if an object *has* a value, it has a satisfaction. To call an object valuable means then, not that it has a value but that it *gives rise to values*. "The bread which I eat is *valuable*, but this means only that under certain conditions it will serve my hunger." [23] It must be nonsense according to Parker's theory to say that the bread *has* a value (except on the basis of the panpsychist assumption that he rejects).

On the other hand, it seems to me that in the writings on valuation both of Dewey and Lepley, the term "valuable" is sometimes used as synonymous with "it is a value." This tendency is found in its most extreme case in such places as department store advertisements that say "this merchandise is a most unusual value." The name of Chapter V in R. B. Perry's *General Theory of Value* has encouraged this confusion and likewise has given rise to some misunderstanding of his theory. It is entitled, "Value as Any Object of Any Interest." This sounds as if he held that the object (such as a sunset or a good deed or a commodity—what I have been calling the real object) is the value. That this is not his meaning is made clear, however, when he says on pages 115 and 116 that the object of interest is *invested* with value, or the object *acquires* value, or the object is *valuable*. I would say that to call a real object a value is a metonymy, but that to call a real object valuable is a literal expression.

Value is always a quality or property of an object, but it is not a *real* property in the sense that an object has it independent of the fact that sensibilities can *care about* it. The caring about is not constitutive of the object, but it is constitutive of the property. Parker's denial of the adjectival character of value results from his failure to make the analysis between real properties and putative properties. Because "in calling bread 'valuable' no new property of the bread is designated—its chemical-physical properties are not added to one jot or tittle"; [24] that is, because the value is not a real property, which bread has independent of the needs, desires, or what not of human sensibilities, he concludes that value cannot be adjectival.

Value is a putative quality or property, not a real one: It depends

[23] P. 227, below. (Italics his.) See also his *Human Values*, New York, 1931, p. 21.
[24] P. 227, below.

upon the relationship that the object which has the value (or is valu-able) can come into with a sensibility. If one wants to speak in meta-physical terms, he would say that the value is a quality or property that is emergent at this level; but the metaphysics is not essential here. The analysis is independent of whatever metaphysical interpretation may be given it.

Parker is quite correct in holding that to call it a putative property is no more an explanation of why the object is held to be valuable than to ascribe a *virtus dormitiva* is an explanation of why opium puts a man to sleep. If the ascription of a *virtus dormitiva* were at all useful in helping us to discover the general characteristics of the chemical-physical properties in opium that puts men to sleep, then the ascription could well be made. It was discarded because it did not prove useful, but in fact, quite the contrary. I have found (in attempting to order my own experience) that the classification of value as a putative property proves useful. Thinking of it in this way, I have analyzed the subjective conditions and the objective conditions necessary to its occurrence.[25] It would be rash to say that very many persons have agreed with my analysis, but that it constitutes an orderly hypothesis I think can fairly be said.

Hahn, on page 119, above, apparently misunderstood my use of the term "putative object." This is the fault of my own expression, for I used the term "object" in the phrase "putative object" ambiguously. The object that has value (the valuable object) is a real object. Re-member that I am not using the term real here in its metaphysical sense. I mean that it is not constituted by my act of attending to it. If, however, I consider my act of valuing, the valuing is directed toward the value in the object. In this sense, and only in this sense can the value be called an object: it is the object of the act of valuing in the sense that it is what the act is about. As I am maintaining that the value is a putative property, then it is, when considered as an object, a putative object. I admit, however, that this use of terms was confusing, and it had better be dropped.[26]

Mitchell, on page 192 of his present paper, denounces the question whether value is substantive or adjectival. I am in agreement with

[25] *Perception and Aesthetic Value*, New York, 1938.
[26] In my rejoinder to Mitchell's criticism of my paper, I give up the term "putative" altogether. See p. 409, below.

his argument at this point in spite of the fact that I have called value adjectival. Mitchell is opposing the substance-attribute metaphysics. One does not have to adopt the substance-attribute metaphysics, however, in order to conduct his analysis along the lines that I have followed. I do not adopt the substance-attribute metaphysics. I made the statement a few paragraphs back that *if* a metaphysical interpretation were given to the analysis, it would best be in terms of a theory of emergence. I do not think that the emergence theory is compatible with the substance-attribute theory—at least not in its Aristotelian form.

Parker's satisfaction or gratification and Rice's joy are very important features in the experience of value. I have already expressed my adverse criticism of Parker's views that the satisfaction *is* the value; yet I hold that without reference to the satisfaction there is no value. The attitude or interest giving rise to value is not complete without reference to its fulfillment. Its satisfaction gives significance to it.

Any particular interest may as a matter of fact be satisfied or fulfilled to a greater degree, to a lesser degree, or not at all. This fact added to the fact that the possibility of fulfillment is of necessary relevance to the interest makes it the measure for comparison of different values. The reference to the satisfaction furnishes the "evaluating factor" for the comparison of one value with another. Often we value a thing and then later decide that we should not have valued it, or at least that we would have valued something else enough more highly so that we would have chosen that something else in preference to what we valued in the first place. I have endeavored to show that the principle for the comparison of aesthetic values (and as the principle of comparison, it also serves to distinguish the positive from the negative values or disvalues) is pleasure.[27] It may be that my attempt is not very successful; and at any rate the evaluating factor in the case of moral values is more complex. Nevertheless, I would maintain that without some such evaluative principle (either explicit or implicit) there could be no comparative ordering of values: neither into the more intense and the less intense, nor into the more preferable and the less preferable. Jessup's "standard value" is at stake here, and it seems to me to be an excellent concept. Without some principle of reference such as I have called the evaluating factor, no standard could be set up. Parker and Rice have confused the evaluating factor with value.

[27] See *Perception and Aesthetic Value*, ch. v.

It has been suggested to me by Lepley in correspondence that achievement, a harmony of interests, or a well-rounded life may also be evaluating factors. I doubt that these would be evaluating factors if they were not conducive to satisfaction in the last analysis. The satisfaction of achievement or of a well-rounded life is perhaps the greatest long-run satisfaction possible.

III

This brings me to a consideration of the problem at issue in the second main question of Dewey's article that originated this symposium: the question of the relation between value and judgment. There must be a given element in all experience. When we make judgments and have knowledge, we make the judgments *about* something. In the last analysis there must be an element in that something that is ultimately given. What is ultimately given in the experience of value is not necessarily the same as what is given in the experience of fact. It makes no sense to call that which is ultimately given either subjective or objective. "Subjective" and "objective" are terms of analysis. Nevertheless, what is in experience as a result of judgment and what is given in experience are not to be confused. Knowledge, truth, and error reside in the realm of judgment. If value were the result of judgment, then value would be a form of knowledge, which is contrary to much of the analysis we have conducted up to the present time. If value is a result of judgment, this analysis has to be abandoned and we have to start over again. Such procedure is not called for unless it is necessary. Is it necessary?

A distinction can be drawn between the immediate apprehension of value and the way that apprehension may be modified as a result of judgment. We would be back in the most vicious form of faculty psychology if we supposed that apprehension of value would not be modified by judgment; but the fact that it can be modified by judgment does not indicate that judgment is a necessary condition of value. Several paragraphs back, I called attention to the fact that often we decide that we should not have valued something that we did, or even that we should not value something that we do. The fact that we make this decision, however, does not alter the fact that we did or even do value the something. The decision does not rob the thing of the immediate value it had or has; it merely indicates that in a broader context of a choice of values, that particular value would not be chosen. We may, however, even make a preliminary choice not to pay sufficient attention to the broader context of values, and go ahead enjoying the value of the present object, although with a "guilty conscience."

If we apprehend value, we apprehend value, and whether or not we judge that it should not be, the valuable object still is valuable. If I care about something, that something has value. There can be no error in the immediate apprehension of value any more than there can in the immediate apprehension of anything else. Error is a quality of judgment, and judgment is not immediate apprehension: it is mediated.[28] Valuable objects are often incompatible with each other. In case they are, a choice has to be made. The choice *is* made on the basis of a comparison of values, whether that comparison is made rationally or impulsively or with a little of each. If the choice is made rationally, and other choices are made according to the same principles, then a standard is set up, and there emerges what Jessup calls standard value. This standard value is the result of an evaluative process. The typical standard values are moral and social values. Dewey is so intensely interested in these that all apprehension of value appears to him to have an evaluative element in it.

There are two kinds of judgments of value. First is what D. W. Prall calls the record of the direct experience.[29] Second is what I have been speaking of as the evaluative judgment, which involves comparison. It seems to me that Dewey's "valuation" partakes of a little of each of these. In so far as appraisal can be understood in the sense of recognizing the value of anything, then it is the record. In so far as appraisal is understood to say how much or how little value, then it is comparative. If one holds that there is a direct experience of value anterior to judgment, or if he holds that there can be a judgment of value that is not an appraisal of it in degree as so much or so little, then he can *not* hold that valuation (as I understand Dewey to be using the term) is necessarily constitutive of the experience of value. To establish the position that valuation is constitutive of value, he must deny both of the conditions. Simply to point out that evaluations do as a matter of fact influence apprehension of value does not establish the position.

[28] See my article "Esthetics and Epistemology," *The Journal of Philosophy*, XXXVI (1939), 281–290, for a systematic elaboration of this point.
[29] *Aesthetic Judgment*, New York, 1929, p. 5.

I do not know any conclusive evidence that would eliminate either of the two conditions. On the contrary, both the logical and the empirical evidence would seem to me to establish them.

Lepley, in correspondence, expresses doubt that there is any apprehension of value that is really unmediated. He says, "May not the simplest, most direct perceptive or apperceptive response involve 'judgment' of some order?" This raises a fundamental problem in epistemology. Psychologically considered, his question may have to be answered "Yes"; adult perception does involve judgment of some order. Any concrete experience of an adult human being includes reference to his past experience. I would point out, however, that in value theory we are trying to understand, and understanding involves analysis. In analyzing any concrete value experience we may find the element in it which is simply apprehended. There must be a core of immediacy around which the accretions from past experience accumulate. Let me further point out that the view that the simplest, most direct response involves judgment of some order can be established only on the basis of an analysis of concrete experience—the same kind of analysis that finds one element to be immediately apprehended and another to be added as interpretation in the light of past experience. If the analysis is not legitimate in the one case, it is not in the other.

The comparative theory of value expounded by Mitchell in his present paper might seem to deny that there is any judgment that is a simple record of a direct experience of value, but I do not think that it does. The statement that "x is good" means "it is better that x is than that it is not" does not involve the comparison of different experiences of value in such a way as to establish a standard. Mitchell's problem is the problem of finding undefined notions in terms of which the logical structure of the whole experience of value can be stated: undefined ideas in terms of which other definitions can be made. It seems to me that his suggestion offers an excellent logical scheme for the analysis of experience. The judgment that is the direct record of the experience may, for logical reasons, well be put into the form that he suggests. To put it in this form, however, does not prove that there is no value without evaluation, nor does it offer any evidence that there is not. I do not suppose that he holds that it does. Equivalent postulate sets may be expressed in terms of different primitive ideas and relations. For example, Veblen's set for Euclidean geometry is in terms of a triadic relation, while Huntington's set is in terms of a dyadic relation. Mitchell would state the logical structure of the value experience in dyadic form whereas some other persons would seem to prefer a monadic form. That is the problem here; it is not a question of judgment being a necessary constituent of the experience of value.

A very important subdivision of the evaluative judgment is the judgment of potential value. I have called value a putative property which an object has by virtue of the fact that it can be an object of interest, desire, or caring about. This does not mean that nothing can have value except as it is the actual object of one of these attitudes at any given moment of time. If the thing is the kind of a thing that *can* be an object of some particular attitude, then it *has* potential value. Of course the only proof of a potentiality is an actuality; but if we have found cases where anything is the object of the attitude, that is enough proof of a real potentiality. Pepper's distinction between the potential object of value and the object of potential value is a useful distinction here.[30] Whatever value a potential object could have would be a potential value, but this value would rest in the cognitive or imaginative reference to the future existence of the object. Actual objects may have either actual or potential values. The potential value depends upon a judgment that under such and such conditions, the thing in question would be the object of an attitude, and thus actual value would be apprehended. There are beauties that are not seen or heard; there are moral values that are never realized; there are economic and political values that seem unfortunately always to remain only in the realm of possibility.

No difficulty arises from defining value as a putative property even when it is only a potentiality. Many of the characteristics we ascribe to things are only potentialities. Anything is dangerous, for example, by virtue of the fact that it may turn out to be disastrous, and it is correctly called dangerous only in the light of this possibility. It is not confusing to call bread nourishing though it is evident that at the time it is bread it is not nourishing anyone. Similarly one can speak of the beauty of a landscape at which no one is looking, or the beauty of music that is not being played. The beauty refers always to the possibility of being looked at or heard just as the nourishment refers to the

[30] See p. 253, below.

possibility of assimilation. Literally, music that is not being played does not even exist, but it can exist. Hence, no confusion arises when I refer to Bach's B-minor Mass, though the probabilities are great that it does not exist at the moment of writing this. The score exists, but that is not the music. The music is sound. Similarly, no confusion arises when I refer to the beauty of the B-minor Mass. It is not being experienced now, but it can be experienced under conditions that can be clearly and precisely defined. Therefore, it is a real potentiality.

The most fruitful source of error in the value-judgment lies in the judgment of potential value. I have said that the direct experience of value cannot be in error although we may make the evaluative judgment that it would have been better (that is, a greater value) if we had not found value where we did. The judgment of potentiality of value may be completely in error, however. Many of our judgments of value are merely cursory, and do not record an experience of value but merely make an assertion of potential value. Such judgments are worth no more than the evidence that can be adduced to support them.

It seems to me that one of the objections to defining value in subjective terms as do Parker and Rice is that it is difficult in these terms to explain potential value; and if one does not have the concept of potential value it is difficult to explain many of the ordinary errors in value-judgments. The concept of potential value applies to instrumental value in Garnett's theory, thus a principle of explanation of errors of instrumental value is available, but it is difficult to see how it could apply to his intrinsic value.

IV

I am quite aware of the fact that if the term judgment is used strictly according to Dewey's definition, then there can be no judgments that are direct records of the experience of value, simply because such records would not be judgments.[31] I call them judgments because, in the first place, they have to be called something if we are to talk about them, and in the second, I think the term is justified because the record is the assertion of a proposition. A proposition is whatever can be asserted or denied (or the assertion of which can be true or false). When we actually make the assertion we are making a judgment. Judgments

[31] See *The Quest for Certainty*, New York, 1929, pp. 213, 261, and 264.

are psychological. Propositions are logical. When I assert that I am
experiencing value, I am making a judgment according to this definition.

Toward the beginning of his discussion of the third question in the
paper "Some Questions about Value," Dewey says that statements
merely enumerating facts already in existence are not propositions. I
can see how he could say this about judgments according to his definition of judgments, but I do not see how he can say it about propositions. He distinguishes clearly between propositions and judgments in
Logic, the Theory of Inquiry, and allows for the singular proposition.[32]
That I see a beautiful sunset when I look out of the window as I am
writing this is the statement of a proposition. That the thermometer
registers 92 degrees Fahrenheit right now is also the statement of a
proposition. That I feel hot and uncomfortable is also the statement
of a proposition. Each proposition can be asserted or denied. Each
one is true or false. The fact that there is a great difference in the difficulty of establishing the truth or falsity of one or the other has nothing
to do with whether they are propositions. I can assert each one in a
judgment. The truth of the judgment depends upon the truth of the
proposition. Hence the difficulty of establishing the truth of any one
has nothing to do with whether it is a judgment.

I suggest that one reason that Question III appears to be a problem
depends upon Dewey's definition of judgment and a confusion of propositions with judgments in this place. It is true that in the first statement of the question on page 5, above, he says, "judgments or/and propositions," while in the discussion on pages 9 and 10 he talks only
of propositions; but this is of no consequence. If he had said, "judgments
or/and propositions" all the way through, I would still think that the
problem is a result of the definition. A definition that gives rise to
unnecessary complications and problems is a bad definition and ought
to be discarded. Propositions differ from each other only in subject
matter or in logical form. There is nothing unique in the logical form
of a proposition about value, and hence nothing unique in the form
of the judgment that is the assertion of this proposition. The difference
is only a difference of subject matter.

Even if the difference between value propositions and other propositions lies only in subject matter, is there something in the nature of

[32] New York, 1938, pp. 283 and 290.

the subject matter that renders them wholly recalcitrant to the application of the scientific method? I would answer "Yes," if the scientific method is defined primarily in terms of observation and experimentation; but "No," if the scientific method is defined logically. As I hold that it is to be defined fundamentally in logical terms, and that where observation and experimentation are essential it is because of logical demands plus special demands of the subject matter, my answer to the fourth question would be an unqualified assertion that value-judgments are amenable to investigation by the scientific method.[33]

Whether or not every valuing contains an element or aspect of evaluation seems to me to be quite beside the point. We can consistently hold that valuing is not cognitive, and at the same time hold that in the process of evaluation a comparative ordering of values according to their intensity, preferability, scope, inclusiveness, and perhaps other dimensions can be worked out. The task would be a logical task—one for reason and intelligence, foresight and imagination. The only method that fits these demands is the scientific method.

V

The question with which Dewey closes his paper is one of great practical as well as theoretic import. A theory of the nature of value such as I have indicated here would point to the same conclusions that I think would be found as a result of a careful examination of the empirical evidence. Value is individualistically determined according to the theory because there is no "caring about," that is, no conative-affective attitude that we know anything about, that is not the attitude of some individual organic sensibility. Thus, there cannot be any value without individual sentient organisms. Only rational human beings, as far as we know, can have a *moral* attitude, because the moral attitude arises in the situation where a conflict of values necessitates a choice made in the light of the possible outcome of the choice. This depends on an intelligent grasp of the relation between means and end. Only individuals can exercise intelligence, foresee ends, and make choices. Thus moral individualism is indicated.

Such a moral individualism does not deny, however, that values are

[33] It is unnecessary for me to go over the arguments about scientific method here as they are presented in the article "Scientific Method and Knowledge," already cited.

determined very largely by the socio-cultural context in which the individual lives. Human beings are not solitary creatures. They are conditioned by coming into contact with other human beings. Through this conditioning, institutions are built up. Institutions are not simple aggregates of individuals, they are organizations. They are the matrices in which social conditioning takes place. Society is not a simple aggregation of individuals. It is organized and is institutional. The individual experiences his value and makes his choices himself; but he can not do so uninfluenced by the institutional context. The exaggerated individualism of the seventeenth and eighteenth centuries, in its extreme reaction against the institutionalism of the Middle Ages, treated men as if they were essentially isolated, and institutions as if they were merely simple sums of separate men. More recently, we have found how inadequate such a view is.[34]

Values are not "definitely and completely socio-cultural." Values are dependent upon an individual sensibility, and thus are individualistically determined. Men are socio-cultural, however, and cannot be adequately theoretically dealt with outside of that context. Therefore human values cannot be adequately theoretically dealt with outside of the socio-cultural context.[35]

[34] See my article "Moral Individualism and Political Value" in *Essays on the Theory of Value and Valuation* (Minneapolis, 1945), by members of the Southwestern Philosophical Conference.
[35] For the Criticisms and Rejoinders which relate especially to this paper see pp. 302–311, 400–404, and 408–410, below.

❧ SEQUEL ON VALUE

RAY LEPLEY

M

Y ANSWERS TO DEWEY'S QUESTIONS are, in general outline, as follows.[1] *Question I:* Liking, disliking, desire, interest, valuing, and
valuation are, like prizing and holding dear, interactional and transactional in character, not independently existing 'subjective entities'[2]
or 'mental states.' These several processes or phases of interaction may
properly be conceived as distinguishable from, and as related to, each
other in the way indicated by Dewey's suggested "behavioral description" of them.[3] *Question II:* Liking, desiring, valuing, and the satisfying
of desire are in many instances necessary conditions for the existence
or experience of value, but are not sufficient conditions; inquiry and
testing ("valuation") are also needed for the discovery or creation of
value in what is in some respects the most distinctive meaning of
"value." *Question III:* If and when value, or valuational, propositions
and judgments are truly judgments or propositions, they differ from
other assertive, or factual, propositions and judgments in subject matter only. *Question IV:* Scientific method, "in its broad sense," is as
applicable in matters of value and valuation as in matters of fact and
fact-finding. *Question V:* It is necessary to view value and valuation
both in their socio-cultural contexts and in terms of the 'total' individual
and social interactions which may be analyzed somewhat abstractly
as 'psychological' in character.

The present essay will assume the general point of view suggested
by these answers. It will consider further some issues brought to
sharper focus for me by Dewey's questions, by the comments on his
questions by other members of this inquiry, and by criticisms and

[1] The answers here summarized have appeared more or less explicitly in recent pub-
lications. See, especially, *Verifiability of Value*, New York, 1944, hereafter referred
to as *VV*.
[2] Words and phrases enclosed in single quotation marks which are not within
double quotation marks are felt by the writer to be particularly ambiguous. Double
quotation marks indicate quotations, or words as words.
[3] See pp. 6–7, above.

suggestions received on my own writings. It will thus constitute a sort of sequel to my previous value studies, and will follow the general order of Dewey's questions.

I

The fact that Dewey's first question is one concerning the nature of desiring, liking, interest, enjoying, and the like, as compared with prizing and holding dear, which he regards as interactive and trans-active in character, raises a number of issues concerning methodology in the study of value. Perhaps everyone will agree that prizing, holding dear, liking, interest, enjoying, and so on, constitute, or are included in, value phenomena. Here, if anywhere, are value and the experience of value. But should it be assumed, without question and careful examination, that human experiences, or even the whole of organic experiences, of desiring, satisfaction, and the like, exhaust the class "value," or "value phenomena"? Whether or not Dewey makes this assumption, it appears that many other students of value do so. Of course, for the practical purposes of human living we need most of all to understand value as it occurs, and is experienced, on the human level. Yet the achievement of such understanding may, as in the case of many other phenomena, depend upon seeing human events in their continuities with other events. Or if not necessary for the practical understanding of human value events, recognition and description of continuities, if there are such, will certainly be significant for other philosophic purposes. That there *are* continuities with other events, continuities which have important consequences for the conception of value and for methodology in 'practical, everyday' value matters will be indicated in subsequent sections of this paper.

By contrasting the conception of prizing, desiring, liking, interest, and so forth, as "behavioral transactions" with the conception of them as "mental states" which constitute or generate value "as an uniquely complete product," Dewey's discussion raises the issue as to what, if any, place introspective analysis and an "internal," "mentalistic," or subjective standpoint and terminology may properly have in the study of value and in the formulation of value theory.[4] Some of the comments

[4] Dewey does not explicitly state this issue, nor does he use the terms "introspection," "subjectivistic," or "subjective." I agree with Lee (p. 148n) that the use of the suffix "istic" is to be deplored. In the present discussion I am using "subjective" as synonymous with what Dewey calls "internal, mentalistic, etc." (p. 6, above);

on his discussion take the line that "value cannot be defined in behavioral terms" or that "terms the referent and definition of which are confined to purely behavioral transactions lose all necessary reference to value." But such criticisms clearly presuppose some non-behavioral conception of value and what is perhaps an unjustifiably narrow view of behavioral. If, instead, the behavioral is regarded as including such processes as liking, enjoying, preferring, and so forth, it will certainly embrace the phenomena, and possibly also include the experiences, generally accepted as distinctly valuative. In this broader sense it appears likely that the behavioral and the subjective are but two somewhat different ways of viewing and stating the same total interactive, transactive processes which constitute human value events. And perhaps as long as the actual interactive processes are kept fully and clearly in mind there need be little danger from the use of even the most "mentalistic" or "subjective" terms. To react emotionally against such terminology is probably as unjustifiable as to react similarly to "behavioristic" or "naturalistic" terms as necessarily involving reductionism.

If value theory is to escape triviality and the ivory tower, it must, I suspect, study and describe actual value experiences as they occur or have occurred in various aspects of social and personal life. Since it is not possible to study all instances, there must be a sampling which, if it is to avoid oversimplification, on the one hand, and undue bias, on the other, must be as inclusive and representative as possible. The samples, to be representative, should be taken from, or in, various human enterprises, such as science, art, religion, education, business, and government. Within these enterprises actual 'adjustments' which occur in social, biological, and psychological contexts and sequences must be studied in, and as parts of, these sequences. The total interactions-transactions which constitute courses of adjustment may be variously designated and 'expressed' in terms of 'behavioral,' or processive, continuities and of 'conative,' 'affective,' 'cognitive,' and other 'qualities' of experience as had, so long as these perspectives and terms are not allowed to generate or perpetuate unjustifiable separations and dualisms. Indeed, it is doubtful whether 'value events' can be fully or adequately studied and described without the use of terms

---

this is the meaning which in VV, ch. ix, is called "subjective(2)," and does not equate all meanings of "subjective" with "mental."

commonly classed as 'introspective' or 'subjective' as well as those regarded as 'behavioral' or 'objective.' Even qualities 'as had' are probably events—processes—which can be viewed and designated or expressed in 'both' ways.[5]

II

The question as to whether desiring, liking, interest, or enjoying is by itself a *sufficient* condition for the existence of values focuses attention on one of the main differences of opinion in current value theory. Some students regard intrinsic qualities, such as are had in desiring and enjoying, as primary or *basic* value and all other value as derived from or instrumental to the intrinsic. Others view desiring, liking, disliking, enjoying, and so on, as being merely qualities or experiences 'as had,' and hold that these become values only as the result of inquiry, judgment, or testing in which the qualities are examined in terms of their conditions and consequences, personal and social. The latter group hold either that the value resides in or *is* the immediate qualities as they emerge approved and rendered more secure by virtue of the critical examination to which they have been subjected, or that value resides in, or is constituted by, the efficacy of the 'objects' which produce or sustain approval and (possibly) enjoyment, or satisfaction.

It may well be that these different conceptions of value result largely from differences of approach and terminology and from rather exclusive emphasis upon some element of the "value situation" which each group is afraid will be overlooked or not sufficiently recognized. If this is the case, it may be possible, by recognizing the different approaches and by bringing the various fears and interests into the open, to see that the several emphases supplement each other and that all are required for a balanced perception of the situation as a whole.

Superficially at least, the different conceptions of value appear to result from the fact that some students of value make an introspective, 'subjective' approach, whereas others make a more descriptive, 'objective' approach. The first group places emphasis upon qualities, feelings, desires, satisfactions, and the like as had; the second group stresses human events of desire, interest, appraisal, and so forth, as being continuous with all other events of nature, both organic and inorganic.

[5] VV attempts, however inadequately, the sort of sampling and description here advocated for the study of value phenomena and for the formulation of value theory.

Value for the first group is thus a matter of qualities as had, either before or after the examination of conditions and consequences. For the second, value resides in, or is, efficacy for the production of the events of satisfaction, enjoyment, and critical approval. But it is likely that this analysis is superficial; each group probably recognizes the total, interactive event character of human value matters and experiences, and doubtless each group recognizes the occurrence of qualities and the frequent need or wisdom of examining (inquiring into, appraising, testing) the conditions and consequences of desires, proposals, and enjoyments. The rather exclusive emphasis either upon immediate qualities as had, on the one hand, or upon qualities or efficacies as 'verified' through inquiry, on the other, is perhaps partly due to recognition of the danger, in view of the character of other historical and current value theories, of failing to give proper place either to immediate qualities or to the possibility and need for inquiry and testing as to whether 'immediate values' really are valuable.

So far as historical factors are involved, those who stress immediate qualities as values are perhaps reacting against strong ascetic and 'puritanical' strains in our culture; the assertion of qualities of experience as intrinsic goods is a continued manifestation of humanistic tendencies and impulses. But this emphasis is perhaps also in part a protest against tendencies in science, philosophy, industry, and international affairs to "devaluate" human experiences, to view them merely as events, and to convert all value into instrumental value.

Those, on the other hand, who have stressed the possibility and need for inquiry and testing in order to discover the 'real' value of immediate qualities have sought to promote wider recognition of the change that has come apace in theory of knowledge with the developments and achievements of modern science, and they seek to resist the complacent acceptance of such intrinsic qualities as are already had. They envisage new horizons for the development and extension of the experimental attitude and procedure in all our human enterprises—in community life, education, government, business and industry, as well as in the arts and sciences.

Now, in so far as it is true that students of value, and certainly all the contributors to this symposium, recognize man as at least a part of nature and his behaviors and experiences (even those of desiring, thinking, having satisfaction, and approval) as at least interactive and processive in character, it will be recognized that the several emphases and conceptions of value which we have noted point to different aspects of the same total situation. As a part of nature, we have needs, desires, strivings for satisfactions; and we find that some things, acts, and arrangements satisfy the needs and interests and, in varying degrees, continue to serve them. The immediate qualities of experience are the inner, personal, 'subjective' way of viewing and having a certain place in, and as being a part of, the whole gamut of natural events. We not only have enjoyments, annoyances, likes, and dislikes; we very frequently find it necessary, wise, or interesting to examine and appraise in "the longest run" and "the widest context" of which we, individually and jointly, are capable.

To give adequate recognition to the facts just mentioned is certainly more important than to maintain any one particular use of the term "value" in referring to these facts. To limit the term to any one of the aspects mentioned—to qualities as had 'immediately,' to qualities as also qualified by criticism, or to efficacies as discovered or created by experimental inquiry and action—would have certain advantages and certain dangers. To regard qualities as basic or primary value seems 'natural' because quality, feeling, or 'affection' is perhaps the initial, all-embracing, and final form of experience; qualities of experience as had may thus appear to be the source, seat, and ultimate test of value. But the conception of value as immediate unexamined qualities easily loses sight of the complex interactive character of value situations and of the fact that qualities arise from, are sustained or reduced by, and can be variously tested (evaluated) by means of, the cooperation of the several processes which constitute the situations. It thus entails the risk of excessive tolerance and an extreme relativism which fails to recognize the possibilities for achieving new and more significantly satisfying levels of satisfaction. To locate 'true' value in qualities as qualified through criticism avoids the dangers just mentioned and keeps the "center of gravity" of value in human experience as had. It also calls attention to the fact that as a result of critical inquiry new qualities are generated and are taken up into the original qualities. This conception may seem, however, to deny value to qualities in their relatively unintellectualized occurrence; moreover, it may appear to remain essentially subjective, failing to emphasize explicitly the basic continuity between human events involving the experience

of value and other organic and inorganic events. The conception of
value as in, or as, efficacy for producing events of enjoyment and critical approval opens the way to recognizing the continuity (as well as
the discontinuity) of human value events with all other events; it
achieves a fully objective 'naturalization' of value.[6] But it is easily
misunderstood as denying the 'uniqueness' of human interest-and-
satisfaction events or as attributing human value qualities to subhuman
and even inorganic events.

It must be clear, however, that the limitations and dangers of each
of these conceptions of value—or of each of these significations of the
term "value"—are not inherent in the conceptions themselves. That
is, there is nothing in any one of the conceptions which prevents full
recognition of the facts stressed by the others. Indeed, it seems likely
that the advocates of each view assume the points emphasized by the
others, but regard the points as too obvious to require special mention. At any rate, there should be no objection to recognizing all the
facts and conceptions cited, if by so doing the various emphases are
seen not only to supplement but to safeguard the 'values,' and to help
avoid the dangers, of each taken separately.

If each of us who has been in the habit of stressing some one aspect
of the value situation to the apparent exclusion of the others and of
using the term "value" with one particular reference can free himself
from these habits and view the situation in all the dimensions designated by these several different significations of the term, we may be
able to achieve a point of view and a syntax of value language which will
further cooperation both in the consideration of theoretical problems
and in the pursuit of practical, everyday interests.

With clear and explicit recognition of the fact that experiences of
intrinsic quality occur within and as total interactive processes, the
syntax of valuation compiled by Rice [7] is an excellent list of ways in
which "value" is, and may be, helpfully used. We may, as his table
indicates, distinguish between more behavioral and more introspective
terminology; between values as positive and negative, intrinsic and
instrumental, conative and perceptual, actual and potential; between
elementary, comparative, contextual, and generic judgments of value;

See VV, pp. 228–232.
P. B. Rice, "Toward a Syntax of Valuation," *The Journal of Philosophy*, XLI
1944), 309–320.

and among different kinds of value, such as the aesthetic and the moral.

But when attention focuses, as it frequently and properly does, upon the intrinsic as in one sense basic to all experienced values, we may easily lose sight of the facts (a) that needs, satisfactions, and the like occur within processes of interaction which can be so utilized as to test and enrich the qualities had and to test the capacity of various objects to sustain events of satisfaction and approval; and (b) that the events of human value experience, which like all levels of events may be unique emergents, are continuous with all other events in being causal and natural in character. These facts may be kept more constantly and clearly in mind if, as a supplement to Rice's list, we distinguish also between untested and tested values, between unexperienced and experienced values, and between human and non-human, and organic and inorganic values. "Untested values" will include all efficacies for events, whether human or non-human, organic or inorganic, which now exist, have existed, or can exist, but which have not been established (ascertained, 'verified') by inquiry; or, from a more restricted and subjective point of view, the term may be said to include all intrinsic qualities, or experiences, as had and liked or disliked prior to examination of the conditions and effects of their occurrence. "Tested values" will designate all efficacies established (ascertained, 'verified') through careful inquiry; or, from the more restricted and subjective point of view, the term may be said to include all intrinsic qualities as affected by processes of criticism. "Unexperienced values" are (subjectively) the possible satisfactions, and (objectively) the efficacies for events of satisfaction or of organic or inorganic occurrence, of which we are not aware. In some instances we may become cognizant of the efficacies and upon occasion aware of their operation; they are then experienced values. Human, organic, and inorganic values are the sorts of values which occur on these respective levels of events—the human, the organic, and the inorganic.

In regard to the character of the intrinsic elements in the experience of value, it may be noted that conceptions of value as immediate qualities have historically and currently stressed as basic either interest desire, conation, and achievement, on the one hand, or satisfaction enjoyment, pleasure, or feeling, on the other. From an 'objective' biological, social, and psychological standpoint it appears obvious that th

first emphasis is correct, and that satisfaction or pleasantness-unpleas-
antness is only a rough guide as to what is safe and helpful for the
individual or group.[8] Yet from a more 'introspective' standpoint it
seems equally clear that feelings, enjoyments, satisfactions, and the
like are the sole source and criterion of value.[9] One who conceives
desire or interest as the primary mode of immediate value rightly
feels that this view makes for constructive achievement, and often
only by foregoing immediate pleasures. Still, an advocate of the view
that pleasure or feeling is primary will retort that the value of achievements and of temporary deprivations can be measured ultimately only
by the amount and kind of enjoyments or satisfactions to which they
lead. So far as there is or can be a solution to this problem of priority
or ultimacy, it may lie along the line of recognizing that the conative
and the affective are two ways of having and of viewing somewhat
different but overlapping or intermingled elements or aspects of the
same 'total' adjustment course, or situation. They are equally immediate
havings, and hence are on a par as immediate values; yet neither taken
singly and apart from consideration of conditions and consequences
in a more inclusive personal and social setting is a sufficient source
or criterion of value in the sense of "tested value." It may usually be
well, as Aristotle saw, to lean away from the direction in which either
our desires or our pleasures propel or attract us—well to consider as
objectively as we can the long-run and widespread effects to which
our actions will lead. In estimating these effects it may generally be
wise to stress interests and achievements more than immediate 'passive' pleasures, but to recognize that usually both achievement and
enjoyment can be and need to be secured together in such ways and
proportions as are approved in the light of critical inquiry.

If the term "value" may properly and helpfully be used to designate
and 'express' all of the above-mentioned areas and aspects of value-
acts, it follows that the latter part of Dewey's second question must
be answered in different ways, depending upon which area or areas
we are designating or expressing in any particular instance. When, for
example, we are designating or expressing immediate qualities which
are not elements in or objects of valuative processes, valuation is *not*

See Pepper's essay, pp. 257–258, below.
See, for example, G. Williams, "The Subjective Nature of Ultimate Moral Author-
," *Journal of Social Philosophy*, VI (1941), 244–253.

a necessary condition for the existence of values. Nor is it a necessary condition when we are designating unexperienced human or non-human efficacies. But when we are designating or expressing critically examined qualities or efficacies, valuation *is* a necessary condition for the existence of values. Moreover, it becomes clear that to choose between the view that values occur prior to valuation and the view that they occur only after, or by means of, valuation may easily conceal or ignore one or other of the areas or aspects of the occurrence and experience of value. Such dangers may be avoided or reduced by explicitly recognizing all these areas and aspects as proper designata of "value" and by remembering that failure to distinguish them frequently results in partiality and confusion in discussions of value.

III

An element of 'appraisal' may be said to occur in all judgment—in even the simplest identification or naming. "This is paper," "The person coming in the distance is Mr. Smith," "It is now thirteen minutes after eight"—each statement, if it results from actual judgment and is not merely a parroting of words or a purely conditioned response, involves appraisal. But in raising the question as to whether "anything in the nature of appraisal, evaluation, as judgment or/and proposition" "marks them off, with respect to their logical or their scientific status, from other propositions or judgments," Dewey evidently intends a particular class or kind of appraisals as distinguished from others. He is doubtless referring to what he has elsewhere [10] called "distinctive appraisal propositions." They are "propositions which lay down rules for procedure as being fit or good, as distinct from those that are inept and bad"; they are "different in form from the scientific propositions on which they rest. For they are rules for the use, in and by human activity, of scientific generalizations as means for accomplishing certain desired and intended ends." The "other" propositions referred to are, or include, the "scientific" ones—"nonvaluative propositions about impersonal subject matter."

The differences, in both form and function, between the words and sentences, on the one hand, which commonly 'express' or designate human needs, wants, and interests and the means for satisfying them

[10] "Theory of Valuation," in *International Encyclopedia of Unified Science*, Chicago 1939, II, No. 4, 22 f.

and the words and sentences, on the other hand, which denote the impersonal objects and processes of nature are so marked that they have given rise to a dichotomy; sentences and words are commonly separated, or classified, as of two kinds: the factual, descriptive, or scientific; and the valuative, normative, or emotive. This separation does not, of course, signify that "values" and "valuative language" are not facts, but that the differences between the two groups of facts (value facts and non-value facts) are sufficient to be conspicuous.

The characteristics of form which distinguish valuative and other factual sentences and words appear to be reciprocally related with their subject matters and functions. That is, some words and 'expressions,' such as "good," "bad," "poor," "excellent," "better," "worse," "right," "wrong," "beautiful," "ugly," "naughty," "nice," "should," "should not," "must," "must not," "ought," "ought not," and so on, have occurred, perhaps at first partly by chance and later because of social usage, in the context of events of need, interest, and the attainment of satisfactions; they have thus become the 'language' of and for these events. Their use in venting, expressing, designating, and motivating in these matters therefore seems natural and spontaneous. The occurrence of these terms in, and as parts of, the processes of need and interest and of attempts to secure satisfactions produce and constitute the particular form characteristic of value sentences and expressions. And, reciprocally, these terms become powerful stimuli for producing, heightening, or otherwise qualifying the events of need, interest, and satisfaction.

Likewise, with regard to the language 'forms' characteristic of dealings with impersonal, factual matters. Such words and phrases as "is," "exists," "causes," "is correlated with," "is a function of," "is true," "is false," and the like occur in the context of the perception, identification, designation, and description of events viewed objectively, or as they are observed or inferred to exist 'independently.' They thus become the 'natural' language of events viewed as existential, and become, in turn, conditioned stimuli for 'objective,' fact-finding, cognitive, descriptive responses, especially with reference to inorganic and non-personal phenomena.

The ability to make significant judgments and propositions, whether in matters of fact or in matters of value, is affected both by subject matters and by language habits. Complexities, inaccessibilities, and changes in subject matter often make it difficult or impossible, even with respect to inorganic events, to perform such operations of critical observation and inference as are worthy of being called judgment or to so formulate and use sentences or statements that they are propositions in a strict logical or scientific sense. In matters of human ends and means the difficulties are frequently accentuated both by the nature of the subject matter and by the language which seems so natural to it. For here the subject matter includes, or is held in the embrace of, personal and group likes and aversions, desires, interests, and preferences—qualitative factors of various sorts; and such emotionally charged 'halo' words as "good," "right," and "ought" frequently prevent open inquiry, critical thinking, and unbiased judgment.[11]

In the appraisal of the effectiveness of ordinary physical means, there are perhaps no more difficulties in formulating and testing valuative judgments than in making and testing factual ones. Indeed, here the same proposition can be expressed in either factual or valuative terms and the same operations are required to test it regardless of the language form (unless there are more difficulties in first divesting ourselves of some of the effects of valuative words). It is also clear that desires, interests, satisfactions, and the like can be "brought out into the open," "appraised," and "compared." Their conditions and consequences can be studied, and decisions and choices can then be made which are often in considerable measure 'informed' and 'enlightened.'

But in the case of choices among desires, interests, and satisfactions, are the final 'judgments' anything more than expressions of refined or transformed feelings or attitudes? In one sense the answer is "No." Feelings or attitudes may be the 'final' determiners of choice. Yet this view of the matter easily obscures the fact that feelings and attitudes sometimes are, and probably always can be, qualified and checked upon by the study of conditions and consequences—a study that can include very careful and objective inquiry and judgments which from one point of view may be called valuative and from another factual.[12] Nor should it be forgotten that all judgments and all formulation and testing of propositions probably include, and even require, elements of feeling;[13] the presence of affective and qualitative factors as *subjec*

---

[11] See also *VV*, pp. 159–160.   [12] See *VV*, pp. 77–78.
[13] See, for example, W. James, *The Principles of Psychology*, New York, 1890, I ch. xxii; A. Rignano, *The Psychology of Reasoning*, tr. by W. A. Holl, New Yor

matter and as elements or aspects of the total interactive, transactive processes of genuine inquiry need not render judgment less careful, objective, and critical. Moreover, a single act of 'judgment,' in a short-span sense of the word, seldom has to be *final;* further interactions may be utilized to check and qualify particular elements of response within the span of a more inclusive judgment.

When and in so far as value judgments and propositions do incorporate or issue from a maximum of care and objectivity, there is probably no justification for concluding that they differ in logical or in scientific status from factual ones. The propositions which occur within the several aspects of value experience noted above [14] have somewhat different character and status, as do various groups of non-value propositions. Like many factual ones, value propositions which designate qualities as having been, or as being, experienced merely assert or state an accomplished fact or occurrence. Examples are "It tastes good," "It is beautiful," and "I love you." Such statements may be genuine propositions in the sense that they indicate, correctly or not, the experience had. But they may have no further logical or scientific basis; any propositions regarding intrinsic qualities in general are, prior to critical testing,[15] "analogous to the undefined notions and undemonstrated propositions of a deductive system." [16] In addition to statements denoting particular experiences, general conceptions of immediate, or intrinsic, value come to formulation and may be used as a basis for further inferences within a system or systems of concepts. Various kinds of value can be defined as species of the intrinsic (say, positive value and negative value, conative value and perceptual value), or as being related to the intrinsic without being a species of it (as in the case of instrumental value and generic value).[17]

A second group or variety of value propositions are formulations regarding the individual and comparative worths of various desires,

---

1923, pp. 391–405, 406–428; and J. Dewey, *The Quest for Certainty,* New York, 1929, pp. 155–156, and "Qualitative Thought," *The Symposium,* I (1930), 1–32.

[14] In section II of this paper, pp. 170–176.

[15] It should be noted that, even in stating or denoting a quality as immediately experienced, the proposition, however spontaneous and impulsive, involves, if there is a genuine experience, an element of appraisal—a judgment, though it may be of a very low order of inclusiveness and care. In the degree that judgment becomes inclusive and critical the first group of value propositions merge into those of the second group discussed in the next paragraph of the text.

[16] A. Castell, *A College Logic,* New York, 1935, p. 315 f.

[17] See Rice, "Toward a Syntax of Valuation."

interests, and satisfactions as these are able to qualify as values via critical examination of conditions and consequences, including the consequences seen and felt through the fullest possible expression, interplay, and scrutiny of various personal and social interests. Examples of such propositions are: "Beauty, truth, and justice are enduring goods; they should generally be given preeminence among our interests," and "This recreational program will yield a maximum of constructive satisfactions for our city at the present time." These propositions are not so much statements of accomplished facts or satisfactions as they are summations made in the light of continued experience—rules which help to direct, and yet are tested by, further experience. Such propositions have perhaps ultimately the status of statements or hypotheses regarding qualities as experienced in themselves and in relation to each other, but this status has a catholicity and security born of continuing experimental inquiry and testing, a status analogous to that of factual propositions which are in some degree verified or established through experimental operations in the various arts and sciences.

The third kind of value propositions are statements and hypotheses regarding efficacies for events, including but not limited to the events of human need, interest, satisfaction, and approval. Examples are "Rain is good for weeds," "For normal prenatal development plenty of calcium must be supplied the mother during pregnancy," "Experience with this recreational program sustains my whole-hearted approval and support," "The more fully and carefully I study the music of Bach the more enjoyment and appreciation it affords me," and "The enjoyment and appreciation of Bach contributes to my mental health." Such propositions are descriptions which also assist prediction and control. They are based upon previous inquiry and testing, and are perhaps best regarded as hypotheses always subject to further testing. They presuppose value not only as events of human experience but as or in *efficacy*—as or in "nature able to do" at all levels of events.[18] They have not only a security which results from continued experi-

---

[18] This conception of value is suggested by H. Lanz, *In Quest of Morals*, Stanford University, 1941, pp. 94–98, 146 f. See also VV, pp. 199–215. A somewhat kindred view is presented in J. Feibleman, "A Short Account of Axiological Realism," in *Essays on the Theory of Value and Valuation*, ed. by H. N. Lee, Minneapolis, 1945, pp. 22–31, though this reference should not be taken to indicate that I subscribe to "axiological realism" in some of the meanings of this term.

mental testing, but a further ground in all the events, or processes, of nature, or reality. Value so viewed is not merely a late emergent, though the organic and especially the human levels of events constitute very distinctive sorts of value events, including those of 'consciousness,' 'feeling,' and 'imagination'—events which may or may not have occurred before or elsewhere. The 'ultimate' logical and scientific status of the third group of propositions is that of relatively verified statements referring to any or all the events and relations of nature, or reality.

Recognition of these several kinds of value propositions must not, of course, be allowed to obscure the actual continuity of the total adjustment courses within which, and as aspects of which, the various kinds of judgments and propositions occur. Nor should the fact that genuine judgments and propositions need to be, and, with proper habits of procedure can be, achieved, blind us to the further facts that in the face of all the complexities and urgencies of actual life it is often extremely difficult to attain genuine judgment and also that value terms and sentences frequently occur and determine behavior on what is largely a non-propositional, non-judgmental level. Full cognizance needs to be taken of the fact that some signs frequently produce or affect 'choices,' or otherwise direct behavior, in a sort of semi-conscious, unquestioning way. This is clearly true of the 'typical' valuative terms and sentences. "Good," "better," "best," "right," and other 'appraisive' [19] terms commonly cause objects to be given preferential status in behavior. "Should," "ought," "need to," and other 'prescriptive' terms generally guide conduct with a minimum of observation and appraisal. Because such terms, through their strong emotional and habit 'associations,' are most likely to be effective without hesitation or questioning, they are used largely for 'emotive' and motivative purposes. Moreover, when there is opportunity and stimulus to investigate and judge objectively, there is often little or no desire to do so; and even when there is such desire and a great deal of effort is made to be objective, affective or qualitative factors of a personal or special character frequently operate in very subtle ways to divert or pervert the process.

[9] For the distinction between designative, appraisive, and prescriptive signs and for clear illustrations of them see C. Morris, *Signs, Language, and Behavior*, New York, 1946. See also my "Fact, Value, and Meaning," *The Philosophical Review*, LIV (1945), 123n.

Full recognition of these facts may, without condoning them or accepting them as inherent or necessary in value-judgments, help to remove the misunderstanding and conflict between students of value who regard value terms and sentences as being essentially and inescapably "emotive in meaning" and those who insist that value-judgments are cognitive and that "meaning should not be extended in such a way that it can be significantly applied to wholly irrational, or non-cognitive, stimulus-response mechanisms." It should be clear that the emotive effects of signs are neither "a mere by-product or effect of descriptive meaning" nor "a wholly distinct and independent species of 'meaning.'" Regardless of how broadly or 'strictly' we may prefer to use the term "meaning," it must be obvious that although both cognitive and emotive elements are probably present in all behavior which is above the level of unconscious reflex, the proportions in which they are present vary widely, even in value choices and appraisals, from a heavy preponderance of the emotive to a very strict dominance and control by the cognitive.

The question as to whether there is anything in the nature of appraisal, evaluation, as judgments or propositions, that marks them off from other propositions or judgments, *or whether such distinctive properties as they possess are wholly an affair of their subject matter,* assumes that the two kinds of judgments or propositions have different subject matters. The distinction is between human value matters, on the one hand, and impersonal, or non-human matters of fact, on the other. These two subject matters are commonly, and quite justifiably and helpfully, set over against each other in what may be called "the contrast relation" of facts and values. But when all human events, even those of the occurrence of events of need and interest and of the satisfying of needs and interests, are viewed as a part of the whole gamut of existential occurrences and relations, and when it is further recognized that each and every event can be viewed both as an existent and as an object of interest, it becomes clear that both factual and valuative judgments and propositions can be made with reference to every distinguishable event or group of events in the whole gamut. The subject matters of factual and of valuative judgments and propositions thus stand not only in the relation of the contrast of the human and the non-human, or of the organic and the inorganic, but also in a sort of parallel relation—in contrast along the whole scale of events as referents.

Also, the fact that in some instances both factual and valuative propositions can and do function either designatively, appraisively, prescriptively, or motivatively with regard to the same referent raises a question as to what extent this is possible. Thorough investigation of this question will disclose, I suspect, that every possible referent, however extensive or restricted, can be designated and 'expressed' by both factual and valuative propositions and that as *referents,* though *not* as statements, facts and values and the subject matters of factual and valuative judgments and propositions are then identical.[20] This ultimate identity does not deny the reality of the contrast and the parallel relations of subject matters, judgments, and so on, nor does it reduce the importance of problems regarding the nature of values and value-judgments as compared with facts and factual judgments in the contrast and parallel relations. But it may afford well-nigh final and conclusive evidence that value-judgments need not differ from factual judgments in any respect, even in subject matter, and that valuative propositions need differ only in verbal form [21] to be distinguishable from factual ones.

IV

If it is true that the subject matter of valuative judgments and propositions, in their fullest possible extension, is identical with that of factual judgments and propositions, there can be nothing "in the nature of values as subject matter" that "precludes the applicability of the scientific method" "in its broad sense," "in determination of judgments and/or propositions in the way of valuations or appraisals." Some

[20] The grounds for this conclusion are given briefly in VV, pp. 215–225; "The Identity of Fact and Value," *Philosophy of Science,* X (1943), 124–130; "Three Relations of Facts and Values," *The Philosophical Review,* LII (1943), 499–504; and "Fact, Value, and Meaning," *The Philosophical Review,* LIV (1945), 115–131, especially 123n. This matter is considered further in the study referred to in the "Foreword" of VV.

Parker very strongly disagrees with my conclusion on this point. See his review of VV, in *The Philosophical Review,* LIV (1945), 78–83; and pp. 239–241 of this book. The general lines of the reply I should make to his objections are indicated in "Mr. Parker's Criticisms of *Verifiability of Value,*" *The Philosophical Review,* LV (1946), 282–288. See also pp. 382–388, below.

[21] For illustrations of these differences see pp. 176–177, above.

serious doubts persist, however, as to the applicability of the scientific method in value matters. These doubts are particularly persuasive and difficult to dispel when 'human values' are set over against 'physical facts,' and facts and values as subject matters and as adjustment processes, judgments, propositions, and so forth, are viewed in this contrast relationship.

For one thing, it may be held that scientific method, in the strict sense of the word, is characterized not only "by the four steps of observation, hypothesis, deductive prediction and verification," but also by the assumption that "the admissible data must be 'public,' that is, directly accessible to more than one observer," whereas in value experiences the subject matters and adjustment processes are essentially subjective, or private.[22] For example, in chemical reactions or in phenomena of heredity the events are public in the sense that they are 'out there' and can be studied repeatedly and checked upon by operations more or less observable, or otherwise performable, by different investigators; but events in which occur such verbalizations as "I like X," "X is good," or "X is better than Y" may appear peculiarly private, subject to direct observation only by personal 'introspection.' It may seem that such propositions are 'given' and 'tested' immediately and by operations open only to the subject himself and are therefore not amenable to scientific treatment.

In stressing this contrast it is easy, however, to work oneself into

[22] The quotations are from the preliminary questions and comments submitted by Rice, and the sentence as a whole indicates the interpretation which I at first made of his point of view; but in a later communication he says, regarding the last clause of the sentence, that it "does not quite represent my view. I would treat 'value experiences' as behavioral or transactional, and would not limit 'experience' to the private aspects of the transaction, or to the perspective on the transaction that is obtainable by introspection. Nor would I say that even intrinsic values are 'essentially subjective, or private,' if this implies that they cannot be got at to some extent by external observation. The 'adjustment processes' in particular are largely open to public observation, though these too may have their private aspects. All that I intended to say was that observations of the private aspects must be admitted along with the public data. This is particularly true in the present stage of our scientific development: if the electroencephalograph is developed to the point where it can give us accurate reports on data that are now accessible only to introspection, I would say that such data will no longer be private to the degree that they are now, though I imagine we will wish to check the objective results of the electroencephalograph by comparing them with reports of observers trained in introspection."

I am glad for this clarification and to know that Rice does not hold the view which I attributed to him. The view is, however, often espoused. See, for example, F. H. Knight, "Social Science and Social Action," *The International Journal of Ethics*, XLVI (1935–1936), 1–33.

a subjective, "mentalistic" point of view and lose sight of important continuities. We may forget that human value events *are* events which occur in and as total interactions and transactions, the various elements of which are interdependent and can, with proper care, be so utilized as to check on each other. "I like X," "X is good," "X is better than Y" may indeed report or 'express' qualitative experiences as had, but if a question arises as to whether I really *do* like X, and so forth, it is usually possible to repeat interactions with X, to shift contexts or perspectives, to bring into play competing likes and dislikes, to consider and test conditions and consequences.[23] Moreover, verbalizations are actual behaviors which other investigators may verify objectively by study of the behaviors of the person or group who makes them. Desires, interests, and satisfactions are actual events the conditions, occurrences, and consequences of which can be observed and studied objectively, or publicly; and because these events are of and with us they are *also* had, and can be viewed introspectively, or privately. Indeed, if we are not to fall into a distorted perspective we must remember that man and his behaviors are a part of the whole gamut of events all of which can be viewed objectively, but the experiencing of all of which—whether the experiencing be factual or valuative—is complexly mediated and in some measure private. Even the most public sensory facts require critical examination and appraisal in relation to one another and to conceptual systems before they may be accepted as real, or true, with some degree of probability. Nor should it be forgotten that when "scientific facts" and perceptions are selected for comparison with "human values" and "evaluations" the tendency is to choose the simplest and most 'public' facts and the most complex and private instances of value experience and valuation, but that actually events of all kinds, whether human or non-human, organic or inorganic, vary from the fairly simple, accessible, and controllable to the extremely complex, inaccessible, and uncontrollable. The subject matters of both factual and valuative judgments and propositions are public and private in the same sense, and both need to achieve, and can achieve, various degrees of experimentally evidenced objectivity.

In the second place, it may be urged that scientific method is not

[23] This is obvious when we remember that the judgments here given are formal and occur only in philosophical discourse. In 'real life' we like or dislike (and compare), not abstract symbols like "X" and "Y," but such realities as apples, automobiles, houses, people, paintings, actions, arrangements, goals, and policies.

applicable in resolving differences of *attitude* which persist no matter
how much factual agreement there is as to the nature and consequences
of any experienced or proposed value, and that our only resort in dealing with such differences is persuasion by means of emotive words
or signs.[24] This is of course not a rejection of scientific method, but an
insistence on its limitations. It is recognized that differences in attitude
often result from differences in factual knowledge; and when and to
the extent that this is so the differences may be removed or reduced
by increase of knowledge. But it is quite correctly insisted that in
some cases—or perhaps in all cases to some extent—attitudes result
from factors other than, or in addition to, differences in factual information.

Even constantly omniscient beings probably could and would differ
in likes-dislikes, aims, and means. If they could exist in separate realms
and chose to do so, their differences of attitude might present no
practical problems. But if they were to exist in such relations that
they affected one another, their differences of attitude—if the differences were on matters involved in their relations—would have to be
adjusted in some way: by coercion, by voluntary subordination, by
division of domain or function, or by some sort of 'compromise.' It is
difficult to see how one such being could be persuaded by another.
Emotive appeal would certainly be recognized and discounted *as such.*
Nor would there be any need for trying to draw attention to unknown
or neglected facts or to make some facts more attractive *as facts.* If
the adjustments were made by compromise, this would certainly flow
from mutual recognition of the need—as a condition for maximum
well-being and success—for accepting a unified and coordinated
program of endeavors. It would result, in short, from knowledge of
conditions and consequences—from recognition of the conditions that
exist and which must be utilized for maximum achievement of the
ends which are not mutually exclusive or which are not rejected in
view of their mutual long-run effects.

Of course we are not omniscient beings, nor do we often (if ever)
have *full* knowledge even in limited areas. Differences of attitude are,

---

[24] This view is forcefully expressed by C. L. Stevenson in his *Ethics and Language,*
New Haven, 1944. See also the second question raised in his review of VV, in *The
Journal of Philosophy,* XLI (1944), 385–388. For some considerations that are for
most part assumed in the present discussion see my "Stevenson's Questions on 'Verifiability of Value,'" *The Journal of Philosophy,* XLII (1945), 434–437.

consequently, in very large measure the result of differences of factual information. In any case, differences of attitude are perhaps mainly due to learnings, which, if they were constantly recognized (by parents, teachers, statesmen, and all others) in their full temporal and spacial conditions and effects, would be so directed as to avoid or reduce those differences of attitude which are not productive of continuing maximum attainment of ends, or interests. As it is, we often can be and need to be persuaded by descriptive presentation of facts, or by use of emotive words which help to arouse us from lethargies, complacencies, mistaken notions, narrow vision, lack of foresight. There is need for extensive and skillful use of emotive appeals, particularly for making knowledge which is already available more widely known and effective.

But increase and application of knowledge will not remove all individual differences in abilities, interests, and frames of reference. These will constitute irreducible and stubborn facts, and indeed their mutual existence may be a necessary condition for maximum creativity in all our human quests. They will continue to be a source of differences of attitude, so that often "X is good" is true (that is, a fact and a positive value) for one person and "X is bad" is true (a fact and a negative value) for another person at the same time; or both statements may be true (a fact, and either a positive or a negative value) for the same person at different times. Yet if we are sufficiently aware of the presence and character of such differences, we shall certainly not go on stubbornly insisting that one perspective is correct and another wrong. Instead, we shall recognize that for different persons and different frames of reference *some* facts and *some* values are actually different, though whether or to what extent this is so is always subject to inquiry. Nor is this recognition "true but trivial." For it can operate to redirect attitudes themselves—away from dogmatism and intolerance and towards mutual understanding and appreciation; and it can do this without reducing emphasis upon the need for persistent inquiry and critical judgment.

Despite the ominous dangers attending advances in science and technology, one of our chief requisites is still for more and better knowledge—'scientifically' established so far as possible—and especially, at the present time, for knowledge with respect to most effective and approvable ways of making knowledge operative throughout our shared human existence. But an equally urgent need is for 'good will' —for mutual willingness to recognize and respect differences of perspective and interest which may persist even in the light of continuous and genuine inquiry.

A final objection to the scientific method is that it is impracticable in dealing with personal and social problems. A more appropriate method, it may be held, is to bring desires, likes, dislikes, and so on, out into the open and let them react upon each other. Decisions thus reached are not, and cannot be, arrived at by strictly scientific procedures, but are 'compromises,' or resultants, which develop from the interplay of various dynamic factors: likes, aversions, needs, and interests. Political and other social goals and policies can seldom be determined by scientific inquiry alone; nor can those of individuals. There must be more or less continuous processes of expression and resolution of needs and interests.[25] The procedure must be more like that of a creative artist, say, a painter or a musical composer or director, than like that of a scientist.

We have already noted [26] the effects of 'value' subject matters and of the interests which enshroud and pervade value-judgments, as compared with the subject matters and the attitudes characteristic of factual judgments in the "contrast relation" of the factual and the valuative. As we have seen, it is not impossible to achieve considerable care and objectivity even in regard to goals and policies. But this third objection affords opportunity to emphasize an important point: Procedure in value matters can become increasingly experimental not only in the sense that questions of personal and social fact can be increasingly subjected to scientific inquiry, but also in the sense that needs, desires, interests, and so forth can be treated 'artistically' or creatively —that is, *studied experimentally in action,* much as is done by the creative artist. In matters of human goals, policies, arrangements, and acts, both facts and values are generated by ever new and changing conditions. What the possibilities are and which possibilities will win approval in view of their consequences can be determined only in part by scientific study of fact in the narrower, or 'stricter,' sense of "scientific"; there must also be creative and careful experimentation in which

[25] See, for instance, R. B. Raup, "Limitations of the Scientific Method," *Teachers College Record*, XXX (1928), 212–226; and E. T. Mitchell, "Dewey's Theory of Valuation," in *Essays on the Theory of Value and Valuation,* pp. 9–12.
[26] Pp. 178–179, above.

formulations are treated as hypotheses and studied critically in such continuing action and interaction as give maximum expression and consideration to different desires, feelings, and perspectives. In so far as such methodology is achieved it becomes at once artistic and scientific in the "broad sense" of these terms. Nor should it be forgotten that such traits of novelty and creativity in subject matter occur and such traits of procedure are needed, in various degrees, in matters of fact as well as in matters of value, along the *whole* gamut of events and relations.[27]

[27] For the Criticisms and Rejoinders which relate especially to this paper see pp. 296–301, 334–339, and 345–348, below.

❧ VALUES, VALUING, AND
❧ EVALUATION

E. T. MITCHELL

DEWEY'S SECOND GROUP OF QUESTIONS are those concerned with the function of valuing and evaluation, the conditions under which they take place, the relation between valuing and evaluating, and the relation between each of these processes to prior values and to emerging values. It is on this group of questions that I wish to concentrate my discussion, relegating to footnotes any side lights I may be able to throw on other aspects of theory of value. Instead of making a frontal attack, I propose to approach the questions indirectly. While we seek to clarify terms, none of us is interested in merely verbal solutions. We are concerned with *theory* of value. It is legitimate, therefore, to present a general theory and then to test its adequacy by its success or failure in answering questions raised independent of this particular theory. It may, however, be necessary to reformulate some of the questions, because questions frequently contain unsuspected assumptions that prejudice the answer.

I

While the main branches of axiology—ethics, aesthetics, economics, and so forth—are as old as philosophy, theory of value as a single, basic science is of recent origin. Progress in clarification and discovery in this new field can hardly be expected by the logical instruments which kept the branches separate for so many centuries. We need a new tool of analysis which will combine them very much as Descartes's analytical technique combined the classical sciences of algebra, geometry, conic sections, and trigonometry.

The development of the logic of relations culminating in the *Principia Mathematica* provides a subtle and powerful instrument for dealing with the transitive and serial nature of value. The more recent studies by Carnap of equivalent language systems may help to resolve misunderstandings arising from different ways of expressing the same facts.[1] G. H. Mead's technique of behavioral analysis was very fruitful in his hands and should be brought to bear with all its power on the problems of the emergence of value qualities and the genesis of value-judgments. Finally, since all scientific and philosophic research eventuates in theory, the method of science as formulated in Dewey's "analysis of the complete act of thought" will be the ultimate tool.

II

The central value term, by common consent since the time of Plato, is *good*. While this term has been appropriated by ethics, we recognize that *beautiful, true, valid, holy, real,* and so forth, are either closely akin to the good or subsumed under it. Though *good* is the central value category it is not necessarily the most fundamental. The question of the logically "primitive" term is mainly one of system building. Thus Brogan defines good in terms of "better than" while Felix Cohen defines the latter in terms of the former. As far as a hierarchy of definitions is concerned, the question is one to be settled by the norms applied in laying down the foundations of a deductive system. For this purpose Brogan's choice of the relational term "better than" has conspicuous advantages. The proposition "*A is good*" is defined thus: "*The existence of A is better than the non-existence of A.*" The definitions of *A is worse than B, A is equal (in value) to B, A is bad, A is indifferent,* and so forth, are readily framed. The transitivity of the relation "better than" is stated as a postulate, and thus the serial nature of value is provided for, and the concept of a scale of values readily follows. A structure of theorems, applying the logic of *Principia Mathematica,* introduces and demonstrates the main structure of the logic of values.

A logical analysis, and a deductive system based thereon, does not constitute a theory, unless the author claims that the definitions are appropriate and the postulates true. Brogan makes these claims and produces arguments and statistical evidence to support his claim. Thus, he argues that *better than* is not only the most appropriate primitive

[1] I doubt that any two systems using different hypotheses are reducible to differences of language. Not only do the data take on different meanings in the two systems but the rival hypotheses lead eventually to different lines of investigation and thus to different data. The two sets of propositions, it seems to me, in all the examples cited, are parallel but by no means equivalent. Nevertheless, it is illuminating and instructive to note how the same data are expressed and explained according to different theories.

value term but the fundamental value category.[2] Because he finds
that all value-judgments, even the proposition "A is good," are the
product of comparisons, he calls his theory "the comparative theory
of value." Because he finds that the relation *better than* is really fundamental he calls it a melioristic theory—in contrast to all perfectionist
and absolutistic theories whose fundamental category is "ought." Because he finds no all-inclusive good, but rather innumerable distinguishable goods and bads, he calls it a pluralistic theory. And because he
maintains that it is validated by objective evidence he calls it an empirical theory. Since Brogan's theory of value together with his logic of
value-judgments are well known through his own writings, I give the
above summary merely to indicate the starting point which I adopt as
hypothesis in attempting to answer Dewey's questions.

From the above point of view the question as to whether "good"
is an attribute or a substance would sound medieval. Its Aristotelian
origin is barely camouflaged by posing it in the form, "Is value adjectival in nature or substantive?" In a comparative theory of value the
question is answered by denying the relevance of the substance-attribute metaphysics or the importance of the grammatical distinction between nouns and adjectives. In propositions in the form, "A is better
than B," the terms may be anything that a person can discriminate—
objects, activities, events, qualities, characteristics, or relations. The
common name for all terms that enter into relations of *better, worse,*
or *equal* is "values," just as the common name for all terms related by
greater, less, or *equal* is "magnitudes." [3]

Under what conditions do objects, activities, and so on, enter into
relations of better and worse? This question is irrelevant to the logic

[2] A. P. Brogan, "Urban's Axiological System," *The Journal of Philosophy,* XVIII
(1921), 197–209.
[3] The point will be obvious from an analogy. In the early stages of theory of number,
numbers were classified as square, rectangular, triangular, etc. Squareness was regarded as a *property* of certain numbers like 9, 169, etc. Up to a certain point this
way of conceiving of squareness was useful and undoubtedly correct, but in time
it became an obstacle to further progress. When the proposition, *a is the square of b,*
came to be regarded as a mathematical function, it was seen that every number was
the square of some number, and also the square root of some number. Squareness
was no longer conceived as a property of certain numbers. Squares are the left-hand
members and square roots are the right-hand members which satisfy the function
a is the square of b. The older view, based on a subject-predicate logic, was not
incorrect; it was just not very adequate. The functional view, based on a relational
logic, was not truer; it was, however, more comprehensive and more adequate.

of value [4] (that is, to formal logic), but *is* important to a comparative theory of value. It is at this point that Mead's behavioral analysis—unfortunately very sketchy, but fortunately very suggestive—can be brought to bear.

III

No doubt all valuing is conditioned by organic and physiological processes far below the level of conscious choice. Medical men use the phrase "the wisdom of the body" to denote the uncanny selectivity by which the almost infinite number of cells composing the animal body are kept in a state of functional adjustment. To crave exactly the right food to restore deficiencies in minerals, salts, or vitamins, to prefer the most advantageous temperature and intensity of light, to find satisfaction in mating and nursing the young—these and many other cases of want, preference, and satisfaction are usually so precisely adapted to the welfare of the animal organism that the creature appears to be endowed with powers of scientific valuation.

We sometimes call the state or the church an organism; but compared with the human body with its trillions of cells even the Soviet Union with its 200 million people is ridiculously simple. And when we compare the fumbling attempts of any state to make up its mind as to what it wants, to maintain a working internal economy, and to adjust itself to the realities of this earth—when we compare these fumbling attempts with the precision of an animal in its wants, its internal cooperation, and its adjustments to environment, we hardly know whether to marvel more at the wisdom of the body or the stupidity of human corporations.

Undoubtedly all valuing and evaluation are traceable to this biological selectivity. Stripping the words of aesthetic connotations, valuing has its basis in the suitable and the fitting. To prefer the unsuitable,

[4] P. B. Rice in his very suggestive article "Towards a Syntax of Valuation," *The Journal of Philosophy*, XLI (1944), 309–320, states the elementary judgments of value in forms like the following: x *is intrinsically valuable to A at time* $t = x$ *is enjoyed by A at t*. But he points out that such a set of elementary propositions contains so many "primitive terms" and so many terms taken from psychology and other sciences, that it would be impossible to base a formal system on this foundation. I suggest that times, persons, circumstances, and mental states are as irrelevant to the *logic* of value as they are to the logic of arithmetic. It would be impossible to list *all* the conditions of the simplest value-judgment.

or that which does not fit the structure and processes of the organism, would be to court premature extinction. There are definite limits to what humankind can prefer in the way of food, drink, temperature, and sunlight. The internal environment admits of very slight tolerance —a fraction of one per cent in the salt concentration of the fluid that bathes the cells, a very few degrees in the temperature of the blood. There are similarly narrow limits to man's choices in the way of light, sound, bodily exercise, physical shock, and so on. What a person likes, prefers, and prizes, if he is to make a suitable adjustment between internal and external environment, falls within the suitable and the fitting. Use and custom cannot alter these fundamental biological limitations. Valuing is definitely conditioned.

The question as to the point at which values emerge is answered by Mead by a behavioral account of a simple appetition. An act is a single process but may be divided into three phases: the want, the means, and the end. Mead chooses hunger as a typical case of organic want. In the complex animal organism a system of cells has evolved the special function of nourishing the body. When this nutritive system lacks some material to convert into nutriment for the non-nutritive cells, these other cells are stimulated to activity. The sensory system is specialized to select from the environment those features that are of advantage or disadvantage to the organism, and the muscular system connected with the sense organs overcomes the distance between the organism and the food object. This phase of the act constitutes the *means*. Grasping and ingesting the food is the *end*, the satisfaction of the hunger and the restoration of the internal balance.[5]

These three phases of the act are devoid of value unless the organism is an object to itself. The want (or deficiency) is a *felt* want, the means are interesting, and the satisfaction is enjoyable only if the organism can divide attention between the food object being pursued or eaten and the condition of the body. The simplest case of such divided attention would require that the organism be able to touch itself—and this would require a nervous system. Another way of stating the condition for the emergence of value is to say that the organism must be part of its own environment.[6] And since, according to Mead's analysis, consciousness

[5] G. H. Mead, *Philosophy of the Act*, ed. by C. W. Morris, Chicago, 1938, pp. 305, 452.

[6] *Ibid.*, *Philosophy of the Present*, ed. by A. E. Murphy, Chicago, 1932.

has the same prerequisite, it would follow that consciousness and value emerge together.[7]

IV

The three phases of a conscious act—the feeling of want, the interest in the means, and the enjoyment of the consummation each has its value. In general the want is bad; it is felt as discomfort, dissatisfaction, or pain; its elimination is better than its existence. The means are perceived as good in varying degrees; they are experienced as pleasurable excitement, a feeling of mastery, or the joy of accomplishment. The absence of any means, or the inadequacy of available means would create a new want and thus be bad. The most commonly prized and cared for objects are the tools and instruments that have proved exceptionally excellent as means. The satisfaction of the consummation is experienced as enjoyment and perceived as good. The consummation would be bad if it were worse than no consummation; if the meal, for example, were worse than no meal at all.

If want, means, and satisfaction flowed together as one reflex act—as they have a tendency to do in cases of habit or routine—they would have no "value-quality" and would not furnish occasion for comparison or valuing. If, again, experience provided no variety there would be no valuing. Thus, so long as we live in an atmosphere of clear and abundant air we feel no want of air, no interest in the act of breathing, and no enjoyment in inhaling. It is only when we experience dust storms or smoke, or have difficulty in breathing because of illness or injury, that we feel the want of air, take an interest in the action of our lungs, and enjoy pure air. Facts like these, so often observed as to be proverbial, lend evidence for the comparative theory of value.

It will be noted that in the simple act we have been describing all the values are direct. No mention is made of instrumental or potential values. The want has its own perceived value of pain or discomfort; the

[7] The above conclusions appear to me to answer satisfactorily Dewey's suggestion (footnote, p. 8, above) that the emergence of "value-quality" is continuous not only with organic processes that maintain life and growth but with physical-chemical interactions that maintain the stability of certain complex molecular and atomic units. The emergence of "value-quality" is continuous with such phenomena in some respects but discontinuous in others, and certainly not identical with them. Two facts about value distinguish it from the inorganic and from elementary organic forms: (1) The value-object is defined in terms of the organism; it is an example of biological relativity. (2) Value emerges along with conscious behavior; it is an emergent at a late stage of evolution.

means has its direct value of interest or pleasurable excitement, the end has its intrinsic value of enjoyment or satisfaction. While such values are private in that they are relative to the organism, they are public in that they exist relative to any similar organism, and are readily communicated and understood by signs and speech. The ontological status of values is well stated by Mead:

They are not perceptual things in the sense of being there as material things, whose reality we can identify by getting our hands upon them. This reality can abide while the values vanish. . . . In terms of these values we can analyze the act. The want as expressed in hunger, the interest that attaches to the means of securing food, and the satisfaction of the food itself are three phases of the act of eating.[8]

I am trying to describe a simple act in which there is valuing but no evaluation. One may compare his present state of want with the remembered condition prior to the want or with the anticipated state after the want is satisfied, thus judging it to be good or bad. Or he might compare the present want with a previous one, judging it to be better or worse. Or he might compare two wants existing simultaneously (for example, his hunger and his sleepiness) judging one to be worse than the other. Such judgments would be perceptual judgments like: The object in my right hand is heavier than the object in my left.

Similarly we might compare the interest in the present means with that of a previous experience. Thus a hunter might rank the present deer hunting as better than last winter's pursuit of rabbits for food, or a worker might rank his present job as better than his former one. Here again the comparison issues in a simple perceptual judgment of better or worse.

The goodness of the end may also be compared with that of previous consummations or of anticipations. Generally consummatory value is experienced as enjoyment or as quiet satisfaction. I do not think, however, that the judgment "A is better than B" is strictly equivalent to any of the following propositions: "A is more enjoyable than B," "A is more

[8] *Philosophy of the Act,* p. 452; by permission of The University of Chicago Press, publishers. This statement agrees with Parker's view that there is nothing particularly "mentalistic" about wanting, liking, preferring, enjoying, and so forth. Mead has no hesitation in using such terms as behavioral categories. They are as much part of a conscious act as are the movements of the limbs. Mead analyzes the physiological conditions of interest, enjoyment, and so forth, but does not make the mistake of "reducing" these emergent phases to the conditions of their appearance.

satisfying than B," "A is more interesting than B." At this level of valuing we compare things or activities like meals, wines, symphonies, games; we are not comparing pleasures. Pleasure, enjoyment, satisfaction, excitement, and interest are our ways of experiencing these objects or activities. I would agree with Paulsen's statement that "Pleasure is not the good; it is our way of experiencing the good." [9] Nevertheless, having had pleasurable, interesting, or exciting activities and consummations, we can desire pleasure, interest, or excitement regardless of the conditions. To set up such states of feeling as ends in themselves presupposes a high (perhaps an abnormal) degree of introspection and sophistication.

To rely wholly on direct perceptual judgments of value would be placing too much confidence on "the wisdom of the body." Even in the matter of eating and drinking, where taste is on the whole reliable, it is necessary to supplement untutored preferences by scientific tests. We cannot be confident that what we like is the suitable and the fitting. Moreover we cannot be sure to what extent our perceptual judgments are colored by use and custom.

The unreliability of sense perception was taken as condemnation of "empiricism" till Bacon and modern scientists showed how observation properly checked and controlled could provide both the foundation and the test of reliable knowledge. Critics of the direct perception of value point out the wide variation of judgments of goodness and beauty among different peoples and even among different individuals of the same culture, and they use this variation either as an argument against the truth or falsity of any statement employing value terms, or in favor of some rationalistic or authoritarian standard of value. It is my contention that ordinary, common sense experience of value is the starting point and ultimate test of the more elaborate evaluations of ethics, aesthetics, and economics. Without this sharable, communicable experience there could be no knowledge of good and evil, no literary or art criticism, and no social science.

The fact that values are relative to the type of organism, that certain values are relative to the cultural level of society, that other values are relative to the individuality of the person who judges does not prove the case of the amoralist, the subjectivist or the logical positivist. It

[9] My main objection to all affective theories of value is that they cannot be generalized to include truth value, validity value, reality value, and so forth. This point is discussed more fully in Section VI, pp. 201–206, below.

proves, on the contrary, that there is a science of relativity in the field of value.

The fact that taste and preference are unreliable guides to value does not prove that direct valuing is illusory. It proves that direct valuing requires checking and testing by repeated trials, by the consistency of observation by numbers of experienced witnesses, and by indirect techniques of analysis and trial.

V

As distinguished from valuing in which experiential facts are compared directly, the process of evaluation (or appraisal or estimation) is one of indirect comparison. Experiential fact complexes, whether actual or imagined, frequently involve too many factors for direct, immediate comparison. The evaluator must be a judge analyzing, sifting, weighing, and summarizing. The final decision in the form "A is good" or "A is better than B" or (in case of moral choice) "A is right," is a summary judgment.

As the term suggests, indirect valuing requires a middle term or series of terms—some norm, criterion, or more ultimate end with reference to which the values can be summed up, or some process of synthesis by which analytic value factors can be formed into organic wholes. Generally judges use one or more of four techniques, which I shall designate crudely as the yardstick, the score card, the ideal, and the hypothesis.

1. By the yardstick technique I mean measuring by any quantitative unit, a method possible only when there is a known relationship between quantity and quality. Thus, in judging wheat the weight, size, hardness, and color of the kernel are indices of quality, and therefore of the value as food. In judging its value as seed, and hence its value in terms of satisfaction to wheat-growers, a germination test is added and recorded in percentages. In general, the correlation between quantitative measure and quality in experience is so high that quantitative data provide a most useful indirect measure of comparative value—an example of the relation between value-fact and other facts.

2. The score-card technique is used when there are numerous value factors in the objects to be compared. One of the entries may be superior in some respects but inferior in others, and therefore the factors are weighted and the separate ratings summed up. Thus, in judging

live stock the score card may have forty or more items. The end is assumed; that is, the animal is for beef or for milk production, or for some other assumed purpose. The rating scale could be based on an imaginary perfect specimen, but again it may be based on actually existing superior examples. In either case, the score card must be constructed empirically so that it corresponds to what has been found satisfactory in experience. It is used almost always in judging comparative worth; that is, in ranking entries rather than for determining absolute worth.

Only a novice uses the score card slavishly, but even an expert judge uses one in order to insure against overlooking relevant factors or giving undue weight to particular items. A slavish use of the score card would neglect the way in which combinations of factors enter into the whole. This feature of evaluation is treated by G. E. Moore under the concept of organic wholes. The summing up is not simply a matter of adding up scores, but of using the analysis to produce a general impression of better or worse.

3. The ideal, an imaginary construct in which whatever is wrong with things as they exist is corrected, may serve as a standard of comparison for existing factual complexes or for proposed objectives. It specifies the conditions under which the wants or desires would be fulfilled, and can therefore serve as a norm for any partial fulfillment. From the ideal one can also deduce the means for bridging the gap between available resources and the ideal solution. Thus it serves as an indirect technique for comparing the value of alternative plans or policies. While it has been the practice to set up ideals of perfection, there are objections both logical and psychological to this procedure. It is methodologically superior to frame the ideal with reference to the particular problem and with due regard to the realities in the matter of resources. The ideal is imaginary but it need not be fanciful.

The practical function of this use of imagination is exhibited in multitudes of examples from everyday life. When we have or anticipate several simultaneous wants, there are two alternatives open to us. We can rank them, give one priority, and suppress the others. The other alternative is to create an ideal solution in which all the wants find fulfillment. Necessarily the first crude, imperious wants will have to be modified, idealized, and socialized in order to harmonize and enhance each other; but they may thus find a better fulfillment than

they would if each was satisfied separately. Thus we may be hungry
and thirsty and lonely and tired; we may crave bright lights and music
and beautiful surroundings; we may feel the need of stimulating conversation and of appreciative listeners. Incompatible though these
wants may appear, the ideal dinner furnishes a satisfactory fulfillment
of all of them. Similarly the ideal of love and home satisfies a variety
of wants while transforming and refining them.

The ideal presupposes prior values. We must know the value of
food, conversation, and so forth, before we can envisage the ideal
dinner. But the formation of an ideal is a process of revaluing these
factors as elements in a more complex experiential whole. We cannot
evaluate the ideal by means of a yardstick or a score card because the
end is not assumed. The ideal is a product of creative imagination or
of artistry; it is a new end embodying old values in a new combination
that modifies, orders, and relates them. The value of the ideal as an
organic whole is not fully appreciated till it is experienced.

The formation of an ideal, viewed as a process of revaluing old
wants and satisfactions, issues in the transformation of old values and
the creation of new ones. The ideal, viewed as a norm for judging
means and partial fulfillments, is a technique of indirect valuing or
of evaluation.

4. If an hypothesis stands the test it is proclaimed to be *true;* if an
ideal stands the test it is proclaimed to be *good.* The hypothesis has
its usefulness in the progress of knowledge, the ideal in the attainment
of the good life. In so far as these ends are related, the hypothesis and
the ideal are related.

Yet there is a way in which hypotheses are used in general evaluation. In proposing policies, programs, five-year plans, and the like, we
seek to achieve the fulfillment of present desires. But we know (or
should know) that the changes proposed will have indirect consequences that are difficult to foresee. They will give rise to new wants
undreamed of by the reformers, and hence to new satisfactions or
dissatisfactions. Our only method of evaluating policies is through
discussion, and the only value of discussion is to bring to bear on moot
questions as much of human experience and technical knowledge as
possible. The debate boils down to rival hypotheses as to the indirect
consequences of the proposed program. The widely diverging views

of Winston Churchill and the Labor Government as to the consequences of the program of the nationalization of certain institutions is a spectacular case in point. The general method of evaluation is to trace the consequences of the proposed policy and compare these with alternative policies. But the truth as to what the consequences will be is quite hypothetical. One hypothesis or the other must be accepted, but like all hypotheses it should be accepted tentatively subject to revision as the actual consequences substantiate or invalidate the predictions.

If we define *right choice* as the best alternative in view of the probable consequences as judged by available information, it would follow that evaluation of alternatives is mediated by the agent's anticipations as to what the consequences will be. But there can be no such rigid deduction of consequences as is possible in the case of physical hypotheses. In so far as the problem situation is similar to others recorded in history and biography, the agent knows the general trend of various alternatives. In so far as he has scientific data on the consequences he has reliable grounds for prediction. But in so far as the circumstances are unique and particular his anticipations are highly conjectural. Nevertheless it is on the basis of such anticipations that he elaborates the alternatives, analyzes the values they embody, compares them, and makes his choice.

VI

One test of a theory of value is its generality. Wherever there is a question of acceptance or rejection, there is a question of better or worse, and wherever there is a question of better or worse there is a question of value. I do not see how anyone can doubt this statement. But if we agree that any situation involving acceptance or rejection is a value situation, we must also agree that questions of truth, validity, and reality are questions of value.

When we weigh beliefs or opinions against alternative options, we are estimating their value—their trustworthiness, reasonableness, and so on. In scientific procedure, we weigh rival hypotheses as to adequacy, suggestiveness, and the like, accepting one as better. The general value term in the field of knowledge is "truth," ranging from ideal trustworthiness or certainty, down to zero value or absolute error.

When we weigh arguments or demonstrations we are estimating

their value in terms of strength, solidity, cogency, and so forth. The general term for ideal strength is "validity," but actual arguments range all the way from strong to worthless.

Questions of reality also involve acceptance or rejection. The very word "real" is an honorific term related to "royal." The real is the reliable, the dependable, and so on. Different periods have interpreted reality in a variety of ways, but always the real has been the good in respect to objective status, and the more or less real has been the better or worse.

If it is agreed that true, valid, and real are value terms, it will have to be admitted that affective theories of value are not general theories. None of those who maintain that the only good is pleasure, or satisfaction, or any other feeling, think that truth, validity, or reality are states of feeling or states of mind.

Similar lack of generality belongs to desire and interest theories. Thus R. B. Perry maintains that an object is good if it is an object of any interest; but he does not hold the interest theory of truth or reality. That is, he does not hold that a proposition is true if it is the object of an interest. Bosanquet maintained that it is the nature of the good to satisfy desire; but he ridiculed James's satisfaction theory of truth. Either, then, the satisfaction and interest theories of value are not general or truth and reality are not value categories. The latter alternative runs counter to common usage. We certainly speak of some arguments as worthless, some beliefs as untenable (that is, unacceptable or ineligible or worthy of rejection), and some objects as apparent or illusory (that is, unreliable, unworthy of acceptance).

The question, then, is whether a comparative theory of value as elaborated by a behavorial, relativistic approach can be a general theory of value. Professor Brogan, in his Presidential Address before the Western Division [10] indicated the general lines by which his comparative or melioristic theory could be extended to all fields of value. The main obstacle to such an extension lies in the two-value systems of logic, epistemology, and metaphysics. The comparative theory is essentially pluralistic, being committed to the serial, transitive nature of the relation of betterness. Two values, like true and false, valid and invalid, being and non-being (or real and apparent) hardly constitute

[10] "Philosophy and the Problem of Value," *The Philosophical Review*, XLII (1933) 105–129.

a series. But it would be in line with modern science and logic to abandon these opposites, except as ideal limits, and to substitute the technique of ranking hypotheses, arguments, and perspectives in the relation of better or worse. Since the task of generalizing the comparative theory of value was undertaken by Brogan, I shall do no more than indicate the lines on which the project must proceed. I am quite convinced, however, of the possibility of developing a thoroughly general relational, melioristic theory as an alternative to all two-value systems and all absolute or transfinite systems.

The next question is, can Mead's relativistic and behavioral approach be generalized? If it can, it will furnish a thoroughly post-Darwinian and post-Einsteinian perspective. Above all it would rid us completely of the Cartesian mind-body dualism and its partner, psychophysical parallelism. In doing so it would not fall into either a one-sided materialism or an equally lopsided spiritual monism. It would free us completely of substance metaphysics.

The survival of the mind-body dualism is nowhere so much in evidence as in theory of value. The consequence is that it deprives all nature and art and industry of value (except instrumental value or usefulness) either driving it into the recesses of the mind or driving it out of this world altogether into a subsistential realm. The case is not improved when one of the two substances is retained and the other dropped. For materialism, value either becomes an unreal epiphenomenon or is "reduced" to its physical conditions. For idealism, its reality depends on an absolute world consciousness. Even radical empiricism, dropping both substances, does not place values where they belong in nature and art, but either explains them away altogether or bases them on the "sensation" of pleasure.

Obviously, if value is not located in the world with which scientists deal, it is no concern of "natural philosophy," and it is no concern of economics or political science. The result is that the determination of values has been left to professional moralists, aestheticists, and clergymen, while scientists, industrialists, businessmen, and technicians have rigorously excluded value from their calculations. The resulting impasse is equally disastrous to both classes.

The behavioral, relativistic approach to the problems of value does not have the problem of extending a theory of the good to the spheres of the true and the beautiful. It does not begin with any such artificial

division. Aristotle's classification of sciences and ways of life into the
theoretical (whose aim is truth), the creative (whose aim is beauty),
and the practical (whose aim is the good) leads us astray, being altogether too simple to comprehend the vast variety of values and too
clean-cut to be close to reality. We must begin far back of Aristotle's
stratified society to trace the emergence of value. We then see that
the social process is a single evolution characterized at once by continuity and emergence.

We see, as Mead puts it that "The emergent life changes the character of the world just as emergent velocities change the character of
masses." [11] Among the changes that take place is the emergence of
value objects and value qualities.

Good, and related values, as applied to objects and qualities, are,
as explained earlier, relative to wants, means, and satisfactions. From
the standpoint of relativity the value, like the color or texture, attaches
to the object, while the feeling of want or interest or pleasure belongs
to the subject. There is no mystery about how an object, without under-
going chemical change, can acquire or lose value. The value of coal
as a resource is relative to our domestic and industrial needs, but the
value is not in our minds, any more than the feeling of need or satisfaction is in the coal.

Beauty has always and rightly been closely associated with the good.
As I understand behaviorism it makes no attempt to explain aesthetic
appreciation in terms of motor responses. It is not interested in reducing either morals or aesthetics to physiology. Behaviorism is concerned
with tracing the emergence of beauty and related values, with showing the significance of artistic creation as a part of social and technical
progress, and analyzing the act of aesthetic appreciation.

There is little doubt that aesthetic values have their origin in creative
activities. The art object, as is true of all emergents, belongs to two
levels. As a tool or weapon, for example, it served merely as a means
an extension of the human body; but as something delighting hand
and eye by its form and finish it had aesthetic value. Similarly the ceremonial dance or religious drama served a useful function while at the
same time ministering to the enjoyment of the senses and imagination
Even where aesthetic creation and appreciation leave the level of crud

[11] *Philosophy of the Present,* p. 65; reprinted by permission of The University
Chicago Press, publishers.

use, it remains and must remain part of the technological and scientific process. The artistic genius does not disdain techniques and social significance; he takes from its narrow setting what has only special use and significance and universalizes it. The history of Greek drama or modern music furnish examples of process of broadening and enriching of religious and folk themes. Even if "the aesthetic moment," as Hegel called it, is characterized by disinterestedness and distance, by absorption and suspended activity, it falls within, and has significance for, the whole life of action. A behavioral account would seek an explanation for this "moment."

Truth, trustworthiness, reasonableness, and related values apply to conceptual structures like judgments and systems of ideas. Whenever action requires more than insight into the pattern of observable surroundings the intelligent person organizes his field of action, both spatial and temporal, by means of symbols. He brings past experience to bear by means of concepts and envisages what is taking place beyond or below perception by means of hypotheses. The general functioning of the mental processes is the same whether in a naval action or in the bombardment of the nucleus of an atom. Both require hypothetical entities to fill in the pattern and to control the response. Truth and the like are the values attached to such conceptual structures. As Mead says:

Knowledge is the process in conduct that so organizes the field of action that delayed and inhibited responses may take place. The test of the success of the process, that is, the test of truth, is found in the discovery or construction of such objects as will mediate our conflicting and checked activities and allow conduct to proceed.[12]

As in the case of beauty, the behavioral project does not consist in explaining mental phenomena in terms of motor responses. Obviously, long chains of mental processes take place by means of symbols. But motor manipulation was essential to the learning and to the final testing. The behavioral project, as I understand it, consists in defining and determining the conditions of conscious behavior, intelligent behavior, rational behavior, and so forth, in terms of the life process rather than in terms of mind or reason.

Reality, as a value, may be considered as a character of particular objects or of broad perspectives. In matters of techniques and science

Ibid., p. 68.

Mead agrees with Berkeley that the manipulatory experience is in a special way the test of reality; it confirms or disproves perception at a distance or imaginative hypotheses. The real is that which the rest of nature, and especially contact experience, supports.

Mead was dubious about the possibility of bringing the whole world within a single perspective. Reality is relative to fields of action within which it is important to distinguish the dependable from the illusory and the fanciful. Metaphysics also has the function of discovering and illuminating the significance of the common things around us instead of relegating value to some distant or supersensible realm, and for this purpose breadth of perspective is necessary. Since fields of action and special perspectives overlap, it is possible for each to take the standpoint of those engaged in other occupations and other fields of science and thus socialize both ourselves and the world community. The real, as the peculiarly metaphysical value, is the character of our most comprehensive organization of the human field of action.

The comparative theory of value as developed by Brogan stands incomplete without an account of the genesis, functioning, and testing of value-judgments. It admits of completion along any one of a number of diverse lines. It is my experience that the behavioral approach with the concepts of emergence and relativity offers the best background for the melioristic theory.

VII

Terminology.—From a melioristic point of view *value* (or *valuity*, if such a word were allowed on the analogy of *causality*) denotes the relation of betterness.

Values (or value-objects) are the objects, activities, qualities, and so on, between which there are relations of better, worse, or equality. In logic, values (or value terms) are the "arguments" or "values" (in the mathematical sense) of a and b in propositional functions in the form: *a is better than b* (or other forms defined in terms of this relation like *a is worse than b, a is good,* and so forth).

Valuing, in the sense of assigning value, is the process of direct comparison in experience.

Evaluation, in a similar sense, is the more elaborate process of indirect comparison.

Value-Objects, Value-Facts, and Value-Propositions.—Value-objec (or values) belong to the general class of natural objects; that is, they do not exist *in* the mind. They are not mechanical objects; that is, they are not defined or determined by other objects. But they are defined in terms of teleological organisms; that is, they are determined by the processes of the organism as extensions of these processes. Value-objects belong to the same general class as food, shelter, resources, enemies, children, possessions, and so forth. Thus a rock, defined geologically, is not a value-object, but it becomes a value-object if it is a rock-shelter or a rock-obstacle or a rock-building block. We might call such objects "teleological objects," meaning that they are objects relative to a teleological organism. I think any teleological object is implicitly a value-object, but we might define a value-object more precisely as a natural, teleological object determined by the wants, interests, or satisfactions of a conscious act.

It follows that value-objects are part of the environment of any organism for which its own processes are part of its environment. In more common, but less precise language, a value-object is a natural feature of the environment of an organism which is conscious of its own wants, interests (means) and satisfactions. In this statement I am following Mead; but Brogan has the same general idea.

So it may be suggested that the better relation does not hold between the objects contemplated [that is, as physical objects], and it does not hold between feelings alone [that is, between wants, interests, and enjoyments], but it holds between the actual complex totalities of my experiencing in certain ways those specific landscapes.[13]

Value-facts are facts about value-objects. Since a value-object is a physical object (or a physical quality, etc.) before it is a value-object, it follows that value-facts are intimately related to other facts. An obvious case is the conversion of valuable homes into rubble by a hurricane or fire. It follows, also, that the control of value-objects or values lies in the control of either the physical environment or the organism or both. Industry is essentially the process of converting physical objects into value-objects; that is, the approach to value from the side

[13] A. P. Brogan, "The Implications of Meliorism Concerning the Relation Between Value and Existence," in *Proceedings of the Sixth International Congress of Philosphy*, New York, 1927, p. 310; reprinted by permission of Longmans, Green and Company, publishers. I think Brogan's statement would be more correct if he had said that the relation of betterness does not hold between physical objects, but between those objects as related to, and defined by, organisms having wants, etc.

of non-value facts. Psychology, practical ethics, and religion include approaches to betterment through control of the organism. Abnormal psychology is mainly the study of the disharmony and isolation of reason, emotion, and the physical or social realities of the external world. The problem of psychiatry is to restore adjustment; that is, to restore realistic evaluation.

Value-propositions, it follows, are in no way different, *as propositions*, from other propositions. Like other propositions they are testable by (1) time (that is, by consistency of judgment or repeated trials); (2) by numbers (that is, by consistency of judgment by disinterested observers); and, (3) by reason (that is, by consistency of judgment after analysis, elaboration, synthesis, and so forth). The fact that value-objects are relative to the needs, interests, and satisfactions of persons or other teleological organisms, introduces a variable feature in some value-propositions not encountered in propositions about physical objects. While the principle of physical relativity has familiarized us with the variability of physical measurements that depend on the velocity of the platform from which measurements are made, we have not become similarly familiar with the principle of biological relativity. The principle is simply this: The characteristics of environmental objects are determined by the act (wants, means, satisfactions) of the teleological organism. Once this principle is grasped we are prepared for differences in value-judgments depending on cultural level and individual differences. This variability has often been misinterpreted, and used as evidence of amoralism and, in general, for the theory that value-statements are not propositions at all, but merely conventional exclamations of indirect commands.

Value-propositions, because they *are* relative (and not just impulsive or emotional or capricious or spontaneous) can be discussed, investigated, and tested. When groups cannot agree, the investigation should perhaps be directed to the cultural differences that underlie the opposing ideals. Perhaps labor and management, America and Russia, could see eye to eye if the standards of living had more in common.

Prior Values, Valuation, and Emerging Values.—Biological selectivity and unreflective preference give a sort of unconscious ranking to features of the environment of every teleological organism. The close resemblance between the nervous system of human beings and that of other vertebrates, as well as their expressions o emotions, makes it evident that these animals feel wants, interests, and enjoyments. Thus, while they cannot express value-judgments, there is no question that to them certain objects and activities *are* better than others. Their ability to compare various value-objects is limited by shortness of memory, but I see no reason to doubt that some of their preferences are formed by trial and retrial of the two or more objects. Defining value in terms of betterness I have no doubt whatever that animals have values. Similarly I see no reason to doubt that children have values long before they can express value-judgments. There is also the fact that they grew up in a world of values; they are conditioned to rate some things as good and others as bad, and to rate some food or clothes or games as better than others before they actually value them for themselves.

My answer to Dewey's question is that all valuing or evaluating takes place against a background of prior values. Much of valuing, then, is revaluing or reranking old values or reorganizing old values in new organic wholes. The emergence of new values as a person matures is one reason for the reappraisal, but the subject is too complex for brief treatment.

Dewey also asks: Does evaluation result in new values? I think the answer depends on where the question mark appears. In the simplest problem of value the question mark is between the two terms, thus: *a ? b.* That is, Is *a better than b, equal in value to b, or worse than b?* In this case the values (or value-objects) are known but the relation is in doubt.

Generally, however, a problem of value is more complex than this. We could determine the relationship if we knew the value-objects fully. If both value-objects exist in the present, as in the case of two paintings, we may have to explore and analyze them more fully. If both stretch into the future, as in the case of alternative courses of action, we will have to project them in imagination. If both value-objects lie in the future, as in the case of two ideals, we shall have to connect them with present realities by plans of procedure in realizing them. These processes of exploration and elaboration will reveal heretofore unperceived features (in the case of two existing objects), and eventuate in modifications and new constructions (in the case of projects and ideals). Thus new value-objects (or values) are created in the process of evaluation.

Dewey's various discussions of the relation of means to ends, and the relation of both to desire are, from my point of view, quite sound. Desire, means, and ends are all modified in the process of evaluation; and consequently new values emerge.

Obviously, also, evaluation and the testing of value-judgments alter our habitual tastes and preferences. To know that our previous liking for an object or activity was uninformed, uncritical, or the product of bad examples, is to have a different attitude, or a new disposition to overt action. New attitudes result in new acts and eventually in new habits. Changes in behavior produce corresponding changes in emotion, and finally in tastes and preferences.

The most annoying argument in favor of the *status quo* is that other people's tastes and preferences suit them just as ours suit us, and therefore both ways of life are equally good. The underlying assumption is that tastes and preferences are ultimate bases of value and nothing can be done about it. One even hears people who are getting fatter and fatter bewail the fact that they like starches and sugar, as if their likes were unalterable natural causes. When people like the unfit and the unsuitable or when their values are dissociated from the realities of the external world, they probably need a doctor or psychiatrist to help them value the suitable and learn to like it.[14]

[14] For the Criticisms and Rejoinders which relate especially to this paper see pp. 339–345, 348–349, 355–360, and 362–365, below.

AXIOLOGY AS THE SCIENCE
OF PREFERENTIAL BEHAVIOR

CHARLES MORRIS

JOHN DEWEY's lifelong concern with the field of value is one of the
major influences which has brought us today to the frontier of a
scientific axiology. His work has helped to remove the terminological
and methodological barriers which have frustrated scientific work in
this field. The main problem which now arises for those who accept
his general orientation is to build the scientific axiology which he has
shown to be possible.

I

A science proceeds by selecting a subject matter for study, by developing a terminology to talk about this subject matter, and by formulating and verifying statements made in this terminology about the
subject matter chosen for investigation. In selecting a subject matter
for scientific study it is not necessary to define in advance the limits
of the field to be investigated. Physics was not preceded by an exact
definition of "physical process," nor mathematics by an exact definition
of "number"; indeed in these studies no definition of such terms is
found or is necessary. In the same way a scientific axiology, as a science
of valuation, need not begin, nor end, with a definition of "valuation."
It is sufficient for a number of researchers to agree upon certain material for study, leaving open the question whether they will later
extend or narrow the field chosen for the initial investigation.

It is proposed that a number of axiologists take as their task the
study of *preferential behavior,* that is, what Dewey has called caring-
for behavior or selection-rejection behavior. All organisms prefer certain things to other things in the sense of behaving so as to secure
certain things and avoid others, whether the "things" be inanimate
objects, signs, other organisms, or states and activities of themselves.
Among a variety of available edible objects an organism eats some
rather than others; a person looks at certain pictures or reads certain

novels rather than others; some persons are reacted to as friends and some as enemies; some states and activities of oneself are maintained, and others avoided. Few axiologists would refuse to accept such "transactions" as relevant to their study, and no more is needed than this initial agreement to begin a scientific axiology.

A scientific axiology will have as its task the development of a verified theory of preferential behavior. It will not merely describe what organisms prefer what things under what conditions, but through observation and experimentation attempt to formulate the underlying laws of such behavior. Axiology so conceived is a part of behavioristics, namely, that part concerned with preferential behavior.

Human behavior in general, and so preferential behavior in particular, is to a great extent sign-behavior, that is, behavior in which signs occur. Things which are sought or avoided are often not present but merely signified, and whether something is sought or avoided is often dependent on how it has been signified by oneself or by others. A behavioral axiology will therefore make extensive use of semiotic conceived as the science of sign-behavior. It must systematically study the ways in which preferential behavior influences the signs which an organism produces or encounters, and how the signs produced by an organism or other organisms influence preferential behavior itself. In *Signs, Language, and Behavior*,[1] an attempt was made to formulate the outlines of a behavioral semiotic relevant alike to the axiologist and the general student of behavior.

If now preferential behavior be called *valuing*, and the process of determining by signs what preferential behavior will be accorded to something be called *evaluation*, and if finally "*valuation*" be used as a term covering both valuing and evaluation, then a behavioral axiology, as a science of valuation, will be the scientific study of valuing and evaluation.

I believe that this analysis embodies the main features of Dewey's position. A number of special points in Dewey's view deserve further consideration before we make some suggestions as to how axiology, conceived as the science of preferential behavior, may be experimentally advanced. In the discussion of these particular problems we will center attention upon the article which Dewey has contributed in the present inquiry under the title of "The Field of 'Value.'"

[1] New York, 1946.

II

The first problem concerns Dewey's rejection of "introspection." The acceptance of a behavioral orientation for axiology does of course rule out any conception of knowledge gained by "introspection" not subject to control by other methods. But such an acceptance does not necessarily mean the rejection of self-observation as a method, for there is no reason why an organism cannot study its own preferential behavior (including the "feel" of such behavior), and its reports on such behavior be used both by itself and by others as data relevant for axiology. As Mead saw, the commitment to a behavioral approach does not as such involve the denial of a "private" aspect to behavior in the sense that certain aspects of behavior (and so of preferential behavior) are more accessible for direct observation to the behaving organism than to other organisms. Two persons cannot observe a chair in exactly the same respects because of their different spatial locations, and a given individual can more directly observe certain features of his behavior (but not all features) than can other organisms. Science does not require that all evidence as to the truth of statements be directly observable by all scientists.

The just criticism of self-observation lies in its unreliability, and consequently in its secondary role as a method. It is simply a fact that human beings are often notoriously wrong in their reports on what they prefer and why they prefer what they do prefer. But to admit this—and hardly anyone would now deny it—is to concede that there is some other method by which the reports of self-observation must be checked if such reports are to be used as data for science.

This means that the primitive terms of a scientific axiology must be so chosen that a number of observers can obtain evidence as to whether or not such terms apply to a given individual. Only then is it possible to check whether the terms an individual applies to himself do in fact denote him. Behavioral terms—such as "preferential behavior"—meet this criterion, and are therefore proper terms for the construction of a scientific axiology. Given such terms it is possible to determine the reliability of the reports of self-observation on preferential behavior by checking them with the reports of others on such behavior, and then to use such reports as admissible secondary evidence for statements about preferential behavior in cases where this check is difficult

or even impossible. Seen in these terms, Dewey's correct opposition
to reliance upon introspection in developing a scientific axiology does
not require a total rejection of self-observation or a general denial of
differences in the degree of accessibility of certain processes to direct
observation.[2]

The second point concerns Dewey's restriction of the "value field"
to only those cases of preferential behavior ("selection-rejection behavior") directed by "an anticipation or foresight of the outcome" of such
behavior. No question of fact is intended in doubting the wisdom of
this restriction. That preferential behavior is often influenced by signs
in which the outcome of a tendency to act is signified before the act
occurs is of course not in doubt, nor is it to be denied that complex
evaluations are an outgrowth of simpler cases of such sign-influenced
preferential behavior. But the restriction of the field of axiology to
preferential behavior consequent upon signifying the outcome of such
behavior seems unwise. For it is often difficult to know whether the
preferential behavior of animals or children or adults being studied
is a consequence of the occurrence of signs; it would be necessary to
furnish a criterion to determine whether this is or is not the case, if
a thoroughgoing behavioral axiology is not to fall back surreptitiously
on introspective criteria in the very process of delimiting the "field of
value." More important, since somewhere in any action involving signs
preferential status is in fact accorded to certain signified outcomes
without a consideration of the effect of such signified outcomes upon
still other signified outcomes, the consequence of Dewey's restriction
of the value field would be to break the continuity between the study
of preferential behavior dependent upon the occurrence of signified
outcomes and the study of preferential behavior which is not dependent
(in the given situation at least) upon the signifying of its outcome. It
seems wise, therefore, to include all preferential behavior within the
scope of a scientific axiology, and not merely preferential behavior
which is influenced by the occurrence of signs.

The previous discussion has already covered implicitly a third item:

[2] Since this methodological issue has been dealt with at some length in connection
with the similar problem encountered in the study of meaning, reference may be
made to the discussion of mentalistic and behavioral methods in the volume *Signs,
Language, and Behavior*. The methodological problem of the choice of primitive
terms for the study of preferential behavior is essentially similar to the problem of
the choice of primitive terms for the study of sign-behavior.

namely, while there is no general dichotomy of means and ends (but
rather, as Dewey insists, a means-end continuum), in any given situation, no matter how protracted the process of evaluation, there are,
or arise, valuings (preferential behaviors) not in fact evaluated, and
these define the ends in that situation with respect to which other
things and plans of action are means. With respect to these valuings
the organism seeks to find or create a situation of the sort to which
preferential behavior has been accorded as a result of reflection. The
fact that the selection of an end is often made in the light of the means
available for the attainment of various ends, or that ends may be modified in a given situation as they are acted upon, does not negate the
fact that at any given moment the distinction between means and
ends is legitimate. Dewey's own recognition of the situational character of evaluation would seem to require this conclusion.

It is also important to point out that while Dewey is correct in maintaining that there is no end which is exempt by its nature from evaluation in some situation or other, there are often relatively enduring
forms of preferential behavior which constitute unproblematic ends
in many diverse situations. Such highly stable preferential behavior
is in part cultural and in part rooted in the biological similarities and
differences of individuals which appear in every culture. Health may
in a given culture operate as such a relatively stable point of reference; and individuals of different physiques and temperaments bring
to various situations relatively permanent dispositions toward preferential behavior in terms of which specific objects and plans of action
make or fail to make an appeal. The domain of the value unproblematic, while still situational, thus often extends through a plurality of
particular situations. All preferential behavior may be evaluated and
changed to some extent in the process of evaluation, but there are
relatively stable preferences which serve as ends in many situations
and with reference to which plans of action in given situations are
selected as relatively variable means. The extent to which preferential
behavior is enduring and changeable, and the respective roles of
constitution and culture in determining preferential behavior, are
important problems for a scientific axiology, and their answers must
not be prejudiced in advance.

The fourth consideration involves the sharpening of a distinction
which Dewey has indicated in his statement that selection-rejection

processes (preferential behavior) serve to maintain the life processes of the organisms which make the selections and rejections. This fact requires a distinction between preferential behavior and need-reducing behavior. For, while in general an organism's selections and rejections do tend to be controlled by and to minister to its motivating drives, preferred objects may not in fact satisfy those drives, or at least not satisfy them as fully as would other objects. Organisms do tend to select those objects, and those modes of action upon objects, which satisfy their motivations more fully than do other objects and modes of action. This tendency follows from the laws of learning, since learning occurs only as a need is reduced. But this process of correcting preferences requires experimentation, flexibility, and time. Even in very adaptable organisms preferred objects or actions seldom satisfy existing needs completely, and in the case of the culturally deviant person or the psychotic the gap may be very great. A society may through its educative process perpetuate preferential behavior when such behavior is not adequate to the needs of its members. And the evaluation of an object by an organism may be wrong in the sense that the signified preferential status of an object or act may not accord with its actual ability to satisfy a given need. Hence an organism may, because of its evaluation of something, accord to an object or act a preferential status which is harmful to the attainment of its ends.

To point out that selection-rejection behavior tends to maintain the life processes of organisms is therefore only a first step. For we must distinguish between the motivations of an organism and the mere continual survival of the organism in time. Survival is not necessarily the dominant drive of an organism, and, in relation to an actual drive, objects and actions may be valued which do not in fact permit the continued existence of the organism.

A fifth and final point centers around the question as to the nature of the signs which occur in evaluation. Dewey has at various times given different answers, or at least different emphases, as to the relation between "judgments of value" and "judgments of fact." In the *Essays in Experimental Logic* [3] all judgments of fact were regarded as "judgments of practice"; in his "Theory of Valuation" [4] appraisals in the "distinctive" sense were regarded as rules of procedure capable

[3] Chicago, 1916.
[4] *International Encyclopedia of Unified Science*, Chicago, 1939, II, No. 4.

of being grounded upon and controlled by "statements" and yet not identical with them; in *Logic, the Theory of Inquiry*,[5] evaluation is not regarded as one kind of judgment over against others, but as "an inherent phase of judgment itself"; in the paper in the present volume Dewey finds "nothing whatsoever that methodologically (qua judgment)" distinguishes evaluative judgments from scientific conclusions. These variations are mentioned only to stress a single point: the resolution of controversies concerning the kinds of signs which occur in evaluations can be settled only on the basis of a carefully developed semiotic. It is at this point that a behaviorally oriented semiotic becomes of crucial importance for the development of a behaviorally oriented axiology.

In *Signs, Language, and Behavior* "evaluation" was defined as "the process of determining what preferential status will be accorded to something or other . . . insofar as it is carried out by signs." It was held further that all kinds of signs (designative, appraisive, prescriptive, formative) may occur in this process, but that the process must eventuate in appraisive signs, and not in the designative signs which conclude the process of descriptive inquiry. The problem then is to differentiate appraisive and designative signs.

Every person accords a privileged place in his behavior to certain objects and to certain ways of acting upon objects. The ordered series of preferences varies with individuals, though it is likely to contain for different individuals many objects with roughly comparable positions in their selection-rejection series. Drinking-water, for instance, will usually be a strongly favored object, and confinement a strongly rejected one. An appraisive sign signifies the position of something within a series of objects or acts ordered in terms of its interpreter's preferential behavior; it therefore disposes its interpreter to preferential behavior toward what is signified. A designative sign does not regularly evoke a disposition to preferential behavior; it signifies properties of objects which are causally efficacious upon sense-organs or other instruments of discrimination.

In terms of this distinction, to say that an object is brown is to signify certain characteristics of the object discriminable by effects on the sense organs or other objects, while to say that an object is good is to signify either that it falls in the upper range of a series of objects

[5] New York, 1938.

ordered in terms of the preferential behaviors accorded to them by the
interpreter of the sign, or to signify that the object reduces the need
of some organism. "Good" in the first sense is an appraisive term and
not designative; in the second sense it is as designative as the term
"brown." The question of the relation of "judgments of fact" to "judgments of value" is confused largely because of failures to make these
and other distinctions (such as the distinction between modes of signifying and uses of signs, and between scientific method and scientific
statements). If "evaluation" refers to the need-reducing properties of
objects or actions, then evaluation is in no basic respect different from
description. If "evaluation" is limited—as we have limited it—to inquiries eventuating in appraisive signs, then evaluative language and
descriptive language are different in important respects, that is, the
interpretant of one is a disposition to preferential behavior, while the
interpretant of the second is a disposition to expect objects with certain causally efficacious properties.

It does not follow—and this is perhaps Dewey's essential point—
that the methods of evaluative inquiry and scientific inquiry are essentially different even if some such distinction is made between
appraisals and descriptions. Appraisals and descriptions may both be
made hastily, carelessly, unreflectively, and both may be made after
careful scrutiny, the utilization of reliable knowledge, the consideration of consequences. In the first case the method in both inquiries is
"unscientific," and in the second case "scientific."

Nor in this perspective do evaluation and description differ with
respect to the possibility of confirmation. Regardless of how carefully
one has been led to formulate the statement "the table is brown" or
the appraisal "the table is good," confirmation or disconfirmation is
still desirable and possible. In the one case observation of stimulus-
properties of the table is involved, and in the other case observation
of whether one does or does not accord a preferential place to the
table when one acts with respect to it in the situation in which it is
appraised. The testing of designative and appraisive signs differs in
accordance with what such signs signify, but in both cases confirmation or disconfirmation is possible.

While I believe that a more careful semiotic than Dewey has developed will make certain distinctions between evaluations and state-

ments that he does not clearly make, it will in my opinion confirm his basic claim that scientific method is as available for the control of evaluations as it is for the control of statements. Evaluations are not, on our use of terms, statements, but the method used for their control may be as scientific or as non-scientific in one case as in the other. Only if "scientific method" is confused with "statements attained by the application of scientific method" does there seem to be a contradiction in speaking of a scientific appraisal. The issue as to whether there can be scientific evaluations or merely scientific knowledge about evaluations is purely terminological. If "scientific" is restricted to statements (designative signs), then evaluations (as appraisive signs) are not scientific; but if "scientific" be applied to the method by which scientists control their statements, then it is possible to apply this method not only to the control of statements about evaluations but to the control of evaluations themselves. It is in this sense that I think Dewey is correct in maintaining that *methodologically* there is "nothing whatsoever" that distinguishes scientific conclusions and evaluative appraisals; the sole distinction is in mode of signifying, and this is capable of formulation within a behavioral semiotic. Both modes of signifying can be controlled by scientific methods.

III

The attainment of a scientific axiology requires not only an operationally defined terminology but the development of experimental programs. The ultimate goal of this axiology would be to uncover the laws of preferential behavior. As an illustration of how a beginning can be made, I have proposed that "preferential behavior" be made the basic term and that "appraisals" be defined as signs whose interpretant is a disposition to preferential behavior. How other terms are to be introduced has been left open.

I would like to describe briefly the method which I am using in a project called "experimental humanistics"; the results obtained in this study will be left for presentation in later writings. The project is more extensive than the study of valuation, and arose out of an attempt to check empirically the thesis of my book *Paths of Life*, and to show how a scientific study of man can be carried on within the framework of unified science. But since valuings and evaluations play

such a central role in human life, the program of experimental humanists must inevitably embrace these topics, and so be relevant to the
construction of a scientific axiology.

Knowledge of the factors controlling preferential behavior requires
the study of actual persons. The problem is not simply that of a Gallup-
poll knowledge of the statistical distribution of valuings and evaluations, but of the conditions under which given persons appraise, and
behave preferentially to, specific objects in specific situations. Such
conditions are obviously numerous. They include the state of the organism, the features of the immediate situation, and the signs to which
the individual responds (whether produced by himself or by others).
A scientific axiology would seek for laws (in statistical form, of course)
stating the conditions under which preferential behavior occurs. These
laws would tell us who prefers what under what conditions.

The immediate need is to obtain data on the valuings and evaluations of specific persons. For this purpose individuals were asked to
assign a number from 7 to 1 signifying the degree to which they approved or disapproved of given items with which they were presented;
7 signified a high positive appraisal, 4 indifference, and 1 a high negative appraisal. In the study the subjects have been given a set of colored
reproductions of paintings, a group of poems, a list of major philosophical beliefs, and a variety of possible ways in which they might
live (these corresponding roughly to the major ethical and religious
alternatives). Each item in these sets was assigned a number by each
subject; in some cases the subjects also ranked the items in the order
of their approvals. Most of the above tests were repeated a year later
so that study of the changes in evaluations could be made. No attempt
has yet been made to compare these evaluations with actual preferences of the subjects in situations other than the test situation. Thus
we do not know the extent to which persons who appraise highly a
given path of life actually live according to that appraisal.

The subjects were mainly university students in this country, though
a number of older educated persons and a number of persons from
other cultures were included. So far interest has mainly been centered
on certain physical characteristics of the subjects: their types of phy-
sique, body-size, sex, and age. This has been done because of the ease
with which objective data is obtainable on these matters, and because
it was felt important to know at the outset if constitutional factor⸀

play a noticeable role in evaluation. As the study is extended it will obviously be necessary to add data on economic status, quality of education, physical environment in which the individual lives, culture group in which the individual functions, the family constellation in which the individual developed, and significant events in the subject's life history. It will also be necessary to compare their actual preferences in concrete situations with their appraisals. All such data must be used in a statistical study of the conditions under which given preferential behavior and given evaluations occur.

Much can be done with such data. It can be used, for instance, to approach the old question as to whether there are patterns of preference, so that liking a certain picture is associated with liking a certain poem, a certain philosophical position, and a certain path of life. This merely requires that correlations be studied between the preferences of individuals. It is also possible to find by the various techniques of factor analysis how many such patterns there are. This will allow us to isolate more objectively than before the various types of art and the various types of philosophical systems. The same can be done with patterns of evaluation, and a comparison made of these to patterns of preferences.

If a study were made of a number of cultures in these terms it would be possible to find the distribution of valuation patterns in various cultures, and so gain a better understanding of the similarities and differences between cultures.

By correlating the data on valuations with the psychological, constitutional, and environmental variables assigned to individuals one could determine the extent to which preference and evaluation patterns are related to personality types, to biological factors, and to cultural factors. One could also find how persistent such patterns are for a given individual, and the conditions under which changes occur in an individual's value pattern.

The method could be extended to include such items as music, novels, choice of friends, choice of various social organizations. In fact, the whole field of cultural phenomena can be investigated from this point of view. Man can in this way be brought back into the humanities.

The method could also be extended to study the relation of preferential behavior, evaluations, and statements. One could find the effect of scientific data presented to persons tested before and after these statements were made available. To what extent do scientific statements influence appraisals, and these appraisals in turn modify preferential behavior? And to what extent are appraisals of one individual affected by the knowledge of different appraisals made by other individuals? Studies designed to answer such questions would greatly increase our insight into the role which various kinds of signs play in the control of preferential behavior.

This is not the occasion to present the results which have so far been attained in studying the relation of valuations to the persons who make the valuations. Our aim here has been simply to show that there are methods by which it is possible to carry axiology from the stage of speculation and terminological analysis to the stage of experimental science. For the method proposed is experimental, the terminology is operationally interpersonal, and the results obtained belong to the natural science of behavioristics. A scientific study of man was impossible without a behavioral semiotic and a behavioral axiology. Now that the foundations for these disciplines have been laid there is no theoretical obstacle to the scientific study of the most complex phases of man and culture, nor to the incorporation of the results obtained by such a study within unified science.

The development of a scientific axiology has not merely a great theoretical importance for the extension of scientific knowledge. It has practical importance as well in providing data of great relevance for the making of appraisals and the forming of preferences. To apply scientific method in the control of preferences and appraisals we need scientific knowledge about preferences and appraisals. As this knowledge is gained it may be expected to exert its influence upon our appraisals about art, about interpersonal relations, about desirable social institutions, and about the choice of paths of life in which we register our ultimate commitments. And in influencing our appraisals a scientific axiology may well affect profoundly our preferential behavior itself. Both for the sake of science and of man we need a science of man. The development of a scientific axiology will be an essential part of the emerging science of man.[6]

[6] For the Criticisms and Rejoinders which relate especially to this paper see pp. 388–395, 428–433, and 437–439, below.

DISCUSSION OF JOHN DEWEY'S
"SOME QUESTIONS ABOUT VALUE"

DEWITT H. PARKER

THE QUESTIONS FORMULATED BY JOHN DEWEY in the article which has been chosen as the basis for the present discussion seem to me so searching and important, and to cover the ground so completely, that I shall limit my reflections almost entirely to them. I shall, moreover, consider them *seriatim*, in the order given, although there will inevitably have to be some movement back and forth from one to another.

I

The first question is stated as follows: "What connection is there, if any, between an attitude that will be called prizing or holding dear, and desiring, liking, interest, enjoying, etc.?" As this question is elucidated by Dewey, we find that prizing is said to stand for a "behavioral" transaction or disposition tending to maintain something in factual (space-time) existence. Desiring, liking, and so forth, on the other hand, unless also given a "behavioral" interpretation, are defined by him as something "internal" or "mentalistic,"—a kind of process sufficient to generate value "as a uniquely complete product." Although, as Dewey states his question in the original form, he asks for the *connection* between prizing and desiring, it becomes clear that his real interest is rather in an option between what he calls a "behavioral" interpretation of value and what he calls a "mentalistic" one, in terms of desire and satisfaction. Now, with the reservations which I am about to explain, my choice would unhesitatingly be for the latter, and for the reasons which I shall offer.

I accept the latter with reservations because I am far from sure that I understand the terms "behavioral" and "mentalistic" as Dewey does or as most behaviorists do. It has always seemed to me curious that the term "behaviorism," with its adjectival derivatives, is so seldom defined by those who use it. I suppose the reason would be that its meaning is thought to be so obvious that definition would be either impossible or superfluous. For me, personally, however, the meaning is far from obvious, and since no definition is given by Dewey, I shall have to try to give my own. (Perhaps some of the other contributors to this volume will help me here, or at least let me know whether my understanding of the term is also theirs.)

Well then, so far as I can understand it, "behaviorism" has two meanings, one epistemological, the other metaphysical. According to the former, whatever be the character of that which may be known privately (if private knowledge be allowed at all), at least everything that can be known publicly, and therefore scientifically, is alleged to be behavior. I may, possibly, know the pain of my own headache privately, but I cannot know anybody else's publicly, and no one else can publicly know mine. But I can publicly know another person's grimaces and other "expressions" of what to him is pain, as well as certain changes in nerve tissue, more difficult to observe—and all such is behavior. And by knowing publicly is meant, I take it, knowing what other people can know. But this whole distinction is, I believe, merely a matter of degree, and therefore, if intended to be a philosophical distinction, is false. For on the one hand, it is false that another person cannot know my pain. If he has ever had a pain (and who has not?), then he can have a concept of a pain and can apply that concept speculatively to something outside of his own experience, thereby knowing my pain "by description." To be sure, he cannot know my pain "by acquaintance," since he cannot confront my pain with his concept of it; yet knowledge by description is a perfectly good kind of knowledge. If it is not a good kind, then knowledge of behavior is no good, since, so far as organized, so far as scientific, it depends largely on records, which are themselves descriptions.

However, in order to see that this is true, we must enquire what behavior itself is. This brings us to the metaphysical meaning of behaviorism. Now empirically, independent of any speculative or metaphysical interpretation, behavior consists of changing configurations, chiefly visual, under external, or what I have called "counter-control," [1] in the experience of someone. What we call a man's grimaces are visual configurations; his cries are tonal configurations; his "tissue behavior" is

[1] *Experience and Substance*, Ann Arbor, 1941, pp. 38–42.

again visual, or possibly tactual, configurations—all in the experience of somebody. But these are, epistemologically, of like status with his pain. No one else can know them by acquaintance except the person who "has" them. And they are no more identical as between different centers of experience than are the pains of various people, and can be known between different centers only "by description." The vaunted publicity of scientific knowledge depends on the fact that certain abstract aspects or factors, such as number and measure, of certain types of experience, are identical, or nearly identical, in different centers; although the whole experiences are never absolutely identical, any more than pains are.

If behavior is understood in this way, it is, *by itself*, incapable of throwing any light on value whatsoever. If I interpret "mother rocking her child to sleep" behavioristically (changing visual *Gestalt* under counter-control), there is no more value there than in a breeze blowing a leaf (another changing visual *Gestalt* under counter-control). The sole reason why I ascribe value in the one case but not in the other, is because I interpret the rocking by analogy in terms of desire and satisfaction—concepts derived from my own experience of desire fulfilled—but do not so interpret the swaying leaf. The strange conclusion to which a pure behavioristic account is led is revealed by Dewey's footnote, in which he ascribes value to physico-chemical interactions that maintain stability in change on the part of some compounds! [2] If panpsychism is admitted, this would indeed be unobjectionable; but are Dewey and his followers panpsychists? I suspect that they are, but I also suspect that they are reluctant to acknowledge it (why, I do not know). Are they or aren't they? I, for one, am, of a sort.

If the behaviorist's account of value is rejected, are we then committed to the alternative suggested by Dewey, namely, that desire, interest, and so on, stand for something "internal," "mentalistic," or the like, and that "some kind of a mental state or process suffices to generate value as a uniquely complete process?" As I have already indicated, my own answer would be "Yes," with reservations. It is "Yes" because, unless value is understood in terms of desire-satisfaction, as these are known by acquaintance in oneself, it has not the slightest shadow of unique meaning, and one would do well to eliminate the term (as well as "good," "beautiful," "right," and "wrong") from the dictionary. I am

[2] P. 8*n*, above.

well aware that argument is possible on this matter; that others have ascribed to "value" a different meaning. But, for myself, let me say that I have found that wherever I use the term "value" or "the good," or any of its equivalents or derivatives, or wherever I seem to find what I or any one else experiences as value or the good, there appears to be, generically, no difference between that and what I experience as desire-satisfaction. There are, to be sure, all kinds of differences in specific quality or tint between various values, but generically, I repeat, they are all the same as being modes of satisfaction.

But in holding to this view, one does not commit oneself to Dewey's interpretation of "mental." To call desire "quasi-gaseous" does not help, for, so far as I know, no one has ever known it as gaseous. On the other hand, that it does, in a real sense, have the strength of triple plate steel, is certain, for desire helped to form steel plate and protects itself in a battleship by means of plate. That desire is efficacious is proved by the ruined cities of Warsaw, Rotterdam, London, Stalingrad, Cologne, Würtzburg, Berlin, Nürnberg, Hiroshima, Nagasaki (and others), for, apart from desire, they would all be standing as beautiful as they were. To characterize desire as "internal," does not help either, for "internal" is non-significant unless contrasted with "external." Since besides centers of experience there is "nothing, nothing, just nothing" (Whitehead), "internal" means what is contained in the center which is oneself, and "external," experiences belonging to other centers. Moreover, to characterize desire and satisfaction as "internal" may be positively misleading, for desire is commonly vectorial in nature (and so aptly symbolized by an arrow) pointing towards and interested in producing changes either in the center to which it belongs (as when I play to myself when all the family are out of the house, thus creating musical satisfactions for myself), or in some other center (as when musical satisfactions are created there when my playing is overheard). This leads me to object most strenuously to Dewey's description of value in terms of the *preservation* of something in existence. I might have expected that of a stand-patter, but hardly of a "radical" such as he is. On the contrary, desire is essentially creative, not preservative, and value is a new flash of satisfaction, shooting up in one's own or someone else's center.

It follows that value is never properly to be regarded as adjectival, "standing for a property or quality that belongs, under specifiable conditions to a thing or person having existence independently of being valued." [3] A person who is loved or cherished may be said to be *valuable* to the person who loves him, but this is merely another way of saying that he is loved, and being loved is no real quality of that person, least of all a value quality. To call a person loved or cherished is merely to say that someone has loving thoughts about him and will perform towards him helpful acts when he is in need. In this situation there are values—satisfactions in thinking loving thoughts and doing helpful deeds, on the one hand, and satisfactions in being thought of and helped, on the other hand. But these are the sole values there. And notice that like all values, they are activities, not properties. It is true that when helpful deeds are performed by the lover, the beloved's experience is changed, but only those changes which are satisfactions are values. Likewise, the bread which I eat is *valuable,* but this means only that under certain conditions it will serve my hunger, and my satisfaction when that occurs is the sole value in the circumstances, unless, in panpsychistic fashion, the bread can be interpreted as finding joy of a sacrificial sort in being destroyed in order to sustain me. Even in calling the bread "valuable" no new property in bread is designated—its chemical-physical properties are not added to one jot or tittle; for it is serviceable to my needs because of its already existing properties. To ascribe to the bread a predicate *valuable* is like ascribing a *virtus dormitiva* to opium: the opium puts a man to sleep because of its present chemical structure, not on account of any extra "dormitive" property!

There is a final point made by Dewey against the mentalistic view, as he calls it, namely, that if it be true, "it must be a matter of an external more or less accidental association that desire hits upon say a diamond, or a young woman, or holding an official position." To me, this is a very puzzling objection. For no philosophy of experience known to me— with the possible exception of Leibnitz's monadology—has held that a center is isolated from other centers, and that there is no interaction between them. There is no more mystery as to how, for example, amorous interest is aroused by the visual *Gestalt* which is under the control of the life and mind of a woman (we call it her "appearance" with absolute accuracy, for that is how she "makes her appearance" in centers other than her own) in terms of a philosophy of experience than there is in terms of the most naive biologically oriented theory of organ-

[3] P. 8, above.

ism and environment. On either view, we have a kind of "pre-established harmony" that has to be explained.

II

The questions raised by Dewey in Section II [4] are as important as any in the theory of value. From my own point of view, they center around the relation between value, simply considered, or satisfaction, and what has been called standard value—the value represented by norms, ideals, standards. As I see it, these two kinds of value are almost always present together in any human satisfaction, forming distinguishable but inseparable components of a satisfaction: the satisfaction arising out of the assuagement of the primary appetitions involved, on the one hand, and the satisfaction in meeting an expectation, on the other hand. Thus, if I am entertaining my friends at an evening party, my primary satisfaction will contain such components as those derived from the conversation, the refreshments, the games, and the like; but, in addition, the satisfaction in the fact that the party "went off" according to my own standard for such affairs. If, on the contrary, it did not go off well according to my standard, my satisfaction will be qualified negatively; it will be a value, but less intense. Or, in reading or writing a poem, I can distinguish the spontaneous values of imagination and expression from the value that arises through the meeting of my expectations regarding poetic experience. It must, however, be clearly recognized that this second component is itself an illustration of the general conception of value now being defended; for a standard expresses a desire for satisfactions of a certain kind and intensity, being what I call a desire of second order—a desire regarding desires, generating a satisfaction in satisfactions.

Memory, comparison of satisfactions, and conflict of desires are all engaged in the formation of standards. Any activity is undertaken against the background of a previous activity of the same kind remembered, which haunts it like a ghost. Such a memory is already a standard —the initial standard for any activity, to which it must measure up. The first poem we read sets the standard for all readings of poetry, the little girl's first party for all subsequent parties. So memory becomes expectation. If, however, the new experience surpasses the initial one, it will, of course, supplant the latter as standard maker. But since satis-

[4] Pp. 7–9.

factions are complex and no one will surpass another in all respects, the standard usually takes the shape rather of a generalized schema than a particular memory. Satisfactions will then be evaluated in terms of this schema as more or less perfect, as good, better, or bad. (Notice that "good" no longer means value in the generic sense, but in the specific sense of standard value.) But I would again emphasize the fact that this schema is not a mere instrument of intellectual judgment, of classing and serializing satisfactions; but, as fulfilled, surpassed, or fallen short of, determines the very quality and intensity of the satisfaction itself. And I do not mean to imply that the standard as schema necessarily takes the place of the standard as memory. Matthew Arnold's criticism is the perfect example of the use of concrete, intense aesthetic satisfactions rather than abstract schemata as norms in the field of poetry.

Standards affect satisfactions not only by qualifying them, but also by functioning as plans or models in accordance with which new satisfactions are created. The poet's poem is determined not only by his need for expression, but also by his conception of the kind of form in which expressions should be cast. Similarly, the kind of party the child gives is determined by his standard as to parties as such. These standards inevitably involve judgments as to the means required to bring values into existence. The means will accordingly be judged as suitable or unsuitable, efficient or inefficient, good or bad. But, I wish to insist, these judgments as to means are not directly judgments of value, but ordinary judgments concerning potential *valuables*. A value is a satisfaction, never a mere *thing*. Yet, indirectly, appraisals of means do affect the existence and nature of satisfactions; for as the means are, so very largely are the satisfactions, as Dewey has so helpfully and constantly reminded us.

However, comparison working through memory can determine only internal standards—the standard of the chess player for chess, of the military strategist for a military campaign, of the poet for "poet's poetry." But every activity has effects, beneficial or deleterious, upon other activities, and enters into competition with them, for the simple reason, if for no other, that a man can do no more than one thing at once. The resulting value, even when great, will therefore be appraised from the point of view of competing interests; each, so to speak, will appraise the other. Hence, even though my game of chess is excellent, I may condemn it because it interferes with my professional activities or excites the jealousy of a young wife whom I love but am neglecting. Or the Battle of the Bulge may have been a fine piece of strategy, long to be remembered and enshrined for study in military academies, yet as instigated by a ruthless tyrant may be condemned.

In the preceding paragraph I spoke of each competing interest evaluating the other. But that is only a half-truth. If it were the full truth, a center of experience would be a loose bundle of interests, independent in much the same fashion as two or more men who quarrel; and one interest would be as "right" as the other, my interest in chess as my interest in my wife, my desire for military victory as my concern for the moral welfare of my people. But, on the contrary, all my interests are closely interwoven, and involved in what I have called the "matrix self," [5] which corresponds roughly to what Royce called the life-plan. It is the matrix self, rather than any one of the competing propensities taken separately, that evaluates. By the matrix self I wish to emphasize that I do not mean anything transcendental, but something strictly empirical and discoverable, named by such indicative words as "I," "self," "ego," "myself," and "me."

The actual procedure of appraising an interest may be formulated in terms of three principles—attainment (or perfection), influence, and rank. By attainment, I mean the degree to which a desire measures up to its own internal standard or goal. If it fails notably to do this, we tend to discontinue or limit it in favor of other interests. Thus, if I take to writing verses and find that I am incapable of achieving what I regard as good poetry, this continual failure will so discourage me that I will probably give up verse writing for, let us say, gardening, with which perhaps I can get somewhere. There are, nevertheless, some desires that may be so strong that they persist undiminished despite failure. The persistent courtship by some men of some one woman who never says "Yes" would be an illustration. By influence, I mean how far one interest helps or hinders another—whether it is, in this sense, relatively benign, malign, or indifferent. So chess playing is malign if it injures the happiness of a wife whom I love; benign if, playing the game with her, it strengthens the tie between us; relatively indifferent if played so infrequently at the club that it has no effect upon our relationship. It is significant to notice that a satisfaction which is good generically may be

[5] *Experience and Substance*, pp. 41–46.

bad in its relation to other satisfactions, that is to say, bad in the specific moral sense. In this same sense, generic evil, that is to say frustration, may be good in so far as it promotes, as it may, other interests. A renunciation may perhaps initiate poetic composition. The necessity for rank as a principle is evident from the fact that, without it, we would not be able to choose between desires when one interfered with the other. Each would be malign from the other's point of view; hence why sacrifice chess to the love of your wife; why not the other way round? The rank of an interest is its relative place in the life-plan.

The extent to which the plan is fulfilled, and the degree of harmony within it, determine what we call happiness. Happiness is the satisfaction of highest order. The ways by which harmony can be achieved I have discussed elsewhere.[6] Briefly stated, it is a matter of the resolution of conflicts through repression, compromise, substitution (including "sublimation" as a special form), and integration of interests, together with the cultivation of the moods (perhaps better, attitudes) of resignation, faith, humor, and/or defiance. Happiness is, I hardly need to say, not something other than the satisfaction of our several desires, for the life-plan is a plan for these desires, and the satisfactions they yield are components in happiness; on the other hand, happiness is not to be identified with a sum of such satisfactions, but is rather a harmonious pattern of them.

Although the life-plan of the individual is in great measure determined by external, especially social circumstances—family situation, economic, political and cultural institutions and arrangements—the relative rank of his interests is a function of certain intrinsic characters of them, especially intensity, scope (inclusiveness), height, and symbolism. Interests are obviously of greater or less intensity; in other words, we may desire something more or less strongly. Thus I take a stronger interest in writing this essay than in learning to read Spanish, and therefore subordinate the latter to the former. But desires also differ in height; for me, my attachment for philosophy is higher than my liking for bridge or chess. Scope is determined by the number of sub-interests or activities which a given interest commands. What we call an "interest" or "desire" is usually a system of minor propensities. The more inclusive interests I therefore call system-desires. What I call my interest in philosophy is an exceedingly complex system of this sort, including the

[6] *Human Values*, New York, 1931, pp. 390–406.

interest in reading certain books, writing books or articles (such as this one), teaching classes, carrying on discussions with colleagues, all bound together by something which I call my desire to understand my own experience in its relation to other centers. So great is the scope of this interest—so large is the "area" or "volume" of myself that it covers —that anything that promotes or injures it has very great significance in my life-plan, and therefore in my evaluation of values. But although the number of interests affected is important, scope is never determined merely by number; it is number as organized that counts. Injury to unorganized miscellaneous interests, while significant, is not so significant. Finally, an interest is important through symbolism. Trivial in themselves, such habits as crossing oneself or saluting the flag are for the Catholic and the soldier, respectively, of immense significance through symbolism.

The relations of these four factors—intensity, scope (number), height and symbolism—are matters for further investigation by students of value. One would like to know whether they are independent variables, or whether some are reducible to others. That they are not independent is clear. Although any interest may vary all the way from zero intensity to enthusiasm, scope, height, and symbolism tend to increase the intensity of a desire. When very tired of an evening my interest in poetry may sink to a low intensity and my interest in a detective story rise to high intensity, but the latter cannot reach the intensity of the former when I am refreshed. On the other hand, it is important to notice that height cannot be reduced to intensity, for even when the higher interests are at low intensity they are still felt as higher; and the lower, when starved, may reach overwhelming intensity.

Or, if not reducible to intensity, one would like to reduce height and symbolism to scope. And that the former are not independent of the latter is certain. Thus compare love with crude sex impulse; it includes the latter, but so much besides; or compare beauty with simple pleasures of the senses where the same relation holds. And the value of making the sign of the Cross for a believer as compared with the value of executing the same movement by a skeptic, depends obviously upon the background of interests represented in the case of the former, which are absent in the case of the latter. On the other hand, it is, I believe, doubtful whether either height or symbolism can be reduced to mere scope; for ambition may cover the whole of a man's life yet is lower than love. And in the case of symbolism, the special pattern whereby one interest becomes a surrogate for others in the background is irreducible to mere number. Despite these relations to intensity and number, there is, therefore an irreducible factor in height and symbolism.

With regard to number it must be recognized that more interests are not by themselves more valuable than few, or even that interest a and interest b are not, as such, more valuable than interest a or b alone. Mere number is no determinant of value, for value is always *for* someone's desire. More of my own interests are in general of more worth than fewer of them, because I am interested in the assuagement of my whole self as far as possible; but only when, through *caritas*, I make the interests of other persons my own can they count for me.[7]

Although scope, height, and symbolism cannot be reduced to intensity, this last has a unique status; for, in the end, what I want most, that I shall do. I place emphasis on the *I* because the interests of a center are not separate, as if the victory of one were decided by its superior intensity as compared with that of its antagonist, each in isolation from the other. On the contrary, the victory of the victorious is a function of its superior intensity after it has struggled with its opponent; only then is its intensity my intensity; in other words, not what it wants, but what I want decides. And, let me repeat, the I, while not other than its interests, is more than they; for it includes the struggle between them, the review and deliberation upon them, and the final emergence into victory and dominance of one of them as the result of struggle, review, and deliberation. When an interest of large scope is in question, there is a sense in which its intensity is a function of the intensities of its components. Just how to express that function, I do not at the moment know. The whole question as to whether and how far values are quantitative is involved. I have much material on this subject, to be embodied in a forthcoming volume on the philosophy of value, but the subject is too complex to treat of here.

III

Dewey puts the basic question of his Section III in a very striking way, admirably adapted to bringing into the open just how value-statements differ from factual statements. He says that if the question

[7] Here I am criticizing R. B. Perry's notion of "inclusiveness," in his *General Theory of Value*, New York, 1926, pp. 617–619, 645–658. See also my *Human Values*, pp. 110, 111.

were raised about the relation between meteor-propositions and comet-propositions, it would not occur to anyone that the "problem" was other than that of the connection between two sets of facts, the implication being that the difference between value "propositions" and other propositions would be simply that of the difference between one set of facts, value-facts, and other kinds of facts, both belonging to the genus, space-time facts. Now, if this is not the case, Dewey asks, why is it not the case?

I think I can show why it is not the case by studying an example. All over the world before August 14, 1945, people were making statements to one another such as these: "I wish the war were over." Here surely is a value-statement; but is it the statement of a space-time fact? One might perhaps think so. For one might try to analyze the statement into two parts (1) "I wish," and (2) what I wish, "that the war is over." Part (2) it might be claimed, is certainly a statement of fact. It was, say on August 10, 1945, a false statement, but still a factual statement, because it was about certain space-time facts. It was a false proposition like, "The Germans won the battle of Stalingrad." Part (1) also, it might be claimed, is a statement of space-time fact, saying, in effect, (1a) "in the organism to which I point when I say 'I' there exists a wish." And that, presumably, would be a true statement. Hence the statement "I wish the war were over" would be the equivalent of the two statements, (1a) and (2), of which the former is true and the latter false.

The foregoing analysis looks plausible, indeed; but its plausibility vanishes when we begin to ask a few questions. First, as to (2). Why should one be interested in stating an obviously false proposition? Usually one states a false proposition for either one of two reasons: either because one wishes to deceive or because one is ignorant of the facts. Neither could have been true in this case; it was known to everyone that the war was on. Now consider (1). Of course there are occasions when (1) might be equivalent to (1a). If on August 1, 1945, someone had asked me, "Have you a wish that the war were over?" I would have given (1a) as my answer; that is, I would have said, "It is true that I wish, and so on." But, of course, nobody would have asked me such a question! And I would no more have stated as a fact the obvious fact that I had such a wish than I would have stated the obvious error in (2).

It is, however, true that *sometimes* the expression of a wish contains a statement that a wish exists. In this case the statement is translatable

into the type of (1a). If the waiter at table has taken my order but forgotten it, he may well ask, "Is it true that you wish coffee?" and my answer would be "Yes, that is true, I do wish coffee," in which case my
statement would be about a fact, namely the fact of my wanting coffee.
But, to follow this same illustration for a moment, when I originally
said to the waiter, "I want coffee," or equivalently, but more politely,
"Please bring me some coffee," I was not making a statement about my
wish; I was voicing or expressing my wish; I was not interested in affirming or refuting a statement about a fact (my wishing something), but in
creating a new fact—the fulfillment of my wish.

It is most important, therefore, to distinguish between expressions of
desires and values, and expressions about desires and values. The verbal
form may be closely similar, yet the meaning is different. Expressions
about desires are propositions like any others, to be verified or refuted.
Most of the statements in this essay, except those in quotes, are of this
kind. Expressions of desires, taken as wholes, are not propositions at all
(although they may contain propositional parts), but are volitional expressions; for their intention, by which their status is determined, is not
to express anything true or false. Even expressions of standard values
are volitional in character, for they express desires regarding desires or
satisfactions (desires and satisfactions of higher order). The intention in
all volitional expressions is to share a desire or satisfaction, or to make a
desire prevail. The former is clearly the case with simple lyrical expressions like "I wish that the war were over" and the highly complex lyrical
expressions found in poetry and the other fine arts; the latter is the case
with commands, and, at least so it has been thought, with ethical expressions, which we shall consider in a moment.

Before doing this, however, it will be interesting to test what we have
been maintaining by a study, brief as it necessarily must be, of poetical
expression. Suppose we read the following lines of Joyce:

> My love is in a light attire
> Among the apple trees,
> Where the gay winds do most desire
> To run in companies.

They have the form of a statement of fact. But who could think them
to be a statement of fact! The poet is not saying that it is a fact that his
love is in a light attire among the apple trees, for surely she is not there

thus attired this winter's day. But perhaps someone might contend that
the verses do, after all, express a proposition, although a false one. Yet
I say once more, why utter a false proposition? Why write a poem about
something that is not so? And there is a third alternative, that the statement is not a proposition at all, but the expression of a dream, which
itself is the embodiment of a wish. By expressing his dream, the poet
finds some assuagement of his desire, and we who read his lines can
dream a like dream and find a like assuagement. However, the opposing
view has a last resort in argument, as follows: the poet, it may be said,
is, to be sure, not saying that his love is in a light attire, but "I have a
dream that she is in a light attire among the apple trees," and that would
be not only a proposition, but a true one. Yet such an interpretation
would be, I fear a *mere* logician's; it could never be a poet's. When a
poet writes poetry, he is not stating that he has such or such dreams and
wishes; he is dreaming those dreams, putting them into order and in-
viting others to dream them, too. Poetry is dreaming, not a statement
that a dream exists.

I do not mean that there is no cognitive element in the experience of
a person who expresses a wish or a command. To clothe a wish in words
is equivalent to clothing it in concepts, for the word and the concept
are one unrent garment. Expression is self-knowledge, but knowledge
by acquaintance, not by mere description. And in knowledge by acquaintance what is known is present to the concepts that know it.[8] The
difference that I have in mind is the difference between "I love you"
uttered by the lover and "He loves her," uttered by an "innocent bystander" who overhears the lover's words. In the former, the lover's love
is a warmth contained as in an envelope of words, and is a force there
trying to kindle a like warmth in the beloved; in the latter, love is absent,
and only a cold, conceptual description, a "knowledge about" the other's
love, is there—not utterly cold, to be sure, since all concepts are echoes
of primary experiences, but the fire is not that of the lover, but of the
embers of some love of the spectator's own. The combination of self
knowledge with pure lyrical expression is characteristic also of aesthetic
expression, as I have argued elsewhere.[9]

[8] See my article, "Knowledge by Acquaintance," *The Philosophical Review*, LI
(1945), 1–18.
[9] "Wish Fulfilment and Intuition in Art," in *Proceedings of the Sixth International
Congress of Philosophy*, New York, 1927, pp. 437–441.

So far I have limited my discussion to the most elementary types of value expressions (with a brief survey of the more complex variety characteristic of poetry) for the reason that the highly complicated kinds, such as the ethical and legal, are understandable in terms of them. I wish now to indicate how this is so.

Both legal and ethical expressions seem to differ from those already analyzed in being impersonal, in which regard they simulate cognitive expressions. But this impersonality is actually a sham, and both types can be shown to be of the nature of wishes and commands. For consider a simple example, of ethical expression "Burglary is wrong," and of legal expression "Whosoever commits burglary (here defined) shall be punished by imprisonment for a period of from five to twenty years." Giving our attention to the legal expression first, one might try to interpret it as a prediction "If anyone commits burglary he will be punished." But if that were the meaning of the law, it would read "If anyone commits burglary and is apprehended and convicted, he will probably be punished," for many persons commit burglary and get away with it because they are not apprehended or convicted, and even if they are, they are not imprisoned for from five to twenty years, since they escape or are pardoned before their sentences have run. This latter statement is, to be sure, true, but is not what the law says. The law says nothing about apprehension and conviction. Moreover, it uses the word "shall," not "will." The law is in effect a command issued to the officers of the law and the citizenry generally, and, although, like other commands, it contains a proposition, it is more than a proposition. The analysis of the simplest commands proves this. Take the command "March!" This is obviously equivalent to "You shall march," which in turn is equivalent to "I wish *that you will march.*" Here the words in italics are a proposition about the future, but the whole expression, since it contains the phrase "I wish," is not a proposition. The intent of the statement, taken as a whole, is to express a wish that something shall happen, and in expressing the wish to others, to become a cause *making the indicated proposition about the future true.* That the expression is not an ordinary cognitive statement to be translated as "It is true that I wish that you will march," is clear from the fact that it is never in question what the officer who issues the command wishes. The private does not raise the question, Does the officer wish that I shall march, and how shall I verify that this is true?; on the contrary, he marches and thereby makes the subsidiary proposition underlined true. The expression is, thus, not something to be verified, but something to be acted on.

This analysis fits the legal expression perfectly. The law concerning burglary expresses the wish that persons committing burglary be punished in a certain way. As in an ordinary command, there are the two parts to the expression, the pure volitional part, "We wish," and the propositional part, concerning the future, "that those who commit burglary will be punished." The use of the word "shall" in the original expression brings the two parts, volitional and propositional, together. And that a law is not a proposition about a wish, but the expression of a wish, not something to be verified, but something to be acted on, is clear for the reason that the officers of the law and potential burglars are not in doubt what the law is. That is no problem for them; the problem is, to act or not to act as the law commands; to enforce or not to enforce it.

It may, of course, happen that there is a question as to what the law is. But then we are no longer concerned with the same expression, but with a correlative propositional expression of the form, "It is true that they, the constituted authorities (notice the change from 'we' to 'they') wish that burglars be punished." The one is an expression *of* value, the other is an expression *about* value.

The analysis of ethical expressions follows closely that of legal expressions, although, as we shall see, there are important differences. The fundamental theme of this analysis was stated by Russell: [10] ethical expressions are commands, or since commands are wishes, let us say simply that they are wishes. "Stealing is wrong" is equivalent to "Thou shalt not steal." It is no accident that the basic moral code of our civilization is the Ten Commandments. One critical difference between legal and ethical commands is that the latter do not assign penalties for the violation of commands, or when they do, as is sometimes true, it is well recognized that they acquire a legalistic tinge. The law says, in effect, "We want you to do or refrain from doing something, and if you don't, we want the officers of the law to punish you"; the moral injunction says simply, "We want you to want to do or refrain from doing so and so. The one aims to create an act through fear, the other aims to create

[10] Bertrand Russell, *Religion and Science*, New York, 1935, ch. ix, especially pp. 24 249.

wish, for the sake of the intrinsic satisfaction that the fulfillment of that wish will bring. The moralist does not merely want that people should not steal, but that they shall wish not to steal. This is the "disinterested-ness" of morality. And the basis of such a wish is liking for a way of life which the wish sustains, and for the persons who participate, with one-self, in that way.

But if ethical and legal expressions are commands, whose are they? The legal are primarily the commands of the "constituted authorities," and secondarily of those citizens who support the authorities out of approval of the law. They express a desire for a way of life which "crimes" tend to disrupt. Ethical expressions originate in the desires of religious leaders or other innovators in the realm of conduct, but have now become the commands of parents and teachers, who seek to build up in the mass of the people desires similar to their own. The legal and the moral tend to coincide, but never do so. The impersonality of these expressions is therefore merely apparent, as I have suggested; the ap-pearance being due to the fact that they are the commands of many persons rather than of a single one. When I say to the child "You should honor your father and mother," I am not saying to him "*I* want you to honor your father and mother," in the same fashion that I would say to him "*I* want you to run this errand for me"; but rather, in effect, "*we* want you to honor your father and mother," meaning by "we" a group of persons that includes me. At the moment I am a spokesman of that group.

The attempt, as by Lepley in his very interesting book *Verifiability of Value*,[11] to reduce ethical to scientific expressions, can now be shown to be impossible. Adopting his general procedure, we would seek to re-express "Stealing is wrong" as a scientific proposition of some such form as this: "Stealing disrupts the social and economic organization of a society." But suppose I were to say this to a hardened thief, what would be his answer? Why, of course. "What of it!" Unless he desired to preserve the way of life sustained by the economic organization of our society, or unless he identified himself with the frustrations of persons who had their goods stolen, the sentence "stealing is wrong" as well as any Lepleyan transposition of it, would have no *ethical* meaning. It is well known that the early Bolsheviks partly supported themselves by the use of counterfeit money, but *for them* this practice was not wrong,

New York, 1944.

for they did not wish the economic organization to continue. Those who think the transposition adequate presumably do wish it to continue, and this wish is covertly embodied in the expression, thereby destroying its purely scientific character. It can be shown that the same analysis applies to the highest generalizations of ethical maxims, such as are found in books on ethics and theory of value written by philosophers. They are not propositions which are self-evidently true, but volitional statements expressing the universal love (or "good will") of the saints as that has entered into the desires of the philosophers. As propositions, they are meaningless, and their form is merely a deceptive disguise for a kindly heart.

A consideration of one of Lepley's own examples will bring to light another aspect of the same matter. "Promises ought generally to be kept" is transposed as "The keeping of promises produces effects which upon careful and continued examination of consequences are felt (by those who make this judgment) to be very important." But, on the contrary, anyone who says that promises ought generally to be kept is not saying merely that he or anyone else has certain feelings, that is, that such feelings exist; he is not stating a proposition about his feelings which his auditors would be interested in verifying. He is expressing his feelings in order to win the sympathy and excite an appropriate action on the part of his auditors. And generally, no statement as to how certain persons feel or have felt (anthropology, psychology, history) can ever be equivalent to an ethical expression, for the reason that the latter contains the attitude of the speaker or writer as a living, active force; while the former does not contain it, but simply affirms its existence. Or, in so far as some of the attitude lingers there, it ceases to be a purely scientific, and becomes a volitional statement.

Nevertheless it is a very significant fact that to every volitional expression there corresponds a propositional statement. We have already noted this fact with regard to such simple value statements as "I love you," to which there corresponds the propositional statement "He loves her." Similarly, to the volitional statement "I wish the war were over" corresponds the propositional statement "He wishes that the war were over." This correlation extends to complex aesthetic, legal, and ethical statements. Thus to "My love is in a light attire," there corresponds the factual statement "James Joyce imagined his love in a light attire among the apple trees." To the legal expression, "Burglars shall be punished

PARKER 241

by imprisonment from five to ten years," there is a corresponding factual statement, "In the United States there is a law to the effect that burglars shall be punished." To the ethical statement "Promises ought generally to be kept" there corresponds the kind of transposition suggested by Lepley. This correspondence is what one would expect in view of the dependence of values on existing desires. Moreover, it explains the constant confusion between volitional and propositional expressions. However, it cannot be too strongly emphasized that correspondence is not identity.

IV

In this part Dewey raises the burning question of the possibility of controlling valuations, especially through knowledge and what are called "rational methods," as contrasted with brute force. He appears to think that those who accept a "mentalistic" theory of value are prone to deny the feasibility of rational methods, at least where basic issues are involved. He puts the question simply by asking whether value facts are "bias facts." My answer, as Dewey would I am sure expect, is that they are indeed bias facts. If the basis of all valuation is appetition (volition) then values are a bias, a specific direction of the self, and so of the organism with which it is connected. This bias is obviously related functionally to elements in the physical environment, and to the institutional arrangements of a society (including the biases of other persons upon whom the initiation and preservation of these arrangements depend), but never so related that the bias of the individual is (or ever can be) eliminated from the value. Values are, as has been claimed, a function of the "situation," but primarily and necessarily of a desire in the situation. Biases are capable of modification, but then new biases supervene. Before entering upon the problem of methods, rational or other, by which they can be modified, a previous question must be asked and answered, Why try to modify them? To this question the more immediate answer is, Because of conflicts with other volitions, and because of conflicts with standardized volitions.

Postulating the existence of an interest of highest order (matrix self), aiming at the realization of the individual's life-plan, which being a plan for our desires, seeks their maximum satisfaction, then the methods already mentioned, of compromise, substitution (sublimation), and integration are available for adjusting conflicts within the individual and between individuals. We seek harmony for the sake of inner peace (a unique satisfaction), but also, and importantly, because conflict interferes with the full realization of the interests in conflict. Consider the case, already cited, of the young man who before marriage spent three evenings a week at the club playing chess, and continues this practice after taking a much-loved young bride. If his wife becomes lonely and jealous, he will find himself beset with a conflict between his fondness for chess and his love of his wife. He may then resolve the conflict through restricting his chess to one evening a week (compromise); by teaching his wife to play chess with him (integration); or by playing bridge with her (substitution). Since presumably his love of his wife will be dominant over his interest in chess, by either one of these methods, and especially by integration (if she learns to play a good game), he will gain, on the whole. Or if, being an industrialist, he finds himself in conflict with the union, which asks a 30 percent increase in wages, while he is willing to offer 10 percent, he may settle the dispute by giving 20 percent (compromise), reasoning that the greater efficiency of contented men may compensate for a lower rate of profit; or, he may make the men shareholders in the business, thus winning their cooperation for as long as the business lasts (integration); or, finally, he may sell the business and engage in a new enterprise where "labor troubles" are not so frequent (substitution). If, besides caring for his own success, he has some interest in the welfare of his men on their own account, the methods of compromise and integration will provide him added satisfaction through the gains to them with which he identifies himself.

All these methods may be regarded as rational in the sense that they provide some satisfaction on the whole to anyone using them, and do not rest on mere force. Notice that they are not the methods of science, although all the knowledge of men and the world that science can offer will help to make them successful. Nevertheless it is clear that the factor of force is not absent. It is not absent in cases of compromise, because where the difference is to be split will depend at least partially on the relative forces involved. If management is in a stronger position, the split will be nearer the amount offered; if labor is stronger, it will be nearer what labor demands. It is not absent in cases of integration, because the economic pressure created by the demands of labor compels the resort to profit-sharing. It is not absent from substitution, because again it is the same pressure that forces the flight to a new type of enterprise. Every peace treaty illustrates the use of all three methods and the inevitableness of force. Take the "peace" that will presumably some day be written for Europe. As a whole it will be a compromise between rival claims. Russia seized Eastern Poland, so Poland was "given" a *substitute* by land "annexed" from Germany. Clearly, if Germany and Poland had been strong enough, this would not have happened. Russia is *integrating* Eastern Germany as far as the Elbe River into her economic system; France hopes to integrate the Saar, as she succeeded in integrating Elsass-Lothringen. The British desire to integrate their "zone" of Germany with the commercial interests of the British Empire. (We who should be trying to integrate the whole of Germany into the Anglo-American commercial and political system [12] are concerned chiefly with hanging war criminals, whose hanging or not hanging will have no effect on the course of history.) But none of these integrations or the resulting grand compromise will occur without some application of force. Does anyone think that they could occur by persuading the Germans? Only when choice is free and no external wills are involved, or only when love (good-will) is dominant, as in my example of the young chess-playing husband, is there no use of force.

But, it may be objected, force is necessary in the European case because the whole situation is wrong. Wrong for whom? For me, yes; and I have my "reasons." Being, in imagination, a "good European," acquainted more or less with the various tribes of Western Europe and with their languages and literatures, and having lived happily at various times among them; and having seen in that part of the Austrian Tyrol stolen by Italy with our consent in World War I, what a foreign occupation and rule does to a people who have to suffer it, I am in favor of a free union of all the nations of Western Continental Europe. But I am an American! I am not a Frenchman with a special love of France; a German with a special love of Germany; or an Italian with a special love of Italy. I do not want more for one than for another, as each of them does. I have none of the desire for power (grandeur) that each of them has. I am not tormented with the fear that each has of the others, with excellent historical justification in every case. I can to a certain extent feel myself into their situations, but the possibility of a transfer of experience is definitely limited. Thus we come up against the irra-

---

[12] Since these lines were written, there is evidence that this has, at last, become our policy.

tional in the realm of values, the "value-centric predicament," the fact that every value—the good and the bad, the right and the wrong—is *for* someone. Through the imagination, mediated by love and art, this predicament may be partly overcome, but never wholly. Where differences in the scale of values are in question, no mere argument stands at avail.

There are still some who cleave to the belief that the social sciences, working hand in hand with the physical and biological sciences, may be able to mold man into an ideal pattern of adjustment and integration. Or, what is more in accord with the pragmatic, temporalistic, and tentative philosophy of our time, it is hoped that by means of these sciences a method can be developed for the resolution of day-by-day problems and conflicts as they arise. But it seems to be far from usually recognized that these methods would have to be employed by real people, acting in a definite social situation, and burdened with all the biases of their inherited biological organization and cultural tradition. Suppose that some over-all global policy was devised by the leaders of the "Big Five," or by their successors. The limitations of their perspectives might be partially overcome by constant discussion and more intimate acquaintance with each other, but in the end any plan for the race would be a compromise between very definite biases. Each would hold somewhat to his own scale of values in opposition to the others. How far each would give way would be determined by the force or wit at his disposal. And in putting the plan into operation, subordinates would have to be used, who would each have his own bias. And all these men, men of good will and men of less good will, might be equally adept at using "social engineering." Even if, as seems not unlikely, the world is some day unified by conquest through the application of atomic bombs, and either Truman's or Stalin's successors wield supreme power, this would remain true. One cannot eliminate the givenness—the "absurdity," if you will—of the historical process. The fate of us all depends upon the kind of men—the kind of volitions—that come into control of the social and physical sciences. These volitions—stronger indeed than triple-plate steel—are the arbiters of destiny.[13]

[13] For the Criticisms and Rejoinders which relate especially to this paper see pp. 381–388, 395–399, and 440–455, below.

OBSERVATIONS ON VALUE FROM AN ANALYSIS OF A SIMPLE APPETITION

STEPHEN C. PEPPER

As in many philosophical problems, so in the problem of value we have to cope first with a term of unsettled meaning. Yet the problem of value is not a problem about verbal usage. We desire to consider the nature of value or the facts of value, not the possible or customary uses of a term. How then do we penetrate through the veil of meanings of the term value, to the facts concerned?

We cannot dispense with the term or an equivalent, since our empirical problem is related to the term. It or its equivalent is bound to crop up again as soon as we try to abandon it. For at the outset we have nothing else to cling to or to hold our problem together. Whatever it is that philosophers and economists have been talking about under the heading of value in the last fifty years or more, that is the area of our study.

So, as a first suggestion about method, let us keep the term and seek out the objects it denotes without, however, letting the search become a study of verbal usage.

As a second methodological suggestion, let us not assume any particular limitations on the meaning of the term. Let us not assume, for instance, that there is one common meaning or common character for all the objects denoted by the term. Let us not assume, for instance, that value is a specific indefinable, or is equated with one sort of activity like satisfaction of interest, or is reducible to such an activity. Let us not assume that value either is or is not relational, or that it does or does not require an object of value. For if we make any such assumptions, we may define ourselves out of some of the most significant material in the field that our colleagues are studying. We may even define ourselves into conflict with the structures of our own denoted empirical materials and so create problems for ourselves that do not exist in the facts. In short, let us admit it to be possible that value refers to a heterogeneous field and that perhaps some quite different though connected experiences are equally named value. The importance of these comments is to keep our attention as students of value on the ways in which the facts studied are actually related, and not be diverted by preconceived definitions.

Lastly, as a third methodological suggestion, in order that we may not be lost in the crowd of materials begging to be studied as genuine and basic values, let us select some one of these candidates—any one that looks promising—and carry our empirical study of this value material to the limits of our knowledge. Having done that, we can proceed to other material in the field, and so on until the field has been covered. Within my experience, however, it regularly happens that a careful factual study of one type of value material automatically draws in most of the others, so that this third methodological suggestion, though sounding very modest, turns out to be nearly sufficient and all-embracing.

In summary, the purpose of the first methodological suggestion is to avoid verbalism in our study, that of the second to avoid definitional or a priori preconceptions, that of the third to direct our study upon factual materials within the field and permit these materials themselves to inform us of the nature of the field.

I

As an example of the method suggested, I should like to show briefly some of the results I have reached from an analysis of a specific common type of purposive activity. First I shall present the analysis, then give a series of observations that appear from the analysis. These observations I shall finally bring to bear on the issues raised in Dewey's article, which was the stimulus for our collaborative studies.

I take it no one would question that values of some sort or some degree lie in human purposes. That is, the pursuit and attainment of an object of human desire is quite surely factual material within the field of our study of values. So I propose to make a careful description of one type of purposive action.

A little observation soon shows that purposes are of two main types—positive purposes in the pursuit of goals, and negative purposes in avoidance of noxious objects. Positive purposes may be called appetitions; negative purposes aversions. The structures of the two are very different. I shall restrict my attention to the structure of appetitions.

Let us take an example of an unquestionable appetition. Imagine a geologist in the mountains bordering a desert where water is scarce, who after a long day's climb in unfamiliar country runs out of water and begins to grow thirsty. His interest in following a line of outcrops has led him farther from camp than he realized and he sees that he is likely to have to stay out overnight. Unless he can find water soon, he will have to go thirsty for a good many hours. He has no idea in this unfamiliar country where water may be found. He therefore climbs to the top of a ridge to get a view of the neighboring valleys. Arrived at the top of the ridge, he sees below him a winding line of bushes which look as if they were bordering a stream bed where water may be had for the digging. When he reaches the bushes, he finds as he anticipated green grass, indicating water beneath. He digs, and water oozes into his hole, so that he can fill his cup and drink to his satisfaction.

Here is a relatively isolated appetition. It began with a slowly intensifying positive drive which spontaneously developed as a result of metabolic processes within the organism. The geologist gradually became aware of his thirst till it reached an intensity where it became the governing motive of his behavior. He then found that though he knew he wanted water, he had no idea where water was to be found. He anticipated that water would satisfy his thirst as a terminal goal, but he had no idea where there was a spring or subordinate goal which would be a means to the terminal goal. His activity then consisted in following out a succession of subordinate acts which he anticipated would be instrumental to his finally getting water, and which fortunately turned out to be correct.

The main features that stand out in the structure of this appetition are a drive, a goal, and a succession of acts connecting the drive with its goal. The outstanding characteristic of positive purposive behavior is this gap between a motivating impulse and its goal, and the necessity of filling in this gap with *learned* acts. And that is why purposive behavior is so adaptable. The gap may be filled in many different ways depending upon the environment and the circumstances.

Among the intervening factors that fill the gap between the impulse and its satisfaction, there are, however, two that stand out above the others—namely, the terminal goal object, water, which will satisfy the thirst, and the idea of (or reference to) the water anticipated by the geologist, which guided his actions towards that goal. The other acts were all secondary to these. If the geologist had not known that what his thirst needed to satisfy it was water, his impulse would have been entirely blind and he would have had to go through a lot of trial and error activity to discover what he wanted. This geologist, however, knew what he wanted as soon as he felt the specific want of thirst. Undoubtedly there was once a time, as a small baby, when his want was blind. He felt the want, the impulse to drink, but he did not have any idea what would satisfy it. In spite of the fact that babies are equipped with innate readinesses to suck and swallow, many babies have to be taught to take their milk. They are hungry and thirsty without any idea what is the goal object that will satisfy their want. Their impulses, their wants are blind.

What gives sight, so to speak, to a drive is the cognitive anticipation of what will satisfy it. Such an anticipation consists of a set of references, and we shall call it an anticipatory set. The drive (the dynamic element) plus such an anticipatory set (the cognitive element) governs a positive purpose and keeps it headed for its goal. Taking a term from R. B. Perry, who uses it in much the sense I intend, I shall call the combination of a drive and the primary anticipatory set for a terminal object to satisfy the drive, a "governing propensity."

Now it appears that as the governing propensity consists of two factors, so does the goal of an appetition. The terminal goal object is the object of the anticipatory set—namely, water for a thirsty man. But this is clearly not the ultimate goal of an appetition (though often assumed to be), for the ultimate goal is the satisfaction of the drive. For if the terminal goal object, water, did not bring satisfaction to the drive then obviously the appetition would go right on in pursuit of whatever goal object it was that would bring satisfaction to the drive.

The acts that fill in the gap between the governing propensity and the goals of this propensity we shall call subordinate acts. These consist of subordinate anticipatory sets for subordinate goals which the drive activates as means to the attainment of the terminal goal and final satisfaction.

This whole structure can now be spread out in a diagram where its dynamics can be clearly seen:

Governing Propensity	Subordinate Acts	Goals
I A_1		O_1 Q
	A_2	O_2
	A_3	O_3
	A_4 O_4	

I = drive (thirst)

A_1 = terminal anticipatory set (anticipation of water)

$\left. \begin{matrix} A_2 \\ A_3 \\ A_4 \end{matrix} \right\}$ = subordinate anticipatory sets $\left\{ \begin{matrix} \text{anticipation of water hole} \\ \text{anticipation of green patch} \\ \text{in valley} \\ \text{anticipation of way down slope} \end{matrix} \right.$

O_1 = terminal goal object (water)

$\left. \begin{matrix} O_2 \\ O_3 \\ O_4 \end{matrix} \right\}$ = subordinate goal objects $\left\{ \begin{matrix} \text{actual water hole} \\ \text{actual green patch in valley} \\ \text{actual way down the slope} \end{matrix} \right.$

$Q = \left\{ \begin{matrix} \text{quiescence pattern or} \\ \text{consummatory act} \end{matrix} \right.$ $\quad \begin{matrix} \text{(actual act of drinking, and feeling} \\ \text{of satisfaction in drinking)} \end{matrix}$

Abstractly, this diagram means that a drive, I, which demands satisfaction in a specific consummatory act or quiescence pattern Q, activates an anticipatory set A_1 for a terminal goal object O_1 which is expected to produce the quiescence pattern, and that this goal object not being at hand, the drive activates a succession of subordinate anticipatory sets, A_2, A_3, A_4, with their corresponding subordinate goal objects O_2, O_3, O_4 filling up the gap between the anticipated terminal goal object and the present location of the organism. On the assumption that all these anticipations are correct, then the organism acts upon O_4, which leads to O_3, which leads to O_2, which leads to O_1, which produces the quiescence pattern and the termination of the appetitive act.

Translating the foregoing diagram in the concrete terms of our example of the thirsty geologist at the moment he was standing on the ridge planning his next course of action, we say that his thirst (I) induced him to anticipate water (A_1) as a means of satisfying his craving, and this led him to think of a water hole (A_2) as a means of obtaining water, which led him to think of the green patch below in the valley (A_3) as a likely place to make a water hole, which led him to think of the way down the slope of the ridge (A_4) as a means of getting to the green patch in the valley. And here at his feet is the actual beginning of the way (O_4) down to the green patch, which he proceeds to have commerce with by walking down the slope, and this act actually brings him to the green patch at the bottom of the valley (O_3), where he proceeds to dig the actual water hole O_2, into which water actually flows, O_1, which then he drinks, and which consummatory act brings satisfaction and quiescence to his thirst and an end to this appetition.

Now, from this description, let us collect the values (that is, the acts and objects that would be accepted as instances of value according to accepted writers on the subject). The total activity may be roughly divided into a succession of segments: the emergence of the drive, and the emergence of the anticipatory sets, and then the succession of subordinate acts leading up to the attainment of the terminal goal object and the resulting consummatory act or quiescence pattern.

Observation 1. We observe that every one of these segments contains an element of wanting or conative value. As soon as a drive emerges there is a want. Behavioristically, this is usually evident in restlessness or trial and error activity, if the organism is not aware of the source of the want or the means of satisfying it; or, if the organism has learned from experience how the want can probably be satisfied, the conation is evident in the directness of the organism's action towards the goal object. Conative value thus extends throughout an appetition.

Observation 2. Obviously conation has its source in the drive, since the conative value vanishes when the drive is brought to quiescence in the consummatory act. When the geologist's thirst is satisfied, he no longer wants any more water for that thirst impulse. If he fills his canteen from the water hole after he has drunk his fill, the motivation for this act is not *thirst,* but *fear* of future thirst. This latter act is a new purposive act. It is not even an appetition. It is a rather complex form of aversion. The conative values derived from the thirst drive stop when the thirst ceases. The consummatory act at the end of this sequence of acts definitely brings this purposive activity to an end. This point should be marked by those who follow some comments of Dewey too literally and deny that there are values which are intrinsically ends. The geologist's drinking of the water may be a means (in some other sense of "means" such as that of causal connections with many other acts in the geologist's life and the lives of his associates), but it is conclusively the end and the terminal goal of the particular series of values set in motion by the emergence of the geologist's thirst on that particular day.

Observation 3. If conative value is defined (as I should advise) as the degree of wanting due to a drive, then it follows that the amount of conative value varies with the intensity of the drive and that this intensity varies from segment to segment of an act. In general, thirst gets more and more intense the longer it lasts, but there may nevertheless be considerable fluctuation in the course of a single appetition. Actual conative value, then, is not constant, but varies with the intensity of the drive.

Observation 4. It becomes fairly clear that if there is an actual object of conative value, this object must exist in the actual segment of the act where the conation is present. By actual object, I mean an existing object actually effective within the valuing act, as distinct from a potential object which is a possibility lying in the future but not actually present or in immediate causal relation with the act. I suggest that an actual object of conative value is an object actually charged with the drive. This means that goal objects with which an organism is not in actual commerce are not actual objects of conative value, but only potential objects. The geologist's water hole, of course, does not exist until he begins to dig it. On this basis an impulse without an anticipatory set (for instance, thirst before a child has any idea what will satisfy it) is a blind conative valuing, a wanting without an actual object. Indeed, whenever an organism is driven to trial and error activity there is some degree of blind wanting, objectless conation, a valuing of the organism knows not what. The trial and error activity is to the end of finding a something on which to concentrate the wanting. What is found is actually an anticipatory set. This is what is then charged with the energy of the drive, and this, I suggest, becomes the actual object of conative value at this stage of a purpose. But when an organism through its anticipatory set comes to be in commerce with a goal object, then that object is the actual object of conative value. And finally when the consummatory act is reached, then the actual object of conative value is the sensuous quality of the quiescence pattern itself. Thus, there is no single actual object of conative value in an appetitive activity, but the actual object migrates from segment to segment as the drive proceeds towards its goal. First the actual object is the anticipatory set, then whatever subordinate goal object the organism gets in contact with, then the succession of superordinate goal objects attained, until the consummatory act is reached, the sensuous quality (or the corresponding behavior pattern) of which is then the actual conative object.

A goal before it is achieved, then, is not an actual object of conative value. It is only a potential object, and does not become actual until it is attained. The realization of this fact will, I believe, untangle a lot of problems that surround the question of the object of value.

Observation 5. Note that goal objects and quiescence patterns are potential objects of conative value at all times previous to actual attainment. Their conative value as potential objects is, however, describable. The conative value ascribed to a potential object is the intensity of the drive in reference to that possible object. Thus as the geologist stood on the ridge just before starting for the green patch in the valley, he wanted water with the intensity of his thirst drive at that moment. The actual object of his conation as regards the reference to water was that actual cognitive reference itself of which his anticipatory set for water consisted at that moment. The potential object of conative value was the object of his cognitive reference, namely the as yet nonexistent water in the nonexistent water hole which was to quench his thirst. I repeat, the water itself that he will drink, though the terminal goal of his appetition, is not the actual conative object of his desire previous to his drinking it. The actual object until he is in actual commerce with the water is the cognitive reference to the water, or the anticipatory set itself.

Observation 6. Let me call special attention to an observation made above in another context, that there may be conative value without any actual object. Clearly so, when a drive emerges without an anticipatory set, but so also in some degree whenever an organism has to resort to trial and error behavior. This fact is not usually provided for adequately in relational theories of value of the form $(I)R(O)$ or value = interest in object. Is the object thus symbolized actual or potential? If the assumption is that the object of interest is actual, the theory is false or definitionally narrow and arbitrary and of little human significance. If the object is regarded as potential, then the exponent of the theory must be prepared to deal with a relation, one of the terms of which by definition does not exist (that is, the potential object). To be sure, conative value always is relational for a basic drive, in that such a drive is always in fact *capable* of being brought to quiescence by some kind of object or act which automatically is thereby the potential terminal object of potential conative value for that drive. Consequently, every segment of an appetition ordinarily has either a potential or an actual object of conative value. But the trouble with defining conative value as relational is that it tends to befog the distinction between an actual and a potential object. *(Interest) in (actual object)* is quite a different relation from *(interest) in (potential object)*. And just suppose (contrary to fact perhaps) that there were a drive for which there was no possible satisfaction—or is it so contrary to fact in certain acquired and perverse impulses where men have wants so constructed out of contrary primitive impulses that nothing in the world could satisfy them?—would not these interests, for which not even a potential object of satisfaction could be described, still be conations and contain conative values doomed to frustration? In short, is not the critical factor in conative value the drive or the conation, and is it not incidental whether or not there is an object for that drive? This is what I at least, hold. It is wanting that determines conative value, and the object of the wanting follows after, and is a thing to be found.

Observation 7. A distinction emerges at this point between a *potential object of value* and an *object of potential value*. These two potential values are often confused. A potential object of value presupposes a drive actually in process or conceived of as in process in reference to which an object is a possible goal. By definition, the object does not exist as an actual attained goal, for otherwise it would be an actual and not a potential object. In contrast, an object of potential value must exist or be conceived of as existing, in reference to which it is estimated that there is some probability that it may be the goal of a drive or become an object of actual value. In this latter case, the object exists; it is the valuing of it that is potential. To avoid the too ready ambiguity of these two types of potentiality, I propose to call the latter *conditional objects,* signifying that these are *objects* conceived as being possible objects of value under certain conditions.

Almost any conceivably existing object could be taken as a conditional object. But conditional objects acquire importance only when the probability of their being valued by some person becomes a reason why another person puts an actual value upon them. Thus a merchant buys a supply of "goods" not because he wants them for himself, but because he judges somebody else will want them and will pay for them at an

advantage to himself, with which proceeds he can then get something
he himself wants. All commodities are conditional objects based on a
belief that they will sometime be valued. From this develops credit
value. Credit value is actual value placed upon a conditional object on
the belief that it will be an actual object of value at some future time.
Apart from credit value, however, a conditional object has no actual
value. Some writers, however, treat it as if it did. The water under the
ground in the valley where the geologist dug his water hole was, of
course, a conditional object for anyone who had the passing thought
that that water might sometime quench the thirst of some passing
stranger. But that thought would not endow that water with any actual
conative value, since no one actually wanted the water at that moment
either to drink or as an investment for the future. No actual conative
value attaches to a conditional object unless it acquires actual credit
value.

Observation 8. Our analysis shows the ultimate ground of the distinction between means and end in value. The ultimate end of the
geologist's appetition was the act of drinking which brought his drive
to quiescence. We call this the quiescence pattern or terminal goal. It
is determined by the nature of the drive, and automatically becomes the
potential object aimed at in the appetition the moment the drive comes
into action in the organism. In relation to this consummatory act, all
other segments of the appetition are instrumental. Even the terminal
goal object (O_1) is a means to the production of the consummatory
act or quiescence pattern, which brings the drive to rest. This latter is the
absolute end of the appetition motivated by that particular drive. (For
the recurrence of a thirst drive is not literally the same drive as the thirst
that was quieted and satisfied. Thirst as a drive in action motivating
an appetition is to be distinguished from thirst as a behavioral disposition of an organism. The actual thirst is an actual drive but thirst as a
disposition is only a potential drive.)

In the progress of the appetition, however, there was a succession of
relative ends—namely the various goal objects. These are ends relative
to acts subordinate to their attainment, but they are means to the attainment of superordinate goal objects.

It appears then that in the structure of an appetition there are two
types of ends: (1) an absolute end, which is not in turn a means to
something else, and (2) relative ends, which are ends relative to sub-

ordinate acts, but means relative to superordinate acts. A quiescence pattern is an absolute end. But all goal objects, including the terminal goal object (in our example, water) are relative ends.

An absolute end cannot be in error. It is the act which in fact brings the drive to quiescence. A drive continues until it reaches its quiescence pattern. Nothing else will stop a drive except death, extreme fatigue, or a stronger drive that blocks it. The geologist might have died in his search for water, might have sunk into sleep from extreme weariness, or might temporarily have forgotten his thirst at the sight of a mountain lion in the valley. But it is still a fact that the drive would only be brought to quiescence by drinking.

Relative ends, on the other hand, may be in error. Goal objects are correct if they lead to their superordinate goals, incorrect if they do not. It follows that attached to all goal objects are, implicit if not explicit, judgments (our anticipatory sets) to the effect that the goal object sought will lead to the goal above it. These are the so-called value-judgments. All instrumental values involve value-judgments. Such judgments are intrinsic to the purposive activity involved in the very structure of the activity, as our diagram in showing the function of anticipatory sets makes very clear. The test of the correctness of an anticipatory set and its goal object is whether in fact the goal object when attained does produce the superordinate goal expected of it.

Putting the last two paragraphs together we see that value does not entail judgment—at least conative value does not. Some acts and objects of conative value involve a value-judgment and some do not. The relation of a drive to its quiescence pattern—which is the fundamental dynamic relation of an appetition—does not entail cognition. The ultimately irrational basis of conative values is thus justified. And justified also is the view that the function of cognition is essentially an instrumental function for the satisfaction of drives in the economy of a biological organism.

Observation 9. This is perhaps the proper spot to point out the relation between value and *evaluation.* If we define evaluation as *a judgment of whether something is an instance of value or not, and of what kind, and of how much,* it follows that an evaluative judgment is a judgment *about* value. It is not necessarily a value-judgment, that is, a mediating judgment within the structure of a value act. In short, it is not necessarily an anticipatory set. It is, so far as defined, an attempt

256 ESSAYS

to obtain a dispassionate scientific judgment of the values present in an appetition—or other situation containing value—quite outside the situation. An evaluation is a judgment. It is not a value unless value gets attached to the evaluative judgment. It is essential to see this distinction.

But as soon as the distinction is clearly seen, it is then equally essential to note that the reason most people are interested in evaluative judgments is precisely that they may use them as value-judgments, as anticipatory sets for the attainment of correct goal objects. An anticipatory set carefully arrived at is nothing other than an evaluative judgment as to the best means of obtaining a value goal. So the geologist on the ridge, considering the best means of getting water, and laying out a plan of action, was making a succession of evaluative judgments, which, after a conclusion was reached, were acted upon as anticipatory sets having the conative values earlier described. An evaluative judgment is not necessarily an anticipatory set, and so does not necessarily have any conative value for any specific purposive act, but when it takes on the status of an anticipatory set then it does acquire instrumental value in the activity it mediates.

Observation 10. I wish now to point out an additional value factor in the appetitive structure we have been studying—namely the affective values (pleasure and pain) it contains. Obviously there is pleasure of high intensity in the consummatory act. When the geologist finally obtained his water, he received much satisfaction and pleasure in the drinking of it. Of course, it may be argued that there is a distinction between the satisfaction of a drive and the introspective quality of pleasure in a consummatory act. But I incline to question this distinction. Leaving this issue aside, there is unquestionably a positive feeling, which I shall tentatively identify with pleasure, which occurs with the release of the drive's tension in the consummatory act of an appetition. The typical classical examples of pleasure are the feelings associated with the consummatory acts of basic appetitions—the pleasures of eating, drinking, sex orgasm, and the like. I am inclined to correlate this pleasure with the release of tension of a drive when the drive is not so intense as to be painful in itself. Likewise I incline to correlate pain in the appetitive drive with high tension of the drive. Consequently, I suggest that every drive has a pain threshold. Below this threshold the drive is active, but without pain. Mild thirst is not painful, but intense thirst is a typical example of pain. Release of intense thirst, I hold, does not give pleasure, but only relief from pain. When the pain threshold is passed in the consummatory act, then from that point down to final quiescence of the drive the release of tension yields pleasure.

On this hypothesis, I think it is clear that the primary motivation of an appetition is neither pleasure nor pain, but the drive. Only with experience does an organism *learn* that pleasure accrues to the consummatory act, and then pleasure as an anticipation becomes an added motivating factor. Pain is an added motivating factor, when the drive exceeds a certain intensity, and the organism learns to be apprehensive of intense drives and tries to satisfy them before the pain sets in.

Psychological hedonism, therefore, does not strictly hold, but there is a degree of secondary truth in the theory. Organisms are primarily motivated by their drives, but they *learn* the wisdom of avoiding pain and seeking pleasure. This may become a sophisticated conscious ideal, as with the philosophical hedonist—and as such is an evaluative factor in his choice of anticipatory sets—but there is some evidence that it is an unconscious emotional factor which directs the development of the personality in its repressed conflicts and is thus very deeply imbedded in our behavior. It is as if we instinctively learned to act on the hedonistic evaluative standard. At least, the direction of individual behavior for the avoidance of pain, so that the resulting behavior in a situation of conflict is such as to produce the minimum of pain under the circumstances, seems to be very deeply imbedded. The pursuit of pleasure may be a mode of evaluative motivation requiring more intelligence and foresight than the avoidance of pain.

We need much more information on these matters, and controlled experiments carried on without an assumption of some identification or some reduction of affection to conation or vice versa. As a tentative hypothesis of the relations between affection and conation in reference to a concept of behavior tensions, I append the following chart:

Tension	Affection	Conation
Increase of tension above pain threshold	Increasing pain	Increasing conation
Increase of tension below pain threshold	Neither pleasure nor pain	Increasing conation
Decrease of tension above pain threshold	Decreasing pain	Decreasing conation
Decrease of tension from pain threshold down	Pleasure	Decreasing conation

My hypothesis is that the primary motivation of purposive action is the conative tension of an instinctive drive. This automatically gives us conative value (positive wanting in appetitions, negative wanting in aversions), and the amount of this value is proportional to the degree of tension in the drive. Over and above this conative value, comes affective value, which cannot be directly correlated with conative value, as the chart shows. However, with experience an organism *learns* to be apprehensive of pain even before it sets in, and to seek pleasure. Pleasure and pain now become superimposed motivations reinforcing the original simple conative impulses and redirecting them towards the attainment of a maximum of pleasure and minimum of pain in the resolution of any individual's conflicts of impulses. The organism, I suggest, learns to act at a very early age and without premeditation for pleasure and against pain because of innate connections between these two types of value. An organism always wants pleasure as soon as he discovers what pleasure is (for that lies in the very structure of an appetition leading up to the consummatory act where pleasure emerges).

But that fact by no means signifies that positive wanting is pleasure; by our descriptive analysis it obviously is not. Nor does the fact signify that the value of the pleasure comes from its being positively wanted; for it comes out in the consummatory act as a sort of sweet surprise, and can only reinforce an original conation by the fact that it has a value of its own. Moreover, the intensity of pleasure in the consummatory act may be steady or increasing, while the wanting is necessarily steadily decreasing. For, in my hypothesis stated above, pleasure arises from *decreasing* tension below the pain threshold, the intensity of the pleasure possibly being correlated with the speed of decrease of tension; whereas conation is directly correlated with the amount of tension. Hence increased pleasure may accompany decreased wanting. So these two positive values cannot be identified in any way. But they are closely connected in the very structure of an appetition in such a manner that instinctively an organism learns to seek pleasure; similarly, on the negative value side, with pain. Thus it happens that pleasure and pain come to take evaluative control of individual behavior.

In short, I find that an analysis of purposive behavior indicates that affective values acquire evaluative priority over conative values in individual behavior, but that nevertheless the conative values are the dynamic and motivating and the more primitive values. It is through

drives that things are wanted or not wanted, and not through pleasure
and pain. But, with experience, organisms soon learn to direct their
drives toward decreasing pain and increasing pleasure wherever choices
or conflicts present themselves. This result is due to the structural connections existing in appetitions and aversions which bind together the
conative and the affective values.

II

Now let us apply our observations to Dewey's questions. Clearly,
from a study of the values of a simple appetition, one cannot assume a
generalized theory of value. There is much more in the value field than
appears in the segment of an isolated purposive act of a certain type.
However, we can at least require that answers to Dewey's questions
shall not be contrary to our findings in our limited analysis.

Let me anticipate one possible objection to my procedure which a
follower of Dewey might be tempted to make. He might try to discount
all my observations on the contention that my description of a *single*
purpose in isolation was a gross abstraction and false to the actual complexities of value situations in real life. In answer, let me say that the
geologist's behavior is taken out of real life. Real life is not always complex. It can become very simple, especially in conditions of emergency
such as the geologist was nearly faced with. Motivation then gets reduced to its lowest terms. All I hold is that answers to Dewey's questions must not be such as to contradict the observations made above, so
far as the latter are true to fact.

With the background of the foregoing analysis, Dewey's questions,
unless I misunderstand them, can be quickly answered:

I. What connection between "prizing" and "enjoying"?

A. If "prizing" is equivalent to my "conation" and "enjoying" to my
"affection," the answer to this question lies in Observation 10.

B. If "prizing" is supposed to imply an object of value and "enjoying"
not, I should agree that an object of value for affection was relatively
accidental. As for the object of value entailed by conation, I refer to
Observations 4, 5, 6, and 7 on the distinctions between "actual object of
value," "potential object of value," and "object of potential value" ("the
conditional object"). I think Dewey fails to distinguish these three, so
that an unambiguous answer cannot be given. I certainly should avoid

defining conative value in any way that would necessarily involve an
object of value.

C. In so far as the introspectionism versus behaviorism issue is contained in this question, I believe we need *all* the information we can
get, and that means we do well to accept both introspective and behavioristic reports regarding both conation and affection. I do not think
the acceptance of introspective reports about feelings of pleasure, pain,
and wanting involves the (for Dewey, vicious) mechanistic categories
and their dualism of mind and matter. Nor do I (consistently with my
views expressed in *World Hypotheses* [1]) regard the mechanistic interpretation as entirely distortive.

II. What relation between "prizing" or "enjoying" and "valuation" or
   "appraisal"?

I take it Dewey's "valuation" is equivalent to my "evaluation." For
my answer to this question, see Observation 9.

Since I should equate value (within the limits described in this paper)
with conation, affection, and the like, I should not consider an evaluation a value. It is a judgment about value. But an evaluation may become an object of value and charged with a drive—specifically whenever
an evaluation is used as an anticipatory set (see Observation 9).

This is, however, in part a verbal question. For what I now call "evaluation" corresponds roughly with what I once called "standard value,"
and what I now call "value" roughly corresponds to what I then called
"immediate value."

I should regard conation or affection apart from any judgmental element as a "sufficient condition for the existence of values" (see Observation 6).

III. Are evaluative judgments different from other judgments?
   Answer: No.

IV. Is scientific method applicable to evaluations, or judgments about
   value generally?

   Answer: Yes.[2]

[1] Berkeley, Calif., 1942.
[2] For the Criticisms and Rejoinders which relate especially to this paper see pp. 293–
295, 371–375, and 377–380, below.

SCIENCE, HUMANISM, AND THE GOOD

PHILIP BLAIR RICE

IN OUR TIME the nineteenth century conflict between science and religion has been largely replaced by, or absorbed in, an equally lively controversy between the upholders of "scientific method" and the defenders of the "humanities." Today's dispute comes into sharpest focus where curriculum-making is in question, but it diffuses into more general discussion in the serious and semi-serious journals. The issue is sometimes stated to be whether the methods of science or the methods of humanism are best fitted to give us knowledge of values. This way of putting the question precludes an answer. It erects artificial methodological barriers between these two major branches of human activity, and at the same time obscures what is distinctive in their contributions. If the dispute cannot be settled, our education and our culture will continue to suffer from the split mind which impairs their effectiveness at the moment. We shall continue to have a profitless squabble between an arid version of scientism, on the one hand, and a flabby humanism or a frightened supernaturalism on the other.

The conflict cannot be overcome by a polite compromise, such as putting large doses of science and large doses of the humanities into the curriculum of the college, or the curriculum vitae of the individual, to flourish side by side in splendid isolation. Such a compromise is often supported by a neat division of labor, in which "intrinsic" values are assigned to the domain of the humanities, while "instrumental" values are held to be the special preserve of the sciences. Dewey, among others, has valiantly combatted this oversimplification of the problem, and, though I sometimes disagree with his reasons, I am in hearty sympathy with his general opposition to such a solution.

I

The solution that I wish to suggest in this paper is along the following lines. The sciences and the humanities draw upon different skills, and

diverge considerably in their aims and functions. In so far as both can
be used to give us knowledge of the good for man, what they have in
common is empirical method, or an empirical logic, as a way of testing
beliefs. They differ in the detailed application of this method to their
respective subject matters, and in the sources to which they look for
their data. Even these differences, however, are for the most part differences of degree and of emphasis rather than sharp divisions of kind.

Empiricism, in its developed form, is the method which employs the
steps of observation, hypothesis, deduction, and verification by experience. It is opposed to those methods which make their final appeal to
authority, pure reason, intuition, or mere uncriticized emotion and impulse. If "scientific method" is restricted to the use of quantitative or
metric procedures, then it is a narrower term than empiricism. But today it is customary to conceive scientific method more broadly, so as
to include those subjects in which exact measurements are of limited
applicability. If empirical or scientific method is, furthermore, defined
in such a way as to admit only "public" data, and to rule out all use of
introspection or self-observation, however careful and controlled, then
there are limits to its adequacy in psychology and the value studies. Such
a restriction would, as I shall argue below, play into the hands of the
adversaries of empiricism. Because of these ambiguities in the meaning
of the term "scientific" it seems to me semantically advisable to adopt
"empirical method" rather than "scientific method" as a slogan, and to
conceive it so inclusively as to make no rigid prior assumptions as to
either the mensurability or the publicity of its data. But the slogan does
not matter greatly if we are clear as to what we are talking about.

Humanism, like the sciences, has sometimes been empirical in its
temper, and sometimes not. Certain spokesmen for the humanities today claim that a selected list of great books can give us intuitive or a
priori knowledge of eternal truths which require no verification. But
if we go back to the Renaissance for a definition of humanism, we find
that the humanists were at least as empirical in their procedures as the
scientists themselves, whom the new wine of mathematics often intoxi-
cated into thinking that they could dispense with the labor of observation. The humanists were, of course, concerned with a great many things
besides acquiring a knowledge of good and evil. They created works
of art, edited texts, and tried to live with gusto. But in so far as they
addressed themselves, directly or indirectly, to exploring what we now

call "values," they drew upon three principal sources: (1) literature, including religious literature, and the other arts; (2) shrewd everyday observation of other people's behavior; and (3) self-observation or introspection. From these sources the humanist can obtain presentations of goods and evils, hypotheses about them, and, either at first or at second hand, data to test these hypotheses. If in practice the humanists sometimes rely upon casual intuitions, and as literary men are more preoccupied with stating their insights amusingly or movingly than with multiplying inductive verifications of them, this springs partly from the fact that they have several functions to perform and are moralists but occasionally. Humanism becomes irresponsible only if it confuses these functions, or if it denies the applicability of the more sober and plodding techniques of the sciences, whenever these are sufficiently developed, to check its somewhat random insights into human motivation and sentiment.

It would be rash to impose definite limits upon the fitness of those subjects conventionally called sciences to investigate the subject matter of values, and equally rash to claim that they will ever crowd out the so-called humanities in performing this function. The arts will probably always be slightly ahead of the sciences in making us aware of certain possibilities and certain discriminations in the realm of personal living, though not only the "artist" Henry James but also the "scientist" William James can give us illumination here. And conversely, we shall probably look for an understanding of society primarily to the anthropologists, economists and political scientists; yet it would be presumptuous to exclude entirely the testimony of poets and novelists as to the repercussion of social institutions in our lives. The ways in which the arts can be used to give us knowledge of good and evil are intricate and indirect, and I shall not here attempt to analyze them in detail. But it is perhaps in order to say that works of imaginative literature should not be used as *sortes Vergilianae*. When we draw upon literature for ethical hypotheses, we shall, if we are wise, seek verification outside the work of art itself, though sometimes the appeal is to other humanistic sources of data, such as everyday observation and introspection, when controlled laboratory or statistical evidence is not available or not conclusive.

Dissatisfaction with the partisans of "scientific method"—and often, in consequence, rejection of the empirical approach to values in general—is most often voiced today, not only by those whose chief interest is in the arts, but also by those to whom the problems of personal values, and of the individual moral struggle, are most insistent. For such persons, literature and religion may seem to offer more that is directly useful and testable in their lives than the sciences. Scientific psychology has as yet developed only the rudiments of a theory of personality, though it has made promising beginnings. Empirically minded philosophers have devoted themselves mainly to exploring the continuities between human and animal behavior, the logical aspects of value theory, and social ethics—in the latter case, sometimes giving the impression that the search for an individual pattern of life can be submerged entirely in the effort to remake the institutional patterns of society. The present vogue of that uncommonly muddled and pretentious doctrine called neo-orthodoxy, and the mass flight of intellectuals to Rome or Nirvana, can be attributed in part to the failure of empirical and naturalistic philoso-phies, at the present stage of their development, to offer ways of re-solving many predicaments of the individual. Consequently those who are concerned over the "new failure of nerve" should devote at least as much attention to putting their own house in order as to exposing the confusions of Chancellor Hutchins and the fulminations of Monsignor Sheen. Until it achieves a more adequate analysis of experience, empiricism will be vulnerable to the attacks of reactionaries.

An individual style of life is fostered by imaginative example and by the kind of dramatic participation that religious practices have afforded in the past, as well as by hypotheses derived from scientific inquiry. The arts, and religion—in so far as it retains or recovers some poetic relevance to the human situation—will probably continue to influence our fundamental valuations in these ways and many more; and it is difficult to see how those activities conventionally classified as sciences could take their place. The role of scientific or empirical method is to test the assumptions that are involved in the adoption of a style of life, and the explicit propositions that state our valuations. A sound and rich culture requires both a lively ferment of imaginative expression and the continual tough-minded scrutiny of its fruits in experience.

Theory of value will remain a technical academic exercise unless it can offer some guidance in the solution of these and similar problems. As a special "branch" of philosophy, value theory is little more than a half-century old. Its rise coincided with the development of the post-Darwinian biological and social sciences, which produced a major revolution in our conceptions of life and mind. It is understandable, and it has been highly fruitful, that such influential writers on valuation as Dewey and R. B. Perry should have taken their basic principles and attitudes from these sciences. But certain limitations have resulted. I am not suggesting that thinkers like Dewey and Perry are insensitive to the role of the "humanities" in our culture. Dewey has written profoundly of the arts in *Art as Experience,* and Perry has attempted a similar service for religion in *Puritanism and Democracy.* There is, however, too little explicit carry-over of these interests into their technical writings on general theory of value; and it may be argued that their basic categories have not been chosen in such a way as to promote the kind of harmonious collaboration between the method of science and the insights of the humanities which is one of the major needs of our time, and which can be clarified only by a philosophical analysis of values. It is to some central issues in this task that the following considerations are devoted.

II

The cleavage between the scientific and the humanistic interests of philosophers manifests itself in the choice of the basic concepts of value theory, which has sought an elementary or, sometimes, a "generic" sense of the terms good and bad on which to construct the more complex and special meanings involved in such notions as aesthetic value, economic value, and ethical value.

This basic sense of good must refer to some very pervasive aspect of experience. Nearly all current theories agree that the experience of value as a whole includes, along with other components, feeling and striving, which are closely related to each other, so that they call value an "affective-motor" phenomenon. When they investigate the relation of these two elements in detail, however, it turns out to be very complicated, so that they are usually forced to take one or the other as fundamental, and to make it central in any definitions that they may offer.

Affective theories treat the basic sense of good in terms of pleasure (pleasantness, enjoyment, joy, satisfaction, consummatory quality, hedonic tone), and evaluate striving by its issue in feeling. Conative theories take striving (Eros, desire, interest, goal-seeking) as fundamental, and treat feeling as its by-product. In general, those who come into value theory from a preoccupation with the "humanities" are predisposed toward an affective theory; and those who take their cues from the biological and social sciences favor a conative definition of elementary value. This alignment is probably unfortunate, but it is historically and psychologically intelligible.

There are also compromise theories which try to keep feeling and striving equal to the end: Jessup's by including them both in the definition of primary value, Pepper's by erecting the affective and the conative into distinct but coordinate species of elementary value.[1]

Conative theories have an initial appeal to the "scientifically" minded because conation is easier to detect and measure in the laboratory than feeling, because it supplies a manageable continuity between human and animal values, and because a view which takes it as central serves to keep in the forefront the emphasis on socially directed effort which is a fundamental concern with these theories.

Striving may enter into the value situation in a great variety of ways, and consequently there are a number of different versions of the conative theory, depending upon which relationship of striving to value is taken as central. I shall divide conative theories into three main classes, which may be called the "teaser," the "satisfaction," and the "maintenance" theories.

1. The teaser theories, represented by Perry and Hobbes, and by Aristotle, Spinoza, and Pepper in so far as they hold a conative theory, formulate a very widespread usage of the term value: the good, in its primary sense, is that which evokes striving, or constitutes the objective of striving. Perry, for example, defines "x is valuable" as "interest is taken in x," and interest in turn is described as an active motor attitude toward an object.[2] The individual "values" the object which he strives to achieve, and therefore, at least at this preliminary stage, the object can be said to have some value for him.

This definition expresses a very common precondition of value. But this sense of the term is not well fitted to serve as the basis for the reflective discriminations which value theory seeks to make, that is, for tested judgments of value. For it frequently turns out that when we get what we want we don't want it. What the individual expects will gratify his desire often proves in the event not to do so. Our strivings may be misdirected, and the judgments of value that grow out of them and

[1] The references are to B. E. Jessup, *Relational Value Meanings*, Eugene, Ore., 1943, and to Pepper's essay, pp. 245–260, above.
[2] R. B. Perry, *A General Theory of Value*, New York, 1926.

guide them may consequently be mistaken. Conversely, the unexpected and surprising elements in life are sometimes recognized as good when they come.[3]

If we are to make this necessary distinction between correct and incorrect estimates of value, it is necessary to equate "x is striven for," not with "x *is* valuable," but with "x *seems* valuable," or "x is believed to be valuable," or "x is responded to as though it were valuable." This sense of the term, then, does not describe actual value but merely *imputed* value.

2. The satisfaction theories offer a criterion to decide when the imputation is correct and when it is incorrect. They locate the actual value, not in the evocation of striving, but in its satisfaction or reduction. In order that an object may be reflectively judged to be valuable, it must not merely be sought but must allay the need which motivates the striving. If it does not do this, we decide that the original object was mistakenly imputed to be good, and some other object is pursued in order to banish the unrest.

Some theories which formally define the valuable as that which satisfies interest—for example, those of Prall, Parker and Aiken—are not strictly speaking conative theories at all. They place the value, not in the termination of striving as such, but in the accompanying enjoyment: they are, accordingly, affective theories. Such an attempt to make the best of both theories has the weakness that it is highly debatable whether the enjoyment always attaches to the terminal, or the reductive, phases of conation and may not occur in other contexts.

A strictly conative version of the satisfaction theory ignores the affective by-products of striving, and adheres consistently to a motor conception of striving. Thus the behaviorist C. L. Hull treats striving, and consequently the magnitude of its reduction, as measurable by the physical energy expended by the organism in getting to its goal.[4] And his fellow behaviorist E. C. Tolman defines the good as "getting to a final physiological quiescence or from a physiological disturbance, or both." [5] We thus have a meeting of the extremes of behaviorism and Buddhism: the good is Nirvana, or extinction of desire.

Perry answers similar objections by saying that when unexpected elements are valuable we strive to maintain them after they arrive. In taking this position he is shifting to the "maintenance" theory discussed below.
C. L. Hull, "Value, Valuation, and Natural-Science Methodology," *Philosophy of Science*, XI (1944), 125–141.
E. C. Tolman, *Purposive Behavior in Animals and Men*, New York, 1932, chs. 2, 17.

The principal difficulty with this view is that we sometimes find the process good as well as its termination: the game as well as the victory, the wooing as well as the conquest. And those preconsummatory phases of the striving to which we attribute value may involve the maintenance and even the increase of striving rather than its abatement. To answer this objection, the defender of the need-reduction theory is forced to postulate a fixed initial quantity of "tension" or latent energy tapped by the arousal of the particular drive, and to hold that this tension is being reduced even while the external manifestations of the striving are on the increase. But such a reservoir of tension would seem to correspond at most to a maximum *limit* of energy-potential possessed by a given drive. Whether the maximum energy will actually be expended depends both on continued stimulation and on the amount of resistance encountered, which are variable quantities.

This version of the conative theory, like the others, is concerned with a genuine cross-section of the valuational facts. Undoubtedly, an important class of the experiences that we hold to contain value is constituted by that final phase of striving in which the goal-object is reached, appropriated or consumed, or by those preliminary phases in which the tension of striving is being abated. But, as I have suggested, these are not the only phases of the process that we find good. And in so far as the terminal phase is preeminent, it also seems to be the phase in which the maximum of enjoyment is experienced, or the final release from suffering is accomplished—so that an affective theory seems at least as well fitted to describe the facts, except where it is ruled out by the assumptions of the more dogmatic types of behaviorism.

The satisfaction theory has the further difficulty that it offers a very shaky basis for judgments of *comparative* value. In estimating the worth of alternative activities, we are concerned not merely with the fact of satisfying an interest, and the number of interests satisfied, but with the manner of obtaining satisfaction. There are notorious differences between the ways in which the average Englishman and the average Frenchman satisfy the interest in food. Satisfaction is a crude but useful index of the bare presence of immediate value, and frustration of immediate disvalue, but the art of life requires nicer instruments of discrimination.

3. In his "Some Questions about Value," Dewey finds the crucial condition of value in still another relation to striving besides the two

already mentioned. He says that that type of "prizing" which constitutes the necessary though not sufficient condition of value (the additional condition required to make it sufficient consisting in the act of valuation or appraisal) is "a way of behaving tending to maintain something in factual (space-time) existence," the object prized being a "thing that exists independently of being valued." Examples of prizing in this "behavioral" sense are "the behavior of a mother bird in nourishing its young or of a mother bear in attacking animals that threaten her young."

He seems to be offering us, by implication, a definition of prizing according to which "A prizes x" means "A strives to maintain x in existence": the mother bird's or the mother bear's prizing of her young is constituted by her striving to maintain her young in existence.

Now it seems utterly arbitrary to limit prizing or valuing to precisely this type of conation. As the other versions of the conative theory suggest, we attribute value to objects that we pursue but never attain, to ideal objects that do not yet exist, to perishable things that we consume, and to transitory goals at which we do not linger. The mother's prizing of her young is *a* genuine type of prizing, but Dewey has not shown that it is the only legitimate type of prizing, or the prototype of all other types of prizing.

His view would seem to rule out, for example, the whole class of aesthetic attitudes. When we are enjoying or prizing aesthetically a picture in the museum, we are not concerned with maintaining the picture in existence, but we are content to leave that to the museum staff. All sorts of conative behavior are involved in aesthetic prizing, such as adjustment of the eye, head, and trunk muscles in the act of perception. But behavior of this sort is directed to preservation of a *perceptual attitude,* the attitude of prizing (or disprizing), and not to preservation of the object prized, such as the picture or the young birds.

A curator's activities are, indeed, devoted to preserving the existence of the picture—not only its bare physical existence, but a proper appreciation of it by the public—and there is, in well-conducted museums, a close relation between those activities and the aesthetic values of the paintings. The curator, if his time is limited, will ordinarily devote more of his loving care to a Rembrandt or a Cézanne than to a Rosa Bonheur; and if the museum catches on fire the casual visitor will try to save the paintings to which he ascribes the highest aesthetic value. In these ways we can sometimes, to use Dewey's words, find a rough measure of the "intensity of the 'prizing'" in the "amount of energy that goes into the nourishing or the protecting behavior." Art critics, however—as Dewey himself has recognized in *Art as Experience*—have considerably more reliable methods of judging the aesthetic values of paintings than are furnished by such gross behavioral tests.

Aesthetic prizing, then, seems to include a striving to preserve something, but only in an indirect way. "*A* prizes (aesthetically) the picture" cannot be equated with "*A* strives to maintain the picture in existence." What is maintained in existence is the perceptual attitude of aesthetic prizing itself. The maintenance theory, consequently, is useful in calling our attention to the fact that, in many instances of prizing, maintenance of something or other is somehow involved (though I should have thought that it was highly obvious that any activity which takes some time has to be maintained during that time); it has not shown that the striving is always directed toward maintaining in existence the object prized. Dewey does not seem, therefore, to have got at the gist of the matter. That which makes the picture valuable, whatever it may be, is something besides the maintenance of a perceptual attitude towards it. The maintenance of this attitude is simply an auxiliary condition of the prizing. An affective view would hold that for the picture to be valuable it must also give rise to a certain kind of delight. In *Art as Experience*, Dewey himself has described the aesthetic experience as one of "delightful perception." Why does he now tell us that it is the maintenance of the perception, rather than the delight in the perception, that is the crucial element in the value? The maintenance of the perception is a necessary condition of aesthetic delight, but the delight is the necessary condition of the prizing: we seem, therefore, to be coming somewhat closer to the heart of the matter by means of an affective theory.[6]

[6] In his "The Field of 'Value,'" Dewey places some altogether gratuitous interpretations on the brief remarks of mine which he quotes (p. 72, above). (1) I was referring—in the case of both the curator and the aesthetic visitor—to the prizing of the picture, and not to the prizing of the prizing of the picture. And I was using "experience" in the sense of a transaction—between a man and a picture—and not in the sense of a mental state. (2) I was not intending to impugn the aesthetic sensibilities of curators, but to point to one of their functions which is not shared by most of the visitors to their museums, the function, namely, of maintaining the pictures in existence. (3) When I said that the visitor "looks" at the picture, I meant as I believe should be obvious from the context, that he is looking at it aesthetically and not in some other way. (4) I would agree that aesthetic looking is a process that takes time and involves a transaction with the object. (5) When I referred to the

On numerous other occasions, Dewey has located the central fact of value in still another mode of striving, that is, not in a striving to maintain something in existence, but in a striving to overcome a "lack," or to eliminate the troublesome element in a situation and to restore harmony.[7]

This brief survey of conative theories, however cavalierly it may deal with each of them, suggests that, although striving comes into the experience of value in a great variety of ways, the relationships of value to striving are so numerous, so diverse, and so complicated that it is a hopeless task to seek, in terms of any one relation to conation, an adequate "generic" conception of value, or even a "basic" conception of value on which a comprehensive and well-articulated theory can be built. When anyone tries this, he gets into epicycles upon epicycles, in the effort to overcome the simplifications which a too-restricted initial choice of categories invariably produces.

The shortcomings of conative theories become especially evident when they try to give an account of aesthetic value or ethical value as a function of striving. They are forced to define the ethical standard, for example, as an "integration" or "coordination" or "harmony" of interests or conations. But attention to the actual experience of ethical deliberation shows that this standard of integration is assumed dogmatically; men often choose an affectively more rewarding but less well-integrated way of life to one that is more harmonious but poorer in feeling. And the standard of integration by itself gives us no way of choosing between two patterns of conduct or two social systems which are equally well organized.

Consequently we seem forced to conclude that conative theories, although they have done a great service in bringing to light the manifold ways in which striving is related to value, have been unable to offer in terms of conation alone an analysis or a definition of a basic sense of value which possesses sufficient scope and precision to guide valuational choices.

---

maintenance of the picture and the aesthetic enjoyment of it as exhibiting different types" of value, I did not intend to "reify" these types into Platonic Ideas, but imply to point to a distinction between the attitudes as classes of individual behaviors.

7. Dewey, "Theory of Valuation," in *International Encyclopedia of Unified Science*, Chicago, 1939; *et passim.*

III

The most important current versions of the conative theory owe their origin to a psychological assumption which was prevalent when these theories were formulated a generation or so ago, but which requires considerable modification as a result of the subsequent inquiries of experimental psychology itself. This assumption is that any complicated activity, such as valuing or learning or instinct or feeling or thinking, must be conceived primarily in terms of its motor elements. Perry's and Dewey's theories treat the motor factor in quite different ways; and neither would accept the crude version of the motor theory associated with the name of J. B. Watson. But all the types of conative theory explicitly stress the motor phases of effort—whether they choose to focus on the evocation of striving, or its reduction, or its maintenance.

The psychologies of the decades leading up to the 1920s brought to light the fact that motor striving played a much greater role in the so-called mental functions, even the "higher" ones, than had previously been recognized. It was seen—for example, in Dewey's early "The Reflex Arc Concept in Psychology" [8]—that sensation or perception is not a mere passive reception of data but usually involves all sorts of motor adjustments such as those of the eye and head muscles. "Emotion" is not an experiencing of inert mental states, but requires an active preparation of the striped muscles, the glands, and the vascular and visceral systems, for flight or combat. Even "thinking" usually includes innervation of the vocal muscles, or, with deaf-mutes, of the finger muscles. But the first flush of such discoveries led to what is now beginning to be recognized by experimental psychologists to have been too simple a conception of the relationship between sensory stimulus and motor response, and to have exaggerated the role of motor activity in some of these processes. The idea of not only the reflex arc but the sensory motor circuit, like the categories of stimulus and response, sometimes led to a rather crude application of the principle of the conservation of energy to the human organism: if you put energy into the organism in the form of sensory stimulation, it was assumed, you must always get energy out of it in the form of motor reaction.

This view ignored the anabolic and katabolic functions of the organism itself, which make it impossible in any given single reaction to equate input and output; it also ignored the resistances—the inner friction, so to speak—that occur in the central portions of the nervous system itself. The cerebral cortex alone contains some ten billion nerve cells, and the rest of the central nervous system several billion more. This would seem to suggest—and recent experimental evidence corroborates the suggestion—that a great deal can happen in the central portions of the neural circuit that does not find its immediate, or even perhaps its ultimate, conditions or expressions in motor activity. Building on the work of earlier experimenters, Rafael Lorente de Nó has given elaborate histological and physiological confirmation of the existence of "closed chains" of central neural activity, to which the independent observations of psychologists in other fields had been pointing for some time.[9] An impulse can find its way from the senses into the central nervous system and chase around there for a long time in elaborate circuits, without issuing in overt response; and conversely the impulse in some cases can be extinguished by the resistances of the central cells and their media without ever innervating the motor cells at all. Meanwhile the impulse may have established a number of central associations, and even have yielded considerable dividends in the way of consciousness, that is, of "thinking" or "feeling." The sensory impulse, moreover, can be amplified a thousandfold.

Whether such "higher" processes as thinking and feeling can take place *entirely* without motor expression and sustained proprioceptive stimulation is not the point at stake. It is undeniable that these higher processes normally, even though perhaps not invariably, do involve more or less motor activity of the sort that the Deweyan theory of perception, the James-Lange theory of emotion, and the Watsonian theory of thinking have stressed, and that these externally observable phenomena supply clues—though less reliable clues than it is sometimes supposed—to the so-called inner states of other people. The question is rather as follows. Granting that these activities normally have motor constituents, can we establish specific one–one correlations between these activities and motor striving, so that the striving can be treated as the exact behavioral expression or equivalent of, say, the feeling or the thinking or the perceiving?

There is an increasing wealth of evidence to the contrary. I shall give

[9] "Analysis of the Activity of the Chains of Internuncial Neurons," *Journal of Neurophysiology*, I (1938).

only a few samples from the mass of evidence presented by K. S. Lashley, who was an associate of Watson in the early development of behaviorism. Lashley is concerned to stress the relative autonomy of the central portions of the nervous circuit, and to show that a considerable segment of the learning process is independent of the motor phases of learning:

If we train an animal in a maze and observe carefully his subsequent errorless running, we find little identity of movement in successive trials. He gallops through one trial, in another shuffles along, sniffing at the cover of the box. If we injure his cerebellum, he may roll through the maze. He follows the correct path with every variety of twist and posture, so that we cannot identify a single movement as characteristic of the habit. . . . We seem forced to conclude that the same motor elements are not necessarily used in the learning and performance of motor habits and that motor elements can be utilized directly when no specific associations have been formed with them.[10]

After a survey of similar experimental observations we find the behaviorist Tolman concluding that there are types of learning in which the motor element is subordinate:

Learning can no longer be envisaged as a matter of building up S-R connections but it must be considered rather as learning of "what leads to what." When the further "whats" resulting in given directions are made good, given the animal's motivation, then, if the animal has also learned, he will tend to go in these directions. . . . Learning *per se* is to be envisaged, in short, as a matter of the animal's acquiring the correct "expectation sets"—the correct "hypotheses" or, to go back to the 17th, 18th and 19th centuries, the correct associations of ideas (not the correct S-R's).[11]

O. H. Mowrer and associates have criticized the motor interpretation of expectancy. They interpret their experiments as indicating that preparatory set or expectancy cannot be treated as a "motor set" but "is primarily a central phenomenon," and is "mediated principally by neural rather than neuro-muscular mechanisms." In criticizing the older behaviorist emphasis on the motor elements, overt or implicit, these writers point to an increasing amount of empirical evidence which undermines the view that "psychologically significant events" cannot occur "in the

[10] K. S. Lashley, "Basic Neural Mechanisms in Behavior," *The Psychological Review,* XXXVII (1930), 5; by permission of the editors.
[11] E. C. Tolman, "The Law of Effect," *The Psychological Review,* XLV (1938), 203 by permission of the editors.

human nervous system without concomitant manifestations in 'motor' mechanisms (muscles or glands)." [12]

In a survey of the evidence revealing that in most animal instincts the motor behavior is extremely variable, Lashley suggests that the core of the instinct consists in a sensory-central rather than a sensory-motor pattern:

It is possible that the nest, or other product of activity, represents a sensory pattern which is "closed" for the animal, in the sense in which this term has been applied to visually perceived forms. The nest might then be built by somewhat random activity, modified until it presents a satisfactory sensory pattern. [13]

In this connection, Lashley cites a study by Hebb which corroborates earlier work by the Gestaltists tending to show that sensation and perception are less intimately dependent on motor response than the older behaviorisms and response theories assumed:

Studying the visual reactions of rats reared to adulthood in total darkness, Hebb has found that the animals respond immediately to objects, as contrasted with background. Something of a figure-ground organization is immediately given. They learn readily a differential reaction to figures which cannot be explored in any way except visually. This means that the figures must be distinguished visually before association with motor reactions can occur. [14]

This very brief summary of the trend away from motor theories of behavior may be summed up in the following words of Lashley:

The James-Lange theory of emotion, the idea that mental attitudes are an expression of bodily "sets," the theory that instincts and serial habits are chains of sensory-motor activity, the doctrine that implicit speech or gesture forms the basis of thinking: these are all expressions of the belief that the central nervous system serves merely for the rapid switching and conduction of impulses from receptor to effector, without long-continued intraneural sequences of activity.

[12] O. H. Mowrer, N. N. Rayman and E. L. Bliss, "Preparatory Set (Expectancy)— an Experimental Determination of its 'Central' Locus," *Journal of Experimental Psychology*, XXVI (1940); "Preparatory Set (Expectancy)—a Determinant in Motivation and Learning," *The Psychological Review*, XLV (1938).
[13] K. S. Lashley, "An Experimental Analysis of Instinctive Behavior," *The Psychological Review*, XLV (1938), 450; by permission of the editors.
[14] *Loc. cit.*, 450.

276   ESSAYS

On the contrary, Lashley holds that the evidence supports the view that

the pattern of organization of the motor cortex can be altered by central excitation and that the altered condition can be maintained for long periods without reinforcement from peripheral organs. . . . The work of Thorson on tongue-movements and unpublished observations of eye-movements during thinking, together with reports of the recovery of speech with the use of an artificial language . . . point to some continued intraneural process as the basis of thinking. . . . The peripheral (including motor) activities are not an essential condition for the maintenance of the central processes.[15]

The more developed types of human behavior are mediated by man's capacity to respond to symbols. These symbols are not always overtly perceived or expressed, but the symbolic act may be central in its crucial phases. The human being's capacity to use symbols in these ways is an outgrowth of the more rudimentary animals' sign behavior. A rat exhibits what Tolman calls "vicarious trial-and-error behavior," or what others call "symbolic exploration." When the rat comes to a choice point in a maze, he makes brief explorations into the alternative alleys, then without pursuing each to its conclusion finally "chooses" one of them—presumably the one which causes the greatest preliminary lessening of the goal-seeking tension which motivates him.[16] Human beings placed in a similar situation can often choose the right path without "running back and forth" after the fashion of the rat; they can respond to the sensory cues as *symbols* of that to which they lead, and fit them into the total symbolic structure which constitutes their knowledge of the situation. Implicit motor responses are often involved, but the evidence we have considered previously suggests that the central processes are more decisive here than the motor, and are to a considerable degree independent of them. In the place of the gross motor response of the rat to signs, the reflective human being makes a largely "internalized" response to symbols.[17]

The rat's motivation is elicited by externally administered rewards and punishments, such as food and electric shocks. But the human being's motivation in valuational and moral situations is to a large exten

[15] "Basic Neural Mechanisms in Behavior," previously cited, 10–12.
[16] E. C. Tolman, *Purposive Behavior in Animals and Men*, New York, 1932, ch. xii; and "The Determiners of Behavior at a Choice Point," *The Psychological Review* XLV (1938).
[17] G. H. Mead, *Mind, Self and Society*, Chicago, 1934.

dependent upon what Thorndike has called the "confirming reaction"
or "O. K. reaction," which in humans after earliest infancy is guided by
the rewards of "self-esteem" and gratified "conscience." [18] The internal
reward or punishment, furthermore, may attach to symbols rather than
to the possession or consumption of external objects.[19]

We may have here the scientific instruments for the recovery of what
is valid in the Socratic, Hebraic-Christian, and introspective-modern
insights that happiness or salvation in its last manifestations is an "inner
condition," and is not to be defined wholly by external happenings.
This does not imply any return to earlier metaphysical and theological
beliefs about the "soul"; nor does it require us to hold that the internal
factors in conduct can be isolated, in the total study of their genesis and
functioning, from the physical and social environment or from the total
"situation"—on the contrary, the internal and external factors are in
constant interaction. The symbols which mediate adult moral activity,
being largely linguistic, are not private but social in their origin. The
individual frequently gives overt utterance to these symbols, and he
uses them to direct his action and reconstruct his environment. We get
evidence as to other people's activity through observation of these overt
acts, aided by inferences from those phases of our own processes which
are directly accessible only to self-observation. What I am suggesting,
then, is that the "internal" phases of the behavioral act can be distinguished from the other phases for the purposes of analysis and description, and that they are to some degree autonomous or central in their
operation, not that they can come into existence in the total course of
the individual's life development, or be adequately understood, apart
from the context of their social conditions and overt expressions.

An account of the "internal" along these lines would be thoroughly
naturalistic and empirical, and it would be "behavioral" in the sense
that it conceives mind not as a separate substance, or a passive mirror
of the external world, but as the unitary activity of the organism developing through its interaction with natural and social conditions. To
assert all concern with the "inner" or "private" aspects of behavior, as
so conceived, to be just a hang-over from prescientific ways of thinking

[18] E. L. Thorndike, *The Psychology of Wants, Interests and Attitudes*, New York, 1935.
[19] O. H. Mowrer and D. Ullman, "Time as a Determinant in Integrative Learning," *The Psychological Review*, LII (1945); and P. B. Rice, "The Ego and the Law of Effect," *The Psychological Review*, LIII (1946).

is to commit the genetic fallacy. Attention to the inner life is no more discredited by the original association of the notion with certain now outmoded theological beliefs than the Pythagorean theorem is discredited by its early connection with a taboo on beans. The major ethical and religious traditions cannot receive the critical reinterpretation that they need, and that the "humanistic" faction claim they deserve, until empirically minded philosophers get over such phobias.

IV

If such functions of the organism as instinct, learning, motivation, thinking and expectancy cannot be exhaustively treated in terms of their motor constituents and accompaniments, it seems initially probable that valuing—which, in many of its forms, includes these factors and is therefore at least as complex as they—may likewise have manifestations in which other factors besides the motor predominate. When we come to what Pepper calls the affective values in particular, we see that recent psychological and neurological investigations of feeling accord with this shift of emphasis from the motor to the central neural factors.

The recent experimental evidence on hedonic tone (pleasantness or unpleasantness) indicates that it is a direct function of stresses in the central nervous field.[20] There are no special sensory receptors for pain and pleasure (the so-called "nociceptors" or free nerve-endings appear to be simply nerves with a low threshold of overstimulation, and because of their ubiquity in the tissue cells easily summate to produce a central disturbance when stimulated over a wide area); and the motor expressions of the milder forms of affect, in particular, are at most rough clues to their occurrence and qualities.

The exact central conditions of positive and negative hedonic tones are not yet known. Pleasantness in many instances seems closely correlated with release of tension—whether this tension is a muscular set or a vector of central neural forces or "expectancies"—but it has not been shown that it can be universally so treated, as Pepper's essay in this symposium assumes. In fact, both common observation and the indirect neurological evidence indicate that in some cases pleasantness

---

[20] W. B. Cannon, *Bodily Changes in Pain, Hunger, Fear and Rage*, 1929; L. T. Troland, *Fundamentals of Human Motivation*, New York, 1928; H. F. Dunbar, *Emotion and Bodily Changes*, New York, 1938; F. H. Lund, *Emotions*, New York, 1939; K. S. Lashley, "The Thalamus and Emotion," *The Psychological Review*, XLV (1938).

is constituted by or correlated with maintenance or increase of activity. We observe that increasing sensory stimulation—such as stimulation of the taste buds by a sweet substance or stimulation of the thermoceptors by warmth—tends to be increasingly pleasant up to a certain point, then to pass into unpleasantness and pain. Likewise with muscular activity and many other types of experience.

A possible clue to an embracing theory of neural action in hedonic tone may be found in Adrian's experiments on single sensory fibres, which show that for certain receptors the transmission of impulses is regular between rates of 25 and 300 or 500 impulses a second, and beyond that rate of stimulation tends to become irregular from inability of the walls of the nerve cells to restore themselves.[21] If the electrochemical operation of the central regions is similar to that of the sensory nerves—and there is increasing evidence to this effect [22]—we may speculate that pleasantness is correlated with smooth functioning in the central regions, and unpleasantness with ragged functioning. Pleasantness may therefore accompany either an increase, maintenance, or decrease of tension, provided that the rate of functioning falls between a lower and an upper limit.

The evidence suggests that hedonic tone cannot be correlated with any single phase of striving, such as its sinking to quiescence, but is dependent upon too great a variety of factors to be treated in any such simple fashion: it seems to be the complex effect of interaction, summation, irradiation, conflict, and inhibition within the rapidly shifting fields of stress in the central region between the spine and the cortex.[23]

Consequently "gross behavioral" observations of externally observable factors are at present unable to give us adequate definitions of affect. Refinement of such electrical devices as the electroencephalograph may some day furnish more reliable clues to these intricate central happenings, but at present we have to use such external clues as we can get in conjunction with the indirect neurological evidence and with "introspection," which at least reports on the presence and the degree of positive or negative hedonic tone, and to some extent permits us to analyze the phenomenological structure of affective experience. We

[21] E. D. Adrian, *The Mechanism of Nervous Action*, Philadelphia, 1935.
[22] See the symposium by D. Bronk, R. Lorente de Nó, and others, "The Synapse," *Journal of Neurophysiology*, II (1939).
[23] K. S. Lashley, "The Thalamus and Emotion," *The Psychological Review*, XLV (1938).

should in any case have to check the findings of the electroencephalograph by our own direct inspection, since a machine would not register
hedonic tone as felt but only its supposed conditions or neural constituents. In the practice of valuation, of course, we have to link enjoyment
and pain with certain types and phases of specific activities and specific
situations, our total knowledge of which comes neither from introspection alone nor from external observation alone, but is an elaborate construction in which the two perspectives on behavior are almost inex-
tricably interwoven.

I have tried, in this section and the last, to give, from my own incomplete knowledge of recent experimental developments, reasons suggesting that the psychological assumptions which underlie the current conative theories of value may be sadly out of date. The motor theory of
behavior was a promising hypothesis thirty years ago, and it has been
fruitful, but its program has required increasingly grave modifications
as a result of the solid scientific work that has been done since that time.
The present state of opinion in scientific circles is far from disclosing
unanimity on these topics, but it at least indicates that a motor theory
of behavior, in its extreme forms, requires some further scientific back-
ing, and should no longer be advanced as a dogma which renders all
alternative theories "unscientific" or metaphysical. And it is significant
that most of the experimental exponents of behaviorism nowadays who
are studying the more complicated human functions are calling this
assumption in question and conceiving "behavior" more broadly. The
divorce between philosophers and psychologists has been particularly
unfortunate for theory of value, and with psychology showing some signs
of intellectual maturity philosophers would do well to cease from purely
a priori speculation on topics for which there now exists some empirical
evidence, however incomplete.

V

Since, as we have seen, conation appears to enter the experience of
value, and to be related to the affective element in value particularly, in
ways that are too various, too devious, and as yet too imperfectly understood to give us a simple basic conception of value, we are forced to
turn back to feeling, and to see if we can find an affective definition of
a primary sense of value upon which can be based an analysis of the
manifold ways in which conation enters into the process. Such an under-

taking must at the same time avoid the errors of those traditional "subjectivistic" or "mentalistic" versions of an affective theory which have caused recent writers to reject it.

Intrinsic good is perhaps best defined ostensively, by reference to certain types of direct experience, just as any synonym for it must itself be so defined. Our psychological knowledge at present does not enable us to define it adequately in terms of its conditions. The stimulus conditions and the gross behavioral manifestations of the affective quality in question are too varied and too variable to give us a manageable definition. If an exact statement of the sufficient proximate conditions of hedonic tone is ever found, it will probably make use of neurological terms; but these will be of limited utility in the everyday practice of valuation. We can, fortunately, recognize the value fact itself when it occurs, even though we are largely ignorant of its precise conditions. Consequently the following definition may be offered provisionally as serviceable:

"An experience x is intrinsically good" means "x contains joy." [24]

Spinoza's word "joy" (*laetitia*) seems to me preferable to such partial synonyms as "pleasure," "enjoyment," "satisfaction" and "consummatory quality," for it connotes, better than these, the whole range of affective qualities found in the variety of experiences prized for themselves, from sensuous delight to relish in the grim struggle for an ideal; it is especially well fitted to describe the feeling component of those activities which

---

[24] In this definition, I have chosen to treat intrinsic goodness as a characteristic of experiences rather than of objects. It is, however, a widespread linguistic practice to speak of certain objects as having intrinsic value. This practice, which employs the figure of metonymy, is unobjectionable so long as we recognize that goodness in objects is a relational property—a property constituted by a relation, actual or potential, to an organism and its experiences—and not a simple quality possessed by objects apart from this relation; though it is somewhat paradoxical to speak of a relational property as "intrinsic" to one term of the relation. While an "experience" is itself in one sense relational or transactional, the paradox does not arise here, because the intrinsic value occurs within the relational nexus (which includes the object, where one exists, as one term), and does not depend on another term for its realization. To avoid the paradox, C. I. Lewis, in his Carus Lectures for 1945 (published as *An Analysis of Knowledge and Valuation*, La Salle, Ill., 1947) has devised the term "inherent value" to designate the relational property of an object immediately concerned in an experience that is intrinsically good, while reserving "intrinsic value" for the experience itself. The properties of objects that most concern us in value theory are, in any case, dispositional properties or potentialities, which constitute a more complex notion than the basic conception of intrinsic value here defined. (In this section of my paper, I am greatly indebted in general to Mr. Lewis' Carus Lectures, of which I was privileged to read the section on value theory in manuscript.)

ESSAYS

are commitments of the whole personality, and these are of special importance for value theory because they take precedence over more segmental interests. A colorless but precise technical equivalent of "joy" is "hedonic tone."

Other conceptions closely related to that of intrinsic good are the following:

An experience is intrinsically bad when it is characterized by suffering, or algedonic tone.

An experience or an object has positive instrumental value when it is a condition of the achievement or maintenance of joy, or when it is a condition of the escape from or avoidance of suffering.[25]

The pervasiveness of hedonic and algedonic tone in all kinds of experience, and the readiness with which we can recognize them and respond to them when they occur, suggest that we have here concepts which are more comprehensive than the various species of conation. Joy and suffering may be the accompaniments of striving, its results, and, when we are reflective, its guiding lights. Furthermore, I am unable to find anything else in experience which can serve to distinguish between those experiences which are good "in themselves" and those which are bad "in themselves." It is significant that many conative theories, such as Perry's and Dewey's, have no place for the distinction between intrinsic and extrinsic value. They are quite consistent in refusing to make such a distinction within their own theories, but they have often misrepresented the meaning of these concepts within an affective theory.

Intrinsic value, as empirical writers use the term today, does not imply any reference to supra-empirical realities, such as Platonic Ideas or "essences," which are sometimes supposed to be their source. It simply refers to the presence of joy or positive hedonic tone in experience. Its presence is a factual matter, to be determined by direct inspection in the case of the individual whose experiences or transactions are asserted to possess it, and by indirect but equally empirical methods in the case of others.

A judgment of intrinsic value is not always, as Dewey asserts, a simple "report that a thing is or has been valued." It is never this when we assert

25 The definitions suggested here constitute a revised form of the elementary definitions of value given in my "Toward a Syntax of Valuation," *The Journal of Philosophy*, XLI (1944), which also suggests the way in which definitions of the more complex senses of value can be erected upon the elementary definitions.

that someone else's experience has intrinsic value, but it requires non-introspective methods of corroboration. When we judge that a future experience of our own, or a class of responses to a certain kind of object in general, will have intrinsic value, we test or verify such judgments in much the same way that we test other types of value-judgments: by induction from past events similar in kind, by inference from empirical knowledge of the connection of intrinsic values with certain conditions and consequences (such as certain types of conation), and so forth. The logic that we employ is an empirical logic.

The distinction between intrinsic and extrinsic value, therefore, is not identical, as it is so often asserted to be, with the distinction between the "had" and the "tested." In order that intrinsic value may *occur*, someone must "have" it; but we may test *judgments* about it in the absence of the having. Instrumental values, likewise, may merely occur, or assertions about them may be tested. We maximize the achievement of both kinds of values when we devise adequate methods of predicting and judging them.

An intrinsic value, moreover, does not imply any temporal or metaphysical "ultimacy" but may be quite transitory: the fleetingness of some kinds of pleasure is notorious. Hedonic tone is a quality in whose realization the functioning of a mind or an organism is a necessary condition: it is not a property of any kinds of objects, physical or "subsistential," apart from their effect on vital processes.

Our valuation of any complex situation is usually more concerned with instrumental values than with positive intrinsic values. Even traditional hedonism, as with Epicurus and Bentham, has recognized that most of our actions are prompted more by aversion to pain than by desire for pleasure. Most of our enjoyments or positive intrinsic values occur as transitory ripples in the process of relieving the discomforting tensions set up by organic and socially acquired drives which are forced on us in one way or another. In so far as we value something merely because it enables us to avoid or to escape pain, we are assigning an instrumental value to it. But we can also, to some degree, by taking thought conduct our hounded activities in such a way that more rather than less joy is achieved in the process; and we can even develop skills and interests whose smooth functioning, under fortunate circumstances, gives us more enjoyment than discomfort. The reflection which enables us to do this does not require any ignoring of instrumentalities and consequences, but rather a weighing of their involvement in the total process. The type of affective theory which I am suggesting does not involve a *separation* of intrinsic and instrumental values but only their *distinction*.

An affective theory would be in complete sympathy with Dewey's insistence that the ideal of life should be to overcome in practice the separation of intrinsic from instrumental values, to eliminate mere "routine" and to give every experience a measure of consummatory quality. In fact, the term intrinsic value as I am using it here is almost synonymous with Dewey's notion of "consummatory quality." Where Dewey seems to me to go wrong, so far as I can grasp his discussion of it, is on the following two points. (1) In his apparent denial that the joy which constitutes this consummatory quality or intrinsic value can be distinguished (not separated) from its conditions and consequences, and hence that we can symbolize it and adopt it reflectively as the goal and justification of the process. (2) In his assumption that, because the ideal aim of moral striving is to eliminate "mere" instrumentalities, it is illegitimate to have a valuational term for them when they occur. In the present state of the world, many acts for all persons are in large part mere instrumentalities. Such are battle, for soldiers; earning a living, for people with uninteresting jobs; faculty meetings, for professors; and the endurance of illness, for everybody. These activities are not pursued or supported primarily for their own sakes, but to avoid discomfort or to achieve a more rewarding life in the future. To deny this is to confuse a stubborn fact about the human situation with a counsel of perfection.

To attribute intrinsic value to an act, furthermore, is not to give it final approval. There are many acts which we value for themselves but repudiate as a whole because of their consequences.

The distinction between intrinsic and extrinsic value is not strictly identical with the distinction between ends and means. Choice of the "end-in-view" occurs before the fact; but such judgments are highly fallible, so that our judgment on the intrinsic value actually realized in the process may, after the returns are in, attach it to some element besides that which was adopted as the end and which served to guide the striving.

The opposition of some contemporary empiricists to the notion of intrinsic value has also sprung from two additional considerations. In the first place, many defenders of the concept, including even such empiricists as Prall, have treated as intrinsic values such moral concepts as those of honor, truthfulness, and self-sacrifice. A thorough analysis of acts so characterized would show that they are initially adopted as means to the achievement of other goods, and, above all, to the avoidance of evil; though they readily elicit the "confirming reaction" which attaches to all values with which the self becomes identified, and thus they acquire some measure of intrinsic value. And secondly, in intuitionist theories, feelings are often held to serve as evidence for propositions dealing with instrumentalities, whereas the view I am advocating holds that the observation of feeling supplies evidence only for those constituents of a value-judgment which make assertions about feeling itself, and does not furnish sufficient evidence for a judgment making assertions about a complicated nexus of intrinsic and instrumental values.[26]

VI

In the preceding section, I have not undertaken a detailed elaboration of an affective theory, much less a "proof" of one. I have simply tried to prepare the ground for such an undertaking by clearing away some of the untenable meanings assigned to the basic notion of intrinsic value both by its opponents and by its defenders.

An affective theory of value cannot be established, as some of the classical hedonisms tried to do, by deduction from the psychological principles of motivation. This is the case even though the hedonistic principle has recently received from the experimental treatments of acquired motivation much more support than was accorded to it twenty years ago. Thorndike's Law of Effect—which is roughly an experimental equivalent of psychological hedonism—has once more come into favor with students of both human and animal learning, and is tending with some investigators to replace the Law of Exercise (the Watsonian and Pavlovian principle of conditioning by conjunction or simple repetition).[27] Thorndike himself has not assigned universal scope to the Law

[26] Lepley's essay in this symposium constitutes a genuine effort by a writer generally sympathetic with instrumentalism to understand what other contemporary empiricists mean by "intrinsic value," and to square this notion with the instrumentalist position. Dewey, Ayres and Geiger, however, continue to assign to "intrinsic value" meanings which scarcely any empiricist who uses the concept today would accept.
[27] "The Law of Effect," a Symposium, by H. A. Carr, E. C. Tolman, E. L. Thorndike, E. A. Culler, J. F. Dashiell, and K. F. Muenzinger, *The Psychological Review*, XLV (1938); and O. H. Mowrer and associates, articles previously cited.

of Effect, but in his latest writings holds that mere exercise or repetition
—even of a punishing character—can establish motivational connections, though these tend to be replaced by rewarding or satisfying connections when they occur.[28] Mowrer and Ullman, while upholding the
Law of Effect generally, show that it does not always lead us to seek the
maximum reward or lessening of punishment, because of the organism's
failure to develop correct sign-responses to the tension-reducing potentialities of a given type of action.[29] A recent comprehensive survey of
the current experimental studies of learning and motivation (*Conditioning and Learning*, by Hilgard and Marquis) [30] concludes that effect or
reward is only one of three distinct principles each of which seems to
work fairly well with certain types of learning but which have not yet
been brought into a unified theory.

What this experimental work does support—though far from conclusively—is the view that the organism tends toward a lessening of
painful tension and an achievement of satisfaction when it learns to
manipulate signs and symbols effectively. It is in this sense that, as
Pepper says, we learn to become hedonists. But we never learn to do
so completely. Whether because of the blind compulsion of our con-
genital drives, or because of the Law of Exercise, or the Death Wish,
or faulty symbolization, we frequently are motivated by something other
than the desire for the maximum of joy and the minimum of suffering.
This makes it impossible to establish such a simple and direct connection between hedonic tone and motivation as Pepper and Jessup suggest.

An affective theory, then, must appeal to the whole set of "value facts"
and not merely to the facts of motivation. It is directly concerned with
outcomes rather than with motives, though in the "rational" human being these tend to be brought ever closer together. The maximization of
joy and the minimization of suffering—whether for ourselves or for
others with whose interests we have identified our interests—is a standard that we adopt when we reflectively compare our activities and
symbolize adequately both the instrumentalities involved in the alternative courses of action and the probable affective rewards to be obtained
from these alternatives.

[28] E. L. Thorndike, *An Experimental Study of Rewards,* New York, 1933, and *Man
and His Works,* Cambridge, Mass., 1943; see also P. B. Rice, O. H. Mowrer, and
G. W. Allport, "Symposium: The Ego and the Law of Effect," *The Psychological
Review,* LIII (1946).
[29] *Loc. cit.*   [30] New York, 1940.

In trying to establish any value theory, we encounter the difficulty that what we are seeking primarily is a set of *definitions* of value concepts; and definitions, though they are indirectly controlled by experience, are never strictly speaking "proved," that is, confirmed or disconfirmed, by it; their acceptance or rejection rests on their capacity to organize the subject matter which they seek to make amenable to analysis, prediction, production, and explanation.[31] To show that the basic definitions above furnish an adequate basis for this task falls beyond the scope of this essay.

I have merely tried to suggest that conative theories are using categories which are too limited to organize the field of value facts with sufficient precision and comprehensiveness, and to recommend that attention be directed once more to the possibility of finding in terms of feeling a basic concept that refers to a more pervasive aspect of the value facts than any specifiable type of conation gives us, and one that enables us to judge the outcome of conations. That intrinsic value is defined in terms of feeling implies no disparagement of the role that striving plays in the total value-situation. Joy is, for the most part, achieved only through effort. In practice, we must frequently accept Dewey's maxim that sufficient unto the day is the good thereof. Painful drives are forced upon us, and our striving is directed to the elimination of them and not to the achievement of freely chosen joys. But we are also granted rare opportunities of choice when we are able to select our patterns of action, not from any urgency of pain, but when instrumentalities are abundant and when the choice ultimately hinges, not on the feasibility of the means, but on the positive intrinsic values that are likely to accrue to the entire process provided that we develop our capacities to achieve them. An affective theory also permits us to include within the value facts those activities, such as contemplation and aesthetic perception, where motor striving of any externally testable kind plays a minor and auxiliary role.

The theory I am suggesting, then, is an "affective-motor" theory, one which, like a number of others, seeks to include the roles that both feeling and striving play in the total experience of value. Only its basic definition of intrinsic value is stated in purely affective terms—and this is done, I repeat, not to deny the importance of conation as a source of intrinsic value, but to allow for the multiplicity of ways in which it so

[31] I have dealt with this question in a paper, "Definitions in Value Theory," *The Journal of Philosophy*, XLIV (1947).

functions. Instrumental value is, of course, more explicitly concerned with conation, and is not intelligible without reference to it. The more complex levels of valuation, such as the economic and the ethical, include a reference to both intrinsic and instrumental values and hence to the interinvolvement of feeling and striving. Furthermore, even though intrinsic value in general is *defined* in terms of affect, the adequate description of any particular occurrence of it must take full account of the strivings operative in the activity.

In choosing the larger patterns of our lives, we cannot abstract the affective elements from their context and perform a calculation of disembodied hedonic and algedonic tones. We have to plan our lives in terms of activities, personalities, and social institutions. We soon learn that, to preserve life itself (the basic instrumental value), and to avoid suffering for both ourselves and others, we must keep these going, and these largely impose our tasks. Our joys and pains are generated in the process, and their precise forms often cannot be foreseen. The feeling component consequently recedes into the background of our concern; but it is always lurking there, ready to give us a standard by which to judge and, so far as may be, to predict the fruits of our activities and our institutions in life and value.

VII

My answers to Dewey's questions, partly by way of summary and partly by *obiter dictum*, would be as follows:

1. "Prizing" as conceived by Dewey designates a type of value fact that is too special and too limited in its range to supply the basic concept for value theory. "Joy" or "hedonic tone" or "consummatory quality" is of much wider applicability. Joy is related to desire, interest, and other forms of striving, in too great a variety of ways to permit it to be accurately and serviceably defined as a function of one of these, although the intelligent conduct of life requires that we seek to discover the connection of feeling with the modes of striving in particular activities. The immediate quality of hedonic tone is "internal" or "private" in the sense that it is directly accessible only to the inspection of the person whose activities it characterizes. Its "internality," however, does not preclude meaningful and verifiable discourse about it, nor does the term used here imply that external conditions play no part in "generating" it. Feeling is a natural event, or quality of natural events, inex-

tricably bound up with other elements in the unitary processes of behavior. If various groupings of such elements may be held to constitute
a "private" or "subjective" or "inner" realm, this latter somewhat metaphorical phrase refers only to an empirically discoverable field determined by the peculiar perspective that an individual self has on certain
aspects of the natural processes that are centered in his own organism.
I should not like to speak of this ordering of events as "mentalistic"—
with the suggestions that the term has of Cartesian dualism or metaphysical idealism—but it seems to me preferable to follow Dewey in
reserving the term "mental" for certain functional characteristics of the
behavioral act as a whole.

2. If this question means simply that immediate values are dependent
for their existence and nature on the past reflective valuations of the
individual and his society, among other conditions, I would agree with
Dewey. The developed individual cannot recover the naiveté of his first
days. But a number of other propositions are asserted or implied in
Dewey's discussion of the question, and especially that goods never
"just come" to us, but are always instituted by a specific act of judgment
or appraisal. This seems to me to be refuted by daily experience. The
gods sometimes toss golden apples in our laps—not often enough, perhaps, that we can sit around waiting for it to happen, but still with
sufficient frequency that we can be grateful for our luck when it comes.
I see no reason to deny value to these experiences, though I agree with
Dewey that most goods have to be achieved, and most evils averted, by
hard thinking and striving. As to the technical issues involved in the view
that the occurrence of all goods is dependent on the valuation of them,
I believe that Dewey has been sufficiently refuted by Perry and Prall in
the 1920s, and by Pepper, Morris, Lepley, Aiken, and others in this
symposium; and that many obstacles to agreement on this problem
might be removed if the more orthodox instrumentalists would try (in
their postscripts to this volume) to reply to these criticisms in detail. It
is hard to explain the underlying assumption, that thought always makes
its referent, as anything else than a survival from the logic of absolute
idealism which influenced Dewey so strongly in the formative period of
his philosophy.

3. I would agree with Dewey that "valuation-propositions" have the
same logical status as other empirical propositions, and that they are
distinguished simply by their subject matter, which comprises values

as a special class of facts. But the further assumption that the communication of "facts already in existence" does not suffice to constitute a proposition seems to me to rest on certain peculiarities of Dewey's quasi-Hegelian logic. It will be rejected by all those who accept the standard definition of a "proposition" as any expression that can significantly be asserted to be true or false; for we can make true or false communications about facts already in existence. But this is no place to argue the logical point.

4. In general, I am in agreement with Dewey, Lepley, Aiken, and others in their rejection of the position that so-called judgments of value are not propositions but ejaculations of emotion. But this position, particularly in the modified form in which it has been stated by C. L. Stevenson, raises so many thorny questions that it might better serve as subject matter for another cooperative inquiry.

5. There is no problem peculiar to value theory here. We can treat some instances of human behavior as simple functions of a "socio-cultural" context; in others, the decisive considerations are to be found in the idiosyncratic personal situation of the individual: in his own reflective and creative activity which transforms the culturally imposed conditions. Attention to the socio-cultural context has some relevance to any larger investigation into values, but it does not always suffice.

In conclusion, I should like to say that too large a part of this paper has regrettably been devoted to disagreement with Professor Dewey. His five questions deal with matters arising in the technical elaboration of a general theory of value, and it is here that my disagreement with him is greatest. A good many of these grounds of disagreement themselves have been suggested to me by his own analyses of specific valuational problems in such fields as social philosophy and aesthetics, where we can all look to him, if discriminatingly, for guidance. It is hardly necessary to add that, whether he will accept it or not, I should like to pay homage to Dewey's leadership in the general task of fostering an empirical attitude toward valuations, and in upholding vigorously the standards of liberalism and reflective intelligence against the cohorts of obscurantism and reaction.[32]

[32] For the Criticisms and Rejoinders which relate especially to this paper see pp. 326–330, 404–408, and 410–414, below.

PART II: CRITICISMS AND REJOINDERS

I

IF ONE COULD DERIVE a theory of value simply from an analysis of appetition, Pepper's paper would take us farther in the direction of an
adequate theory than any other account of the subject with which I am
acquainted. For he has differentiated the several factors or phases of
appetition more carefully, perhaps, than anyone else. Unfortunately,
no such simple derivation is possible. What basis, other than sheer stipulation, is there for identifying *value*—the subject matter of evaluations
—with each "positive" phase of an appetitive process? Even if Pepper's
definitions were sound, he would still have to provide arguments to support them. But such arguments, I surmise, would take him beyond
mere factual observations concerning the differentiae of appetition
itself.

Pepper thus seems to me to beg the all-important questions: (1) How
is one to *define* value, and (2) What are the criteria of a successful
definition of value? His paper, despite its valuable suggestions concerning the psychology of motivation, gives no real clue whatever to the
solution of our basic philosophical questions, since it provides no method
for deciding what a *correct* definition of value would be.

The seriousness of this weakness in Pepper's analysis may be seen in
the fact that although he professes to "discover" by means of his study
of appetition two modes of value, namely, conative value and affective
value, he utterly fails to show why we should accept either or both of
these factors as specifications of value-meaning. Moreover, when the
problem of evaluation or appraisal is raised, he provides no way of determining the order of priority with respect to these "types" of value.
Indeed, he suggests no basis whatever in terms of which they could be
compared at all as values. No value theory, I submit, can be regarded
as satisfactory which affords no answers to such basic questions. I, for
my part, have found no clear reason elsewhere for attributing intrinsic
value to mere conation. And I fear that Pepper's "observations" con-

cerning appetition have not brought me appreciably closer to this end.

At the same time, I am in considerable sympathy with Pepper's opening remarks concerning the purpose of value theory. The problem of definition, as I have already implied, is of very great importance; but it is not the sole end of a theory of *values*. Indeed, it is merely ancillary or preliminary to the problem of developing factual criteria and laws of valuation. Unfortunately, so much energy has gone into the task of defining terms that most theorists have left the substantive problems of value theory largely untouched. One of the great merits of R. B. Perry's work is that it has gone beyond the definitional problems to a development of a theory of values. Unlike Pepper, however, Perry is careful to preface his interest theory of value with a long prolegomenon in which he tries to establish the *validity* of his definitions.

I agree, also, with Pepper's point that we should not assume at the outset that "value" has one and only one meaning, or, in other words, that there is some unique characteristic which is common to all objects to which value is attributed. But two ways are open to the theorist who takes seriously the possibility of plural value-meanings. He may come to the conclusion, as Pepper has virtually done, that the *word* "value" is simply ambiguous: it refers to more than one distinct and logically independent kind of entity. In this case the theorist would have on his hands not one general theory of value, with one subject matter, but several theories of value, with several different subject matters. Such theories would not be alternative or competing theories, but different theories of different states of affairs, no more intimately connected, perhaps, than chemistry and politics. The other possibility is, I think, more interesting and more important. Pursuing it, one would try to develop, as Rice has done, a syntax of valuation which would define these several modes of "value" in relation to one another. In this way, one could accept the plurality of value-meanings without becoming involved in the position, which I would adopt only as a case of last resort, that there is no such thing as a general theory of valuation, but only special theories which have no logical connections with one another. In short, one may differentiate intrinsic and extrinsic value, instrumental and inherent value, potential and real value, and so on, without falling into the type of pluralism in which, I fear, Pepper's observations seem to have landed him. The real question, here, is not whether there is one and only one meaning to "value," but whether there is one and only one meaning for intrinsic value. On this point, in spite of Pepper, I shall remain, at least tentatively, a monist. This is why I would be unwilling to regard both conative and affective value as modes of intrinsic value unless it were shown that there is some characteristic which both share in virtue of which both are *modes*.

So much for the definitional problems raised by Pepper's paper. I turn now, all too briefly, to one or two comments on his psychology of motivation. In the first place, it seems to me that he equivocates with respect to the "goal-object" of appetition. In terms of his example, he suggests that the terminal goal-object of his thirsty geologist is "water." But he also says of this goal-object that it is one which "will satisfy the thirst" of the geologist. If so, then it would seem that satisfaction of thirst is the real terminal goal-object, and drinking of water is merely a subordinate act which, it is believed, will bring about this result.

The point is that Pepper appears to hold that the terminal goal-object of an appetition is never the consummatory act which is the "quiescence-pattern" of the drive which motivates that appetition. This seems to me quite exceptionable. I see no reason to suppose that one may not directly aim at the realization of such quiescence-patterns themselves. In fact, I think that the quiescence-pattern itself, in cases of appetition such as Pepper has described, *is* the goal-object which is usually aimed at. But if so, it is the satisfaction and not the water which is the final *object* of value.

My second comment upon Pepper's psychology has to do with his rather curious notion that blind drives can have "goals." Granted that drives have quiescence-patterns which, unless realized, will leave the organism unsatisfied, I fail to see in what sense the latter are to be regarded as "goals." I have pointed out elsewhere that to maintain this theory in its present form requires acceptance of a doctrine of immanent teleology which I, for one, am not prepared to accept. I am well aware, of course, that many contemporary psychologists, and particularly the proponents of psychoanalysis, do tend to employ a language which strongly suggests some such view as this. But I suspect that this is merely an uncritical way of talking which is not intended to imply a doctrine of immanent final causes. In any case, it seems to me that the relation holding between "drive" and "quiescence-pattern" may be given an analysis which would avoid these difficulties. However, this would take us beyond the scope of the present remarks.

II

The general point of view of Lepley's paper seems to me to be admirably free from the narrowness of most contemporary writings on the subject. He displays little trace of the fallacy of "initial predication," as Perry called it, which has vitiated so much discussion of value theory. If he has a characteristic weakness of his own, and I am not at all sure that he has, it is perhaps the opposite tendency toward an overly hospitable desire to gather together within the confines of an inclusive system all of the insights of the hitherto conflicting schools of axiology. The sweep of Lepley's work is apparent. To me, at least, the price of a certain indefiniteness on crucial points may have been paid. Thus I feel a certain hesitancy, even after several rereadings, about the relevance of my criticisms, such as they are, for I am not at all sure that they are criticisms of the position which, in the end, he wishes to defend. On most questions, clearly, the differences between us concern matters of comparative detail. There are one or two considerations, however, that I may mention which will point up the places at which I feel a certain lack of clarity in Lepley's views, as set forth in this "Sequel," or, at any rate, a certain need for further instruction before I can judge the extent of my underlying agreement with him.

In the first place, then, I feel that Lepley, like Dewey, has not made a sufficiently sustained attempt to come to terms with what appears to my mind as the fundamental concept of value theory, namely, that of "intrinsic value." Both of these writers have admirably adumbrated a great many of the causes and conditions of value. They have clarified the contexts and functions of valuation and appraisal. They have shown the ways in which valuations correct, chasten, and modify our interests, and, hence, our values. They have not, I believe, provided a clear and unequivocal definition or criterion of intrinsic value itself. But failing this, they seem to leave up in the air the problem of the justification of conduct and the validation of normative judgments. It is clearly desirable to emphasize the continuity and interaction of means and ends, just as it is essential to stress the use of appraisals for the direction and control of behavior. Still, every *given* means serves some ulterior purpose which alone justifies it as a means. But without the conception of that which is valuable or good, per se, it would be impossible to ascertain the validity of the ulterior purpose itself. It is the function of the idea of intrinsic value to give us a criterion, in the light of which alone we may determine whether our instrumentalities are instruments of value. Without this, the justification of choice or action has no conceivable ground, and appraisals are left without a clear conception of their proper subject matter.

There is, then, a problem of relevance, when consequences and means are being appraised, and this relevance, I submit, cannot be established without a definition of intrinsic value. And this requirement is not at all mitigated by our recognition of the continuity of means and ends, or of the fact that no given action is free from consequences which, from the standpoint of morality, must be taken into account in any complete appraisal of the action itself.

It is possible that I have not grasped as clearly as I might what Lepley's position is on these matters. In any event, I should insist that the controversies between the proponents of the interest theory and the satisfaction theory, inconclusive as they may perhaps be, are not idle, even though both may be calling attention to factors which any fully adequate theory of value would have to take into account. I agree with Lepley, as I also agree with Rice, that a fully developed syntax of valuation may enable us to resolve many of the issues which, at present, prevent a more complete agreement amongst present-day theorists. Such a syntax may well enable us to assign a significant place to such factors as "drive," "expectation," "object of interest," "satisfaction," and so on, which would remove the necessity for a great deal of the contemporary debate which all too often arises from an obsession with some exclusive or particular sense of the term "value." Nevertheless, I do not believe that in granting this, one is forced to give up the attempt to arrive at a clear, unequivocal definition of intrinsic value.

My second comment has to do with a point that both Morris and I have previously stressed, namely, the importance of distinguishing carefully between use and meaning in the analysis of language. In view of the fact that judgments of value are characteristically used to modify conduct, it is peculiarly important that this distinction be kept constantly in mind in attempting to affix the meanings, or modes of signification, which are to be assigned to valuation statements. Because the distinction has been so frequently ignored, many writers have tended to argue that since appraisals affect attitudes and behavior, their characteristic *meaning* must be construed in emotive or motive terms. To me, such an argument is illicit. I shall not say that Lepley has himself employed this type of reasoning, but I get the impression from his paper that he may have been to some extent influenced by others who have employed it. Thus, while he says that "If and when value, or valuational, propositions and judgments are truly judgments or propositions, they differ from other assertive, or factual, propositions and judgments in subject matter *only*," he seems to me also sometimes to suggest that the characteristically normative or appraisive meaning of such judgments is emotive or attitudinal, and this because the functional context of these judgments is emotional or volitional. In short, while he holds that value-judgments may contain a descriptive or factual component, which differs from other factual propositions only in subject matter, he also appears to maintain that their "final" meaning is emotive or prescriptive. What I should like to have more clearly answered by Lepley is this question: Is the meaning of evaluations, as well as their causes, uses, and effects, emotive or prescriptive, or is it, qua evaluation, purely descriptive? I confess that I find no clear idea as to just where Lepley stands on this point.

My third comment concerns what I believe to be a reference to a review of C. L. Stevenson's *Ethics and Language* by myself. In that review I had stated that Stevenson had not clarified the meanings of such crucial terms as "belief," "attitude," "cognition," and "emotion," and that because of this he had failed to give any clear conception of their dynamic interrelations and, consequently, he was in no position to give an adequate account of the precise ways signs operate in arousing, articulating, and modifying beliefs and attitudes. The question of "emotive meaning" in ethics cannot, to my mind, be adequately explicated, and the ways in which ethical judgments enter into the modification of attitudes and actions cannot be fully understood, until we know more precisely the functional interdependence, or lack thereof, of cognition, attitude, and belief. Just what to make of the "emotive theory," as Stevenson has described it, is hard to know until it has been ascertained whether and to what extent the emotive effects of ethical and valuative expressions are dependent upon or independent of cognition. Now Lepley has said that both cognition and emotion are probably present in all behavior above the level of the conditioned reflex. And he argues from this that the emotive effects of signs are neither an effect of descriptive meaning nor distinct and independent. But I think that his own solution of what strikes me as a problem of first importance seems to be both unclear and inadequate. The question is not whether emotion and cognition are both present, but how and if they are related; it is not whether signs are emotive in their effects but how they are so. Granted that evaluations function to modify attitudes and actions, how precisely do they do so? Stevenson himself appears to maintain that although both elements are present, one can be independent of the other, and that there is such a thing as independent emotive meaning. Indeed, if there were not, his "persuasive" methods in ethics could not arise, even in principle. And I also would hold that there is no cognition without motivation. But this is beside the point. The question is simply this: Is the emotive effect of valuational statements an independent mode of meaning or is it not? I cannot see how anything that Lepley has said obviates the necessity of answering this question or removes its theoretical importance.

One final comment: In arguing that the basic difference between statements of fact and evaluations is primarily a "difference in verbal form," does Lepley mean to imply that this difference implies no difference in meaning whatever, and that valuation statements can always be translated without remainder into corresponding factual statements? Or, to put the matter in other words, are valuative statements *merely* descriptively synonymous with certain corresponding statements of fact? If the answer is positive, then does not his position entail that the emotive aspects of evaluative *judgment* are (a) not a matter of meaning at all, and (b) byproducts or effect of what the judgment descriptively asserts or implies?

Rejoinder by Lepley

My replies are numbered to correspond to Aiken's criticisms of my paper.

1. May it be assumed, as in the criticism, that it is either possible or necessary to provide a "clear and unequivocal definition or criterion of value itself" (intrinsic value), "in the light of which *alone* [1] we may determine whether our instrumentalities are instruments of value"? For both practical and theoretical purposes we need of course to strive to achieve the fullest possible clarity regarding the nature of value. But

---

[1] Italics mine. For explanation of my use of single and double quotation marks see note 2, p. 167, above.

the quest for clarity should not result in the acceptance of an over-simplification or arbitrary abstraction. I had hoped that it would be clear from my paper [2] that I think interest in achievement (of personal, social, and possibly cosmic 'welfare') should be given preference over short-range satisfaction, if and when the two are actually in conflict; but that I also hold that a complex experimental process of inquiry and testing (in which 'having,' 'feelings,' and the weighting of consequences interact) is needed in order to establish, in the fullest possible sense, the value of both satisfactions and achievements.

2. In his *Signs, Language, and Behavior*, Morris makes clear that 'signs' may 'signify,' or prepare behavior, in several different ways. If by "evaluate" we mean (as Morris does) the giving of a preferential status to something (however unreflective the giving may be), and if in "meaning" we include such giving of preferential status, I should say that the *meaning* of evaluations, as well as their causes, uses, and effects, is often 'emotive' or 'prescriptive'; but if we limit "evaluate" to reflective judgment as to what consequences will follow and as to whether these are and will be desired and approved, the *meaning* (in the sense in which Aiken apparently prefers to use the term "meaning") of evaluations is, qua evaluation, purely descriptive—or at least as purely descriptive as judgments can be. The words "evaluate," "mean," "signify," "signification," "emotive," "prescriptive," "use," and so forth are extremely equivocal. I am disposed to agree with Morris that no one has gone to fundamentals in dealing with the semeiotic aspects of axiology, and with Rice that another cooperative inquiry might well be devoted to these problems.

3. It was not my intention to hold that the emotive effects of signs may not be effects of descriptive meaning. No doubt in many cases the emotive effects are at least in part the result of descriptive 'meaning.' In some instances the emotive effects of 'evaluative statements' are entirely or nearly devoid of descriptive content, and may then be said to be an independent mode of meaning. Here again semeiotic difficulties similar to those mentioned in point 2 above beset us. I wholly agree that the issues raised in Aiken's third criticism are in need of much further consideration.

4. Yes, I believe that "valuation statements" can probably always be

[2] Especially pp. 174–175, above.

translated without remainder into corresponding factual statements.[3] This does not necessarily entail that the emotive aspects of evaluative judgments are not a matter of meaning: this depends upon what we mean by "meaning" (see point 2 above); nor does it imply that the emotive aspects are by-products or effect of what the judgment descriptively asserts: they may be by-products or effect of personal or social factors rather than of what the judgment "descriptively asserts."

[3] See my *Verifiability of Value*, pp. 216–220, and "The Transposability of Facts and Values," *The Journal of Philosophy*, XXXVI (1939), 290–299.

IN THE SECOND PART of my paper I have remarked that the significance of emotion derives from the past conditioning of our emotions by the myths and mores that have played so large a part in the social experience of mankind. This may seem to suggest that investigators who focus their attention on the emotional, or conative, or appetitive aspects of the experience of value do so because they are themselves obsessed by these ceremonial aspects of human experience; and that suggestion may be further reinforced by my citation of Adler.

Nevertheless, I doubt if that is the case. Certainly I see no evidence of any such motivation in any of the papers in this volume. These papers do fall into two groups: those which find the distinguishing character-istic of value experience to be emotional, or conative, or appetitive; and those which do not. If the papers of the former group were indeed moti-vated by ceremonial (or shall I say theological?) considerations, I should expect them to take an overtly theological turn sooner or later, as Adler's lucubrations do—and sooner rather than later. But they do not do so. Not one of them does. Indeed, the most striking characteristic of all the papers of this group is their truncation. Each of them seems to have been at great pains to lay a foundation, and then to have stopped short, giving no indication of what might be built on it. Each seems to struggle mightily to establish what nobody denies, that the experience of value is in some sense or other emotional, or conative, or appetitive, or all of these; and since nobody denies that appetite, effort, and feeling do indeed enter into all experience of value (which is as much as to say all human experience), the presumption is that these writers attach some special significance to what they have so laboriously established. But what it is they do not say. Not one of them does.

Since I have been asked to comment on Lee's paper, I will take it as a case in point, although it may seem a bit odd to speak of so good-humored and relaxed a writer as having been engaged in a mighty struggle. Lee identifies himself as a methodologist, and he does seem to have gone methodically to work at the task of tightening the loose joints in our language and sharpening the cutting edge of our analytical tools. In view of his closing paragraphs it may even seem ungracious to locate him on the far side of "the great divide"—that "veritable chasm," as Geiger calls it, by which these two groups of papers are separated.

But if "men are socio-cultural" creatures, and if "therefore human values cannot be adequately theoretically dealt with outside of the socio-cultural context," as Lee says in his closing sentences, why does the entire preceding substance of his paper lie outside that context? In a certain sense values are indeed "dependent upon an individual sensibility, and thus are individually determined." But if nobody denies this (and I know of nobody who does), and if this sense is not the significant one, why has the entire body of the paper been devoted to it?

Why does Lee start out by trying to dissociate caring from knowing? I say "trying" to do so because it seems to me virtually axiomatic that these two aspects of experience, though they are logically distinguishable, are existentially indissociable. I should agree that truth is a matter of knowing and that value is a matter of caring; and I should further agree that things may happen about which one neither knows nor cares. But to say that it is not necessary to one's knowing that he should care is to misconceive knowing quite as much as caring. I may care very little about the stranger who has just passed my window, but I know correspondingly little; and what little I do know is evidence that I do care that little bit what is going on outside. To say, as we often do when discussing some neighbor's affairs in considerable detail, that we don't care at all, we are only interested to know, is to deceive ourselves—as we likewise very often do. Surely it is an a-b-c of the theory of knowledge that knowing is caring, and that the psychopathic who doesn't care likewise doesn't know. Why, then, does Lee propose to dissociate caring, and why does he do so at the very outset, making this dissociation virtually the basic postulate of his value theory?

Why does he say [1] that "the direct experience of value" (that is, dissociated caring) "cannot be in error"? Why does he say [2] that "the fact that it [apprehension of value, or dissociated caring] can be modified by judgment does not indicate that judgment is a necessary condition of value"? Doesn't it? That, it seems to me, is precisely what it does indicate. Nobody denies that caring, like knowing, is often virtually instantaneous; but surely it is so because of previous experience. Instantaneous caring

[1] P. 163, above.   [2] P. 159.

involves instantaneous recognition, and recognition—however quick—
involves judgment. In *The Meaning of Modern Sculpture*, Wilensky
relates an incident that occurred during one of his public lectures. He
had showed his audience a number of slides representing various contemporary works, all of which had been rather coolly received. But
when he showed a slide of quite a different character, it elicited an
immediate burst of applause. With heavy irony he then remarks that it
was a photograph of a costumer's dummy. Clearly the audience *thought*
it recognized a piece of sculpture in the classic style. Surely the fact that
an audience who cared enough about sculpture to attend such a lecture
was nevertheless capable of making such a mistake is a comment, not
only on the knowledge and taste of that audience, but also on the heavy
reliance of classical sculpture upon what we would now call "photo-
graphic" representation of the human body—which, of course, was
Wilensky's point.

Such being the case, what in the world does Lee mean by saying [3]
that "If we apprehend value, we apprehend value, and whether or not
we judge that it should not be, the valuable object is still valuable"?
Does he imagine that the members of Wilensky's audience remarked
later to their friends, "I had a wonderful experience this afternoon. I saw
a picture of a costumer's dummy. What a thrill!" Would he expect them
thereafter to haunt the windows of ladies' dress shops in the hope of
repeating this thrill by catching sight of an undressed dummy? Isn't it
more likely that their instantaneous response to "lifelike" sculpture
would be conditioned thereafter by this experience—as Wilensky intended that it should?

I ask these questions in all seriousness. Lee, and his companions on
the far side of the chasm, seem to attach some special significance to the
emotive aspect of the experience of value. They do not say why they do
so, nor even exactly what it is; but they seem to imply not only that
emotive responses are independent of judgment and even of recognition, but also that such emotional experiences are higher and finer than
"mere" understanding.

In probing the motives of such writers I do not mean to be imperti-
nently personal. They represent a climate of opinion that is very general
today. None of them, I think, would contradict Lee's declaration to the
effect that all human behavior is socio-cultural. The amazing thing is

[3] P. 160.

that, recognizing this as we all do, we can still give virtually our exclusive attention to one aspect of social as well as of individual behavior
and virtually ignore another aspect that is certainly no less extensive,
whatever may be said of its importance. Why do students of the social
sciences, no less than the philosophers, devote themselves almost altogether to the study of attitudes and sentiments and the coercive relationships which they accompany, as though that sort of thing were the
whole substance of human life and the whole structure of society?

This is indeed an interesting and important question, and I am going
to take advantage of the opportunity which the writing of this postscript
offers to suggest an answer to it. The supposed importance of emotions
and sentiments and "direct apprehension," and all that sort of thing,
certainly derives from "the three m's" (myth, magic, and mores) by
which immemorially emotions have been conditioned; and the effect of
exclusive concentration on that sort of thing is to declare, "Great are
the three m's; nothing else in human life is of any account!" But, as I remarked at the outset, I see no indication in any of these papers—nor in
the current literature of the social sciences—that their writers entertain
any such idea.

How, then, shall we explain this singularly motiveless preoccupation?
I propose to venture the suggestion that the motive is intellectual. We
are, all of us, seeking to understand human behavior in its (related)
individual and social manifestations. We give little thought to the technological aspect of behavior because it seems to require no explanation.
We know that it goes on. Indeed, we love to watch skilled artisans at
work—in garages, on construction jobs, in the engine rooms of ocean
liners, and so on; but nobody regards their operations as a Great Mystery. They may do things we can't do; but we know quite well how they
learned to do them, and we assume that (barring physical disability)
any one of us might have learned to do as well. This, I think, is what
Dewey has had in mind when he has remarked upon the singular prevalence of the word "mere" in the writings of his critics. All his emphasis
has been upon matters which strike his critics as "mere"—for just this
reason. Though we marvel at the atom bomb, we soon come to realize
that "there isn't any secret." It is only a vast extrapolation of the commonplace. The technological-instrumental activities of mankind are the life
process of the race. As such they are virtually coextensive with life itself.
Consequently they are commonplace; and since they are commonplace,

they seem to pose no problem of understanding; and since they pose no problem, we ignore them.

But sentiments and attitudes, commitments and coercions, superstitions and illusions, are perpetually disturbing. What are these seizures by which we are all so persistently upset? What is the mysterious force by which men are coerced, as it were, against their will, sometimes for good and sometimes for evil? As my wife used to reiterate through the days and years of the great depression, why do people put up with it all? Doubtless the orderly processes of organized society are good; but it seems no less obvious that starvation in the midst of plenty is superlatively bad.

Here is a conundrum to challenge understanding. That we should have tried to solve it is altogether right and proper. I have no complaint to make on that score. My complaint is rather that we have failed precisely because our attention has been fixed on this problem so unswervingly as to produce a sort of astigmatism. This, we have said in effect, is *the* problem of human nature (and of social organization), thereby overlooking the whole of that vast congeries of activities by which men have always lived and developed their amazing powers of hand and eye and brain; and we have said it not on the basis of careful assessment of these two aspects of human experience but as an a priori dictum which in effect makes of our own astigmatism a universal law.

Furthermore, it is by this astigmatism that we have insured the failure of our efforts to understand that aspect of human nature which has been the object of our exclusive preoccupation. As I said at the outset, the most striking thing about all these efforts to explain value in terms of "individual sensibility," as Lee calls it, or satisfaction, or even animal appetite, is their amazing inconclusiveness. In spite of all their care to escape the bonds of philosophical traditionalism (well illustrated by the passage in which Lee shies away from "faculty psychology"), and in spite of their assiduous honing of their analytical tools, they seem to me to find nothing and get nowhere. The reason for this failure is a limitation of perspective which no amount of observational precision can possibly correct. As Geiger has very well said, the extravagant care which has been lavished on these definitions is largely wasted, since definition as such isn't "basic." Indeed, it may be "no more than a semantical stop-gap"—or, perhaps, a sort of stop-view: a blinder, in short, which seeks to improve the vision in one direction by shutting out all the rest of the horizon.

As Geiger goes on to say, what is basic is "approach." I agree, and this also seems to me very well said. Obviously, Geiger's approach is the same as my own; and although neither one of us finds as much as he could wish, I think we are moving in a direction in which there is a great deal to be found. If you set out to explore "caring" as distinguished from "knowing," or "individual sensibility" as distinguished from its "socio-cultural context," then all you can find is that valuing is caring and vice versa. But if you set out to explore the socio-cultural substance of human behavior (and social structure) in which value relationships obtain, and if you regard caring as an aspect of knowing and doing (and vice versa), then you find that there is no special problem of value and that the general problem is coextensive with the life process of mankind.

All that I have tried to say might be put in terms of feeling and achievement. Values are felt. No one denies it. But are not values invariably achieved? It seems to me that nobody can possibly deny that such is the case; and yet this aspect of the problem is completely ignored by what might be called the "sensibility school." As my final word in the present debate I therefore propose the following challenge. Either values are achieved or they are not. If any member of the sensibility school is prepared to argue that they are not, let him do so and see what kind of a case he can make; and unless he is prepared to do so, let him address himself to the analysis of the process by which values are achieved. If he will do that, I believe that he will find a trail across the chasm which divides us.

REJOINDER BY LEE

Ayres, in his Criticisms, complains of the truncation of many of the theories presented in the papers of this symposium. The truncation is admitted on my part. Limitations of space prohibit laying a foundation and building a structure both at the same time. When there is as much inconclusive argument about values as there is at present, a discussion of methodology is necessary as a foundation for a more complete theory. Too great haste to complete the superstructure may lead to the construction of inadequate foundations. Dewey is anxious to reach the applications of his theory to social and political conditions. I think that some of the foundations on which he builds are theoretically inadequate. Parker also is eager to reach applications, as is shown in his recent paper "Reflections on the Crisis in Theory of Value." [4] I think that some of his foundations too are theoretically inadequate. There is nothing to do but to argue it out. By the time I had finished, my space was filled.

If the truncation of my paper is a necessary consequence of the theory there proposed, Ayres is correct in condemning it. In my paper, I refer, however, to articles that show the significance of the kind of theory I expound. In the last section of the paper "A Precise Meaning for Objective and Subjective in Value Theory," [5] possible applications are indicated in aesthetics, ethics, and politics. The paper entitled "Moral Individualism and Political Value" [6] briefly sketches possible political applications. The only detailed elaboration I have made is in *Perception and Aesthetic Value*.[7] I hope that it is more than an indication of how the theory can be applied to aesthetics. In considering the truncation of the present paper, these applications should be taken into consideration.

Ayres suggests that the truncation results from the preoccupation with theoretic considerations, and asks "How, then, shall we explain this singularly motiveless preoccupation? I propose to venture the suggestion that the motive is intellectual." [8] I plead guilty; but would add the following: there are some of us to whom fundamental theoretic questions seem to be of great importance even if they are motivated only by intellectual curiosity. History apparently shows that sometimes man can do things better if he theoretically understands them.

I do not think that the division into sensibility theories and non-sensibility theories is as serious as Ayres thinks it is. If it could be shown that a sensibility theory necessarily leads to the truncation of which he complains, perhaps it would be. I do not think that it does so lead. On the other hand, if the emphasis on individual sensibilities yields a hypothesis useful in explaining some of the phenomena of value experience, such, for example, as the individual differences in the apprehension of aesthetic values (tastes), then it is a good theory. I think that too much emphasis on conation apart from affection does lead to a truncation. It makes it difficult to account for aesthetic value. Aiken shows this in

[4] *Ethics*, LVI (1946), 193–207.   [5] See note 13, p. 152.
[6] See note 34, p. 166.   [7] See note 25, p. 157.   [8] P. 305.

his paper. The conative theory is constructed to account for moral and socio-moral values, and does not serve well to account for other kinds.

Ayres borrows a metaphor from Geiger and says that the sensibility theories lie beyond the "great divide" by which the two groups of theories are separated.[9] I take exception to this metaphor. This is not the great divide. The great divide lies between the absolutists and the relativists in value theory. There is no paper in the present symposium written from the absolutistic point of view. The present papers are separated only by a minor divide that does not run even parallel to the great divide. They are all in the same watershed, but in different branches of it.

If the absolutistic point of view had been represented among these papers, it is not likely that Ayres could have said that he knows of nobody who denies that values depend "upon an individual sensibility and thus are individually determined."[10] All absolutists deny it, and in so doing become authoritarian. This may be either a religious authoritarianism, a traditional authoritarianism, Nazi, Fascist, or what not.

I cannot agree with Ayres' estimate of the place of analysis in value theory. Perhaps knowing and caring are never experienced apart from each other. I shall not argue the point, because whether or not they are does not influence the validity of the course of thought in my paper.[11] If knowing and caring may vary independently of each other (and I think that the evidence shows that they may), then they are legitimate terms of analysis. It would have been better if I had expressed it this way in the first paragraph of my paper, instead of saying that it is not necessary to one's knowing that he should care.

Ayres is correct[12] in adversely criticizing my paper if it dissociates knowing and caring, especially if it makes such dissociation a basic postulate of the theory. I do not mean to dissociate the two, and I do not think that the term "dissociated caring" is a very good synonym of "valuing." It is true that in the opening of my paper, I take my point of departure from the vague notion of caring, but I hope that my analysis advances beyond its starting point.

As caring and knowing, although they may not be found apart from each other in concrete experience, may nevertheless be treated as analytically distinct because they vary independently, so valuing and judg-

[9] P. 303.   [10] Ibid.
[11] See my Criticism of Pepper's paper, p. 373, below.   [12] P. 303.

ing may also be treated as analytically distinct. Ayres' example, taken from Wilensky, where recognition altered appreciation, does not show that they are not distinct. I have always maintained that judgments may affect one's valuations. That they may does not deny the validity and usefulness of the distinction between the two.

The illustration from Wilensky does not show that one's immediate and direct sense of values may be in error. Instead, it presents a complex case where judgment and evaluation affect and change one's sense of values. Such changes take place, and this is a fact that must be accounted for in any value theory. In my paper it is accounted for on pages 158–160, above. Any appreciation of representative or partly representative sculpture involves a large proportion of "derived aesthetic values." [13] In addition, the case at issue in Wilensky's illustration probably involves an appreciable amount of what I call (following Santayana) "aesthetic vulgarity." [14] It may be presumed that Wilensky chose a reasonably well-made dummy and was careful to get a good picture of it. Thus, there were aesthetic values involved, though not of the kind that the audience may have expected. The audience's mistake was a mistake in judgment.

The fact that the audience changed its attitude when it was told that the picture was of a dummy shows that there was a mistake somewhere. The question is, where was the locus of the mistake? I maintain that it was in the judgment, not in the direct experience of value. I suspect that the dummy really looked good to some at least of the members of the audience. I suspect that costumers' dummies look better than sculpture to many people, even though they would not admit it for fear of being thought "lowbrow." Ayres' conclusion that members of the audience would not boast of the experience or haunt shop windows seems to me to be an admirable illustration of the point of my paper on page 160.

The many more details of my possible agreements or disagreements with specific points in Ayres' Criticism are of little import. The whole question at issue is the place of analysis in a theoretic understanding of the field of valuation. The task, as I see it, is to construct a hypothesis which will serve to explain the facts of the value experience in as far as we all agree on the facts. Where we disagree on what we are going to call the facts, the hypothesis must go farther and enable us to delineate

[13] My *Perception and Aesthetic Value*, New York, 1938, ch. vii.
[14] *Ibid.*, pp. 143–146, 167–168.

and describe the facts more clearly and articulately so that we can agree. The hypothesis must be constructed on the basis of categories that are neither vague or confused. The derivation of such categories is a work of logico-empirical analysis. It is empirical, because the material with which it works is furnished in experience and must apply back to experience. It is logical, because the conceptual ordering and organization of the material must be according to logical relations.

CRITICISMS BY GARNETT

THE PAPERS by Dewey and Geiger are written from the Instrumentalist point of view and, as most of what I have to say is relevant to
both, I shall discuss the two together. Dewey's paper is confined to
certain methodological issues but his discussion is relevant to, and
touches on, the larger issues with which Geiger deals more explicitly
and very vigorously. What seem to me to be the merits and defects of
both papers are those of the whole school of thought they represent.

The chief merits of the Instrumentalist point of view are (1) the
insistence upon the relevance of all values to the active and satisfying
life of sentient creatures such as ourselves, and (2) the insistence that
this relevance makes questions of instrumental value amenable to investigation and decision by the methods of the physical and social
sciences. The defects are (1) a phobia against everything called mental,
resulting in neglect of subjective analysis, (2) the rejection of the distinction between intrinsic and instrumental values, and (3) the failure
to carry the analysis of the active and satisfying life sufficiently deep to
discover the real nature of the distinction between pseudo-values and
real values.

These defects are inherent in the Instrumentalist approach to the
problems of value and cannot be remedied until that approach is surrendered for the phenomenological. The trouble with Instrumentalism
is not that it emphasizes too much the need of intelligence and the assurance that intelligent inquiry, and it alone, can solve our value problems.
The trouble arises instead from the limitations that Instrumentalism
imposes upon intelligent inquiry, stopping short just as it reaches the
threshold of the crucial questions—the nature (not the consequences)
of what is really good in our own present experience, and the reasons
why we should be concerned with social good, the good of others besides ourselves.

The phobia against the mental is manifest in Dewey's attempt to
restrict "the field of value" to what he calls the "behavioral." This, he
says, rules out appeal to *introspection* "when that word is used to desig-

nate observation of events which by definition are wholly *private*." To attempt to *discuss* what is "wholly private" is "one of the Irish bulls of philosophy."

But what is it that Dewey is here rejecting? When he finds it necessary to distinguish between animal carings-for, which are not valuings, and human, which are, he points to the fact that human carings-for are accompanied by "anticipation or foresight of the outcome" and "recognition of the result as the ground or reason" of the caring-for. This admits that unless we have reason to believe that an action involves such "anticipation" and "recognition" we do not know whether it belongs in the "field of value." Morris says that this criterion of the field of value is inconsistent with a "thoroughgoing behavioral axiology." Certainly it would seem that without resort to introspection one could never know that such events as anticipation and recognition existed anywhere in the world.

In similar fashion, Dewey has resort to what are ordinarily regarded as introspective criteria when he needs to distinguish aesthetic from non-aesthetic activity. "The art *becomes* aesthetic in qualification when the seeing is cherished or prized as something *worth* sustaining and developing." If we need to know this much about the way we are looking at a picture before we can know that aesthetic values are involved, then surely introspection is necessary.

But apparently this is not the sort of introspection Dewey means to reject. He appears to have so narrowed the term "private" that our own mental processes are not "wholly private" in his sense if we can talk about them. It is only the claim to introspective awareness of experiences that cannot be brought into *discussion* that is ruled out. Either this must be so or Dewey's reference to the "Irish bull" is an irrelevant argument and his criteria of the field of value and the nature of aesthetic activity are inconsistent with his rejection of certain claims for introspection. But if this is all Dewey means, then why trouble to say it? All he has said is that when we speak of values, we are not referring to something *ineffable*. But there is no need to attack "introspection" or "mentalism" to maintain that. This attack therefore is misleading. For the sake of clarity it ought to be abandoned. It has already conceded all that any "absolutist" or "mentalist" needs to ask.

The second defect of the Instrumentalist point of view to which I wish to call attention is the refusal to distinguish between intrinsic and instrumental values. Since common speech uses the terms "good" and "valuable" in these two different senses the refusal to recognize both is an endless source of confusion. The value character of *objective* things and the objective things that have value are both *instrumental*. The thing that is said to be valuable in this sense is prized, not for what it now is, but for what it does to something else, for effects that it is expected to produce in the near or distant future. This is an unobjectionable and common usage. But Instrumentalists seek to confine the notion of value to this usage. Yet there is a persistent tendency to use the terms "good" and "bad," "value" and "disvalue," to mark another distinction— a distinction in the present character of immediate experience. There are some things (some phases of present experience) which we prize (or value) for what they now are; and we seek to retain or increase these phases of experience. These phases of immediate experience also are "values." But their value character is something intrinsic to their present nature, part of their present content or structure.

Dewey's rejection of intrinsic values is connected with a perfectly valid insistence on the illegitimacy of the separation of means from ends. This, however, is not the real question at issue. The question is not whether the value of an end can be considered as such, apart from the means to its realization. It is rather the question whether present experience in its immediacy contains the distinction of good and bad apart from reference to its further consequences. To Dewey the term "good" never seems to mean anything else but "good for." "Of what good," he asks, "is a 'final' value unless it also has 'instrumental' value?" If "good" only means "good for" then the answer is "None." But if "good" and "bad" are used to mark the distinction between the sort of experience we prize (in the sense of seeking to maintain it) when present, then the answer is different. If it is the last moment of a man's experience (and thus has no consequences for him), it is better for him that it should be a moment of joy and content than one of pain and disappointment.

This latter sense of value (as an intrinsic character of immediate experience) is its most fundamental sense. For objective things only have value by reason of their effect upon the value content of subjective experience. The thing that we value as instrument, for what it *does*, we value for what it probably does to some immediate experience of the future, as tending to create the sort of experience that is prized for what it *is*. It is in the analysis of immediate experience, therefore, that the final solution to every problem of evaluation is to be found. The discrimination between real values and pseudo-values thus requires an analytical examination of the intrinsic distinctions within immediate experience as well as an inquiry into the ever-receding further consequences of the thing evaluated.

This leads to the third defect in Instrumentalism. It does not clearly distinguish between real values and pseudo-values. Both are equally "values." Instead of recognizing that we may mistakenly value things that really have no value (or have disvalue) it is assumed that anything that is valued must therefore have value, more or less. "Values," says Geiger, "are the products of human choices." "Choices can produce values, 'any old' values," though "there is a further problem of discriminating between the values themselves." Anything chosen, apparently, thereby becomes a "value," even though the choice was a "bad" one. On this point Dewey, in the *Ethics*, is more careful. "The Good," he says, "is that which satisfies want, craving." But he goes on to say "Not every satisfaction of appetite or craving turns out to be a good. . . . The task of moral theory is thus to frame a theory of Good as the end or objective of desire, and also to frame a theory of the true, as distinct from specious, good." [1] This is better, but is still confusing. The object of desire is still, *ipso facto*, a good, though it may turn out to be a specious good—a good but not a good. Clarity demands that we recognize that it is not the mere fact that an object is an object of desire, want, craving, or choice that constitutes it a good, but rather that an object is a good (instrumental) if it has a certain effect on life; and it is *potentially* an instrumental good if it *can*, by appropriate use, have such an effect upon life. But this throws us back upon a further question: What sort of effect upon life must a thing have in order to be an instrumental good? And this involves us in the problem as to what phases or features of life are good in themselves, as immediate experience.

This leads us to the major weakness in the Instrumentalist position—its failure to disclose an adequate ground for distinction between values and for ethical decision. There is insistence (rightly) on the necessity of intelligent inquiry as to the results of our choices, the assumption being that we should guide our present choices by the prospects of future choices, avoiding "conflict of choices," securing "federation

[1] J. Dewey and J. H. Tufts, *Ethics*, revised edition, New York, 1932, p. 205; by permission of Henry Holt and Company, publishers.

of choices," preserving the opportunity of "free intelligent inquiry."

This statement of the method of decision of value questions, however, is inadequate for two reasons. In the first place, it directs intelligence only to the *means* of satisfying desire, the criticism of desire being concerned only with the avoidance of conflict in their expression. What is required is the addition of a critical introspective analysis of the roots of desire within the self. The problem of value is not merely: "How can I best satisfy all my desires, present and future, most completely?" It is also: "Are all my desires equally worth cultivating and strengthening? Are the strongest and most persistent really the most important? Are there any possibilities of cultivating new desires or strengthening present ones which would make my life the richer?" The terms "worth," "important," and "richer" in these questions refer not to the problem of satisfying all desires as they arise but to the interrelationship of all desires in the inner structure of the self.

The investigation needed to answer these questions is primarily an honest searching of one's own soul illuminated by intersubjective intercourse on the results of such soul-searching by others and by sympathetic effort to understand and appreciate the literature in which the greatest spirits of all time have expressed their deepest insights. Such investigation reveals a remarkable kinship of the human spirit amidst all the differences. And it learns to allow for the differences and even cherish most of them as contributions to the richness and variety of social life. It leads to the recognition that what is intrinsically valuable in life is activity that is positive in form and quality—enjoyable, free, creative activity, integrated and harmonious within the self, integrated with and contributing to similar activity in the lives of those whom it touches. In practice Dewey, Geiger and their Instrumentalist associates do not neglect this sort of inquiry, for they arrive at the same conclusion. I am inclined to believe that, in spite of all their differences, such an evaluation of what is most worthwhile in life would find agreement among all the writers of this symposium. This part of the task of investigating values is therefore not neglected in practice by the Instrumentalists or other contemporary philosophers. But it is taken for granted by the Instrumentalists and not given due place in their theory. And because the results of this subjective inquiry are taken for granted the theory that lays explicit stress only on objective inquiry into instrumental values seems to them more adequate than it really is.

The failure, however, to lay explicit stress upon the process of subjective analysis leaves the Instrumentalist in difficulty at a still more
important point in his theory. This is the second place at which the
Instrumentalist method of deciding value questions breaks down. It is
frankly faced in Geiger's paper. "Suppose there is a clash between his
continuities or between his technologies (if this is really possible) or
between two value systems within the same culture. What then?" He
answers: "But men have to live, and they have to live in some sort of
social community. If these continuities are unrecognized, value discussion becomes no more than a philosophical exercise. The clash between
'technologies' must first be resolved on the level of whether men can
live and live well."

The trouble with this "solution" of the problem is that it solves nothing when one of the two parties to the clash decides that it can live better
by living at the expense of the other. History reveals all too many instances wherein a group that controls the instrumentalities of power
has done this, not merely for years and decades, but for generations
and for centuries; and it is still being done. "Free, intelligent inquiry"
into the means of maintaining the values they cherish only confirms
such groups in their exercise of the power to exploit. Nemesis may come
eventually but it is commonly too far ahead and too uncertain to enter
into a calculation of the relation of means to ends.

It is therefore not by any such "Instrumentalist" inquiry that such a
group can find that its actions are wrong. Those in such groups who have
seen that such conduct is wrong and have urged or preached the need of
a change of attitude have reached that conclusion, not by far-sighted
calculation of the ultimate effects of exploitation upon the predominant
interests of the exploiting group, but by soul-searching reflection upon
the inner spiritual stultification and disintegration it wreaks upon themselves in the present or immediately past act. It is thus that they discover
the spiritual values lost or destroyed by otherwise intelligent selfish
exploitation. They then express these insights in speech and literature
which drives others to reflection, and gradually the moral consciousness
of the group is sensitized to the realization that certain things ought not
to be.

If value theory is ever to get beyond mere counsels of prudence on
how to get what we want, and how to promote the welfare of those in
whose welfare we are interested, then it is to an analysis of this process

whereby spiritual insight is developed that it must turn. It requires all
the exercise of intelligence, all the experimentation with new instruments and techniques, all the freedom from traditional absolutes that
Instrumentalists have so strongly advocated. But it will not be done so
long as the now traditional phobia against everything that can be
branded as "mentalistic" and the preference for "behavioral" (if not
"behavioristic") terms and data are maintained, nor so long as "scientific method" is confined to the experimental study of the relations of
means to ends. In the last analysis the problem of evaluation is a problem of the relation, not merely of means to ends, but also of ends to
ends. And that calls for an analytical understanding of the human spirit.
The method, therefore, must be primarily phenomenological. Secondarily, since the spirit gives itself expression in words, it can be aided by
the techniques of semantics and logical analysis.

REJOINDER BY GEIGER

Garnett's comments on my paper are indeed generous and forbearing
and I thank him sincerely for his restraint. I can easily imagine other
critics handling my remarks in a much less patient manner. I also appreciate his saying that my deficiencies are the general ones of instrumentalism, not mine in particular. Of course, I cannot accept that since
I certainly do not speak for instrumentalists at large (as Garnett himself
notes when in a later page he observes that I am less careful than
Dewey). My errors are my own, not those of a school.

Instrumentalism is lacking, Garnett feels, in discovering "what is
really good." To be sure, What is really good? is not only the sixty-four
dollar question; it is the top question in the entire human scene, and
were the contributors to this inquiry able to answer it definitively
they would have larger tasks than writing for this symposium. To accuse
instrumentalism of being unable to answer such a question is not exactly fair. Garnett suggests that this superlative question must be approached phenomenologically (his precise use of that term will be considered later), and he seems to imply that instrumentalism ignores the
present character of immediate experience, in which dimension must be
located the concept of value.

I do not believe that instrumentalism ignores immediate experience
—no philosophy of radical empiricism can do so. But I do not see how
immediate experience is of any particular help in locating the dimension

of value. For what does "immediate experience" per se give us? What standard of discrimination does it *itself* propose? How can it divorce itself from the social context which molds any human experience, however immediate or private it may be? These questions—and they may seem outrageous ones—all have been raised before, in my original paper and in my comments on Rice's paper. But Garnett forces them into relief when he insists that the (phenomenological) "examination of the intrinsic distinctions within immediate experience" is the clue to every problem of valuation. He also forces them into relief when he accuses the instrumentalist of himself being unable to distinguish between values and pseudo-values. Perhaps instrumentalists like Dewey and Ayres are wrong when they propose criteria such as continuity of the life process, cultural survival, and expansion of intelligence; but they are not ignoring the challenge to distinguish between values, nor are they by-passing immediate experience. Rather, it seems to me, are they trying to understand that experience *critically*—which is what they mean by evaluation. Garnett is not impressed by my own suggestion that the locus of "choice between choices" is to be found in the understanding and control of the world in which man finds himself—that "world" being a matrix of biological, psychological (even "psychic"), physical, and cultural elements. This, too, may be naive and misguided, but at least the attempted distinction between values and pseudo-values is not being blinked.

It is true that criteria such as these fail to separate intrinsic values from instrumental. This is, of course, deliberate and not simply a missed cue. (It also is what tends to divide the participants in this venture more than anything else.) For instrumentalism can discover nothing over or beyond the *continuity* of human experience, nothing ultimate—in the sense of being outside a process; or intrinsic—in the sense of being so unique and induplicable that it can be the judge of everything else, dividing into neat piles the instrumentalities and the finalities. There is nothing which clicks shut for the instrumentalist as does hedonic tone for Rice or spiritual insight for Garnett. Not that these experiences are ignored or denied; nor would instrumentalism refuse to go along with Garnett in his contention that perhaps all of us would find agreement in what is most worthwhile in life. But whatever that may be called or however it is to be arrived at, it is surely not something separate from a context, something which ruptures the continuum of experience, or which is extrapolated from that experience as an end-in-itself.

This refusal, not to discriminate within experience but to hypostatize discriminations into final entities, may be regarded, as Parker regards it, as a sentimental and unrealistic perversion of "experience," one which evades the entire impact of force and power politics upon man's choice between values. And Garnett himself inquires what avails the "free intelligent inquiry" of instrumentalism when coercion and exploitation take over. It is no sign of defeatism or incompetence to admit that here, too, instrumentalists do not have the tested and certified recipe for inaugurating an era of sweetness and light in the world. Nevertheless, I should think it much more plausible to look for the possible answer to exploitation and coercion in the operational approach which has always claimed the allegiance of instrumentalism. The concern with economic, political, educational, and sociological patterns of group behavior seems much more pertinent in understanding social conflict and in preparing techniques to control that conflict than the "soul-searching reflection upon . . . inner spiritual stultification and disintegration" counseled by Garnett.

It would be easy to caricature Garnett's sovereign remedy of "spiritual insight" and to question the efficacy of his "solution" of power politics— discovery of "the spiritual values lost or destroyed by otherwise intelligent selfish exploitation," and expression of "insights in speech and literature which drive others to reflection, and gradually the moral consciousness of the group is sensitized to the realization that certain things ought not to be." I do not intend to caricature. But I should like to inquire what change, except verbal, is introduced by his "phenomenology" (the "analytical understanding of the human spirit"), what change, that is, over good old "introspection"; and to inquire, furthermore, how the "traditional phobia" against "mentalism" (which must have reasons behind it) can be cured by substituting a new word for an old.

Garnett is asking for a fundamental change of heart on the part of the instrumentalist, for a conversion which will give him a different taste in universes and in values. But I do not need to remind him, or any one of the writers here, that the temperamental foundations of philosophy (whether tough- or tender-minded is not the point) are not so easily moved. Which is perhaps the chief point demonstrated by the present "inquiry."

THE MANY POINTS OF VIEW to be found in these papers were to have been expected. What might have been somewhat less expected is the extraordinary persistence of a theme, the strains of which are rarely absent. It is not an unusual theme, although the variations on it, which the papers provide, make for some discordance. The theme is interrogative rather than declarative, and inquires about the preciousness of values. Are they unique, different from anything else in the world, and do they require special treatment? The affirmative answers to this question seem to stand out, although not monotonously so. There seems much less interest in what might be regarded as a more "popular" theme: Are certain values to be preferred over others, and why?

But this is only a repetition of what has already been said in my original essay. There is little point in saying it again. There is also little point in getting disturbed about what is felt to be the serious, almost tragic, occupational limitations of a number of papers in this volume. The area of value has apparently come to be regarded as simply one more exercise of professional ingenuity. Since the present approach makes no such assumption, the following remarks will have to be limited to brief, specific, and admittedly incomplete comments on what seem to be several outstanding issues.

I

One of those issues might be regarded as minor, even trivial, yet it may well characterize a dominant mood of much of this book. It is the rather threadbare identification of "behavioral" with "behaviorism," a confusion that appears especially unpardonable in the light of Dewey's express repudiation of it. Parker's paper, for one, inflates the confusion to such proportions that he almost succeeds in making himself angry. He insists flatly that the two words refer to the same "philosophy," then he dissects the "epistemology" and "metaphysics" of the behavioristic philosophy, and finally he asserts that values are not a matter of behavior at all but of desire and satisfaction. The same kind of argument is found in several of the other papers, notably those of Lee and Garnett; and, it should be added, the mistaken identity of "behavioral" and "behaviorism" is also carefully exposed by Hahn and scrupulously qualified by Rice and Morris.

Perhaps this is a prime illustration of the need for a linguistic analysis such as that proposed by Morris. An organism can study its own preferential activity—that is the basic assumption of his paper, the basic assumption, also, of any sound use of a term like "behavioristics." The extravagances of John B. Watson are not intended just because there is a similarity in vocabulary; neither is there any necessary affinity for strictly "motor" theories of behavior, which Rice shows to be out of date. (He does not appear exactly generous, however, when he assumes that Dewey's reading in psychology—also that of other instrumentalists—stopped with the reflex-arc concept.) The use of "behavioral" by instrumentalists should be clear enough. It implies that there is a continuity in human experience and that the continuity has some intelligibility. It admits—indeed insists—that certain aspects of human experience may be analyzed separately, although whether they should be identified by the dated terms of "conative" and "cognitive" is questionable; but such separability is one of analysis and does not imply any ontological dualism. Self-observation is a legitimate tool of psychological investigation, but, as Morris points out, introspection does not demand the hypothesis of an inner and disinfected realm; it does not presuppose fundamental discontinuities in the human dimension. "Behavioral," then, seems to stand for the premise that man's experience is an understandable unit of psychosomatic and social factors, that it is subject throughout to investigation and modification, and that disintegrations in that experience (for example, frustrated desires or social evils) are remediable and not simply the occasion for a mind-body, or a good-bad, dialectic.

II

All of which is familiar enough to be banal. But the blurring of the distinctions between "behavioral" and "behaviorism" is not to be understood as just a signal example of linguistic confusion; after all, the writers of these essays are, if anyone is, semantically sensitive. Therefore, as was suggested some paragraphs back, this seemingly minor point of language is not minor at all if it is looked upon as a capital illustration of a temper of mind, one that insists on a decisive separation of values from facts.

That temper is found in a number of the papers, Parker's essay again being as incisive on the matter as any. He rivals Bertrand Russell in his belligerent insistence that values are biases, that "volitions are the arbiters of destiny," and that verifiability plays no meaningful part in discriminating between biases. This is frank, intelligible—and makes nonsense of any attempt to choose between values.

Yet papers like those of Ayres, Dewey, Hahn, Lepley, Mitchell, and Morris do not seem to be nonsense. Nor do Northrop's recent books. Perhaps, then, a naive question may be risked: What is the real point of value theory anyway? If values are fundamentally unverifiable, induplicable, and isolated, then discourse about them, as about any exclusively mental quality, is frustrating. They are immediate experiences, about which there can be neither argument nor decision. Analysis—at any rate, scientific analysis—can be nothing but perverse, and comparative evaluation of values only a waste of time. If values are indeed unmodifiable bias-facts, choice between them is only a thin variation on a theme of power politics, and discussion about them, to quote earlier words, "turns into a demonstration of professional competence." However ingenuous, this question about the value of value theory needs answering.

It is a far from ingenuous question if phrased differently. Is there no way of reconciling the "immediacy" interpretation of value with the critical? Cannot there be, in Northrop's terms, a fusion of the "aesthetic and theoretic components"? As these papers demonstrate, fusion is enormously difficult; yet without it, the two contrasting interpretations of value turn into gross caricatures. For example, to see the so-called instrumentalist approach as insensitive (or even opposed) to the immediately experienceable and aesthetic components of human experience is an almost libelous distortion. (Even Parker will admit that Dewey, Kallen, and others have paid some attention to aesthetic theory.) To see, from the other side, the intrinsic exposition of value as no more than a bald euphemism for mystical escapism is to be equally purblind.

The quarrel here is not about the existential status of immediate or intrinsic experiences, but about their *value*. For—at least according to the present assumptions—value depends upon choice, upon e-valuation, upon judgment between alternatives, upon a process of comparison. These assumptions in no way deprecate immediacy; they do suggest that aesthetic components or hedonic tones are not by themselves complete, since they provide no way to establish themselves over other claims. An unanalyzed liking for x is just that; it becomes a potential value when it has to compete with some other liking, say for y.

Now, Rice, for one, insists that all this has long since been repudiated by Prall and others in their familiar controversies with Dewey; but that, as Rice would admit, is a matter of opinion. His own opinion is that these premises are neo-Hegelian, and his reason seems to be that in his youth Dewey was sympathetic to Hegel. This is as apt an example of the genetic fallacy as any Rice himself exposes. There is nothing Hegelian about the idea that value is a special kind of experience, that it is not just any old interest or any old "good." There is nothing of dialectic or *Negativität* in the contention that man is above all a preference-making animal, that he inevitably chooses between interests or between hedonic tones. Interests and joys are what they are: they do not have to be values, too. When Rice and Garnett (in his comments on my paper) challenge the "orthodox instrumentalists" on this point, they are doing no more than refusing to accept a definition of value that attempts to discriminate and differentiate. Joy and interest (as R. B. Perry uses interest) are so catholic and ubiquitous that they are worthless in determining their own worth. The word "value" seems an important enough term in philosophy to represent something sharper than a kind of affective bath. This, and not Hegel, is the reason why value is being accepted as a special kind of good, and not as good-in-general; and this is why any "reconciliation" between the comparative and intrinsic elements in value determination would seem to afford some kind of priority to *theory*, to an approach that seems the more inclusive because, while acknowledging the uniqueness of immediacies, it does not grant their insularity or their inviolability to scrutiny and judgment.

III

The basic discrepancy revealed in the present work shows itself in many forms, all of them related. For instance, the intrinsic-instrumental, subjective-objective variance is reached, in some of the papers, through a comparison of the concepts "life" and "value," the results of such comparison being, however, poles apart. Where Ayres sees the area of value as continuous with the entire life process, Jessup assures us that, although values occur *in* life, life itself is not value, and life as a whole is in no way to be connected with the value situation. This seems an amazing kind of disagreement. Garnett's position on this problem is interesting: the more abundant life is indeed a final end, but, since it is intrinsic and ultimate, it must be sharply separated from "value" as we commonly understand that term, for intrinsic "value" is not moral value; it is amoral. Here, of course, is the thesis (rather, the antithesis) underlying so much of this book.

Garnett's ultimates are distinctly generous ones: his over-all intrinsic good is nothing less than that of an unobstructed sentient and conscious life. The various ways by which such a life can be reached he regards as instrumental goods. Garnett also distinguishes between *moral* good and evil (that indicated by praise and blame) and *natural* good and evil (for example, food and poison). The danger in this kind of approach seems evident, even if Garnett realizes it and tries to avoid any decisive split between ends and means. To avoid that split is, however, extraordinarily difficult when ultimates and instrumentalities are given a fundamentally different status, and especially when the final things of life—the things that must be argued about and judged between—are made amoral. For just any old "unobstructed sentient life" cannot be ultimate (waiving the question whether anything can). And if it were, there would be no escape from the dialectical travesty of ends-justifying-means.

To break the continuum of ends-and-means must be regarded as one of the disallowable practices of ethics. At any given moment, as Morris shows, a legitimate procedural distinction can be drawn between what is an end and what is a means, but that is not to insulate them and create two impervious dimensions. Really more than two dimensions are involved, for, according to Garnett, there are nice distinctions even between "subjective," "intrinsic," "ultimate," and closely related terms. (The different kinds of "subjectivity" found in these papers begins to get confusing. For example, Lee, who maintains that "caring about" is clearly subjective, nevertheless criticizes the "subjectivity" of Rice and others.) No one challenges the need for semiotic discrimination or the importance of glossaries, but verbal distinctions are one thing and ontological dichotomies and trichotomies another. It should not be arrogance to assert that the separation of instrumentalities from ultimates is the mortal sin. Narrow as the original fissure may be, into it seep all the ingredients that so often have made ethics a utopian fantasy or a bald apologetic.

IV

Rice's paper deserves particular notice in this inquiry because of its yeoman efforts to justify some kind of distinction between "empirical method" (which he accepts) and "orthodox instrumentalism" (which he does not), and because of its elaborate psychological exposition and defense of an affective theory of value. Also worthy of attention are his opening remarks: they stand out, in the context of these essays, because they aim at extending the field of value beyond the confines of professional philosophy to problems as wide as the contemporary conflict between "scientism" and a "frightened supernaturalism." The failure of nerve which the latter alternative points to, Rice likes as little as does Sidney Hook. Furthermore, the solution proposed by Rice is one that employs the methods of scientific empiricism.

This is all to the good. Equally welcome is his insistence that both the humanities and the sciences need to avoid the extremities of doctrine that would tend to make the one "flabby," and the other "arid"; in other words, each of the disputants must put his own house in order. At this point, however, two items seem to suggest themselves, one of clarification and one of more than mild protest. How far would Rice carry his empiricism? For example, does he accept the naturalistic idea of continuity?—the idea that all experience lends itself to scientific applicability and control, that, in the words of W. R. Dennes,

There is for naturalism no knowledge except that of the type ordinarily called "scientific." But such knowledge cannot be said to be restricted by its method to any limited field of subject-matter—to the exclusion, let us say, of the processes called "history" and the "fine arts." For whether a question is about forces "within the atom," or about the distribution of galaxies, or about the qualities and patterns of sound called Beethoven's Second Rasumowski Quartette and the joy some men have found in them—in any case there is no serious way to approach controlled hypotheses as to what the answers should be except by inspection of the relevant evidence and by inductive inference from it.[1]

[1] W. R. Dennes, "The Categories of Naturalism," in *Naturalism and the Human Spirit*, ed. by Y. H. Krikorian, New York, 1944, p. 289; by permission of Columbia University Press, publishers.

At times, Rice seems ready to subscribe to some such statement; at other times, he emphasizes the "limitations" of a scientific approach to value, especially when it poaches on the precincts of private emotional struggles, the struggles that are allegedly resolved only by the solace of literature and religion, not by the administrations of scientific method.

This brings up the point of protest. How should scientific method put its own house in order? What is disorderly about it? To aver, for example, that scientific naturalism is to be criticized because it has not yet helped to solve the great ethical problems (a criticism which is now the rallying point for all enemies of naturalism) must come under the head of hitting below the belt, whether from naturalist or antinaturalist. No one can deny, as Rice shows, that much of today's frustration, the frustration that (literally and figuratively) has turned so many to Rome, Moscow, or Nirvana, stems from unresolved moral problems. But to assert that these riddles are still unanswered *because* scientific naturalism has its limitations is to beg the entire question. It would be to assume—as was suggested in my original paper—that "scientific man" is the dominant figure in contemporary culture, and to assume further that his medicine has already been tried and found useless. Rice must accept some such premise to feel dissatisfied with the efforts of the "orthodox instrumentalist." But that premise cannot possibly be permitted. The assumption that the scientific and naturalistic temper already characterizes man's approach to moral and social affairs may be meant to be flattering to instrumentalists; it is hardly realistic. Naturalists would be the first to insist that, in the field of values, their efforts have been those of persuasion, not of celebration. Yet without that assumption, the assumption that free, intelligent inquiry is in full swing throughout the areas of economics, politics, and ethics, this kind of suspicion of naturalism is meaningless.

A more plausible premise would be to the effect that where naturalism has yet to make its impact, where it has encountered bias, stereotypes, vested claims, and introverted aloofness, there the great questions have remained fatally unanswered. Rice's unwillingness to see the importance of the socio-cultural factors in value theory may partially account for his view of the "limitations" of scientific method. For the reasons why there has been a tragic separation between morals and technology, between the humanities and the sciences, are to be found most significantly in the context of human history, in the social and cultural setting against which natural science developed, in the philosophical and theological tradition which has so hampered the struggles of naturalism.

The point of this protest is not one of sanguine assurance that nothing is wrong in the house of science. Self-inspection and self-correction (themselves, the very hallmark of scientific method) are always in order. But it is premature to begin to "limit" science before it has had a real chance—and it has not had a real chance, not, at any rate, in the very field where it is looked upon with more than a little suspicion.

The focus of Rice's paper is on an empirically directed "affective" theory of value, which places great reliance on joy, or, less colorfully, "hedonic tone." Here is the locus of "intrinsic" value to which instrumentalities lead. In this part Rice agrees with Garnett; however, he points out that "intrinsic" values are not necessarily "ultimate," that they may indeed be quite transitory, which would not, I think, agree with Garnett. Intrinsic value does not have to signify final approval; it is, following Rice, what Dewey seems to mean by consummatory quality. What does not seem clear, though, is—how shall we regard joy? No moral bell rings when hedonic tone is sounded—because literally anything can sound that tone. No help in choosing between values, or even in discovering values, can be found here any more than in a quantitative felicific calculus.

Classical hedonism is repudiated by Rice. Yet what Ayres in one of his books has said about happiness seems unusually appropriate: happiness has meant whatever culture has meant. It is a term so broad as to be ethically useless. Man finds his happiness in the activities the mores celebrate. Rice's statement that the "socio-cultural" context has little or no relevance for problems of value appears somewhat shortsighted, here as elsewhere. Joy may indeed be "internal" and "affective," not "conative" in essence. But *what* joys are to be chosen? Hedonic tone can be accounted for in a chapter of a volume by Krafft-Ebing as well as in the raptures of the Christian mystic or the saintly Yogi. *Which* joys are important? How can we choose between the (merely) instrumental means that bring about hedonic tone, if almost anything will suffice? Undiscriminated joy may or may not be "inner" and "affective"; it may well be an immediate and consummatory experience, and one should regard it highly. How does it help judge between totally different ways of life, each of which achieves hedonic tone? However impertinent, questions like these can be neglected by the value theorist only at the risk of making value theory preciously futile.

"Joy," or any other immediate intrinsic "good," is, after all, a symbol, a word given to an event extrapolated from its conditions. Concentration upon this sort of abstraction lends itself to hypostasis, a danger not removed just because Rice disclaims dualism, "mentalism," or any attempt to "separate" intrinsics from instrumentalities. "Joy" is like "truth," "health," "wealth," "the weather"—in William James's examples —a name given ex post facto to a group of specific happenings. Those specific happenings are what they are: they are like data. Yet we don't wallow in data. We use them, among other things, to verify our hypotheses, to make beliefs and ideas "true." The data themselves are neither true nor false—they are what we have to take into account. (This is still, of course, along the lines of James's analysis.) Similarly, it can be argued, hedonic tones (not some substantialized Laetitia) are immediate experiences which have to be taken into account. They are not automatically *values*. Values, like truth, are names given to processes, to happenings, to choices men make. All this is admittedly iteration (although hardly vestiges of Absolute Idealism, as Rice seems to suggest), and it is undoubtedly not the "defense" he has in mind when he challenges the "orthodox instrumentalist" on this point. But repetition is indicated, for this wholesale immersion in immediacies, in undiscriminated ultimates, is frustrating, it seems, for anyone who is attempting to delimit the realm of *value*.

As a postscript to this discussion of hedonic tone, a word or two may be ventured on Rice's formidable array of physiological and neurological data. The present writer is certainly no expert in experimental psychology; yet one aspect of the evidence seems overlooked by Rice when he suggests that "we may have . . . the scientific instruments for the recovery of what is valid in the Socratic, Hebraic-Christian, and introspective-modern insights that happiness or salvation in its last manifestations is an 'inner feeling,' and is not to be defined wholly by external happenings." That omission is the interesting work on muscular tensions during learning, and on the connections between tensions and "mental" relaxation,[2] the point of which is to show precisely the

[2] Much of this work has been done by G. L. Freeman. See his articles in *The Journal of General Psychology*, IV (1930), 309–334; V (1931), 479–494; *The Journal of Experimental Psychology*, XV (1932), No. 3; *The Psychological Review*, XXXVIII

intimate and functional connection between "external happenings," i. e., muscle tonus, and the most private ratiocinations and intimate states of "peace of mind." I do not see how studies like these—and they are but a sample of a large literature—give much comfort to Rice's suggestions. Furthermore, Rice admittedly speculates on the physiological nature of pleasure when he hints at its correlation "with smooth functioning in the central [nerve] regions." So far as I can discover there is no evidence for this; nor is there any for the idea that the free nerve-endings are simply structures with a low threshold of overstimulation. As I understand it, free nerve-endings initiate sensory impulses we call pain when the membrane is punctured and the tissue fluids undergo redistribution. The reason that intense stimulation in any modality may seem to pass over into pain appears to be simply that eventually the energy delivered to the organism becomes sufficient to break the membrane surrounding the free nerve-endings.

These, however, are peripheral points, not to say pedantic. They are mentioned simply to suggest to Rice that he continue to be cautious about reading too much into his neurological exposition of hedonic tone; for his whole approach is cautious. But far from peripheral is Rice's abrupt statement that "there is no problem peculiar to value theory" in its socio-cultural context. He admits, it is true, that "the socio-cultural context has some relevance to any larger investigation into values," but just what this "larger investigation" refers to he does not say. This is not the place to go into a long defense of the relevance of cultural determinism or to show the immense significance for value theory itself of hypotheses like those of George Mead and his concept of the "social act." But the notion that values, or any other activity of the human animal, can be fully understood without taking into account the conditioning factors of man's social surroundings seems extraordinarily one-sided. One has opportunity here only to counter an abrupt statement with one equally abrupt and say, with Dewey, that values are "so definitely and completely socio-cultural that they can be effectively dealt with only in that context."

(1931?), No. 5; *The American Journal of Psychology*, XLV (1933); and an article by Freeman and S. L. Lindley in *The Journal of Experimental Psychology*, XIV (1931), No. 6. The connection between mental relaxation and muscular tension is to be found, of course, in the important (if semi-popular) work of E. Jacobson, *Progressive Relaxation*, Chicago, 1938.

V

The essays in this collection range from one end of the value spectrum to the other, from the ultraviolet to the infrared. The paper by Ayres might be placed in the latter category. Despite, or because of that, his essay would appeal—at least in this corner—precisely where some of the others would not. But the purpose here is not to laud what is felt to be an incisive and provocative paper. In fact, just because the present writer is so much in agreement with the over-all point of view, it may be helpful to raise specific questions on points where Ayres may possibly be weakening his case by overstating it.

In this essay, as in other of his recent writings, Ayres can be said to out-Dewey Dewey and to out-Veblen Veblen. There is nothing outrageous about this, but it will necessarily shock those to whom Dewey and Veblen are still strange and unappreciated (and some of "those" could be philosophers). Ayres' central argument might be presented this way: Values relate to the continuity of the life process and to the pattern of organized human behavior. That process and that pattern are technological ones, that is, tool-using—tools being conceptual as well as manual. Therefore, values relate to technology. This general argument is sound, although it must be confessed that it probably raises at least verbal blocks in many minds that otherwise might be receptive. For despite Dewey's own acceptance of them, words like "technology" and "tools" are hardly in philosophic repute, and they tend to be misinterpreted and misjudged, no matter how carefully defined. Such a handicap, however, is less serious than that of possible overstatements like "nothing but science is true or meaningful" and the idea of "best" or "higher" values makes no sense. These, of course, are being taken out of their context; in their context they are by no means so sparsely covered. Nevertheless, they seem to suggest more than Ayres intends.

Even this is not as important as the difficulties that Ayres leaves untouched. Is there only one life process, only a single continuum? Does technology, science, or even intelligence exhaust the locus for value? Can a synthesis between the "theoretic" and "aesthetic" components of experience be achieved if one of them is underscored as strenuously as it is by Ayres? These questions are no more than different ways of pointing out that technology itself—no matter how broadly defined—has competition, intramural competition from even Western culture, and extramural from other cultures. It is the very technological continuum itself that is challenged, say, by mystics, Eastern or Western. Now, mysticism—using the word as a rough symbol for non-technological value patterns—may be aberrant and misguided. But that cannot be decided, it would seem, upon a technological basis without begging the whole question of *which* values are to be pushed and which rejected. For it is precisely science, intelligence, inquiry, and theory that are themselves being suspected, and to justify them it would seem necessary to get *outside* a technology and judge among several cultural continua.

A similar difficulty might be found in Ayres' repudiation of the notion of ends, of "best" or "highest" values. His insistence upon a continuity of ends and means is unquestionable. Yet his general argument can be understood as itself offering us a "best" value, that of tool-using. Ayres cannot mean that tool-using *is now* a complete locus for value. He would certainly admit that in great areas of human experience, for example, those of ethics and the social problems, scientific procedures are conspicuously absent. That they *should* be employed there appears indubitable; that they can be employed there somewhat less so. But in any event, they are being proposed as *oughts*, as better if not best values, as ends whether or not ultimate. Ayres appears more allergic than necessary to the ordinary vocabulary of morals.

These questions, it will be recognized, are addressed to the present writer's original essay as much as they are to Ayres'. They are questions, difficult ones, that any instrumentalistic approach must raise; and they are being made articulate here for purposes of future clarification and discussion, with full realization that even the "orthodox instrumentalist" has not come to the end of his quest for certainty!

REJOINDER BY AYRES

I concur fully in everything Geiger has written both in his essay and in this note, including his comments on my own stylistic asperity. However, I doubt if anybody has ever been put off by terminological harshness, or, for that matter, by any merely intellectual difficulty inherent in the identification of the fine arts, science, and reflective thinking generally with the tool-using activities of mankind. The difficulty has its origin elsewhere, and would not be lessened by any amount of stylistic appeasement. On the contrary, I am convinced that our only hope of resolving the present confusion is by making the alternatives as clear as possible. That means calling a spade a spade; and if anybody says that is tantamount to calling it a damned shovel, I would point out that it is he who is damning a tool but for which none of us would be here to argue, toolwise, about anything.[1]

[1] For the Rejoinder by Rice, see pp. 410–414, below.

❧ CRITICISMS BY HAHN[1]

I

LEPLEY's "Sequel on Value" seems to me to be an unusually persistent attempt to see and consider seriously the relevant data, to avoid neglecting the facts behind each basic emphasis of these studies, whatever words of caution about their interpretation may be necessary. The fundamental type of interpretation offered, I should say, is pragmatic or contextualistic, and though I am not sure that the logic of this position and the relevant facts require pushing some points as far as he does, I find myself in agreement with the general direction of his thinking.

In answering Dewey's first question, he seems to me to be on sound ground in adopting a broad behavioral description of liking, disliking, desire, interest, valuing, valuation, prizing, and holding dear, and in terms of this description characterizing them as interactional and transactional rather than as independently existing "subjective entities" or "mental states." At least two methodological issues, he asserts, are raised by Dewey's first question: (1) that of whether the class "value," or "value phenomena," is exhausted by human or organic experiences of desiring, satisfaction, and the like; and (2) that of the place of introspective analysis and an internal, mentalistic, or subjective standpoint and terminology in the study of value and the formulation of value theory. The first issue turns about the place to be given efficacies for events, instrumental values. If they are dismissed as being of merely secondary or derivative importance, the class "value" may be limited to certain human or organic experiences of desiring, satisfaction, or the like. With his characteristic doctrine of the relativity of means and ends, however, the pragmatist has objected to any such limitation. If any end may be viewed as a means to some further state of affairs and any means may become an end, to exclude means is to exclude too much. And if means or instruments are included, the field includes

[1] I am grateful to the University of Missouri Research Council for a summer research appointment which freed me from teaching duties to write my set of Criticisms.

more than the human or organic experiences mentioned, for the means-end principle goes far beyond them, affording a basic continuity between human and non-human events. Far from excluding instruments or means from the field of values, the pragmatist finds in them a key to an understanding of it; and his emphasis upon instrumental values helps counteract a tendency to isolate values from each other and from everything else and thus to neglect significant continuities. With reference to the first issue, then, Lepley and I agree that the class "value" is not exhausted by human or organic experiences of desiring, satisfaction, and the like.

In regard to the second issue raised by Dewey's first question, a behavioral as contrasted with an introspective analysis or conception of value, Lepley follows an essentially behavioral procedure which is broad enough to include immediate or had qualities. Some writers apparently hold that one must make a choice between behaviorism and doing justice to had qualities, subjective experience; and, such being the case, they reject the former. Lepley sees that an adequate behaviorism has a place for these facts. What has been primarily objectionable to the pragmatist in connection with immediate experiences, or so-called introspective data, has not been these facts as he sees them but rather an interpretation of them which gives rise to either the traditional metaphysical dualism or a subjective idealism of some sort. Though it may find it necessary or desirable to reinterpret some of them, an adequate behaviorism should omit no relevant facts. Something like this, I take it, is Lepley's main point in this connection; and it seems to me a sound position.

Certain of his statements, however, suggest that he may be going somewhat beyond this position. Just how far I am not sure. He asserts, for example, that in the broader sense "it appears likely that the behavioral and the subjective are but two somewhat different ways of viewing and stating the same total interactive, transactive processes which constitute human value events." Or again: "Indeed, it is doubtful whether 'value events' can be fully or adequately studied and described without the use of terms commonly classed as 'introspective' or 'subjective' as well as those regarded as 'behavioral' or 'objective.' Even qualities 'as had' are probably events—processes—which can be viewed and designated or expressed in 'both' ways."

I am left wondering whether Lepley wishes to suggest, (1) in line

with my interpretation of his main position above, that though common
sense value facts are stated in terms some of which are usually classed
as "introspective" and some as "behavioral," an adequate behaviorism
can give a full treatment of them; or (2) that both behaviorism and
introspectionism are partial truths, each of which needs the supplementation of the other to give an adequate account of value events;
or (3) that either the introspective or the behavioral approach may
be formulated broadly enough to include the relevant value events,
and when so formulated, they are roughly equivalent; or (4) some
combination of these possibilities.

Alternative (2) has a good deal to recommend it. At any rate, Watsonian behaviorism and the introspective procedure which generated
the traditional metaphysical dualism of disparate "inner" and "outer"
realms both seem to me inadequate in spite of the fact that we may
learn from each of them.

Alternative (3) is an interesting possibility which has the merit of
suggesting that neither the behavioral nor the introspective version of
values is as restricted or unreasonable as its opponents might have us
believe. There is some question, however, of whether interpreting the
views thus broadly does not rob each of what is distinctive and prevent
our learning as much as we might through pushing each to the limit
in its more distinctive form. The pragmatic restatement of the behavioral approach, however, does look quite promising to me. But re-
stating introspectionism in such fashion as to prevent its generating
or perpetuating what Lepley or I might regard as unjustifiable separations or dualisms might require abandoning a metaphysical framework
which some would think was amply justified on other grounds.

Apparently no place would be left for the sort of metaphysical dualism set up by many of those who have started from the primacy of
introspective data and then attempted to go on from there to some
sort of outside world. To restate the introspectionist's case in this fashion might seem to some not a revision or development of his position,
but its complete abandonment. Or it might be held that in this case
introspection is included only on the behaviorist's terms. At any rate,
so far as I can see, no restatement of introspectionism which preserves
the traditional dualism is the equivalent of Lepley's broad behaviorism; nor does justification of the treatment of felt qualities, which I
agree should have a place, require maintaining that the behavioral

and the introspective are but two somewhat different ways of getting at the same facts. I question, moreover, whether the subjective approach affords as adequate coverage of the interactive, transactive processes as the behavioral.

In view of such considerations as R. B. Perry advances in connection with the long history and many inadequacies of introspectionism, I favor attempting to develop and refine a behavioral approach to value problems. If, as he maintains,[2] "the limitations of the introspective theory of consciousness have been most flagrant in the region of the will and the affections . . . in that department of human nature with which theory of value is primarily concerned" and "almost every recent advance in the motor-affective field of the mental life has resulted from the more or less complete abandonment of the introspective method," there would seem to be a great deal to be said for adopting a broad behavioral approach to see what could be accomplished through its development.

In answering Dewey's second question—Is an attitude of prizing or holding dear, desiring, liking, interest, enjoying, or some experience of valuing, "by itself a *sufficient* condition for the existence of values? Or, while it is a necessary condition, is a further condition of the nature of *valuation* or *appraisal*, required?"—Lepley, if I correctly analyze his account, distinguishes three basic types, areas, or conceptions of value—(a) qualities as had, (b) qualities as had and as qualified by criticism, and (c) efficacies for events—and asserts that the question may be answered differently for the various areas. The basic point that the question, or group of questions, can best be answered after making certain distinctions in type of value seems to me sound, and his classification is similar to one which I developed in my constructive paper. He would probably agree that in part this is a verbal question of what we are to mean by value, as suggested by these sentences: "When, for example, we are designating or expressing immediate qualities which are not elements in or objects of valuative processes, valuation is *not* a necessary condition for the existence of values. . . . But when we are designating or expressing critically examined qualities or efficacies, valuation *is* a necessary condition for the existence of values." If we call one set of things value, valuation is not a neces-

[2] *General Theory of Value*, New York, 1926, pp. 143, 145; by permission of Longmans, Green and Company, publishers.

sary condition; but if we define value as *critically* examined qualities or efficacies, *criticism,* or valuation, becomes a necessary condition of membership in it.

Though a question of how we shall use terms may be part of what is involved here, I think Lepley would agree that more significantly it is a factual question, difficult to answer, of the place which reflective or critical factors have in value situations; and here the crucial area, that of immediate value (Lepley's "had qualities"), is one on which we may differ. The first sentence of the above quotation suggests that he thinks that there are immediate qualities which constitute values but which are not elements in or objects of valuative processes. Is this to be interpreted as asserting that there are cases of pure having, enjoyment, or prizing, into which no element of judgment, appraisal, or cognitive reference enters? Do having, enjoying, prizing, and the like, occur without an inferential, judgmental, or appraisive factor present? Do we prize or demand, say, purely arbitrarily, quite apart from any cognitive or evaluative considerations? On a view stressing the interactive character of transactions and rejecting a faculty psychology, can some activities be allocated to pure feeling or willing, and others to knowing? If an affirmative answer be given to these questions, are the qualities thus had, enjoyed, or prized thereby (that is, through such having, enjoyment, or prizing and not through contributing to some end) made values?

I incline to answer these questions in the negative. Immediate value for me is not produced by a having or prizing which contains no element of judgment, appraisal, or cognitive reference, though such having or prizing might constitute a kind of limiting case. On my view the difference between immediate values and reasoned, tested, or critically evaluated ones is highly significant, but it is a difference of degree rather than of kind.

It would be possible, of course, to give a negative answer to the first questions above and still avoid my position. One might maintain that, though having, prizing, and the like, never occur apart from a cognitive or appraisive factor, it is nonetheless the non-cognitive aspect which is responsible for value. I should want to know why, if more than a question of terminology is involved.

In the remaining sections of Lepley's paper I find much of interest and little with which to disagree. In fact, in view of the little I had to say in my constructive paper regarding Dewey's third question, perhaps I should say that though it is one which I have not yet thought through to my entire satisfaction, I am at present inclined to accept Lepley's answer to it. I might add that his discussion of it contains a suggestion of an interpretation of immediate experience much more acceptable to me than the one I attributed to him in connection with Dewey's second question. Though he is discussing propositions and may intend the statement to apply only to them, it appears to include reference to a necessary condition for any sort of experience. The statement, quoted from note 15, follows, with my italics: "It should be noted that, even in stating or denoting a quality as immediately experienced, the proposition, however spontaneous and impulsive, involves, *if there is a genuine experience,* an element of appraisal—a judgment, though it may be of a very low order of inclusiveness and care."

II

In "Values, Valuing, and Evaluation," which I found to be one of the most interesting essays in our collection, Mitchell builds on Brogan's work to develop a general theory of value in terms of which to answer Dewey's questions, concentrating his discussion on the second group of questions. The basic metaphysical framework of his theory seems to me to be a pragmatic naturalism along Mead's lines, a position with which I am, of course, in fundamental agreement. For progress in clarification and discovery within the field of value theory he looks to three intellectual instruments: (1) a relational logic, (2) Mead's technique of behavioral analysis, and (3) scientific method as formulated in Dewey's analysis of the complete act of thought.

I shall not attempt a detailed commentary on this highly suggestive paper but shall rather limit myself to two or three sets of questions and comments. First, Mitchell reinforces in at least three ways, I was pleased to note, the view that metaphysics may be of crucial relevance for value theory: namely, by (a) showing certain undesirable consequences of accepting an Aristotelian substance-attribute metaphysics, (b) performing a similar task for Cartesian dualism, and (c) indicating various differences it would make to substitute a post-Darwinian, post-Einsteinian perspective of the sort he advocates. The Aristotelian substance-attribute metaphysics, he suggests, has hindered develop-

ment of an adequate theory through encouraging what he regards as
artificial divisions and absolutistic conceptions of value. That such a
view continues to influence value discussion long after the Middle
Ages he indicates by the fact that we, amusingly enough, still debate
questions couched in its terms. For example, the question—"Is value
adjectival in nature or substantive?"—he treats as a barely camouflaged
survival of the question of whether "good" is an attribute or a substance, and in terms of a comparative theory of value he answers it
"by denying the relevance of the substance-attribute metaphysics or
the importance of the grammatical distinction between nouns and
adjectives." Though the terminology may be significant as indicating
the pervasive influence of the substance-attribute metaphysics on our
language and perhaps our ways of thinking, I suppose that Mitchell
would agree that Dewey, in this context, is not offering us a choice
of relevance only within an Aristotelian system but rather is raising
a wider issue concerning the conditions of "value." In any event, however, I should be glad to see a fuller statement by Mitchell concerning the influence of this metaphysics and the subject-predicate logic
on value discussion.

Perhaps the most significant consequence of the Cartesian mind-
body dualism, which "is nowhere so much in evidence as in theory of
value," is the mislocation, from the point of view of the pragmatist
or contextualist, of values, which are taken out of art and nature,
where they belong, and placed within the recesses of the mind or in
some subsistential realm. And not the least of the virtues of the theory
Mitchell sets forth is that it would free us from this dualism as well
as certain other troublesome features of traditional accounts. If the
view does enable us to avoid or solve certain of the traditional difficulties without falling into equally bad or worse ones of its own making, that is reason enough for exploring it further; but Mitchell also
suggests certain positive advantages, which give promise of carrying
the view beyond the negative virtues of not having some bad features
of various other positions; and perhaps these positive values might
well be given greater emphasis.

A second set of problems arises in connection with the determination
of the field of values on Mitchell's view—with the difficulties of doing
justice to the continuities between values and the rest of reality without neglecting relevant discontinuities; and though I shall center my

comments on his account, many of these problems are equally pertinent and at least equally difficult for my position. In stressing the
continuities Mitchell sometimes seems to be offering a very broad
field of values, but when he directs attention to significant discontinuities the field seems much more restricted. Broadly speaking, the
field of values for him, as for Dewey and Morris, seems to be that of
situations involving preferential behavior. "Wherever there is a question of acceptance or rejection," he writes, "there is a question of better
or worse, and wherever there is a question of better or worse there is
a question of value." This sounds quite inclusive, but even so there
is some question as to whether it would include all of the class of
efficacies for events, recognized by Lepley and myself as constituting
a type of values; for this class includes certain extensions beyond the
organic realm. One might maintain, however, that wherever there is
a question of means or instrumentality for a given result, whether
organic or inorganic, a question of better or worse is involved and
hence a question of value. Possibly Mitchell would regard these utilitanda, or efficacies for events, as implicit values, possibly no more than
conditions.

At any rate, at times he seems to be suggesting an area broad enough
to include them. In particular, some of his distinctive arguments against
affective, desire, and interest theories of value turn about their lack
of sufficient generality to include true, valid, and real as value terms.
If these terms be included, as Mitchell argues they must, efficacies
for events seem to me to be thereby included. "But if we agree that
any situation involving acceptance or rejection is a value situation,"
he declares, "we must also agree that questions of truth, validity, and
reality are questions of value." The real, to take the broadest of these
terms, "is the reliable, the dependable," "the good in respect to objective status," "that which receives support from the rest of nature,
which is confirmed in the life of the individual or community, and
which helps maintain the concord of values." Such values as reliability,
dependability, trustworthiness, and the like I should call utilitanda, or
instrumental values, and that the real is so characterized I should agree;
but is it not much more besides?

Are not reliability, dependability, and other such utilitanda or instrumental values which characterize things in relation to the goals of
successful action or the end of "objective status" only a portion of

being, existence, or reality? It may be maintained, of course, that reality can be given a generic meaning on this basis and that anything whatever can be given some rating—good, bad, or indifferent—with respect to ends so that nothing would be omitted from the real. Even the unreal might be said to have some place in this conception of reality. This use of value, however, might prove rather confusing; for we do—do we not?—speak of reality or existence with reference to non-value aspects, and it is convenient to have the term "reality" to include both these value and non-value aspects.

The difficulty here, of course, may be largely one of terminology; but in any event some clarification seems to be needed. By questions of reality Mitchell may have in mind much less than the most general questions possible. Just as certain value terms—as, for example, "moral" —may be used in either a generic sense to indicate an entire field— say, morals—or in a more restricted sense to indicate something ranking high within the field—moral as contrasted with immoral—so, he might hold, "real" may be used in either an inclusive sense or in the restricted sense of something possessing in superlative degree certain traits. If "real" is used merely in the restricted sense, it becomes a subdivision of the field of values, and it might appear that there is no special problem; but once "real" in this sense is defined in value terms or recognized as possessing value in superlative degree, the rest of the field of reality in the general sense seems to be swept into the domain of value, and the generic reality, which we ordinarily think of as including values, becomes a subdivision of the latter (or identical with them). Once a portion of the field of being or existence is viewed as occupying a place in a scale in so far as it is real, it is difficult to avoid applying the same scale to the rest of the field; for if some things as members of a given area are reliable or dependable, others within the area become unreliable, undependable, or indifferent, and even the indifferent is determined on the basis of value criteria. If "real" is used in a generic sense, it may still be interpreted in value terms as suggested above, and due respect for the evidence may require something of the sort; but I wonder if it would not be less confusing to reserve for the generic term a domain sufficiently broad to include both values and non-values. If "real" is used merely in a restricted sense, there is no special problem so long as a way is left open for a generic sense which includes both values and non-values; but if it is used even in a restricted sense and defined as value, it becomes difficult to retain this restricted meaning.

In spite of my misgivings regarding speaking of values when reality or truth or validity is what we mean, I think Mitchell has a case. He performs a service in directing our attention to the value coloring of these terms and to the continuities involved, and his conception may provide the basis for clarifying many historical questions and issues with reference to these areas; but if all these be recognized as values, something more seems to be needed by way of stressing significant differences or discontinuities between any one of them and values in the more usual sense of the term.

Though one wonders how a field of values broad enough to include the real will be able to exclude any reality, Mitchell's section on "Below Valuing" is devoted to subvalues. In it he seems to be offering a much more restricted field than in the sections stressing the need for a generic view. Here he asserts that though all valuing is conditioned by biological selectivity, by organic and physiological processes far below the level of conscious choice, values, I assume in the sense of immediate values or critical developments of them, emerge only with consciousness and are defined in terms of the organism. In speaking of valuing here, I take it, he is concerned with behavior on a molar level. Valuing and evaluation in this sense are grounded in the suitable and the fitting, "stripping the words of aesthetic connotations." The suitable and the fitting limit the range of preferences an organism can have without bringing on premature extinction and afford a basis of judgment of the wisdom of preferences. Though I agree with Mitchell's version of value here, the suitable and the fitting seem to me to be utilitanda, or instrumental values; and such values not merely condition molar level preferences, they seem to me to be essentially the kind of values Mitchell is getting at in his more generic conception and to be subvalues only in the sense of being below (or at least different from) the values emerging in connection with the molar level valuing and evaluating.

Speaking in terms of molar level valuing, Mitchell defines a value-object, or a value, as "a natural, teleological object determined by the wants, interests, or satisfactions of a conscious act"; and on this basis he declares that "a rock, defined geologically, is not a value-object." If we revert to the conception which includes the real as value, I wonder if even the geologically defined rock, some instances of which existed prior to organisms, could be excluded. Would it not be the geologically acceptable or reliable, that which is acceptable or dependable in terms of the purposes of the geologists? Are we to assume that rocks, defined geologically, are not abstract extensions of behavior objects but rather something radically different in kind?

The question of the extent of the field of values is raised in yet another form by Dewey's second question (or group of questions) as formulated in the introductory rough listing— Is an attitude of prizing or holding dear, desiring, liking, interest, or some experience of valuing, "by itself a *sufficient* condition for the existence of values? Or, while it is a necessary condition, is a further condition of the nature of valuation or appraisal, required?" I assume that the question concerns immediate values and their critical refinements and that two of the main issues involved are the extent of the field of values and the relation of evaluation to valuing. Since Mitchell does not answer explicitly the question in this form and would presumably prefer a different formulation, I cannot be sure of my interpretation; but he discusses both problems. Naturalists agree that some experience of valuing is a necessary condition of the existence of immediate values, and the question of whether it is not merely necessary but sufficient —and of a narrower or broader field of values—usually turns about their interpretation of the nature of valuing or the relation of the latter to evaluation. That such experiences as those enumerated in the question are concerned somehow with value probably all would agree. Hence it might be better to agree that the field of immediate values, at least, is determined by some experience of valuing, and then we can work on our differences of interpretation in regard to the field so delimited.

Mitchell's view, I think, is in accord with this suggestion. I agree with his "contention that ordinary, common sense experience of value is the starting point and ultimate test of the more elaborate evaluations of ethics, aesthetics, and economics. Without this shareable, communicable experience there could be no knowledge of good and evil, no literary or art criticism, and no social science." In stating that values are "determined by the wants, interests, or satisfactions of a conscious act," he is asserting, I take it, that an experience of valuing is a sufficient condition for the existence of immediate values. He is thereby giving a basic place to the felt good and admitting the fundamental character of tastes and preferences, wants, satisfactions, enjoyments, prizings, demands, and interests.

Valuing for him, however, as for Dewey and me, is no purely arbitrary affair. Instead of interpreting it as pure having, enjoyment, or prizing into which no element of judgment or cognitive reference enters, he views it as differing only in degree, not in kind, from evaluation. Whereas the latter involves indirect comparison, valuing is direct comparison. Since Mitchell recognizes it as a comparative, judgmental process, he presumably finds in it a critical, appraisive factor, what Dewey calls "an element of recognition of the properties of the thing or person valued as *ground* for prizing, esteeming, desiring, liking." In thus holding that valuing has such an element, he denies that tastes and preferences are ultimate bases of value such that nothing can be done about them. Though they are in a sense ultimate—in the sense that we appeal not from them but from the less enlightened to the more enlightened preference or taste—we can do something about them. We can refine and check on them, for they contain the seeds of possible improvement. Mitchell's account of the ways in which we can check on them, both directly and through his four techniques of evaluation, I might add, offers some of the most interesting material in his essay.

REJOINDER BY LEPLEY

Hahn focuses attention upon two points which I feel may be least satisfactory in my paper. The unsatisfactoriness arises not, I hope, as Parker's remarks [3] may suggest, from an evasion of issues, but because I have not been able, despite considerable reflection on the issues, to arrive at answers which seem to be entirely clear or complete. Nor have I seen how to make much further headway in dealing with the problems. I am therefore indebted particularly to Hahn for the pains he has taken to delineate the possibilities in each case.

In regard to the 'behavioral' versus the 'introspective' I am not sure that I can say more than I have already written in my main paper [4] and in the second and third paragraphs of my Criticisms.[5] In the

[3] P. 395, below.
[4] Pp. 168–169. For explanation of my use of single and double quotation marks see note 2, p. 167, above.
[5] P. 381.

sense that I accept the hypothesis of continuity in all events, even in the occurrence and experience of qualities, I suppose I am fundamentally a 'behaviorist.' In this sense, I prefer the first of the positions which Hahn notes as possible: the view that an "adequate behaviorism" can give a full treatment of all value facts. But can behaviorism, however liberally interpreted, be adequate—in all respects and for all purposes? Can it give full recognition to, and make full use of the data of, the qualitative, affective, experimental "as-hadnesses"? Or must we employ words such as "like" and "dislike," "right" and "wrong," "good" and "bad," "ought" and "ought not," and so forth, in more than 'behavioral ways,' if we are to succeed in designating and expressing some aspects or dimensions of our behaviors-experiences? It seems to me that such words must be used, but that they are extremely dangerous terms, which easily create delusions of epistemological and metaphysical dualisms. I doubt that there is basically any dualism between behavioral events and the 'as-hadnesses' or the 'givens of experience.' So, although I feel that Hahn's second alternative ("that both behaviorism and introspectionism are partial truths, each of which needs the supplementation of the other to give an adequate account of value events") is correct in that neither 'behavioral' nor 'subjective' terms alone (nor perhaps the two combined) are adequate, I suspect that there is more danger than ultimate truth in this alternative.

The solution of the 'mind-body problem' which I most favor is a variety of the one often called "the identity theory," a variety which seeks to recognize that awarenesses, and perhaps the events or relations of which there is awareness, are 'emergent,' somewhat (to use a crude analogy) as light emerges from and is more than the vibrations or electronic activities of the filament of an electric bulb. I find, therefore, a certain amount of merit and also of demerit in the third possibility which Hahn mentions: that either the introspective or the behavioral approach may be formulated broadly enough to include the relevant value events, and when so formulated, they are roughly equivalent. This alternative is correct, it seems to me, in that the fundamental interactive, transactive processes of adjustment (some phases of which are often largely 'subjective,' or 'inner') can perhaps always be read throughout—so far as we *can* read them—either as physical-physiological-behavioral or as given-had-awarenesses, and therefore as *both* of these. The two readings are probably identical only in the sense that they are different ways of viewing and bodying forth the same events. The third alternative is dangerous, however, in that it may be interpreted to mean that either the behavioral or the introspective perspective and formulation may be so developed as to be adequate (as a metaphysical description) in itself apart from the other. I do not mean to say that the behavioral and the introspective are *but,* or *merely,* two different ways of getting at the same facts (the actual, underlying events); for both they and the facts got at (inferentially) are real and should be as fully recognized as possible, not lost by reduction.

In regard to whether having, enjoying, prizing, and the like, ever occur without there being present, also an inferential, judgmental, or appraisive factor, which is Hahn's second question on my paper, I am also uncertain. The issue here seems to be like that in regard to whether we have any sensory experience which is not also perceptive. It may be that only in earliest infancy are sensory 'experiences' (and feelings, likings, enjoyments, and so forth) had without perceptual or judgmental elements. But it appears to me that some of our experiences, or many phases of them, are wholly, or almost wholly, affective or qualitative. Occasionally, we find ourselves emerging from a state which seems to have been one of complete absorption in qualities, and we may judge that the state was good in itself or was good as a means to some end, say, our mental health. We feel, also, that without such intrinsic elements of experience, whether they may occur singly or only along with other more 'cognitive' elements, much—if not indeed all—value would be lost, or at least would be unexperienced. Thus both from our experiences of 'pure' feeling and from contemplation of qualitative elements considered in isolation (as G. E. Moore puts it), or in abstraction, these elements may be recognized as good in themselves, or 'intrinsically.' Of course, it may be insisted that a feeling or quality as had or in isolation becomes a value only through judgment and that it possessed no 'real value' prior to or apart from the judgment. But this would be merely to insist on one use of the term "value" to the exclusion of other uses, and is not the basic issue Hahn is raising. For the most part, I agree with him that the difference between immediate value and reasoned, tested, critically evaluated value is a difference of degree rather than of kind. And I hope that my main paper and my other writings on value make it clear that I attach very great importance to the need and possibilities for achieving value "in a most distinctive sense" through experimental procedures. But with sufficient recognition of the almost perpetual need for critical examination and testing, I see no real objection to regarding the immediate qualities, or 'givens,' of experience as values 'in themselves,' whether they ever actually occur in isolation or not. Indeed, the recognition of the immediate elements of experience as among our most precious values avoids what otherwise often appears as an overintellectualization of value—a denial of value to the affective or qualitative elements which seem so fundamental and pervasive in nearly all our value experiences. I am quite aware, however, that to regard these as *sufficient* elements in the discovery or creation (as contrasted with the 'having') of value is extremely dangerous. The three conceptions of value distinguished in my paper need to be kept in close—perhaps integral—relation, for they may be but abstracted aspects of actual value situations or adjustment courses.

Rejoinder by Mitchell

Hahn is concerned with the limits of value, finding me somewhat vague on the subject. Since objects take on value qualities relative to organisms capable of conscious selection, I think it reasonable to maintain that values emerge along with the evolution of consciousness. It seems to me to be unduly stretching terms to ascribe value to the conditions that maintain or complete the orderly arrangements of atoms, molecules, or elementary biological forms. While chemists use the words "satisfy," "complete," and so forth in describing the behavior of atoms and molecules, they realize that their language is metaphorical and they could define their terms mechanically. But one cannot define terms like food, shelter, enemy, resources except as involving the processes of some organism. It is in the selective action of conscious creatures that such objects are better or worse than an alternative object and therefore have value qualities. I think Parker has a point in wondering whether Dewey and, presumably, Hahn are panpsychists.

Having fixed the lower limit of the realm of value, I see a realm that is almost coextensive with that of perception. If we agree with Bergson and Mead that the perception of an object reveals its possible action on us and our possible reactions to it, and that the perceived qualities are therefore invitations or warnings, it would follow that value qualities are coextensive with perceptual qualities generally. Those theories which identify value with hedonic tone or some other subjective feeling fail to take account of the exceeding wealth of value terms in our language, most of them applying to the objects of nature and art. Our own states, of course, are also objects of attention and are describable in value terms.

Hahn is dubious about including truth, validity, trustworthiness, reality, and the like, in the realm of value. He thinks of these as instrumental values or utilitanda. Apparently he does not follow Dewey, as I do, in maintaining the relativity of means and ends. There are many reasons why it is necessary to place truth and reality on a par with the good and the beautiful as value categories. For one thing, it is obvious that we compare and evaluate arguments as better or worse; that is, as sound or less sound. And similarly we compare and evaluate statements as better or worse, the truer being the better and the less true or adequate being the worse. The same is the case with the objective status of things as ultimately real or mere appearance. In the second place, while the true, the valid, and the real are undoubtedly useful for extraneous purposes, it is quite possible to set up the pursuit of truth, consistency, or ultimate reality as ends in themselves. Furthermore, I agree with Ayres that positive values form a concord mutually supporting and enhancing each other and the total life of the community. Surely among these values, science (concerned with truth), logic (concerned with validity and consistency), and metaphysics (concerned with reality) are an integral part.

I

AIKEN's "Reflections on Dewey's Questions about Value" are much too extensive and closely reasoned to be covered in any commentary as brief as this needs to be. An adequate discussion of them would require an at least equal space. My remarks are therefore confined to two of his central points—points which challenge basically my own thinking about value, or at least my way of talking about value. They are:

1. The view that will and cognition interpenetrate in such a way that each is a factor in or a constitutive component of the other, with the result that no sharp distinction can be drawn between conation and cognition.

2. The view that desire or interest determines only "trial" value or "ostensible" value, while satisfaction or enjoyment determines "real" value.

I am not sure that Aiken will accept my phrasing of point 1 as a correct statement of his view, but it seems to me to express what, in spite of a number of qualifications, he in the main argues. His chief interest in this matter is to show that "value-judgments are verifiable," that they are "factual" and not mere expressions of decision—or, finally, to show that value-judgments are propositions. "The *only* question is whether so-called value-judgments are propositions at all."

Aiken in his discussions bearing on this question makes use of three terms, the relationships of which constitute the problem. They are (a) valuing, (b) evaluation or appraisal, and (c) judgment of fact. The problem is taken up in the form of Dewey's question: What is the relation between "valuing" and "evaluating"?

In his first sections Aiken defines or describes "valuing"—though with a certain tentativeness, as an act or an attitude which institutes value. The distinction, he says, between "a *judgment* of value and an *act* of direct valuing . . . is a crucial one, and it seems desirable . . .

to restrict 'value' to the act of desiring or being satisfied . . . and 'evaluation' and 'appraisal' to judgments about values." He says further, "A value, as such, is . . . a-rational, in the sense that it *may* exist apart from evaluation and deliberation." Again, he observes that value, though perhaps not unaffected by appraisal, has "meaning apart from or prior to the act of appraisal." It has meaning relative to want, need, choice, and interest.

The meaning which I understand Aiken initially to assign to "judgment of value," that is, to "appraisal" or "evaluation," is clearly expressed in the following statement:

I suggest that appraisals and evaluation are essentially estimates and predictions, which are merely probable, concerning certain types of human behavior which we call "values" or "valuings." Whether they turn out to be valid or not depends, not on anything which the appraisal or evaluation can fix or determine in advance, but rather, upon the preferences and interests which are the springs of conduct.

Interests themselves, he says elsewhere to the same point, "give force" to appraisals.

With these definitions or meanings I am in agreement, but I am not sure that Aiken himself adheres to them in his subsequent discussions. Pursuing the question What is the relation between 'valuing' and 'evaluation'? in the larger frame-work of "fact and value" and "conation and cognition," he observes that an "element of decision . . . goes into any judgment of fact that passes beyond what is given in experience" and that "evident cognitive factors . . . are present in most if not all attitudes and decisions." If it were merely meant, as Aiken sometimes does seem to mean, that most *experiences* are descriptively complex in containing both cognitions and conations in significant relation, as when I want something I also usually know in some measure what it is I want, then I would still be in agreement. Knowing is ordinarily a condition of wanting, or, in Aiken's term, cognition "mediates" valuing. Finally, however, although he maintains that "valuing" and "judgment of fact" are separate "in the *logical* sense," he seems to hold that cognitions *are* also conations, and that conations *are* also cognitions.

Aiken may not accept this interpretation because his discussion proceeds, not in terms of the *logically* distinguishable "attitudes of approval" and cognitions, but in terms of the "expressions" and "statements" of a total experience, such as "This object is good," in which both attitude and cognition are clearly "involved." But it seems to me that the radical problem is not whether both are involved, but rather what each *is*. On this question, though there is no direct statement such as I have given, Aiken seems finally to stand on the position indicated, namely, that each is in some measure the other. In an act of valuing, he holds, we must "acknowledge the presence of a cognitive factor" which is "for the most part, a judgment to the effect that the object in question is harmful or dangerous or friendly or useful." Now, if it were meant that a typical value *expression,* "This object is good," reports both the act (which is not itself a judgment) and knowledge of an object toward which the act is directed, then there should be no dispute. But this seems not to be the meaning. Rather it is that we do or can cognize the values of an object (its harmfulness, friendliness, and so on) prior to or even without (in the logically distinct sense) actually *valuing* them. This does not agree with a previous statement that "values are logically prior to appraisal."

The problem may be reduced to the question: Are values facts, or are judgments about values judgments of fact? The answer can be, "Yes—depending on the further sense to be clarified." I agree that judgments about value are judgments of fact, the fact in question being *valuing,* or, if it be preferred, the relational properties of things of the nature of being harmful, friendly, and so on—"harmful, friendly, and so on" meaning in turn "being felt as such." In brief, judgments about values are judgments about felt fact or known-and-felt facts. But the judgment about value is not about itself, it is not a part of the fact which it reports.

The crux of Aiken's position is best seen in his approach to the problem from the cognitive side, in which he urges "the normative factor, the element of decision," involved in "judgments of fact." By judgment of fact is meant "the verifiable propositions of science." That is, judgments of fact are theories, hypotheses, laws, and so forth—the generalizations of science. Belief in these judgments, it is said, is always conditioned by an initial act of choice—an attitude or valuing. "The act of postulation . . . is itself the *free act* or decision of the scientist. No one can force me by logic to believe in a world beyond what is immediately given. . . ." Thus "an element of choice or decision goes into the constitution of any fact which is more than a judgment of immediate experience."

The ultimate insight into the postulatory nature of rationality may be granted. It is philosophically familiar. It is found in James's pragmatism—the passional element in belief, or the will to believe; in Bergson's intuitionism—"the normal work of the intellect is far from being disinterested"; in Santayana's skepticism—"science is superstition firmly believed in"; and in pure mysticism—in which "truth" is non-logical. But this insight which uncovers the limits of rationality has its own limits. If "decision" or faith, whether pragmatic, spiritual, animal, or logical, is to condition experience, it must do so forwardly and not retroactively—that is, if it is to remain the decision or faith which it is. If we are freely committed to the enterprise of experience in the way of thinking logically, by means of evidence and inference leading to conclusion, we cannot produce at will a special or unique skepticism, mysticism, or voluntarism for each new case or item of experience. We may in some last-ditch sense will our world, but we do not then separately will each fact in it. An element of decision may ultimately condition rational thinking, but rational thinking does not *go on* in terms of it. The element of decision is conditional, not operational in experience of fact. But in matters of value the reverse is true, and it is for this reason that a "sharp distinction between decision and fact" can be drawn. In valuing, the will is the constitutive act recurrently and not merely the ultimate condition.

To maintain the distinction between value and fact makes no straining necessary in the further explanations of what we actually do and say in our cognitive and valuative experiences. For example, if we say pragmatically that reality is such that we can do a number of different things with it, and that what we specifically know of it is what we do do with it (the element of decision), we are also saying in effect that we know (purely cognitively) that it is that kind of reality which might support some other knowing-doing. Or if we have as absolute options two different theories about a given phenomenon (say light), we do not make a choice at all, but recognize that our real knowledge in this matter consists in knowing that the phenomenon in question, as so far experienced, can be explained in either way—or that our knowledge is incomplete.

Further, to maintain the distinction between fact and value does not conflict with the fact that "as F. S. C. Northrop has pointed out: 'One cannot deduce the theories of science from the facts . . . One deduces the facts from the theory.'" If it be granted that a theory is decided upon or chosen because it is "satisfactory," it can still be urged that a theory is satisfactory, not in the sense of being variously congenial or as we would altogether wish, but only in the sense that it works in consistently with our other knowledge, or, briefly, that it squares with the facts. That is to say, we demand finally that a theory chosen be satisfactory *to the facts,* that the theory in question imply the facts which we know independently of that theory.

Satisfaction of fact (truth) and satisfaction of person (value) are independent variables. Facts which square with a theory and are therefore accepted may be affectively indifferent, unfriendly, or even deeply inimical to our very continued existence—as, for example, the "exploding universe," if a fact, finally may be. But we do not revise our cognitions, or call them bad choices on such considerations. If we unambiguously chose or decided upon a theory as we consciously choose as good what is agreeable to us or what unconsciously accords with "the wisdom of the body" in preserving itself, we would in all probability not have chosen the theories which modern science on the whole offers us. The disparity between stubborn necessity and ultimate human want is a constant burden in modern thought, philosophic as well as poetic and fictional. It is found in Kant's *Critiques* and Russell's "A Free Man's Worship" as well as in Thomson's "City of Dreadful Night" and Mark Twain's *Mysterious Stranger.*

It may be granted then that every theory reflects an ultimate choice, but not that every theory is a choice. Every particular theory is judged by facts not of its choice. And no theory is a good one that does not allow a clear distinction between fact and value *on that theory,* or on its own conditions. It is not a good theory which does not allow that at any moment of experience what we further want is not necessarily commensurate with what we are further obliged to accept as true.

My second point of comment, which I make very brief, is on the view that only satisfaction or enjoyment, and not desire determines "real" value. Aiken writes: "An object of desire is . . . properly speaking, a 'trial value,' and it should retain this status until its realization brings the satisfaction which transforms it into an actual good."

The suggested usage does have certain advantages; for example, it does nicely mark the fact that it frequently "takes time and effort to know what we want." In another respect, however, it is seriously inadequate. In calling objects of desire merely "ostensible" or "trial" values and allowing only satisfactions to be *real* values, one disallows the familiar possibility that some real values are never attained or realized, that an ideal, for example, may be forever an ideal.

In confining real value to satisfaction, Aiken confines it to actuality or to the existent. But he himself says that "there is no reason why, in order that valuation propositions, as propositions, should be regarded as factual, that they must be 'about' something already in existence." This statement is sufficient to validate "objects of desire" as real values.

It may be added, however, that a further consequence of denying real value to objects of desire is to deny value meanings to such well-established value terms as "disappointment," "defeat," "failure," and "frustration," and also "responsibility," "blame," and so forth. That is to say in general, that to experience negative satisfaction, or dissatisfaction, is also to experience the "contrary to fact conditional," which would have been the value realized if the disappointment or defeat had not occurred. And this value not realized is still the real positive value. Without it the negative would have no meaning. Similarly, a person who blames another does so with a positive and real though unrealized value in view. He blames because some satisfaction expected, hoped for, or demanded, has not been given; the person blamed has not done what he *should* have done, what was *desired* of him. Dissatisfaction is thus desire unsatisfied, and the correlative positive value is defined in such cases purely in terms of the desire.

II

I think I am in basic agreement with Mitchell on what might be called theory of value theory, but I am in disagreement with him at some fundamental points on the actual theory of value which he offers. I shall not take much space to rehearse my agreements in detail. Basically, they center upon the position that inquiry into value which results in a general theory is empirical, that in order to frame an adequate hypothesis about value we have to *investigate* value, not prescribe it, and that in order to do so with a reasonable expectation of success, we need not only to employ a rigorous and many-sided care in describing values, but also an appropriate method or logic in the analysis of value. My agreement with Mitchell's study is not, however, charily limited to acceptance of this general approach. His descriptions and analyses of what goes on in the field of value activity and what must be taken account of in value theory are convincing and instructive.

My disagreements are with the following points:

1) That the sufficiently or exclusively appropriate logic for analysis of value is the relational, non-Aristotelian logic;
2) That "better-than" is an adequate primitive value term;
3) As corollary to (2), that value is neither substantive, nor adjectival, but "relational," (that is, that it is a relation); [1]
4) That the real and the true are, as such, values;
5) That an affective theory, or a motor theory, or by presumption, a motor-affective theory, cannot be a general theory of value.

These points are all interrelated, and my statements of disagreement with them will, therefore, overlap, but I shall attempt to deal with them severally and in the order listed.

Point 1 in this set of objections should perhaps rightly come last in order of consideration, for if we adhere to the basic and agreed principle of empirical procedure, we cannot tell at the outset which specific method or which particular logic will best enable us to deal with our object. The only empirical method of deciding on *method* is to try one method out in competition with others, and then judge by the results. Accordingly, the question here has specifically to wait upon questions 2 and 3, whether the primitive value term is "better than" (relation), or whether it is "good" (substance or quality). To decide at the beginning that the correct logic for value statement is either the subject-predicate or the relational logic (and not both) would be to force the answer to the other questions. My answer will, therefore, have to be found in what follows.

Points 2 and 3. Mitchell, following Brogan, holds that "better than" is the primitive term in the logic of value. And this means that all value statements can be reduced to and find their accurate expression in a "better than" form, or in an immediate cognate, such as "is equal to"

---

[1] Mitchell does not say that value is relation. In fact he makes several statements and pursues lines of thought which import that values are *things* in relation. With this I am in agreement, and accordingly, hold to a relational value theory. However, I make the interpretation stated in point (3) in view of his direct denial that the substantive-attribute way of speaking about value has any relevance. If this is maintained consistently then I do not understand how it could also be held that value is anything other than relation. What I criticize is this manner of speaking.

or "is worse than." In brief, he holds that value *is* a relation. Against that view, I should maintain that value occurs *in* relation. My answer to the question (taking Dewey's and Mitchell's together) whether value is substantive, adjectival, or relational, is that it is all three. We may take a substantive view of value, an adjectival view of value, or a relational view of value. We may ask the same kind of question of "cause," as Mitchell suggests, but contrary to his intent, get the same kind of answer. We may say with complete adequacy in each case that (a) substantively, an object "X" is a cause; (b) adjectivally, "X" is a causal object, and (c) relationally, that object "X" stands in a causal relation to object "Y." Similarly, we can say substantively in a class-membership proposition that a given value-object is a good; adjectively, in a subject-predicate proposition that it is good; and relationally, in a relational proposition that it is better than another value-object.

This threefold way of making statements about values is the empirically complete way, and any way short of it is inadequate to the data —or, worse, distorts them. If we talk of value as only substantive we land in the absolutistic way of that medievalism which Mitchell rightly rejects. But if we talk of it as only relational we fall into the opposite error of asserting relations without relata. If something is to be better than something else, it must be better in respect to some at least contextually determined property or substance. Quantification without quality certainly applies to nothing that we experience. And to be better than, is in the first place to be a substance or to possess a quality which is quite specifically and simply *good,* that is, in context. But this does not commit one to a metaphysically absolute good. The good which is found substantially and qualitatively in a given place or a given time may be very different in substance and quality from goods in other places and times. They will still be defined as Mitchell rightly says "in terms of teleological organisms"; they will still be descriptively pluralistic, and as various as the factual things in the world, in which they will still be found.

Among the advantages which Mitchell claims for the better-than theory of value is that it takes account of the pluralistic and serial nature of values, which two-value systems allegedly do not do. Two-value systems oppose good and bad, true and false, valid and invalid, and so on. Two values "hardly constitute a series." He writes further, "it would be in line with modern science and logic to abandon these opposites, except as ideal limits." But doesn't this qualifying phrase, "except as ideal limits," give away the contention? If there is an ideal limit,[2] is it not that to which reference is finally made in making actual comparisons of better and worse? Thus, for example, in the scale of truth or adequacy as applied to an hypothesis, must we merely and always compare one actual hypothesis with another? Can we not rather say that an ideal, that is, a completely good and not simply better hypothesis is one which accounts for all the facts, and that an ideally bad hypothesis is one which accounts for none of the facts?

The whole section V,3, on the ideal, with which I fully agree, seems to me to argue away from the better-than view. "The ideal . . . ," we read there, "may serve as a standard of comparison for existing factual complexes or for proposed objectives." It can "serve as a norm for any partial fulfillment." The whole section III, "Below Valuing," bears a similar import away from the better-than interpretation. Moreover, the language there used to denote the biological and physiological selectivity which is the basis of conscious valuing is strikingly adjectival, and even substantive. The following are examples: ". . . valuing has its basis in the suitable and the fitting." "The sensory system is specialized to select from the environment those features that are of advantage or disadvantage to the organism." "To crave exactly the right food . . . to prefer the most advantageous temperature and intensity of light . . . these and many other cases of want, preference, and satisfaction are usually so precisely adapted to the welfare of the animal organism that the creature appears to be endowed with powers of scientific valuation."

One may ask, if the unconscious "selections" of the organism can be properly described as directed upon objects which are such adjectival and substantive goods as "the suitable and the fitting," "exactly the right food," and "the most advantageous temperature," why cannot conscious valuings, which are continuous with the unconscious, be expressed or reported adequately in the same language and logical forms?

Points 4 and 5. A further advantage claimed for the better-than view is that it is a general theory, one which can accommodate all types of acceptance and rejection. Certain other theories, namely affective and

---

[2] Cf. a preceding statement, in Section V, 3 of Mitchell's paper (pp. 198–201, above): "The ideal is imaginary but need not be fanciful."

motor theories, fail on this test of generality. Specifically, it succeeds and they fail in dealing with questions of truth, validity, and reality —all value questions.

My disagreement here is on both points: (a) The alleged inadequacy of motor-affective theories, and (b) the value status claimed for truth, validity, and reality. My discussion of point (b) will support my stand on point (a), which I first state without argument: I do not agree that "true, valid, and real are value terms" and hence do not accept the only grounds on which it may be held "that affective [and motor] theories of value are not general theories."

On point (b) I limit my comments to the status of the real in respect to value. I think the question of the real is crucial to the questions of the true and the valid.

Mitchell writes, "Wherever there is a question of acceptance or rejection there is a question of value." I should say instead that wherever there is a question of value, there is a question of acceptance or rejection. That is to say, to value something is to accept it *as desirable,* not merely to accept it as real. Bare acceptance is *too* general to determine or define value; it means mere recognition of the factual status of something. It consequently permits no distinction in the quality of value as positive or negative, that is, as good or bad, as value or disvalue. As for adequacy, it is twice as inadequate as the two-value systems are charged with being. It is a one-value system. For if the real, as such, is value, then everything is value, and in equal degree. But this does not accord with actual valuings and evaluations. To say that something is real, is not to say that it is good; neither is it to say that it is bad. Also, to say that something is real is not to say that it is better that it exist than not. Many evils are real and are accepted as real, but it is better that they not exist. Many inconsequential things are real, and it makes no difference whether they exist or not. Again, the real is not only "the reliable, the dependable, and so forth"; it is sometimes the horrible, the ugly, the frightful, and the like. It is even sometimes, both in nature and in human character, in earthquake, drought, and hurricane, and in deceit, irresponsibility, and lawlessness, the unreliable and the undependable. They are real but unwelcome when they occur, and their mere reality or factuality does not mark their value. The specific affective attitude in which they are received does.

In sum, reality has to be qualified in a certain manner of acceptance or rejection before it is valuable. Affective and motor theories recognize this necessary qualification. They are in principle adequate as general theories of value. The theory of bare acceptance is not.

REJOINDER BY AIKEN

Jessup suggests that while I do acknowledge a logical distinction between "cognition" and "volition," I regard the two as mutually involving one another. This is true. My point is, in part, that, although we may distinguish the cognitive factor and the motor-affective factor in judgment and volition, both factors are present in both activities. But I maintain, also, that cognition, in so far as it claims *validity*—in so far, that is, as it is represented as "correct," "veridical," "warranted"—clearly presupposes criteria which are normative. Principles of "meaning" and "truth" are not themselves factual. They lay down the very conditions of factuality. In this sense, empiricism itself is not an empirical doctrine, but, rather, a determination to proceed empirically in the analysis of concepts and in the validation of statements. Given a sufficiently unambiguous set of epistemological or logical norms we can proceed to the determination of the meaningfulness or truth of any statement; but the determination of meaningfulness or truth presupposes norms with respect to which alone it can be made.

Jessup maintains that such standards are "conditional" but not "operational." This is perhaps a useful distinction if not pressed too far and if taken as a matter of degree rather than one of kind. What it signifies, to my mind, is that "conditional" norms are continuously operative throughout the activities which they govern. But as in the case of government by consent, acceptance of the norms of knowledge must be implicitly reaffirmed at every step. Indeed, like Rousseau's "general will," the free choice of standards of meaning and validity is inalienable. Like all standards, these remain binding only so long as they are accepted. Hence, while I agree with the letter of Jessup's distinction, I do not think it blunts the point of my analysis.

Jessup says that a theory is "chosen" when it is "satisfactory to the facts," and he argues that "satisfaction of fact (truth)" and "satisfaction of persons (value)" are independent variables. Now, of course, provided that certain methodological or epistemological norms are accepted, the question whether any particular statement "satisfies" these conditions is independent of the question whether such a statement is also "satisfactory to persons." But this has no bearing upon my argument. The only relevant question, it seems to me, is whether methodological or semantical principles are themselves normative rather than factual. If the former is true, as I maintain, then I don't care whether Jessup's agreement with me is a "last ditch" agreement or not. I have not said that *some* distinction between "value" and "fact" cannot or should not be made. My contention is merely that values may, for all of this, be regarded as facts, and that value-statements may be factual. In saying this I do not at all imply their identity, any more than I imply the identity of "murder" and "punishment" when I say that all murderers should be punished.

As for Jessup's second criticism, I confess that he seems to me to beg precisely the points at issue: (a) If "real values" may be "real" and yet never realized, then it follows analytically that my distinction is badly formulated. But Jessup has not shown this. In any case, I care very little for the terminology in which my distinction between "real" and "trial" values has been expressed. My interest is in the distinction itself. I don't deny that "trial values" are "really" values—in some sense. What I assert is that their function is instrumental to the business of satisfying wants. I deny intrinsic value to ideals merely as such. My point is simply that an ideal which never conduces to satisfaction is without real value. I see no reason whatever for granting intrinsic or real value to every ideal, however silly, however futile, however vicious. It seems to me, in fact, self-evident that an ideal is worth to be realized only if it would conduce to human well-being; but if it *is* worth in this respect, it is worth as an instrument or end-in-view alone. (b) I cannot see that the satisfaction theory "confines" value to "actuality" in any way that does not hold, by analogy, for any naturalistic theory. The interest theory, for example, limits "value" to actual interests. The self-realization theory limits value to actual states of self-realization. My theory does not imply that objects may not be potentially valuable, even though no one is now deriving satisfaction from them. Nor does it imply that nonexistent "objects"—Hamlet, for example—may not possess "real value" if actual satisfaction is taken in contemplating them. I cannot, for the life of me, see that the satisfaction theory is involved in any peculiar difficulty on this score—no more so, certainly, than the interest theory. Moreover, when Jessup says that my statement that "there is no reason

why, in order that valuation propositions, as propositions, should be regarded as factual they must be 'about' something already in existence"
is "sufficient to validate 'objects of desire' as real values," he is simply
guilty of a non sequitur.

REJOINDER BY MITCHELL

Jessup's comments on my paper include suggested restatements, some
of which I could accept, misunderstandings which I can, I hope, readily
clear up, and one or two real issues on which we shall perhaps have
to agree to disagree. On the whole, I think we are not fundamentally
far apart.

His first criticism is that I have arbitrarily selected an instrument in
the logic of relations and formed the comparative theory of value to
fit the instrument instead of adopting the proper procedure which is
to select instruments to fit the empirical data. I reply that the whole
history of science exemplifies the bearing of new instruments on new
and fruitful theories. Given a new instrument one naturally tests its
application in various fields. There is no point in using a stone axe
to fell trees if a power saw is at your disposal. Such is the history of the
application, by Brogan, of the logic of relations to the data of value.
I adopted it because it works. Any value-judgment that can be handled
by the subject-predicate logic can be handled better by the relational
logic; and, where judgments are obviously comparative, as "Wisdom
is better than rubies," the S-P logic is either incompetent or exces-
sively cumbersome.

The suggestion that the comparative theory of value was devised
to fit the relational logic may or may not be true; but, in any case, the
point is irrelevant. The only question is, Is the theory adequate? Jessup
claims that it is inadequate because it omits the substantive and adjectival aspects of value. He says "We can take a substantive view of
value, or an adjectival view of value, or a relational view." If I understand what Jessup means, we are talking about entirely different things.
By a substantive theory of value I understand a theory that maintains
that the good, the beautiful, and so forth, are substances; that is, they
are Platonic forms or essences, or absolutes. By an adjectival theory
I understand the theory that values are attributes inhering *in* substances.
By a relational theory I mean the theory that value (or valuableness)
is a relation *between* objects. So interpreted, it would be absurdly

inconsistent to maintain that the good is a substance (always a subject) that it is an attribute (always a predicate) and is relational (always implying two terms in relation).

Jessup doesn't mean to say anything so absurd. He means that value terms ("values," as I shall use this word) are sometimes nouns, denoting things, sometimes adjectives, denoting attributes, sometimes relations. With this assertion I agree. But the question is wherein lies the valuableness—is it an ultimate reality (substance) in its own right (in itself and not in another), is it *in* something else as an attribute, or between two terms as a relation. My theory is that where the relation of betterness exists, valuableness exists; and where there is value, there exists the relation of betterness: valuableness *is* the relation of betterness.

A certain misunderstanding of the comparative or melioristic theory runs through all Jessup's criticism. He confuses the statement "Value is relational" with the statement that "Values are relations," which I am careful not to make. In the proposition "*a* is better than *b*," value is designated by the relational phrase. The "values" are the relata *a* and *b;* they may be things, classes, universals, qualities, relations, or anything else that may be discriminated and compared in the relation of better or worse.

It is true that when suitable adjectives can be found, many value-judgments can be expressed in S-P form, as, health is good; money is useful; ale is refreshing. But in the first of these examples there is the implicit comparison between health and the lack of it. The second and third examples are not value-judgments without the unstated additions "the useful is better than the useless" and "the refreshing is better than what isn't refreshing."

These explanations should remove most of Jessup's objections. Thus, he asserts that propositions involving betterness are incomplete without specifying the respect in which one object is better than the other. This is to say that betterness involves some standard value as a basis of comparison. Let us examine a case where the standard is indicated; for example: "Dark bread is better than white bread with respect to nourishment." But here there is the implicit addition "nourishment is better than its deficiency." In general, wherever there is a "standard value" that, too, is relational.

The same considerations apply to an ideal when used as a standard in valuation. The ideal embodies a combination of values, each of which, and the organic whole, is relational. Ultimately, as I have explained, we come to direct comparisons in experience without reference to any standard value or ideal.

With regard to my alleged swing to an adjectival or substantive view in the later parts of the paper, it is true that I frequently use the S-P form of statement. In expounding the relativity of value, it became convenient to return to the elementary distinctions of good and bad. Having defined "A is good," it is not necessary always to substitute the definition for the proposition defined. To do so would be pedantic and wasteful. I could rewrite all sentences but I see no reason for doing so. Thus when I say "The good is the suitable and the fitting" it seems unnecessary to erase the sentence and write: "Relative to the needs of the organism, certain foods, certain temperatures, certain intensities of light, and so forth, are more suitable and thus better than others." My point was that the organism selects the more suitable with uncanny precision.

Jessup rejects my suggestion that truth and reality are value terms and that the relational theory of value might be generalized to include the fields of logic, epistemology, and metaphysics. He spotted my difficulty in regard to truth and falsity. If true and false are ideal limits, here would be a special case of a series generated by the relation of "better than"—a case with an upper and lower limit. We could deal with such a series by defining the statement "A is true" in some such way as this: "There exists no statement B, such that B is better than A relative to the situation." If, however, truth is a matter of degree with no ideal limit, the melioristic theory would apply without special treatment.

Jessup's comment with respect to reality as a value term strikes me as exceptionally inappropriate. It is rather obvious that historically "the real" has had a value connotation. For example one can hardly fail to notice in Plato that Being is better than non-Being and that in Plotinus and Thomas Aquinas The One is separated by infinite degrees of betterness from outer chaos. Generally speaking, reality has an honorific status compared to appearance. I use the word real in contrast to the illusory, the real being obviously the better with respect to dependability, reliability, and firmness of support.

Jessup objects that the real is not only the reliable and dependable;

it is sometimes "the horrible, the ugly, the frightening." The same may be said of the true, and yet truth is on the whole better than error. Why should we, as philosophers, search for the real as opposed to the illusory, if the real is not better on the whole than the unreal. Even when we praise the ideal in contrast with the real, we add that the ideal would be better *if it were realized.* When the real is frightening and ugly, it is better to face it and base our actions on it than to escape into an insane world of hallucinations. If this were not so we would have no need of psychiatrists.

To say that truth and reality are value terms is not to say that they are the sum total of all values. There are other value categories such as beauty, justice, and moral goodness. Each field has its own value categories but the common term is the relation "better than."

As a result of criticisms so far made, I see no reason to change my two fundamental theses, (1) that wherever the relation of better or worse is involved we have a case of value; and obversely where there is no question of better or worse no value whatever is involved, and (2) value is relative to the wants, interests, and satisfactions of organisms.

I

AIKEN'S PAPER makes many acute analyses that help clarify fundamental problems in value theory. His remarks on the use and
limitations of a strict behavioristic method are to the point. His analysis
of the relation between the meanings of "valuing," "appraising," and
"evaluating" is discerning. Dewey's use of the term "appraisal" tends
to introduce into the direct experience of value an element of conscious
estimate of the measure of the value, and this is true whether or not
Dewey intends it. Aiken has well shown that this is a confusion.

On the other hand, Aiken sometimes confuses me, but I think that
this is due not to his analysis but to a use of terms. For example, in
agreeing that value may be called a property, he calls it a property of
persons; [1] and again,[2] he says that it is desirable to restrict the meaning of the word "value" to the *act* of desiring or being satisfied. I shall
return to this question later.

He says that he suspects the distinction between "thing" and "property" to be not clear, and largely verbal.[3] I agree. It is the same point
that I attempt to make by insisting (in my Rejoinder to Mitchell's
Criticism of my paper) that when I call value "adjectival" I am not
implying the substance-attribute metaphysics. The distinction is more
than verbal, however, if "verbal" is taken to imply "arbitrary." It is
an analytical distinction that serves well in the ordering of our experience, and it can be made quite clear in a given context, but it is not
assumed to be a reflection of "the nature of things."

I am not sure that I follow Aiken in his analogical reasoning on
pages 27 and 28, but to pick it to pieces would be petty, for he admits
that its details are doubtful. This much is evident, however; persons who
argue that judgments of value are not factual either assume an inde-
fensibly narrow conception of fact—too narrow for the purposes either
of science or of common sense, as Aiken declares—or they display

---

[1] P. 22, above.   [2] *Ibid.*   [3] *Ibid.*

a naive lack of comprehension of how difficult an epistemologically adequate definition of fact is.

In illustrating that we do not, in ordinary discourse, identify value with volition,[4] he does not choose his examples well. It cannot be said that they have no connection with choice or desire. It is true, however, that they have no necessary connection with ends-in-view or deliberative decisions, and I suspect that Aiken, in this place, tends to think of volition a little too much in the latter terms. Again, however, this point is not worth elaborating, for if his examples do not aid, neither do they hinder his argument.

What Aiken is calling attention to in his "contrary to fact conditional"[5] is, I take it, that value must be defined in terms that apply to potential values. The potential value may be either of an actual object or of a potential object, as Pepper points out. Aiken uses different descriptive categories than does either Pepper or do I in my paper, but which are used is of little importance so long as the covert assumptions that Aiken calls to attention on pages 15 and 16 of his paper are not smuggled in by way of the categories. I have no adverse criticism of Aiken's categories on this score. The point is that potentialities are facts, as Aiken points out in regard to contrary to fact conditionals. It is no paradox that the conditional expresses a fact even if it is "contrary to fact." The conditional expresses a relation between an antecedent and a conclusion. It does not assert the antecedent. The relation expressed may be a fact even when the antecedent does not express a fact.

The most important questions raised by Aiken are those concerning the place of satisfaction in the analysis and understanding of the value experience, and the distinctions such as that between trial or ostensible values and real values which grow out of his treatment of satisfaction.

Aiken's paper has convinced me that reference to satisfaction should occupy a more important place in value theory than it does in the usual statements of the interest theory or of any conative theory. (I suppose that Ayres will deplore this confession as marking my further defection in the direction of the "sensibility school.") Although Parker and Rice emphasize satisfaction, I cannot agree with their *identification* of value with satisfaction for the reasons set forth in my paper. In

[4] P. 36.   [5] Pp. 17 and 26.

addition, all the objections that can be made to the definition of value in terms that are wholly subjective can be brought against their theories.

I cannot agree with Aiken's statement of the details of his theory, partly because of the reasons given in my criticism of Parker and Rice, and partly because his statement gives rise to many confusing applications of terms such as those to which I called attention in the second paragraph of the present Criticism. There are others in addition to the ones cited there. For example, on page 39 Aiken says that an *object* of desire is a value, but on page 40 he says that *satisfaction* is a value. (The fact that the first is a trial value and the second a real value does not lessen the difficulty.)

The distinction between trial values and real values cannot be generalized to cover the whole range of value experience, and in addition it seems to me to be at least somewhat incompatible with findings in the earlier part of his paper. Perhaps I make these statements only because I have misunderstood the distinction, and it is possible that my misunderstanding is due only to his use (somewhat careless at times) of his terms. Nevertheless, the fact that I have these misunderstandings indicates that Aiken's statement of his theory can be improved. The improved version might convince me.

The distinction between trial and real values is well suited to moral, political, and economic values, but not to aesthetic values. I cannot see how an aesthetic value could be a trial value in Aiken's sense. If an aesthetic object does not yield satisfaction, it is not an aesthetic object (that is, not an *actual* one—it may be a potentially aesthetic object in the sense that it may be judged that to other persons or at different times or under different circumstances it might give rise to satisfaction). The concept of trial value is suited to instrumental but not to intrinsic value. Perhaps Aiken would agree (see pages 36–37) but he does not say that the two distinctions coincide.

Furthermore, the distinction between trial and real value is judgmental and hence evaluative. The trial value is one that promises to become a real one. If the satisfaction ensues, the promise is borne out. Therefore, the trial value arises in a situation in which one judges that the satisfaction will ensue. The trial value, then, cannot, in the light of Aiken's clear analysis of the difference between valuing and evaluating, be a case wherein there is a genuine immediate apprehension of value. A trial value refers to the potentiality of satisfaction. Potentialities cannot be experienced, they can be only judged. The *experience* of a trial value that remains ostensible and yet genuinely a value while it is being experienced sounds strange. The trial or ostensible value is a value that a person expects a given object to have, and it remains ostensible only so long as the expectation remains an expectation. If it is mistaken, then there is no value there to be experienced. If it is realized, then the only value there is a real value. Perhaps I am pushing this point too far, but it indicates why I think there is something the matter with the detailed working out of Aiken's theory.

I still agree with Aiken, however, that the element of satisfaction is an essential component of the nature of value. In the kind of a situation wherein arises what he calls conative value, Pepper has shown that a drive always refers ultimately to its satisfaction or "quiescent pattern"; and he defines what he calls affective value in terms of pleasure or satisfaction.[6]

The question is: Where in the categorial scheme for value theory does the necessary reference to satisfaction fit in best? I have suggested that the reference to satisfaction can be adequately handled by using it as the evaluating factor,[7] and this fits in well with the fact that the difference between trial and real value depends on judgment. Instead of Aiken's terms "trial value" and "real value," I would use "trial value" and "tested value." The tested value is one where the evaluative judgment is seen to be borne out. "Real value" connotes that only this kind is genuine, but I hold that one's apprehension of an object to which he imputes satisfactoriness is a genuine value experience even though it might turn out not to pass the test according to which the object will continue to be valued in comparison with other things or in a larger context.

The foregoing consideration gives the reason why I cannot agree unqualifiedly with Aiken when he says "Not just any '*prima-facie value*' is therefore worth realizing."[8] It *is* worth realizing until it is considered in the wider context of all potential values realizable in a given situation, but such consideration requires judgment, comparison, and evaluation. As I have pointed out, we often continue to value an object that yields a lesser satisfaction by refusing to turn our attention to the wider context or to the considerations of judgment that show something else to bear the promise of yielding greater satis-

6 See pp. 248 and 256–259.   7 See pp. 158.   8 See p. 40.

faction.[9] Aiken's conception of trial value (which may or may not be worth realizing according to his statement) sounds as if the *experience* of value in this case is itself only a tentative experience. A direct experience that is only tentative does not make sense. *Judgments* can be tentative. This is another consideration that makes it appear that the distinction between trial and real (or as I would rather call them, tested) values refers to judgments and hence evaluations. As the reference to satisfaction determines the difference between the two classifications of value, it appears again that satisfaction best fits into the theory as the evaluating factor.

Whenever we value anything we impute to it the quality of being possibly satisfactory. Although the word is somewhat awkward, let me call this imputed quality "satisfactoriness." I continue to call it an imputed quality although I agree with Mr. Mitchell that the term "putative," which I used in my paper, ought to be given up.[10] I do so because the language used must emphasize that it is a relational quality —one that the object does not have independent of its relation to an active and sentient organism.

Satisfactoriness names a potentiality. If one thinks that anything has this quality (that is, if he imputes this quality to anything, whether it be an actual or a potential object), that thing has value for him. Nevertheless, the only final test of a potentiality is an actuality. Unless there were actual satisfactions there could be no imputed satisfactoriness. The basis for one's imputation of satisfactoriness in the case where satisfaction is not experienced is a judgment, and as such may be in error. Thus there may always be error in the judgment of value. This takes care of Aiken's trial or ostensible values. In case the satisfaction is experienced, however, the imputation of satisfactoriness cannot be in error. This takes care both of the immediate apprehension of intrinsic values (such as aesthetic values) and Aiken's real (or as I would rather say, tested) values.

Some degree of satisfaction is always present in any actual experience (apprehension) of value. To say this, however, is not to identify the value with the satisfaction. To make such an identification does not take care of potential values. Satisfactions are feelings, and as such are actual. If value is not explained in terms that include potential

[9] See my paper, p. 160.
[10] See Mitchell's Criticisms, p. 402, and my Rejoinder, p. 409.

values, then it follows either that there is no explanation of error in value-judgment or else that there are no genuine value-judgments. Aiken sufficiently refutes [11] those who would maintain the latter position.

Value may be identified with the imputed or relational quality of satisfactoriness, however, and none of the above objections may be brought. Whether or not anything has the characteristic of satisfactoriness in a given situation can be factually determined, and as a result of the determination its value to me may utterly change. This does not mean that it really did not have value to me before the change. It must have had value, or the value could not have changed. I may even come to the decision that I should not have imputed the satisfactoriness where I did, or that in the consideration of a wider context the satisfactoriness evaporates. Thus, I may conclude that my judgment of value was in error, but even in this case, my apprehension was what it was even though my judgment may have been erroneous. In Aiken's language, the trial value does not turn out to be real; but I maintain that it was quite real; the point is that it does not qualify under the test. The trial value is not a tested value.

II

The methodological assumptions with which Pepper begins his paper are excellent. They do not, of course, constitute a theory of value, nor do they indicate one. There is no theory until a hypothesis emerges, but there must be a thorough analysis of the field before a fruitful hypothesis can be made. Pepper presents a fine piece of preliminary analysis, and indicates, in his observations, many important characteristics of the hypothesis that would emerge from it.

A question might be raised as to whether this is a sufficiently broad example to bring out a completely general hypothesis. It is an example of a deliberately purposive act. May there not be value experiences not connected with deliberately purposive acts? For example, one may, while walking through the woods, come across a completely unexpected but beautiful little waterfall. The experience of beauty often is not connected with consciously purposive acts. The analysis of a purposive act is not sufficient to bring out a general theory of value. Pepper, at the beginning of Section II of his paper, indicates that he

[11] In Section IV of his paper, pp. 31–36, above.

is quite aware of this fact. His readers must keep it in mind, however, or else many irrelevant criticisms may be made.

If one formulates a hypothesis on the basis of an analysis of purposive acts, his hypothesis is apt to be weighted in favor of instrumentalism. I hasten to add that Pepper's is not. Moral value is closely connected with purposive acts, and those writers who take their whole point of departure in value theory from the experience of moral value and who consider it to be the example of value *par excellence* are making a mistake. Aesthetic value is a better example of intrinsic value than is moral value. A theory of value that does not cover the aesthetic experience as well and as completely as it does the moral experience is inadequate.

Pepper's analysis of the place of pleasure or satisfaction in the value experience is illuminating.[12] He calls attention [13] to the fact that a distinction may be made between "the satisfaction of a drive and the introspective quality of pleasure in a consummatory act," and doubts the importance of the distinction. In this I agree with him. One is not always self-consciously aware of his pleasure, and need not be. Whether or not he is, is irrelevant to the question of the place of satisfaction in the value experience.

Satisfaction marks the end of a particular drive, and without reference to possible satisfaction there can be no understanding of the value connected with that drive. In the course of his exposition of this point, Pepper effectively disposes of Dewey's blurring of the distinction between means and end, and thus of the distinction between instrumental and intrinsic value. Satisfactions do exist, and thus there are intrinsic values. In Pepper's language, the drive leads to a quiescent pattern, and there is no quiescent pattern without satisfaction as a concomitant.[14]

Pepper shows in what sense an end can be regarded as an absolute end. He does not mean that the end is "absolutely absolute." It is absolute *for the drive under consideration.* He says that the consummatory act or quiescent pattern is "the absolute end of the appetition motivated by that particular drive." [15] This is the only sense of "absolute" that is necessary to establish intrinsic value. The end may be relative

[12] See p. 248, and Observation 10, pp. 256–259.
[13] In the first part of Observation 10.
[14] See Observation 8, p. 254.   [15] *Ibid.*

to other drives or other ends, but this is a sense very different from the relativeness of what he calls the subordinate goals, and is not to be confused with it.

Another problem of this symposium on which I think Pepper's analysis sheds a good deal of light is the relation between cognition and valuation. It is true without a doubt that the anticipation of either terminal goals or anticipatory goals involves cognition.[16] In fact, the recognition of any goal in a purposive act involves cognition. This fact, however, offers no ground for blurring the distinction between cognition and valuation. I suppose that there is *no* articulate adult experience in which cognition is not involved, and I suppose that the same thing can be said of conation. Concrete adult experience is the manifold out of which these analytic distinctions are made and to which they refer. The purposes of understanding are not furthered by declaring that everything is everything else on the ground that something is always found along with something else in concrete experience, yet it appears to me that this is perilously near what some of the followers of Dewey do when they deny the possibility of sharp distinctions between cognition and valuation, cognition and conation, ends and means, instrumental and intrinsic values, and so on.

The only important adverse criticism that I have to make of Pepper's paper concerns his use of the word "value." I cannot get used to the way he uses it. This is probably my fault rather than his, yet I think that the way he uses the word makes it mean something so different from what it means in ordinary speech that I wonder if the resultant theory applies to ordinary experience as well as it ought. I have a prejudice that ordinary speech serves reasonably well to record our common sense and precritical experience.

An example of the usage to which I object may be found at the beginning of Observation 3 in his paper, where he advises the definition of conative value as "the degree of wanting due to a drive." Earlier (Observation 1) he uses the term conative value in apposition to wanting. In Observation 4 he says that "an impulse without an anticipatory set . . . is a blind conative valuing." In Observation 5 he says that "the conative value ascribed to a potential object *is* the intensity of the drive." [17] In Observation 10,[18] conative values are positive wantings in appetitions and negative wantings in aversions. And so on.

16 P. 243.   17 Italics mine.   18 On p. 258.

What I object to here is the identification between the wanting and the value.

Similarly for affective value: at the beginning of Observation 10 Pepper calls the affective values pleasure and pain. Later [19] he refers to pleasure and pain as two types of affective value (the positive value and the disvalue). In the next paragraph, however, he says that pleasure *"has* a value of its own." [20]

In the light of these uses of the word "value," I wonder what "valuable" means. Usually, when Pepper uses "valuable," he seems to mean what I think I mean. I think that an object that *has* value is valuable. My valuing, I should suppose, is my apprehension of the value of an object, whether the object is either actual, potential, or an object not clearly envisioned. In case there is *no* reference whatever to any kind of an object, I do not see why my wanting should be called a valuing at all. The point is that in the cases Pepper describes, the wanting is a necessary condition of the valuing, but the recognition of this fact need not lead to an *identification* of the two. In the case of conative value, the intensity of the drive *measures* the intensity of the possible satisfaction, and hence the intensity of the value, but it *is* not the intensity of the value.

Pepper uses an expression [21] that can lead, I think, to the resolution of all these difficulties. He suggests that "an actual object of conative value is an object actually *charged* with the drive." This is an excellent metaphor. Soda water is ordinary water charged with carbon dioxide. It has a zip and a tang that the ordinary water does not have. So, the valuable object has a characteristic that it does not have out of relation to the drive with which it is charged. This metaphor, when reduced to literal expression, says that the quality of the valuable object that makes it valuable exists only in the relation in which we find or put it. This is what I attempted to express in my paper by saying that value is a putative quality, but having been persuaded by Mitchell to give up this expression, I am willing to call it simply a relational quality.[22]

May it not turn out that Pepper's conative values are instrumental values and that his affective values are intrinsic? If this is the case, it explains Dewey's objection to the concept of intrinsic value. Pepper finds the satisfaction in the end, and Dewey is skeptical of ends. Dewey

[19] P. 258.   [20] Italics mine.   [21] On p. 251.
[22] See Mitchell's Criticisms, p. 402, and my Rejoinder, p. 409.

tends to insist that all the value is to be found in connection with the conation. As Aiken points out, the usual expression of the interest theory also does this.

If the affective value is intrinsic, or even more closely connected with the intrinsic, then Pepper also suggests that pleasure or satisfaction is the evaluating factor in intrinsic value. He says that "pleasure and pain come to take evaluative control of individual behavior." [23] Perhaps I am unfairly interpreting Pepper's text here, however, for he makes the statement in the context of his treatment of psychological hedonism. Incidentally, I should say that it seems to me that his analysis of the situation which psychological hedonism purports to explain is excellent.

In the above discussion I have endeavored to use the verbal noun "valuing" consistently to name the act of apprehending the relational quality or attribute of an object by virtue of which we call it valuable. "Valuation" names the resultant of the act of valuing. The noun "value" names the relational quality or attribute by virtue of which the act is performed. (It may be said that by "value" I mean "valuableness," but the awkwardness of this term is objectionable and wholly unnecessary.) Where "value" ("to value") is used as a verb, the syntax shows it unequivocally. "Evaluating" names the act of making a judgment (either recording or comparative) of value. Finally, "evaluation" names the resultant of that act.

REJOINDER BY AIKEN

Lee's criticisms seem to me primarily queries concerning my *meaning*. Such criticisms are helpful since they indicate inadequacies in the formulation of my theory. In some instances perhaps they suggest confusions of thought or failures of analysis. I am grateful to him for pointing out a certain slackness in the expression of my position. I can only defend this by saying that in the earlier parts of my paper I was, as I thought I had made clear, not attempting a definition of value, and therefore permitted myself the use of phrases which, I gladly admit, might, if pressed, lead me into ambiguity or even contradiction. I assure Lee, however, that I was aware of this. When, for example, I seemed to vacillate between an interest theory and a satisfaction theory, it was only because at that point in my discussion it did not matter which

[23] P. 258.

376 CRITICISMS AND REJOINDERS

view was upheld. I do say later, however, that intrinsic or real value is to be defined in terms of satisfaction, and that "objects of interest" are merely "trial values." I don't, in short, attempt to settle everything at once. And I aim at finality or precision, in any given section of my paper, only with respect to the topic under consideration there.

I did not say nor wish to imply that the distinction between "trial" and "real" values covers the whole range of value-meanings. Of course it does not. It does not, for example, coincide with the distinction between instrumental and intrinsic values.

I do not agree, however, that just any kind of "prima-facie" value is worth realizing "until it is considered in the wider context of all potential values realizable in a given situation." Some are not worth realizing in any situation, although, unfortunately, we may not find this out until too late. My reason for rejecting the interest theory, for example, is different from that of Dewey. I do not deny that objects of interest are *ipso facto* valuable simply because they have not been appraised or simply because they have not been found to be compatible with other interests. I do not, in short, confuse the question of "value" with that of "moral value." I reject the interest theory (among other reasons) because (a) some interests are worthless, (b) there is never more than a presumption that any given object of interest, if realized, will conduce to satisfaction, and (c) some satisfactions are unanticipated. Value is logically prior to appraisal. Some values are rejected, and quite properly, when they conflict with other, presumably greater, values in a situation. But a value may be a value and still be rejected on moral grounds.

I agree that perhaps "satisfactoriness" rather than "satisfaction" *may* be a better way of defining the generic concept of value. This would take care of the problem, which also bothers Jessup, of denying "real value" to potential values. I do not see, however, why a recognition of the distinction between "real" and "potential" value is not sufficient to account for the point that Lee has in mind. After all, granted that an apple is an apple, we do not confuse real and potential apples. Why should we blur this distinction in the case of values?

In conclusion, let me say again that I heartily agree with the spirit of most of Lee's criticisms, that is, its demand for clarity and consistency. And I could wish that I had been as clear or consistent as I might have been. But I am not moved to give up, as yet, any essential position which my theory involves; and I do not think, although I may well be mistaken in this, that this is due to proprietary interest in the views which I have expressed. I will be delighted to give them up when it is shown that they are untenable.

REJOINDER BY PEPPER

With all of Lee's remarks in the first part of his Criticisms, I fully agree. My analysis of an appetitive act was presented as a sample only, not as a comprehensive description of the value field. Like Lee, I find there are gratuitous satisfactions not preceded by anticipatory strivings.

About his comments on my definition of the term "value" in contrast to his, there still remains, however, some possible disagreement. The question Lee raises here is a fundamental one. Some regard it as purely a verbal question—merely a matter of clearly deciding on one's meaning for words. But I suspect it is also in large degree a material question— one bearing on matters of evidence and inferences from evidence.

To bring out the problem, I have made the accompanying chart. The first column refers to a number of fairly widely accepted facts. These facts are named in terms that do not necessarily denote any value. Then, in columns (2), (3), (4), and (5), I venture to set against these facts the value terminology suggested by the views of myself, Lee, Perry, and Lewis.

For me, I and II are two appropriate uses of value proper. Neither is reducible to the other. But connections between them can be stated for evaluative purposes. III and IV are simply relations in which values can stand to objects. As a result of these relations we may appropriately speak of "objects of value."

For Lee, if I follow him correctly, value proper consists in IV B, "the relational quality" of a person's being pleased or displeased with something. Conation (I) is merely instrumental to IV B. I wonder if he would not deny the existence of II, the fact (?) of objectless pleasure or pain, or of pleasure and pain as values independent of their objects. III would be a derivative conception from IV.

For Perry, value proper consists in IV A. Perry seems to deny the existence of I (conation without necessarily an object) and of II (pleasure or pain as elementary affective data). Perry reduces affections away, turns them into sensations of various kinds, such as sweetness or bitterness. IV B would, in the form of "recurrent value," be reduced to IV A,

		(2) PEPPER	(3) LEE	(4) PERRY	(5) LEWIS
I. CONATION	A. Wanting	Conative *Value*	A Kind of Instrumental Value	(Does not exist without object)	
	B. Non-wanting				
II. AFFECTION	A. Pleasure (Satisfaction)	Affective *Value*	Affection (Possibly Acknowledged only as IV B)	(Does not exist without object)	Immediate *Value*
	B. Pain (Dissatisfaction)				
III. PROPERTY OF OBJECTS ACTUALLY OR POTENTIALLY	A. Being { i—Wanted ii—Non-wanted }	Object of Value (Actual or Potential)	A. Instrumentally Valuable	(Not specially distinguished from IV A)	Inherent *Value*
	B. Being { i—Pleasant ii—Painful }		B. Intrinsically Valuable		
IV. RELATION OF	A. Subject { Wanting Object Non-wanting Object }	Object Being Valued	A. A Kind of Instrumental Value	A. *Value*	Act of Valuing an Object
	B. Subject { Pleased with Object Pained at Object }		B. *Value*	B. Recurrent Value	

Note: Wherever *Value* appears in italics, the Author's basic definition of the term is indicated.

or else to mere sensory qualities perceived, such as, "I sense coffee as bitter," which is not a judgment of value unless another judgment is added, expressing the fact that I want it or do not want it.

Lewis, in his latest book, equates immediate value with I and II indiscriminately and equates inherent value with III, the property of an object's being immediately valuable. Being greatly interested in the predication of value, Lewis gives inherent value a place in his view so prominent that one almost takes this as the ultimate definition of value, for which "immediate value" is only a necessary condition.

Even if this chart is not quite true to the views referred to, it does graphically exhibit the discrepancies involved in the shifting uses of the term "value." I think it also shows clearly that these discrepancies are not "purely linguistic." A man's definition of value affects his perceptions of the data (?) and his descriptions of the surrounding field of experience, and his evaluations. There are factual issues involved in the ways "value" is defined, and these issues go much deeper than questions of usage.

How are such issues to be resolved? If the issues go deep enough, they will not be resolved, I believe, nor even clarified without bringing into the open the categorial presuppositions of a man's whole philosophical approach. The issues among the four views in the chart, however, probably do not go as deep as that.

Could Lee and I, for instance, resolve our issues without going outside the field of fact referred to in the chart? Let us assume that we have no serious disagreement over column (1), in spite of some question as to Lee's admission of II. On that assumption, is there any evidential basis for my considering my definition better than Lee's?

I think there is. The issues come to a head over evaluation. His definition of value requires him to exclude in his evaluative judgments objectless affections (for *by definition* these are not values since they are not *relational* qualities). His definition also requires him to describe the values of purposive activity solely in terms of satisfactions attained. It requires him to exclude in his evaluative judgments acts of pure efficiency in the support of life. Now, my contention is that an evaluative theory which excluded these two sorts of acts in its judgments would in fact prove impracticable. Men would not, and do not, follow such evaluative practices.

Or put the matter another way. If a writer defines as a value criterion something no man would ever employ as a standard of judgment for his acts, then that definition has no empirical justification. Suppose I define value as heat, meaning that the hotter a thing is the better it is. Then it follows that the best thing a man can do for himself would be to get himself as hot as he can as quick as he can—that is, to leap into a fire. To which any sane man would say, "Phooey!"

Does this example make my point clear? I simply believe that my definition of value is closer in accord with what is in fact aimed at in human evaluative activity than Lee's is. Not that I am interested in establishing that point just now. I am simply exhibiting the nature of the issue over what should be taken as the basic definition of value. The issue is, I believe, a material one. The evidence which can settle it is the facts of human evaluative activities. Does Lee's definition, or mine, conform most closely to what in fact is involved or aimed at in evaluative activities?

❦ CRITICISMS BY LEPLEY

I SHOULD PERHAPS REPLY to Parker's paper,[1] lest my silence be misinterpreted. I shall give special attention also to the contribution by Morris, for it raises some issues in which I have become particularly interested.

I

In response to Parker's invitation that other participants in this inquiry indicate their conceptions of "behavioral," [2] I wish to say that I find myself in complete agreement with Morris's interpretation and his reasons for preferring a behavioral to a "mentalistic" or purely introspective approach to value problems.[3] So far as a behavioral approach thus interpreted makes any metaphysical assumptions, it appears to me to stress the hypothesis that there are continuities within and among inorganic, organic, and distinctly human events, including the events of need, desire, interest, satisfaction, appraisal, and the like —continuities which can be discovered and 'utilized' most fruitfully by a methodology which *combines* sensation, perception, thinking, motor action, and other like elements of response in such a way that they check on and 'test' each other within and as continuing transactional processes. In such a methodology, knowledge by acquaintance and knowledge by description are intimately conjoined, if indeed they are distinguishable except for convenience. In this inclusive sense of "behavioral," Parker's treatment of value problems appears to me to be perhaps as behavioral, or empirical, as that of other members of the symposium.

Parker finds that a "behavioristic" account of "mother rocking her child to sleep" discloses no more value than is present in a breeze blowing a leaf. But certainly a full "behavioral" account of the mother rock-

[1] Especially pp. 239–241, above.
[2] As in my main paper, single quotation marks which are not within double quotation marks are used to denote words and phrases which I feel are particularly ambiguous. Double quotation marks indicate quotations or words as words.
[3] Pp. 213–214.

ing her child to sleep will, if the account includes, by aid of both 'objective' and 'subjective' terms,[4] all the continuities of events commonly termed "feeling," "caring for," "foresight," "planning," and the like, disclose marked differences which certainly *can* be taken as distinguishing value phenomena from non-value phenomena. Also, may we properly *assume* that "breeze blowing a leaf" is not a value phenomenon or involves no value? Even on the level of the human events of desiring, enjoying, approving, and the like, the essential nature of value may be inferred, from one point of view, as being the capacity of objects (things, acts, arrangements, qualities) to produce and sustain events which constitute or are experienced, from another point of view, as feeling, satisfaction, recognition of relations, and so on.

In fairness to Dewey it should perhaps be noted that Parker appears to misinterpret footnote 5 [5] of the article which occasioned this symposium. It seems clear that Dewey does not ascribe value to physico-chemical interactions that maintain stability in change on the part of some compounds; instead, he says that if the interpretation of value as a property or quality which occurs when an object is actively cared for were carried out, "it would indicate that the appearance of value-quality is *genetically and functionally continuous*, not only with physiological operations that protect and continue living processes, but with physical-chemical interactions that maintain stability amid change on the part of some compounds" (italics mine). In his present paper, Dewey makes it quite clear [6] that he restricts the term "value" to those cases of "selection-rejection behavior" directed "by an anticipation or foresight of the outcome" of such behavior.

A chief merit of Parker's paper is the clarity with which it recognizes the pervasiveness of the volitional element in our human activities—particularly in the life of aesthetic imagination, but also in matters legal and ethical. If we are to see the value situation steadily and see it 'whole,' we must recognize the pervasiveness, and often the almost exclusive presence, or at least the decided dominance, of wish—of the lure for feeling or of the desire for security, recognition, or any of a myriad variety of satisfactions. But if we are to achieve such balance and wholeness in vision, we must recognize also (a) that "the wish to share a desire or satisfaction or to make a desire prevail" is by no means the only function of value words and sentences, especially of legal and ethical ones; (b) that the non-volitional functions of words and sentences can be increased and a more distinctively valuative (and legal and ethical) level of judgment and language can thus be achieved —a level on which the subject matter is usually in part volitional but the judgment and language are not determined in outcome or validity by volition; and (c) that the same words and sentences may in different contexts signify in different modes and perform also different non-significative functions, and, conversely, that different words and sentences can, in the same context (of which intent and interpretation are parts), perform the same significative and non-significative functions and are, under these conditions, interchangeable or translatable.

Although Parker's paper seems to recognize these three points in some measure, it does not, I believe, make them sufficiently explicit or give them sufficient emphasis. The position taken is, as Aiken says,[7] too voluntaristic.

All our human activities, even those of science and mathematics, spring up and operate within the embrace of desires and purposes. But it is clear that although all sentences arise and function thus, they are not therefore always expressions of desire or attempts to make a desire prevail. In poetry and drama, words and sentences are predominantly expressive; they are dreams or aids to dreaming—aids to imaginative activities engaged in largely for the satisfactions they afford. They are mainly expressions of desire. Also, the words and sentences which arise in human affairs where legal and ethical judgments emerge are initially, and in considerable measure persistently, expressive of desire or are attempts to make some desire prevail. But in these affairs words and sentences come to function also in predominantly, perhaps at some points completely, propositional ways, and their content and character are not then determined constitutively by desire.

Analysis of what may be called a "complete value experience," or a "value adjustment course," indicates that "value" sentences perform at least three distinguishable propositional functions. These functions are likely to occur, or can be achieved, at successive stages of the adjustment course, though they may alternate rapidly with each other and with non-propositional functions and they may or may not recur one or more times during the adjustment process. All three of these functions can be performed by the same or by different sentences.

[7] P. 42.

Sentences which arise largely as exclamations, as expressions of feeling or desire, or as spontaneous commands (say, "I wish the war were over!" or "Stealing is wrong!"—to mention only two of Parker's examples) may then be viewed as denoting an actual state of affairs—an attitude expressed and either 'held' or simulated. When the sentences are viewed thus, either by the 'speaker' or by a 'listener,' they are functioning propositionally in the first sense.

When the sentences are viewed in this way, such questions as these may arise: Do I really wish the war were over? Would I wish it to be over even if its ending meant victory for the enemy? Is stealing wrong? —always? What is meant, and what should be meant, by "wrong"? What is the basis of the "should"? Are right and wrong, good and bad, merely conventions? and so on and so forth. Here the sentences, which at first may have been voiced almost wholly as an expression of feeling or desire and which next were taken as denoting something that the sentences specified, have come to be regarded as statements which need to be investigated. They are conceived as making assertions that are subject to inquiry. They express hypotheses; they are formulations which may or may not be true. When viewed and treated thus, the sentences are functioning propositionally in the second sense.

After inquiry, however long and careful it may be, the final judgments may be 'voiced' (designated) in the same sentences that arose at the beginning of the adjustment course, or in different sentences. If the same sentences are used, they will almost certainly carry somewhat different significations than they did at the beginning and at most of the earlier stages of the adjustment course. "I wish the war were over" may now be intended to signify that, after consideration, the conditions of defeat are judged to be more acceptable than the horrors attending continuation of the war; or it may signify that the desire for peace is now recognized to be only one among several closely related wishes, and indeed, as compared with some of the other wishes, to be a less worthy one. "Stealing is wrong" may not now be or signify a cry of protest or command, but may state a carefully reasoned conclusion (a) that stealing is regarded as wrong by most of the people who live in the particular culture in reference to which the sentence is uttered; or (b) that if a society of such and such character is to be maintained, certain "property rights" must be respected; or (c) that stealing is a mode of behavior which runs counter to the fullest achievement or realization of the "life-plan" or the inherent potentialities of each or all persons.[8] In the degree that the sentences body forth, or designate, conclusions which are the result of careful inquiry and critical judgment, the sentences are functioning propositionally in the third sense.

The point I wish to emphasize here is *not* that since the same sentence or combination of words can perform different sorts of non-propositional and propositional functions they are equivalent or transposable; it may be that the same sentence is not used throughout a particular adjustment course, or if the same words are used, it may properly be urged that the sentence is not really the same in the different contexts in which the words occur. Nor do I intend to say that once the sentence, or pattern of words, is functioning propositionally it may not return to non-propositional functions or that it may not function both propositionally and non-propositionally at the same time. What I do want to stress is, instead, that value sentences usually do in some measure, and nearly always can in larger measure, function propositionally. In other words, they perform propositional functions, and when and to the extent that they do so they are genuine propositions.

Indeed, sentences become genuinely "value" sentences and genuinely legal or ethical sentences, just as sentences become genuinely "factual" sentences or scientific ones, only as they come to function propositionally and are subjected to careful inquiry and testing. As Dewey recently said, "As far as non-cognitive, extra-cognitive, factors enter into the subject-matter or content of sentences purporting to be legitimately ethical, those sentences are by just that much deprived of the properties sentences should have to be genuinely *ethical.*"[9] There is nothing inherently or distinctively valuative or ethical about expressing desire or about persuading people or motivating them to action. The expressing, persuading, and motivating take on valuative or ethical quality only so far as they are toward ends, and by means, chosen in view of carefully and factually grounded consideration of consequences—a consideration which takes into account 'all' our knowledge, including our experiences of the intrinsic qualities and characters of competing possibilities.

[8] The objectivity and validity of conclusions such as (c) are defended by Parker in his *Experience and Substance*, Ann Arbor, 1941, pp. 308–311.
[9] J. Dewey, "Ethical Subject-Matter and Language," *The Journal of Philosophy*, XLII (1945), 701–712. The quotation is from p. 709; by permission of the editors.

Parker may agree that value terms and sentences perform propositional functions, and that the role which these functions perform can
be markedly increased. But he may still insist [10] that, nevertheless,
"every value statement expresses a wish or satisfaction and an invitation to a hearer to share in it," and that the greater breadth of vision
and the greater precision of language attained by even the specialized
axiologist and ethical theorist do not render valuative or ethical statements purely descriptive. Moreover, he may urge that, though we can
know the goodness of an act only by trying it and by considering its
consequences, "preference can never be wholly determined by them.
The intrinsic character of the action itself will be the deciding factor."
For example, "the contribution which courage makes to the preservation of a good life, together with the honor and compensation which
it may command, add to its worth; but the quality of the experience
when we are courageous, as compared with that when we are cowardly,
is decisive."

Let us consider this last point first. Do qualities, say, courage and
cowardice, exist apart from a total setting in which there are recognitions of interdependencies and consequences, recognitions which enter
into and help to constitute the qualities themselves? And if it be granted
that the qualities may be abstracted from the larger situation and had
"in themselves," do the qualities as experienced have value except as
they are able to produce and sustain recognition that they are good,
or that one is better than another, considered either in itself or in its
larger context? In any case, if it be recognized, as by Parker, that
quality and consequences must be considered together and not separated, it seems to make little difference whether we say that value
resides in or is the quality as had or resides in or is the ability of the
quality as experienced to sustain recognition of the quality as good
or better. Parker does not seem to recognize, however, that finding a
quality to be good "in itself," or better than some other quality, is an
instance of an object (the quality) sustaining events of recognition
and approval, and that in this respect the events of liking, enjoying,
appraising, approving, and so on are continuous with the events of all
levels of nature.

[10] As in his recent article, "Reflections on the Crisis in Theory of Value, I: Mostly
Critical," *Ethics*, LVI (1946), 193–207. My quotations are from p. 206; by permission of the editors.

Which leads back to the first point. Perhaps every sentence is in some measure an expression of desire, even the sentences of 'pure' science. But it is probably also true that no sentence is ever merely, or purely, an expression of feeling or volition. In so far as a sentence is only such an expression, devoid of cognitive content or determination, it is neither a factual nor a valuative sentence. The pervasiveness of affective and volitional factors does not, however, render futile and entirely ineffectual man's attempts to increase the objectivity and the correctness or adequacy of inquiry and judgment regarding what exists and what is desired and approved, what courses of action are judged to be most satisfactory and which satisfactions are found "in themselves" (actually in their contexts) to be superior or most approvable. Although we should avoid overoptimism about the amount of 'objectivity' that can be achieved and about the ease of achieving it—especially in more complex subject matters, the hope for maximum achievement would seem to lie along the line of recognizing the possibilities and conditions for the achievement and in stressing its importance rather than in deprecating or ignoring it.

It was recognition that accepting and rejecting, approving and disapproving, and so on can, like all other events, be viewed either from a more 'subjective' or a more 'objective' standpoint and bodied forth in more subjective or more objective language, which led me to the conclusion [11] that the same referent can perhaps always be designated in both "factual" and "valuative" terms. At no time have I held that a factual sentence and a valuative sentence are identical. I have repeatedly emphasized that two sentences are translatable, transposable, or interchangeable only when used with the same intent; and by "used" I have meant to include the interpretations placed upon sentences, as well as any purpose (significative and/or non-significative) for which the sentences were produced.

I agree completely with Parker, therefore, that the members of the pairs of sentences which he mentions [12] (for example, "I wish the war were over" and "He wishes that the war were over"; and "Stealing is wrong" and "Stealing disrupts the social and economic organization of society") are not equivalent or interchangeable when used as he conceives them as occurring. When the first sentence of each pair arises in the context of the intent to express desire and/or to influence be-

[11] In *Verifiability of Value*, ch. x. [12] Pp. 234 ff., above.

havior and the second sentence of the pair is intended almost exclusively to signify a state of affairs (a 'fact'), the two sentences would
obviously not be equivalent or functionally interchangeable. Nor does
it seem likely that the sentences of the first pair ("I wish the war were
over" and "He wishes that the war were over") would ever, except
possibly in very rare circumstances, be produced or interpreted with
the same intent. Dissimilarly, the sentences in the second pair ("Stealing is wrong" and "Stealing disrupts the economic and social organization of society") might very commonly be used with precisely the
same significative and non-significative intent and would, under these
conditions, be equivalent and interchangeable; but if and when the
two sentences have different signification or perform other functions
differently—however slight these differences are, the sentences are not
equivalent or interchangeable. This latter condition does not mean,
though, that if in a particular case "Stealing is wrong" is largely expressive of wish, some other sentence may not serve equally well the
same function should the language habits of the speaker or interpreter
permit. Such a sentence can, however, be no more distinctively valuative or factual than is the sentence with which it is interchangeable.

II

Morris recognizes clearly that preferences often need to be and
can be corrected; [13] that the methods of evaluative inquiry and scientific inquiry are not essentially different; [14] and that a word or sentence
may in one context signify appraisively and in another context signify
designatively, [15] and that all kinds of signs (designative, appraisive,
prescriptive, formative) may occur in evaluative processes. [16] With
these and many other points in Morris's treatment of values, I find
myself in hearty agreement. There are, however, some matters upon
which I should be glad to have his position clarified or made more
explicit.

In the first place, the emphasis which Morris puts upon the fact
that the way in which a sign prepares behavior (the mode in which
the sign signifies) is different from the use made of the sign (whether
informative, appraisive, incitive, or systemic) seems to result in failure
to recognize that, although some signs may come to signify in most
cases designatively, others to signify appraisively, others to signify

[13] P. 216.   [14] P. 218–219.   [15] P. 217–218.   [16] P. 217.

prescriptively, and still others to signify formatively, signs do not in themselves have, *in any particular case of actual signification,* a mode of signifying except as they are produced for a certain purpose (consciously or not) or are responded to ('interpreted') in a particular way. Hence, Morris is led to say, "From the present point of view the fact that a statement can be used valuatively and an appraisal used informatively does not make a statement an appraisal or an appraisal a statement." [17] But is a sign, say a sentence, inherently a statement or an appraisal, apart from the signification intended (consciously or not) by its producer or its interpreter? Just as Morris admits that the sentence "This is a good table" may signify (apparently when produced or responded to with different intents or in different ways) *either* appraisively to give the table a certain preferential status in behavior, *or* designatively to signify that the table is able to reduce, or satisfy, some need of an organism, is it not also true that a somewhat different sentence (say, "This table reduces this need") may, if produced and interpreted as having the same signification (whether appraisive or designative) as "This is a good table," be used interchangeably with this latter sentence? Indeed, is it not true that, for any sentence whatever, some other sentence or sentences, whether they be what are commonly classed as "factual" sentences or "valuative" sentences,[18] may occur, and be responded to in the same way, and that the way each sentence signifies determines whether the sentence is (wholly or in some degree) a statement or an appraisal in each particular context?

To recognize fully the extent to which different words and sentences can 'function' (in mode and/or use) interchangeably or equivalently need not, it seems to me, result in any confusion of designation with appraisal or prescription (or vice versa) nor of statements with appraisals or prescriptions. Whether these modes of signifying and these kinds of sentences are absolutely different from one another, or whether any one mode can occur in the complete absence of the others, may be open to question; but that there are often at least very marked relative differences of mode, kind, and use is made quite clear by Morris in *SLB.* Also, we should certainly strive for all the clarity that can be achieved in value theory, say in regard to the relation of so-

[17] C. Morris, *Signs, Language, and Behavior,* p. 263. I shall hereafter refer to this work as *SLB.*   [18] See pp. 176–177, above.

called facts "and" values. But we do not seek a spurious clarity which conceals fundamental continuities by assuming inherent or complete differences of mode, kind, or use. Morris agrees, I believe, that facts and values occur in what I have called the contrast relation and the parallel relation, but if he is willing to admit an affirmative answer to the last question in the paragraph immediately preceding this one, must he not also recognize what I have called the "identity relation" of fact and value? [19]

A second point may be only a terminological difficulty, or it may result in some measure from overabstraction or oversimplification. According to Morris, a sentence (say, "This is a good table") signifies appraisively only when it prepares behavior for giving the table a preferential status. Yet, to *evaluate* the table or the sentence is to conduct inquiry as to whether the table does or does not reduce some need. This inquiry, he seems to admit, may eventuate in designative signs, but to be evaluative the process must then *terminate* in appraisive signs. So we seem to have the paradoxical view that evaluation is evaluation only as a process of inquiry terminates in appraisal, but that evaluation occurs only when we move from an appraisive to a designative role of signs. The position may be put even more paradoxically by saying that when or in the degree that a sentence functions (signifies) appraisively, it does so without 'appraisal'! By this I do not mean that Morris excludes inquiry from the total process which may lead up to a final designation and then produce also an appraisive signification, or functioning, of the same or of a different sentence. For as noted before, he quite clearly recognizes evaluative inquiry and the fact that appraisals may be made "either hastily, carelessly, unreflectively or after careful scrutiny, the utilization of reliable knowledge, the consideration of consequences." What I mean is, rather, that appraisal, in the sense of critical inquiry and testing, appears not to enter constitutively into the appraisive signification of a sentence as this mode of signification is conceived by Morris. Appraisive signification appears to be regarded as purely an emotive or volitional response, which, though it may be based on knowledge, is itself devoid of cognitive elements.

[19] See my "Three Relations of Facts and Values," *The Philosophical Review*, LII (1943), 499–504.

A third point, very closely related to the second, is that by distinguishing sharply between the appraisive and the designative functioning of signs and by stressing [20] the idea that the dominant traits of moral discourse are its appraisive mode and its incitive use, Morris may appear to accept and to support the view that what makes a sentence distinctively valuative or moral is its appraisive *rather than* its designative (propositional) role. If this view is the one accepted, the same criticisms as were made [21] of Parker's position would seem to apply to Morris's also. Briefly, the criticism is that sentences become distinctively valuative and distinctively ethical only in the degree that they achieve more than volitional, 'appraisive,' or prescriptive significations or uses and are determined in their character by genuinely designative, or cognitive, responses.

A fourth and final point. The conception of axiology as the science of preferential behavior may appear to exclude from axiology some of its most important problems. Would it not be better to conceive axiology as the study or theory of value, and to leave it for inquiry to decide whether value occurs only as or in preferential behavior? May we assume without careful examination of the nature of value on the human or organic level and of the relation of value phenomena here to the nature of other events that value is properly limited to preferential behavior, human or organic? Also, the conception of axiology as the science of preferential behavior may suggest that more scientific knowledge about preferences and appraisals, their correlations with personality and cultural patterns, and the like, is all that is needed in order to apply scientific method in dealing with our human value problems. Doubtless such knowledge will be of help, but is there not a danger of "psychologizing" axiological problems? Should it not be emphasized, for example, that the application of experimental inquiry and testing in the formulating and reformulating of goals and procedures in economic, political, educational, and other social activities is as much a part of axiology as is a descriptive study of preferential behavior; or that the application of experimental attitudes and procedures in these matters needs to become, and can perhaps be made, an integral part of the study of preferential behavior when such behavior is adequately conceived?

[20] *SLB*, pp. 138–140.   [21] On pp. 383–385, above.

III

In conclusion, I should like to express the opinion that it need make little difference whether we use the term "value" in a 'strict,' limited sense (as Parker seems to do) to signify only (human?) satisfaction; in perhaps a somewhat more inclusive sense (as does Dewey) to designate, as we have already noted, selection-rejection behavior which is directed by anticipation or foresight of the outcome of such behavior; in a still more inclusive sense (as Morris does) to embrace all preferential behavior; in a yet wider sense (as do some who uphold a conative or affective theory of value) to include all animal striving and feeling; or in a very wide sense (as still others do) to signify a factor or phenomenon which pervades the inorganic as well as the organic levels of nature, or reality. What does actually matter is whether or to what extent we have an adequate over-all conception of reality on all its 'levels.' If, or in the degree that, we hold such a conception, we are not likely to overlook for long the actual continuities among and within the various levels. From a personal, subjective point of view the theory of value as satisfaction is particularly appealing, and I am convinced by my experiences in the present inquiry that this theory in no way prevents its ablest advocates from having a sound over-all philosophy.[22] But I must confess that a theory of value along the lines which I have suggested above [23] appears to me to give explicit recognition to more of the important value-facts than do the other theories. Also, I feel very strongly that, if in our Atomic Age there is to be maximum possibility for social survival and advancement, there must be increased recognition of the continuities between the character of the most distinctively value phenomena on the human 'level' and the character of phenomena on other levels of nature, and also increased recognition of the continuities of the methodology by which we can know, control, and create most fruitfully on all levels.

REJOINDER BY MORRIS

The present embryological state of axiology calls for blood, sweat, and tears. Until a more widely accepted terminology appears, the problem of "translation" between the languages of axiologists will

[22] See, for example, the papers by Parker, Rice, Lee, and Aiken.
[23] Pp. 167–189.

inevitably take up much of our time. That is why each writer in this field should make clear his or her own terminology, specifying the conditions of denotation for the basic terms and defining the other terms on this basis. Only in this way is it possible for us to understand each other at present, and to know whether our differences are terminological or factual. Lepley is aware of this need. And his comments on my paper are an invitation to relate my own position to his. I believe the issues he raises are largely terminological, which does not mean of course that they are unimportant.

In my analysis of signs I attempt to distinguish between the mode of signifying of a sign (whether it is designative, appraisive, prescriptive, or formative) and the uses to which a sign in a given mode of signifying may be put. Differences in mode of signifying are determined by differences in the dispositions to respond which the signs produce in the person for whom they are signs; differences in uses arise from the varying purposes which an individual may try to achieve by the production of signs. Signs in any mode of signifying denote if their conditions for denotation are met; signs in any mode of signifying are adequate to the extent that they further the purposes for which they are used.

Lepley has some doubts about this distinction. He does not deny that some signs "may come to signify in most cases" in some one mode of signifying. But he is afraid that my emphasis upon the distinction of mode of signifying and use makes me fail to see that "signs do not in themselves have, *in any particular case of actual signification,* a mode of signifying except as they are produced for a certain purpose (consciously or not) or are responded to ("interpreted") in a particular way." This means presumably that in any particular case of signification the mode of signifying of a sign may be dependent on its use. Thus it is maintained that "This table reduces this need" and "this is a good table" may in two specific instances have the same signification (be "translatable") since they may be "used interchangeably."

It is however clear that "use" in Lepley's terminology is different in signification than in my terminology. For he specifically says that "use" includes "the interpretations placed upon sentences, as well as any purpose . . . for which the sentences were produced." Since his "use" includes both my "signification" and "use," it is analytic in his language that signification cannot be distinguished from usage, but it is not analytic in mine. Whether my terms are operationally sharp enough to distinguish use and signification, or designative from appraisive signification, in a particular instance remains of course an open question—but it is another question. My point is not to defend here my approach, but to show how intrusive terminological questions are in the present state of axiology.

The paradox which he claims to find in my position (that evaluation terminates in an appraisal but occurs only when we "move from" appraisive to designative signs) rests on a misunderstanding. I have not said that evaluation "moves from" appraisive to designative signs, but merely that it may include all kinds of signs. Inquiry is evaluative to the extent that it is directed to the control of the inquirer's preferences; such evaluative inquiry may involve inquiry as to the truth or falsity of designative signs without being evaluative only while this occurs. I think that the pattern of our inquiries is the same, and that we call a specific inquiry evaluative, or designative, or prescriptive in terms of whether the problem it aims to solve is what we are to prefer, or what we are to believe, or what we are to do. In the first case inquiry terminates in appraisals, in the second in statements, in the third in prescriptions.

In saying that on my account appraisive signification, "though it may be based on knowledge, is itself devoid of cognitive elements," Lepley has forgotten that in my scheme denotation is as possible for appraisive signs as for designative signs. And since appraisive signs denote or do not denote, they may be confirmed or disconfirmed. In this sense they have "cognitive content," even though the data by which they are confirmed or disconfirmed differs from that of designative signs.

Lepley raises the question whether an orientation of axiology around the study of preferential behavior may not exclude some of its most important problems. I made clear in the first pages of my paper that I did not define "valuation" and so did not limit the field of axiology by stipulation; I merely suggested that the study of preferential behavior may give us a starting point for cooperative work. The problems Lepley fears may be excluded seem to be problems of specific evaluations of educational practices, political institutions, and the like.

As I see it, the term "theory of value" (or "axiology") is ambiguous. It may signify a system of designative statements about valuings and evaluations, or a system of evaluations, or both. If there is no difference between designation and appraisal, then these alternatives collapse. If there is a difference it is important to keep the distinctions clear. Whether there is or is not a difference depends upon more careful work in semiotic than has yet been done. In terms of the present stage of my analysis the difference seems genuine. Hence I should favor some such distinction as designative and evaluative axiology. An attempt to advance the former by experimental procedures does not exclude or depreciate the latter. The point is merely that we must distinguish the study of evaluations from the making of evaluations.

REJOINDER BY PARKER

Lepley's fairness and ability to find elements of truth in various points of view seemingly opposed to his own make it not too easy to write a rejoinder. It is difficult to feel sure that one is not agreeing with him, or, on the other hand, that one is. And in his capacity to look all around a subject, and in the direction of those thinkers who are not officially arrayed on his side, his writing seems to me especially valuable. Nevertheless, in my opinion he shares the defect common to most thinkers strongly influenced by Dewey—an inability or unwillingness to carry through to the bitter end that art of making just distinctions, which, as I recall, was Coleridge's definition of philosophy. There results an elusiveness in his thought which he has in common with Dewey himself, a quality in the latter noticed by others. I am sure that I have been influenced by Dewey more than I realize. My students at Columbia last fall (1946) surprised me by pointing to resemblances between my thought and his—some were even claiming me as one of his school! Yet because of his elusiveness I have often found it very hard to read him and to know exactly what he means or where he stands, and where I stand in relation to him and to those close to him in their philosophy.

One illustration of the failure to make just distinctions is the ignoring of the distinction between what is commonly called extrinsic and intrinsic value. Lepley, to be sure, recognizes the existence of felt qualities, of felt desires and satisfactions, but for some reason which I cannot divine, he appears to be averse to saying that, for example, courage has intrinsic value for me when I enjoy being courageous, and, on the other hand, is *valuable*, has extrinsic value in so far as it protects my aims and possessions. Now it is true that I enjoy being courageous partly, but not wholly, because I know that by being so my aims and possessions will be protected, yet the *causal effects* of my being courageous are not the same as my satisfaction in acting courageously. Of course, if one so chooses, one may reserve the term value for such effects, but that would not alter the distinction between them and felt satisfactions. And, if one does choose to use the term so, it follows, provided all things have effects on all things, which I am willing to grant (what a metaphysical mouthful, though, for a pragmatist!) that all facts are values. But this would only show that they were extrinsic values, in the ordinary way of speaking. That all facts are also intrinsic values requires another and different line of argument, "metaphysical" in character.

Lepley's minimizing of such an elementary distinction is undoubtedly due to his adherence to the principle of continuity. Ends and means, intrinsic and extrinsic values, knowledge by acquaintance and knowledge by description, behavior and felt value, seem to Lepley interlacing parts of one continuous process. The acceptance of a behavioral interpretation of value is based on this principle, for the reason, I suspect, that, if man and nature are continuous, one ought to be able to treat man as one would a physical phenomenon, where all that is given is behavior, and find his values there, nevertheless.

Well, I myself am, equally with Lepley, enamored of the principle of continuity, so dear to Leibniz and in our time to Whitehead. I chose to contrast "mother rocking cradle" and "wind blowing leaf" *not* for the purpose of denying value in the latter, but in order to make clear that *if* one does contrast them, one does so because one interprets the former in terms of desire and satisfaction as known by acquaintance in oneself, but refuses this interpretation in the case of the latter. And if, on the other hand, one does ascribe value to "wind blowing leaf," then one must interpret it also in terms of desire and satisfaction, which is precisely what I myself should do, maintaining that the phenomenon "wind blowing leaf" (in the literal sense of the term "phenomenon") is the way some striving-satisfaction, however lowly or exalted, makes its appearance in our experience.

I wish to insist, however, that the principle of continuity cannot be pushed so far as to blind one to the distinctions that exist in the world —of ends and means, closed and open experiences, so-called extrinsic and intrinsic values, levels of being, kinds and degrees of satisfaction and frustration, happiness and misery. Nor should it blind one to the distinction between volitional and propositional statements. To try (once more) to push home how real and important this distinction is, I will examine Lepley's interesting analysis of the statements which, according to him, arise in the three stages of what he calls "an adjustment course." It should be noticed, however, that Lepley does not deny this distinction categorically, but he does tend (I feel) to blunt it.

He uses as illustrations two sentences from my essay, but in this rejoinder I shall use only one of these ("I wish the war were over"), for the sake of brevity and simplicity. As first employed, he admits that this statement may be volitional—a direct expression or voicing of a wish. But even in the first stage he claims that it may come to function propositionally by *denoting* [24] the speaker's state of mind. But this I should strongly doubt, for the following reasons. Take the sentence from the hearer's standpoint, first. For him the sentence is immediately transformed into what is, to be sure, a genuine proposition, "*He* wishes the war to be over," for he cannot say or think "I wish," since "I" is always self-referential. But this is not the same as the original sentence. Next, consider the matter from the speaker's standpoint. Does the original sentence not merely express but also function propositionally towards the speaker's state of mind? I doubt this, for the reason that at this stage it is not in question for the speaker whether or not he wishes the war to be over; at this stage he is not reflective and engaged in the process of self-examination or verification. Only, it seems to me, when we reach Lepley's second stage in the adjustment process could this possibly be the case. Then our speaker begins to ask the question—do I really wish the war to be over—and to weigh the pros and cons of the ending of the war, in the light of its consequences. At this stage, according to Lepley, "I wish the war to be over" is held by the speaker himself as a hypothesis to be investigated, a proposition to be proved or disproved. Now here Lepley has certainly specified a very interesting and real process which might easily be described as he describes it; for, seemingly, the speaker does not himself know whether he wishes the war to be over or not. In other words, he raises the question—is it true that I wish the

[24] Technical problems regarding denoting are involved here which I do not have space to discuss.

war to be over?—where "that I wish the war to be over" looks like a genuine proposition, something either true or false.

I fear that some of my readers, if such readers there be, will accuse me of splitting hairs, but I must insist that we have here two different expressions, as follows: (1) I wish *the war to be over,* and (2) Is it true *that I wish the war to be over?* The part italicized in (1) is a proposition, as I have explained in my essay, and (2) is also a proposition, but (2) is not the same as (1) taken as a whole, which, as a whole, is volitional. Moreover, their difference is not purely verbal, but corresponds to a difference in state of mind—(1) to a volitional, (2) to a propositional, state of mind—the difference between yearning and inquiring. And this leads me to express a doubt whether the situation has even now been properly described. For when I say to myself or to some friend, "Is it true that I wish the war to be over?", am I in a purely cognitive mood? Is there not an underlying conflict of wishes within me, which has led to my framing the propositional question? A conflict between a wish for the continuance of the war (for whatever reasons) and a wish for peace? Here is no mere debate of a disinterested spectator but a struggle between desires which might express itself thus: "I both want and don't want the war to be over," which would be volitional and not merely propositional. (As when a girl says to herself or to a friend, "Do I love him or do I not love him?" because she both loves and does not love him.)

When, moreover, we reach Lepley's last stage, after the struggle within has been completed and the inquiry as to all the consequences has been made of the truth or falsity of the proposition "the war is over," and come back to our original expression, giving it emphasis perhaps as "Yes, indeed, I do wish the war to be over," then it seems to me that the sentence is still volitional, as in its first appearance. Only, and this is what Lepley would rightly insist on, it is a volitional statement backed up by a lot of relevant material in the way of known causal consequences of war or peace. Yet I, on my part, must insist that, even as so enriched, it remains volitional essentially, an expression of preference, a deed overflowing into words, but a deed that has now adjusted itself more fully to the world in which it has to function. Hence I would have to disagree with the quotation from Dewey "as far as the non-cognitive . . . factors enter into the . . . content of sentences . . . these sentences are by just that much deprived of the properties sentences should have to be genuinely ethical." For every ethical sentence is an expression of love (*caritas,* not mere *libido*), no matter how much investigation of consequences may have preceded its formulation. On the other hand, I do (I think) agree with this much of Lepley's own statement, as follows: "The expressing, persuading and motivating take on . . . ethical quality only so far as they are towards ends . . . chosen in view of carefully considered and factually grounded consequences—a consideration which is in view of all of our knowledge, including our experience of the 'intrinsic' qualities and characters of competing possibilities." And in rereading the last few pages of Lepley's criticism of my essay, I suspect that after all we are much nearer to agreement than might appear from the disputatious character of this my rejoinder; for we both appreciate what an uncanny mixture of diverse elements our experience is. And were I right in my suspicion, I should be pleased.

THE PAPERS of Lee and Rice are both serious attempts to modernize old theories by incorporating an abundance of new and interesting features drawn from contemporary science, but in each case, I try to show, the new version does not basically alter the working parts of the old model.

Thus Lee, beginning with the common sense distinction between what *is* and what *matters* naturally winds up with the assertion that value qualities are not real like physical and chemical properties, but are "putative," being attributed to objects by the mind. He thus agrees with Hamlet that "there is nothing either good or bad, but thinking makes it so." While he insists that value qualities exist in art and nature rather than in the mind, he just misses the sound conclusion that they are relative and objective, and thus spoils his paper by making values dependent on the quirks and whims of opinion.

Rice, on the other hand, appears to accept frankly the dualism between the realm of value and that of the outer world, locating value in the inner life of experience while allowing only causal or instrumental value to the objects of nature, art, and industry. He suggests a parallelism, however, between the smooth or rough form of the nerve impulses and the experience of pleasure and pain which condition value. In pointing out the similarity of this view to that of Aristippus of Cyrene, I had no desire that Rice should share in the disrepute in which Aristippus has been held. In spite of the ancient gossips, the psychological foundations of the ethics of Aristippus are singularly plausible. His theory of the nature of pleasure and pain may well be sound, but the theory of value based on this psychology has the weakness of rendering the whole world worthless except pleasure and pain; that is, except smooth or rough internal motion. Rice has responded to my criticism in a spirited reply but I fail to find an answer to my main objection.

I

Common Sense Realism.—Common sense does, as a matter of fact, frequently make the distinction between what is and what matters—

the distinction with which Lee's paper commences. But common sense is notoriously inconsistent and crude, and while making the distinction also repudiates it. In most cases what *is* also matters, and what matters also *is*. What a person knows, he cares about, and what he cares for, he knows. Moreover values exist or could be brought into existence; and existence in some cases has value and in some cases is a value factor. A person knows his values, and values his knowledge.

The questions here raised are very basic to theory of value, and it is exceedingly bad practice to settle a technically important issue on the basis of common sense at the very start of the investigation. The author (and the reader, in so far as he assents) is henceforth committed to a sort of naive realism according to which existence and certain physical properties *belong* to objects whereas value qualities are merely attributed to or read into objects by individuals.

Into this very old bottle Lee pours the new wine of emergent evolution, objective relativism, instrumentalism, and the like—with results not unlike those indicated in the parable.

Half-and-Half Behaviorism.—I agree with Lee's criticism of certain methodologies incorrectly called behavioristic. He asserts, and I assent to his assertion, that those "behaviorisms" that exclude relevant "private" data are preserving in method the Cartesian dualism which they reject in metaphysics. Descartes's reason for accepting primary qualities as real and objective was that one can attain clear and distinct ideas of these mathematical properties, whereas of the secondary qualities he cannot. The fundamental dualism is therefore methodological and scientific rather than metaphysical. It is precisely this dualism between the objective and subjective, the public and the private, which is preserved in psychophysical parallelism. And a "behaviorism" which rejects the "private" as unscientific in method is not overcoming the dualism but implicitly preserving it.

The Cartesian dualism can be overcome only by finding a common ground. Mead accomplishes this unification by interpreting both mind and its object, both primary and secondary qualities, in terms of "the act." The distinction between primary and secondary qualities becomes mainly that between manipulatory and distance qualities, and these are intimately related in the interaction between an organism and its evironment. Again, the range of objects which Mead calls teleological objects, which are defined in terms of the activities of the organism, helps break down the sharp dichotomy between mind and object. A third important feature of the unification is the fact that in a certain sense the organism, by its "sensitivity" defines all the objects of its environment.

Real and Putative Properties.—I think that this is a most unhappy distinction—and one into which a person is likely to be led by a false start such as that criticized above. Value, the paper asserts, is a putative quality, not a real one. Now the word "putative" means (from *puto*—I think or I fancy) "supposed," "reputed," or "fancied," as opposed to the tested, validated, and well-grounded. To make such a distinction is to give away the whole case for value theory.

There are, of course, putative values. Veblen used the term frequently in discussing economic value. But when you speak of putative values, the contrasting term is real or trustworthy values.

Now Lee does not really mean that value is a putative property in contrast to real properties. He means that value properties are relative to the wants, interests, and satisfactions of an organism. So is color relative to animal sensitivity. So too are size and number relative. But the relative is not the putative. It isn't thinking that makes meat a good food for human beings or salt water bad; it is the human physiological system. If, wherever Lee has the word "putative" he will substitute "relative," he will find his statements improved.

Standard Value.—I do not like the concept of "standard value." The gold standard in business and hedonic value in ethics should warn us against the hankering for eternal, immutable standards for calculating value. If, by standard value, you mean any and all of the tested and undisputed values in all the fields of value, which serve as reference points for our thinking, there is no objection to calling them "standard values"—except that they are not really "standard." If by "standard value" you mean some unitary measuring stick, there simply is no such thing. You might as well search for the "standard truth" by which you could measure all other truths.

The Comparative Theory.—Lee, commenting on the comparative theory of value, writes: "Mitchell's problem is the problem of finding undefined notions in terms of which the logical structure of the whole experience of value can be stated." [1] Not so. I adopt Brogan's logical calculus because it fits the actual structure of value-judgments. But I

---

[1] P. 161, above.

make it plain that such a logic does not constitute a theory of value. The comparative theory of value claims to be an empirical theory justified by the data of observation and by its fruitfulness. My paper reads:

A logical analysis, and a deductive system based thereon does not constitute a theory, unless the author claims that the definitions are appropriate and the postulates true. Brogan makes these claims. . . .[2]

Lee continues:

The statement that "x is good" means "it is better that x is than that it is not" does not involve the comparison of different experiences of value in such a way as to establish a standard.[3]

It is quite true that the abstract definition as part of a logical calculus does not involve actual comparison. But the comparative theory of value, as a theory, claims that this definition is an appropriate one conforming to the common meaning of the proposition "x is good." When you make a statement in this form you may mean more than the definition states but you never mean less. Similarly when you say that anything is evil you always mean at least that its non-existence is better than its existence.

Appropriate definitions have usefulness in directing attention to important features and thus guiding action. If the above definition of "x is good" is appropriate it does involve finding and testing value by comparison. Notice how many of the Proverbs are in the comparative form: "Wisdom is better than rubies"; "A living dog is better than a dead lion." And notice that judgments of evil either suggest or actually state that the evils would be better annihilated.

Value as Adjectival.—If it is true that value is adjectival, as Lee insists, it is most unfortunate. This fact would deprive axiology of the flexibility and power of the denotative and relational logic. The subject matter of value would have to be handled by the cumbersome and confining Aristotelian logic (whose propositions are in the form: P is attributed to all S). It was Aristotle, by the way, who pointed out that "the good" included things, qualities, activities, forms, relations, and many other kinds of entities.

Here, I think, is the crux of the whole subject of axiology. It seems clear to me that "valuity" or valuableness is identical with the relation of betterness; and that values are the terms of this relation. So conceived, the whole question as to whether value (which is a vague word covering both the foregoing) is substantive, adjectival, or relational becomes clear and sensible.

There is actually no metaphysical distinction between things and attributes. "Objects" get their status as things by our acts of perception, discrimination, and naming; attributes get their status in the same way. There is a strong prejudice, traceable (as Bergson and Mead have pointed out) to our spatializing and manipulating needs, to erect some features of the environment into objects and others into attributes. But a little effort, or a different interest, reverses the classification.

It is worth bearing in mind that there are value-objects, value-qualities, value-events, and value-relations. There are also value-actualities, value-possibilities, and value-impossibilities. The general name for all these is "values."

Potential Value.—I would give a slightly different account of potential value from that of the paper under discussion. I think that here, again, Lee's initial common sense assumptions have led him into error.

I think it absurd to say that bread is potentially nourishing, that a badly constructed building is potentially dangerous. Bread *is* nourishing, even while it is still in the bread-box. When eaten, it ceases to be nourishing bread; it becomes chyme and chyle and eventually blood —if I remember my lessons on physiology correctly. A badly constructed building *is* dangerous while it is still standing. When it falls it ceases to be dangerous and becomes a tomb. The actual value lies in the capacity of the object with its qualities to satisfy need. It is only the consummatory value (of pleasure, and so on) which Lee regards as real value, all else being potential, instrumental, or putative value.

I do not think that Lee intends to place himself in the class of hedonists or other affective theorists. But the logic of his initial paragraphs leads straight to this consequence. A thorough objective relativism would have saved him and been consistent with what is new and valuable in his paper.

II

Science and Humanism.—Rice's approach to theory of value through a discussion of the current strain between the sciences and the humanities is an excellent means of showing the pertinence of our subject, a subject that is too often treated in the abstract. He shows that the whole problem of value comes to a focus in education, in the aims and content of the curriculum. With equal cogency he shows how it converges on the question of the use of atomic energy and on other contemporary problems. Value is, as Nietzsche said, *the* modern problem.

I shall anticipate my whole criticism of this paper by expressing disappointment that an approach so broad and just should end in a theory which, in my judgment, offers no new vantage point from which to fuse the scientific and humanistic perspectives. While Rice develops a motor-affective theory of value, he emphasizes the hedonic and algedonic tone of the subjective experience. And feeling tone, according to the hypothesis he favors, is a matter of smooth or rough functioning of the central regions as indicated by the graph of the nerve impulse. Thus Rice joins hands with Aristippus of classical antiquity. If this theory is sound, a little gadget to record the form of the electrochemical nerve impulse is all that is needed to measure intrinsic value.

Admitting the relevance of joy and sorrow to the experience of good and evil, this theory seems exceedingly remote from the diverging standpoints of the sciences and the humanities, and from the problems of education, industry, international relations, and commodious living.

Classification of Theories.—In preparation for the exposition of his own theory of value, Rice classifies and criticizes historical and current theories. I found this classification and criticism very interesting and instructive. I am not at all sure, however, that he is correct in identifying affective theories in general with the humanistic approach, and conative theories with the biological and social science approach. I think that as good a case could be made for the reverse association. In so far as the mind-body dualism has prevailed in science—and it has prevailed very widely—value has been excluded from physical nature and from biological mechanisms and located in the soul or the inner processes. Similarly materialistic science has relegated value to the status of an unreal epiphenomenon or phantasm. Positivistic science likewise denies the reality of value qualities. The sociological tendency has been to locate value in the mores or in subjective attitudes. Humanists (artists, poets, dramatists), on the other hand, being more interested in describing and creating than in explaining, see value in activities and outer things, or else in the object of striving. The point is not important except as indicating the alliance between affective theories of value and mechanistic science, whether dualistic or materialistic.

The conative theories classified by Rice as "teaser" theories are, in my judgment, the most wholesome historical concepts. They do greater justice to man as a vital organism, as a rational creature, and as a part of a significant world. In various ways, they interpret value as that which calls out purposeful activity, which fulfills purpose, and which makes life meaningful. These theories include those of Plato, Aristotle, Plotinus, the Stoics, the main philosophers of the Christian tradition, Spinoza, and so forth. Their weakness is the arbitrary—and often supernatural—character of what they set forth as the summum bonum; their strength lies in their wholeness. In this respect they contrast with the comparatively trivial affective and "satisfaction" theories.

It will be noted that Rice does not classify his own theory as affective; he calls it a motor-affective theory. His definitions of good and bad, however, make it necessary for him to list almost everything which common sense and social science and creative art refer to in value categories as "extrinsic" or instrumental value.

Rice criticizes Dewey's "prizing" as too narrow a term to cover the wide variey of valuing. I think that Dewey must be interpreted liberally in this connection. Valuing, I understand him to say, is not a mere state of the viscera or of smooth or rough functioning of nerve impulses; valuing is an act. If you want to know what a person or a group really values, observe what they prize, what they lavish care on preserving and improving, what they make sacrifices for, what they put strength and effort into, what engages their minds and emotions. Thus he tries to connect, as any sound theory must, human valuing with the inter-action of human individuals and groups with their environments. He uses the word "prizing" with some hesitation, realizing the difficulty of finding *one* comprehensive term for the infinite variety of activities involved in valuing and evaluating. But it is the right *sort* of word, and that is the main thing.

Behaviorisms, Adequate and Inadequate.—Rice's discussion of the rise and decline of certain kinds of behaviorism is most interesting and enlightening. I do not have his familiarity with the more recent literature, but I have taken the opportunity of checking a good deal of it. His conclusion is not that behaviorism should be abandoned, but that it should outgrow the earlier crudities and refine its main concepts. With this discussion I find myself in agreement.

I think, however, that a behaviorism like that of G. H. Mead is not guilty of the crudities exposed by the more recent investigations. Mead never assumed that input must equal output or that every stimulus must have an overt motor response. The fact that action is inhibited, that mental activity goes on in terms of symbols, that in the aesthetic moment action is suspended, that the consummation is simply enjoyed —all these facts are obvious. It is their explanation in terms of the life process or "the act" that Mead is concerned with. In perception at a distance, for example, the meaning or value qualities of an object are grasped without contact or manipulation; but in the life of the individual or the race those meanings have been built up by manipulatory experience and in case of doubt they are tested by contact experience. Thus the ground may look soft, the fruit ripe, or the bush prickly; and the organism can act or refrain from acting according to the appearance. It is in this sense that Mead describes perception as a collapsed act.

I do not think that Dewey means to say that value must be defined in terms of motor responses to the exclusion of interest or satisfaction or feeling. But the unity and continuity of science requires that these inner aspects, instead of being taken as ultimate, be explained as aspects of the life process. I think, therefore, that in so far as Rice's criticism of behaviorism is sound, it is a clarification of Dewey's behaviorism rather than a repudiation of it. I am glad that he ends by aligning himself with a modified, refined, and more adequate behaviorism.

An Affective-Motor Theory of Value.—Rice's own theory of value as expounded in this paper needs to be supplemented by his published articles. Here the affective aspect is too strongly emphasized. If we divide experience into its two phases, doing and suffering, Rice finds the value in the suffering; that is, in the hedonic tone.

While it is undoubtedly true that all experience of value is characterized by feelings of joy or sorrow or some such affects, it does not follow that feeling tone gives any explanation or fruitful concept of value. Just because feeling tone is an obvious, surface quality makes it suspect as a scientific concept. In any case the feeling of joy does not explain the value, but only describes the experience of value. It is much more reasonable to suppose that the value lies in the object (as conditioned and determined by human life processes). When people look upon the world of nature, of industry, and of art as having value and significance, then the philosophy of value and the creation of value becomes a part of every science that modifies the world, and every art, and every industry. But when people look upon value as pleasure and pain, joy and sorrow, then it is the direct concern of only one science (psychology), and the direct concern of no industry and no art.

Rejoinder by Lee

In my paper I start from common sense experience and thought because there is nothing else to start from. This is our precritical apprehension and expression. In critical thought, common sense is subjected to analysis: it is the point of departure, and if the analysis does not depart, our thinking does not get anywhere. I conceive that I am using the same general method that Pepper does in his paper, and which he has stated more fully at the beginning of his book *World Hypotheses*.[4] Of course the danger of this method lies in the possibility that our beginning assumptions weight the whole theory in favor of preconceived conclusions, in the way that Aiken warns against in the first paragraph of his paper. I agree with Aiken's warning. Mitchell and Ayres think that my conclusions are unduly tainted with my initial assumptions. Whether they are and to what extent is up to the reader to decide.

Mitchell thinks that the conclusions are tainted with the substance-attribute metaphysics. I do not think so, but I may not have made my case clear at this point. He thinks that I am committed to the substance-attribute metaphysics apparently because I maintain that value is best understood as a property or attribute of an object. Yet I agree (I think unqualifiedly) with the paragraph of his Criticism beginning "There is actually no metaphysical distinction between things and attributes."[5]

I think that Mitchell is in error in saying that if value is conceived to be adjectival, axiology is deprived of "the flexibility and power of the denotative and relational logic." If this logic could not deal with adjectives and predicational attributes, it would be sadly circumscribed. The monadic form does deal with them, however, and *Principia Mathe-*

[4] Berkeley, Calif., 1942.   [5] See p. 404.

matica conceives the monadic and the dyadic forms to be generally parallel. C. I. Lewis points out in *An Analysis of Knowledge and Valuation* [6] that a function of two or more variables may always be conceived as a function of one variable. Modern logic deals quite adequately with the predicational attribute, and the fact that it holds monadic and n-adic forms to be parallel indicates that it furnishes no foundation for a metaphysical substance-attribute theory.

I think that my theory is a relational theory, but Mitchell has convinced me that my use of the word "putative" is unfortunate, and I agree that it had better be dropped. On pages 85–87 of *Perception and Aesthetic Value* I called value a relational property, and I had probably better go back to that mode of expression, as Mitchell advises. In my present paper, I did not mean "putative" in the sense of "fanciful" as opposed to "well-grounded." I meant that value is a property imputed to an object by virtue of the relation it is in. It may be and is very properly so imputed.

"Father of" is a relation. When a man is in this relation to someone else we very properly say that one of his characteristics or attributes is "fatherhood." This is a relational property or attribute in that it cannot be possessed outside of the relation. This fact, however, does not make it fancied or unreal. The illustration differs from the question of value under discussion in that the terms of the illustration are father and child, whereas in the case of value the terms are a sensibility and an object; but the attribution on the basis of the latter relation is no more fanciful than that on the basis of the former.

The fact that the terms of the relation in Mitchell's theory and those in mine are different is not of fundamental importance, because they can be logically correlated. I say that x in relation to y (where x is a sensibility and y is an object—not necessarily a "thing," but whatever can be held before attention) [7] gives rise to a property of y that can be symbolized by a monadic form, Vy (y having value), and this itself can be symbolized by a dyadic form, y B non y (y better than non y).

I agree with Mitchell in what he says about "standard value." If it connotes what he takes it to connote—something absolute—then the term had better be given up. I do not think it needs to connote this. Our thinking uses standards constantly, but these may be relative instead of absolute standards. Nevertheless, if it sounds as if it refers

[6] La Salle, Ill., 1947, p. 60.   [7] See p. 154, above.

to absolute standards, it should not be used, because I do not want to be open to that misunderstanding. Perhaps a better term would be "tested value," as I have suggested in my criticism [8] of Aiken's paper, and as other participants in this inquiry use it.

One more point. I do not say in my treatment of potentiality that a building is potentially dangerous or that bread is potentially nourishing. I say that the building *is* dangerous and the bread *is* nourishing. This is an important difference. We often do attribute properties to an object by virtue of a potentiality, and the attribution is perfectly proper. The building *is* dangerous because it might fall down even if it does not. The bread *is* nourishing because it might become chyme and chyle and eventually blood. Thus we attribute beauty to the B-minor Mass or to the landscape that is not being looked at, and again, the attribution may be quite correct.

Rejoinder by Rice

The criticisms that Mitchell and Geiger make of my paper are various, but I take it that they agree in offering as their main objection that I exaggerate the importance of feeling for value theory. Mitchell sees me as a companion of the disreputable Aristippus, and Geiger protests that the view I favor makes value "a kind of affective bath." Their criticisms on this score are made for the most part in such a general fashion—and apparently in Geiger's case out of such an intense affective state—that a general rather than a detailed answer seems to be called for.

Again, I repeat that I do not propose to define value *überhaupt* in terms of feeling alone. Only intrinsic value is so defined, and Mitchell complains on the other side (it seems to me with some inconsistency) that my set of definitions as a whole makes it necessary "to list nearly everything which common sense and social science and creative art refers to in value categories as 'extrinsic' or instrumental value." When the wind is nor-nor-west, then, I overemphasize intrinsic values, and when it is sou-sou-east I exaggerate the prevalence of instrumentalities.

My views on this point may be summarized as follows. The life process as a whole is a tissue of both intrinsic and instrumental values, wherein they are for the most part inseparably interwoven. But in order to judge it and to maximize the achievement of the good, the intellect must distinguish characteristics of the life process which in

[8] P. 369.

their brute occurrence are often found in intimate union. The process cannot be justified by its mere continuance, and by the instrumentalities thereto, but by its phases of consummation, its moments when it is capable of being prized, not for its consequences alone, but for its constituent quality. I have called this quality intrinsic value, and I have suggested joy or hedonic tone as the least unsatisfactory equivalent for it. To use Geiger's language, I have "abstracted" it—how could we have value theory or any other kind of theory without abstracting? —but I have not made a "hypostasis" of it. I have repeatedly insisted that affective tone is not a thing, or a substance, and that it never occurs apart from a life process and its physical, neurological, and social conditions. But affective tone is a characteristic of experience which occurs under highly variable conditions, and to recognize the quality when it occurs is much easier than to give a general statement of its conditions.

I have hazarded the conjecture, backed by a certain amount of evidence, that an adequate general statement of its conditions, if one is ever found, will be in neurological terms rather than in terms of such gross behavioral concepts as drive and interest. This is not to deny that needs, drives, and interests condition value; but, since man is a cerebrate animal (a truth which some psychological and philosophical schools are rediscovering rather belatedly), the needs and drives operate through a highly organized central nervous system in which the various influences and activities are compounded and given direction, and in which such a global phenomenon as feeling could be expected to find its proximate conditions, even if there were no experimental evidence to that effect.

If, as Mitchell puts it, this view implies that "a little gadget to record the form of the electrochemical nerve impulse is all that is needed to measure intrinsic value," I do not see why this should be a priori scandalous. Granting that the central tracts do have the role in determining affective tone to which the current empirical work is pointing, such a gadget, provided it could be devised (and I leave this an open question), would be at least as useful for our purpose as whatever gadget would be required, on Dewey's theory, to find a rough measure of the "prizing" in "the amount of energy that goes into the nourishing or the protecting behavior." [9] A scientifically minded behaviorist should not

[9] P. 7, above. Dewey is presumably referring to some such experiments as those by Warden (reported in O. Klineberg's *Social Psychology*, New York, 1940, pp. 66–

412 CRITICISMS AND REJOINDERS

object to gadgets. But I have also tried to make it clear that such a
gadget would not enable us to dispense with introspection—among
other reasons, in order to check up on the gadget—nor with the elaborate task of correlating intrinsic values and disvalues with their manifold economic, social, and aesthetic conditions—for which no gadget
could suffice.

The foregoing indicates the reply that should be made to Mitchell's
statement that an affective theory of intrinsic value makes value "the
direct concern of only one science (psychology), and the direct concern of no industry and no art." Although in the division of the sciences
psychology is usually assigned particular responsibility for clarifying
such terms as "interest," "desire," "satisfaction," and "feeling"—terms
which I believe all contributors to this symposium conceive to be of
special relevance to value theory—the psychological functions designated by them are not to be understood as operating in a vacuum.
Values and disvalues in one fashion or another interpenetrate the whole
of experience, and there is no science and no art on which we cannot
levy for an understanding of their sources and manifestations. Hence
an answer to Geiger's charge—which has been explicitly repudiated
in several places in my paper—that on my view "the 'socio-cultural'
context has little or no relevance for problems of value." Social factors
are among the most important and ubiquitous of the sources and
manifestations of value. But they operate only through individual
organisms, and the process comes to fruition in the conscious experience of individuals. What I am objecting to is the tendency of instrumentalists and other Hegelians to use "social" as an infinity-word and
an incantation which lulls analysis.

Geiger, similarly, ascribes to me the view that our moral problems
"are still unanswered because scientific naturalism has its limitations."
His argument: "Rice must accept some such premise to feel dissatisfied
with the efforts of the 'orthodox instrumentalist.'" What my paper
actually said was that the present revolt against naturalism "can be
attributed in part to the failure of empirical and naturalistic philoso-
phies, *at the present stage in their development,*[10] to offer ways of
resolving many predicaments of the individual." Geiger's spirit in

---

68), showing that a mother rat under optimum conditions will cross an electric grill
22.4 times to get to her young, 18.2 times to get food, 13.8 times to obtain sexual
satisfaction, and so forth.
[10] Italics added here.

interpreting my remarks confirms the fear that instrumentalism, with some of its younger representatives, is congealing into a Church, which conceives its doctrine as final and finished in all essentials, which arrogates to itself the sole right to act as spokesman for naturalism, and which is more concerned with extracting lip service to the creed of "scientific method" and "socio-cultural" conditioning than with pursuing the analysis of these concepts in the dispassionate and cooperative fashion which would ordinarily be regarded as scientific.

The readers of this symposium will, I believe, take as better founded Mitchell's criticism that my paper does not carry us very far toward its professed aim of relieving "the current tension between the sciences and the humanities." I must acknowledge that I have tried only to propose some general considerations pointing to the direction which such a difficult and complicated enterprise should take. Most important of these considerations, on my view, are, first, the extension of the conception of empirical method to make room for critical use of the three means of access to values—the arts, everyday observation, and self-observation—traditionally employed by "humanism," and second, the need for reinterpreting the notion of an "inner" life of feelings, symbols and self-rewards—phenomena which before Freud, Mead, and certain living psychologists such as Thorndike and Mowrer, were dealt with almost exclusively by the humanistic and religious traditions —in the light of concepts and methods which are emerging in the biological and social sciences. I am willing to concede to Mitchell that scarcely a beginning has been made in these tasks. But I hope that I have also offered somewhat detailed reasons for suspecting that my instrumentalist friends will not be able to help with these problems —or indeed to recognize their existence—until they outgrow some of the arbitrary and a priori limitations which their variety of behaviorism imposes on our investigation of mind.

Other, and less central, points made by my critics will have to be dealt with briefly.

1. Mitchell argues that there has been a closer historical correlation of affective value theories with the sciences, and of conative theories with the humanities, than vice versa, as my paper suggested. There is a great deal of historical support for his view if we consider the classical systems of ethics. But the context of my paper will show, I believe, that I was referring to the recent development of value theory as a

special branch of philosophy, in which, for example, Dewey and Perry have been on the scientific and conative side, and such men as Santayana, Prall, and Parker, taking their cues from aesthetics, have given more emphasis to the affective and "subjective" elements.

2. Mitchell holds that while Dewey's concept of "prizing" is not exact, "it is the right *sort* of word, and that is the main thing." For a view which stresses scientific method, I should think that exactitude were considerably more important than this statement indicates. But pragmatism, as it has often been pointed out, has not been agonizingly concerned with exactitude hitherto. The time may have come, however, when pragmatism can no longer advance by continuing to conceive itself as a kind of philosophical youth movement.

3. I was not attributing to Dewey, as Geiger implies, an early adherence to the doctrine of the reflex arc. Dewey's influential article on that topic which I cited attempted to *refute* the doctrine of the reflex arc, in favor of the doctrine of the "sensori-motor circuit," which emphasized equally but in a different, and I believe more tenable, fashion the importance of muscular movement in the perceptual act.

4. Muscular tension is, as nobody denies, an important factor in affective states. But Geiger fails to see my point that the proprioceptors, like the other sensory nerves, discharge into the central nervous system, where their effect is integrated with that of other factors.

5. Geiger asks for my sources on the question of the "nociceptors." The neurological evidence is summarized in E. D. Adrian's *Mechanism of Nervous Action;* [11] it is confirmed by everyday observation that lacerations of tissue are not always painful. When the laceration is confined to a very small area, or when the organism is absorbed in such activities as strenuous sports, the laceration may not be noticed, or may be felt as a pleasant tingle. My colleague in psychology, Professor S. B. Cummings, points out as an additional confirmation of this view, that we often see children picking a slight wound with apparent enjoyment—and that adults can verify the point introspectively by a similar experiment. The conclusion is that the discharges of the "nociceptors," as of the other sensory nerves, have a hedonic threshold, and produce pain or pleasantness only through their contribution to happenings in the cerebrospinal tract.

[11] Philadelphia, 1932, ch. iii.

CRITICISMS BY MORRIS

I

IT IS HARD to bring my reactions to Ayres's paper to a focus. Ayres is always explosive, and an explosion is good for this symposium. An exciting paradox emerges: the defenders of individuality, feeling, and emotion among us have proceeded with calmness and circumspection; Ayres defends sociality, science, "the tool-and-instrument-life process" with emotion and vehemence. It becomes difficult to untangle issues when those close to the artist write with the detachment of the scientist and the champions of science write with the enthusiasm of the poet. When we are told that from the point of view of science there is no problem of value, and that "nothing but science is true or meaningful," lo, we find that value problems, instead of being laid away as quiet ghosts, arise with even stronger tumult to plague us.

With what is perhaps the major emphasis intended by Ayres, I find myself in agreement. In so far as he is asserting that science is the most reliable method for attaining warranted assertions, and proposing that we extend this method boldly to the solution of personal and social problems, I accept his Deweyan statement and evaluation. Looked at in this way, his campaign is directed against those philosophers who claim to find in emotion a superior guide to science for getting reliable knowledge which is relevant to our personal and social ills. That there are still many persons who make this claim goes without saying. And I applaud the vigor of the campaign which Ayres conducts against them.

Nevertheless, it seems to me that Ayres has not focused his sights sharply enough. I fear that his shotgun tactics will wound some of those who might otherwise be on his side. I think he is not precise enough, not scientific enough, in his approach to value.

The notion of "life process" in which all values arise seems to me very vague. We are practically asked to choose between mystery-making or tool-making. Making love, making poems, making a dramatic life, if not explicitly condemned, are at least brushed aside by neglect. One gets the impression that our predominantly technological society is the unquestionable matrix into which men must fit themselves and their evaluations. There is no suggestion that individual men and women may be dissatisfied with aspects of this society, and may evaluate it negatively in terms of what it does to them. Scientific psychology today is exploring the depth and importance of individual differences; Ayres seems to be suggesting that any attempt of an individual to take account of his own individuality is to retreat to "emotion."

But we must not lump together uncritically those who appeal to emotion as a source of truth higher than science, and those who emotionally protest against identifying the scientific universe of discourse with "the universe of discourse of human life and action." For the life process is incredibly complex and pluralistic; and its future course is still, within limits, to be determined by human decision; the existing form of the life process is itself an occasion for evaluation and not an unquestioned standard for settling value problems.

Science is one factor in this life process, and a very important factor in determining its future. But the scientific study of the scientific enterprise shows us (scientifically) the importance of human activities other than those of science. To say that science alone is "meaningful" will only serve to alienate those persons who are not scientists, and may drive them into the ranks of those who are enemies of the scientific enterprise and of technology in general.

Ayres uses a very loose semantics. For, a good case can be made to support the view that a scientific study of signs shows us (scientifically) the importance of other kinds of signs than those used in science. And to admit this need not involve the claim that such areas of meaningful discourse as occur in the fine or applied arts are hostile to science or give us a knowledge superior to science. Mystery-making and scientific tool-making do not exhaust the alternatives of life-making. And we are not likely to avoid "mores nihilism" by limiting men to this choice.

The "present hubbub over value" cannot be dismissed so lightly. It arises from contemporary man's dissatisfaction with some of the results upon himself of his tool-making achievements, and his concern for what direction he shall henceforth give to the life process of which he is a part. He needs help not merely from science as it has existed; he needs, as far as it can be obtained, a science of man which will include a scientific axiology and a scientific semiotic. He needs this not in order to become simply a scientist or a tool-maker, but in order to do a better job of life-making. The elimination of the pseudo-problems in axiology is but a preliminary step, wholesome but insufficient. Dewey realizes this more fully than does Ayres. For to dull the edges of the problem of value is poor service to the scientific enterprise, and poorer service to man.

II

The significance of contextualism for axiology lies in its suggestion that value—like magnetism or meaning—is a field-phenomenon, that is, that specific value terms apply to something or other only in virtue of its place in a value-field or value-situation. So from a contextualist point of view the task of the axiologist is to distinguish a value-field from other types of fields, and to show the signification of specific value terms in relation to this field.

In this enterprise the methodological problem is where to begin: Should one first isolate the value-field and then attempt to relate specific value terms to discriminable aspects of the field, or should one first attempt to establish the signification of specific value terms and then identify the value-field as the field in which such terms are used? These two starting points may of course converge to the same result, and in the end this is what they must do if the contextualist analysis is cognitively adequate. But present contextualist approaches to value show considerable differences, and the question is why they do so.

Hahn suggests that differences in axiology may be dependent on differences in the various axiologists' world views. But since these differences occur also among contextualists it seems likely that something else is involved, namely, the confusion of the axiologist's own evaluations with what purports to be pure description. Just as the great historical treatises in ethics are at crucial points defenses of ethical systems rather than studies of moral behavior, so I suggest that present differences in axiology—even among contextualists—are, at crucial points, defenses of different evaluations rather than disagreements on the truth of statements about valuations. I believe that this is so even in the current controversies concerning the relation of evaluations and statements. I see no way out except by much more careful semiotical analyses and studies than axiologists have yet undertaken.

Hahn and Pepper, for instance, both begin with the account of pur-

posive behavior developed by Tolman, and both explicate the signification of value terms with respect to such behavior. But for Pepper, "whatever is intrinsically positive or negative in appetitions and aversions is
positive or negative purposive value" (so that value terms apply to any
animal's purposive behavior); [1] while Hahn, influenced by Dewey,
writes: "we find . . . that value experiences involve reflection or critical appraisal in varying degrees" [2] (or again, "Enjoyment of qualities
without some reference, anticipatory or retrospective, does not seem to
me to involve value").[3]

Now such differences within a contextualist approach need explanation and resolution. If our aim is to report, then we cannot avoid the responsibility of empirically investigating the conditions under which
persons do in fact employ the term "value"; if we can find a common
set of conditions we can report a common signification for the term; if
we find various sets of conditions, then we can report with some precision the ambiguity of the term. But if our aim is to construct a terminology for axiology, then we must make clear that fact and not confuse
the analytic sentences in our language with empirical sentences about
purposive behavior or about the signification which value terms actually
have to other persons.

Axiological writings today seem to me to be full of such confusions.
In other words, I believe not merely that many of the value terms used
by axiologists are themselves appraisive and not designative terms, but
that many of the basic "doctrines" of axiology are tautologies. And one
reason why this may be so is that the analytic sentences in the language
of a given axiologist are often analytic evaluations which serve to advance the strategies of the given axiologist, and so are presented as if
they were designative statements rather than the form of basic evaluations. To say with Hahn that prizings (or "immediate values") contain
some measure of reflection may (or may not) be a true account of the
(or a) signification of the term "prizing"; but it may also serve to tip
the value scales away from "enjoyment" toward "careful reflection,"
that is, may be an analytic evaluation quite different from those which
appear in the writings of C. I. Lewis, or Parker, or Rice. This suggests
that the domain of the analytic within axiological systems needs careful
exploration. We have learned to distinguish analytic and synthetic state-

[1] S. C. Pepper, *A Digest of Purposive Value*, Berkeley, Calif., 1937, p. 49.
[2] P. 122, above.   [3] P. 121, above.

ments; we must as axiologists learn to be as careful in distinguishing analytic and synthetic evaluations.

In concentrating on the single point that axiology must become more semiotically and observationally oriented, I have of course not done justice to Hahn's paper as a whole. With the direction and intent of Hahn's contextualistic approach I am in basic sympathy, and I find his paper rich in specific suggestions. It is only because I share so fully his conviction of the importance of contextualism that I have stressed the problems which a further development of this position must meet. It must carefully isolate the value-field, it must develop a terminology to talk about this field, it must experimentally determine the signification of value terms in current use in their connection with other phases of the value-field. As this is done, a scientific axiology will arise. Today we are merely at the frontier of such an axiology.

Rejoinder by Ayres

The charge of "loose semantics" is an old one. Many years ago Morris Cohen attacked something I had written with the charge, that "Ayres' thinking is as loose as his syntax," and only a couple of years ago Henry Hazlitt brought in much the same indictment. In every case, however, the balance of the criticism has made it abundantly clear that what the critic really objected to was what I was saying; and I think that is true also of Morris's comments on the present article.

At different points in my paper I have raised the issue of supernaturalism and the issue of philistinism. As I think every reasonably careful reader would agree, it is with regard to the former issue that I have proposed to accept Professor Adler's challenge and to declare that "nothing but" science is true or valuable. Morris says that "Mystery-making and scientific tool-making do not exhaust the alternatives of life-making." I would reply that the issue of supernaturalism is indeed not the only one that science raises. There is the issue of philistinism, and there is also, for example, the issue of university organization. To divide a university curriculum into the sciences, the social studies, and the humanities may be a useful and reasonable procedure; and the same may perhaps be said of the assignment of philosophy to the humanities. But that does not mean that philosophy (or the humanities generally) is another alternative to science in the sense in which supernaturalism is alternative to science. Surely Morris does not mean that, with regard to the issue of supernaturalism, there are three alternatives: mystery-making, scientific tool-making, and philosophy!

I do not believe that any reasonably careful reader could conclude from my article that in drawing the line at supernaturalism I mean to leave the fine arts and human personality—in sum, everything that lies outside the curricular limits of the sciences as defined by university organization—on the far side of that line; or that in drawing the line at supernaturalism I mean to brush aside, if not explicitly to condemn, making love, making poems, or making a dramatic life.

It may be that we would be saved these misunderstandings if we were to use a notation which employed distinct symbols for (a) that which is distinguished from supernaturalism, (b) that which is characterized by instrumental techniques, and (c) that which, at the University of Chicago, is pursued in Ryerson, Kent, Rosenwald, and the buildings of Hull Court. But I doubt it; for these meanings, a, b, and c, interpenetrate each other, so that we would have just as much trouble in picking our symbols as we now have in keeping our meanings clear.

I sometimes wonder, as Geiger does, whether excessive concern with notation is not at least partly subterfuge: an escape from substantive issues into an algebraic looking-glass land where, like the Lady of Shalott, one deals only with reflections. This suspicion is stirred by something Morris says in his present comments—or rather, by something he has led up to and then failed to say.

In his last paragraph Morris says that our present difficulty "arises from contemporary man's dissatisfaction with some of the results upon himself of his tool-making achievements, and his concern for what direction he shall henceforth give to the life process of which he is a part," and I agree. Indeed, I think nearly everybody would. But does this mean that we have carried tool-making too far? That is what the form of the sentence suggests; and this suggestion is intensified by the next sentence, which remarks that man "needs help not merely from science as it has existed. . . ."

I think Morris ought to be quite point-blank in saying whether this is what he means; for if it is, he is in serious difficulties. The sentence which I just broke off goes on to indicate our further need of "a science of man which will include a scientific axiology and a scientific semiotic." If this isn't tool-making, what is it? Is it just an escape mechanism? What is the point to accepting science as "the most reliable method for attaining warranted assertions," and then saying that man's need is not simply to become "a scientist or a tool-maker, but . . . to do a better job of life-making"? Is this a proposal that life-making shall be conducted on the basis of unwarranted assertions?

I do not really suppose it is. But unless it is, I do not see that Morris has any quarrel with me. For I think, and I think I have said with a fair degree of precision, that tool-making can be conceived to be carried too far only with reference to the superstitions and coercions by which men have been immemorially bound (that is, too far for existing institutions); that there is no conflict between tool-making and love-making, beauty-making, and life-making—on the contrary, that tool-making (including Morris's axiology and semiotic) is the way of life and love and beauty for all mankind; and that our dissatisfaction and confusion can be resolved, not by dispensing with closed plumbing or atomic fission (behind which there always lie the "insufferable gadgets" of an earlier day), but only by dispensing with the tyrannies and superstitions which engender confusion and dissatisfaction today just as they have always done throughout the past. If Morris knows how to be clearer about these matters than I have been, I only hope he will be quick about it!

FURTHER COMMENT BY MORRIS

Ayres has lessened some of my worries: he has made clear that his basic opposition was science and supernaturalism, and not that of science and other human activities. His original paper did not make this clear enough to me, and I welcome the clarification.

Let me in turn try to reassure Ayres. I do not think we have carried tool-making too far; I do not think we can carry science too far; I do not propose that life-making be conducted on the basis of unwarranted assertions. My point was merely that since life-making is not exhausted by making science and making tools, we should not depreciate or make more difficult the work of artists and statesmen and prophets by saying that nothing but science is meaningful, or by saying that from the scientific point of view there is no problem of value.

REJOINDER BY HAHN

The issue raised by Morris in connection with my paper is a fundamental one which would require more space for an adequate answer than is at my disposal. His main point, I take it, is that "present differences in axiology—even among contextualists—are, at crucial points, defenses of different evaluations rather than disagreements on the truth of statements about valuations."

In my constructive paper I suggested that metaphysical differences may be responsible for many basic differences in axiology. Morris asserts that something more than different world views—namely, different analytic evaluations—is required to account for the axiological differences and cites as evidence the differences between Pepper's position and my own. Both of us start with Tolman's account of psychological facts, but influenced by Dewey, I give one interpretation, and Pepper gives another. Here Morris apparently thinks that I have confused an analytic evaluation with what I take to be pure description: that is, my assertion that value experience involves reflection or critical appraisal in varying degrees is analytic rather than synthetic and expresses my high estimate of careful reflection rather than designates any facts.

I am quite willing to grant that world views are not the only factors responsible for axiological differences, but my variations from Pepper's *Digest of Purposive Values* hardly demonstrates this point; for in this work Pepper is developing a mechanistic position rather than the contextualism of *Aesthetic Quality;* and at least part of the difference between us may stem from the fact that as a contextualist I do not think I can make as sharp a distinction between cognitive and causal references as he apparently thinks possible on mechanistic grounds.

For that matter, however, for reasons which I shall not attempt to outline here, I am not sure that Pepper has given a large enough place to cognitive factors even on mechanistic grounds; but I think this is in the main a matter of interpreting the evidence rather than simply expressing an analytic evaluation. It is true that I give a high rating to critically accepted or evaluated prizings and enjoyments—would not most of us do so?—but I do not think I am merely expressing this appraisal rather than designating or clarifying factual material. The facts concerning the place of reflective or appraisive factors in value experiences are not, I confess, as clear and unambiguous as I should wish, and purity is not one of the distinguishing traits I should claim for the more helpful facts or descriptions offered.

As I have indicated in my comments on the papers of Lepley and

Mitchell, I do not wish to settle the question of the place of reflective factors in value experience on a purely definitional basis. Perhaps we might agree initially that the field of immediate values, at least, is determined by some experience of valuing and then work on our differences of interpretation in regard to the field so delimited. At any rate, I quite agree with Morris on the need for careful exploration of the domain of the analytic within axiological systems.

I

WHAT A PLEASURE IT IS to read Jessup's paper! So empirical and straightforward, free of the indirections and dogmatisms of the typical behaviorist or instrumentalist. Let me quote certain sentences which deserve to stand as mottoes for any serious treatment of value: "Judgment of value can be verified only by value, not by fact simple." "For value-judgment, the relevant consequences of value are values." "A specific feeling may be deferred, sublimated or sacrificed, but only always in the interest of another or other specific feelings." "The surrender of life . . . is no exception. Surrender of life is not a denial of felt value, but rather the distillation or concentration of it in one supreme moment."

It is, I suppose, much more exciting to write a commentary on a philosophical paper with which you do not agree than on one with which you are in basic agreement. On the other hand, it is of the utmost importance for further work in a field to discover areas of agreement with other students of that field, so that time and energy may not be wasted in polemics and explanations, and progress may be made in a cooperative fashion from a common standpoint. I shall, therefore, begin my commentary by setting down briefly and succinctly the points where I believe myself to be in agreement with Jessup. It will be seen that they are crucial for the further development of the subject. I will then consider certain matters with regard to which I am not so sure of agreement, or at least of understanding.

First, then, the points of agreement.

1. The field of values is an "inspectional" field. I should say—but it is only a difference in language—a field of knowledge by acquaintance for the investigator, and knowledge by description for his associates.

2. This field consists of desires, satisfactions, frustrations and evaluations.

3. The elements of the field are, if private, no more private than the data, sensations, of the physical sciences. But, I should add, they are not merely private, since, if knowable by acquaintance by the person who has them, they are knowable by description by people who do not have them; they are as public, therefore, as stars and atoms.

4. A distinction must be made between a descriptive value-judgment and an operational value-judgment. The former states or predicts the existence of a value in the generic sense of a desire or satisfaction; the latter is itself a *value-charged* judgment about a value, and aims at reconstructing the value itself—it is appraisal or evaluation. Appraisal or evaluation is never a pure factual judgment, but is itself the expression of a value of the person who makes the judgment. The descriptive value-judgment, on the other hand, is a judgment of fact like any other. My own distinction, which is, I think, parallel with Jessup's, is between judgments or statements *of* value and judgments or statements *about* value.

So far so good, but right here I am not wholly confident of my understanding of Jessup or of my agreement with him; yet, on the whole, I am inclined to think that any misunderstanding or disagreement is due to differences in terminology. What I seem to miss is the emphatic recognition of a judgment of value more immediate than evaluative, operational value-judgment; but doubtless what Jessup calls "value predication" [1] is what I am looking for.

For example, we have the following discriminable types of statement:

1) Descriptive judgment simple—"Wine is alcoholic."

2) Primary or simple statement or expression *of* value—"I like wine" or "Wine is good." This is Jessup's value predication.

3) Descriptive value-judgment—"He likes wine" or "It is true that I like wine" or "He finds wine to be good." This is the same as what I call judgment *about* value.

4) Operational value-judgment or evaluation—"an operation upon given values such that it modifies or qualifies their further character." [2] For example, "I ought not to like wine."

Now sometimes I am not sure whether Jessup recognizes all these distinctions, owing to his inclusive use of the term "value-judgment." This is a matter I should be glad to have him clear up.

There are two other matters about which I am even more in doubt, but perhaps with regard to them also I am really in agreement. The first concerns the problem of the confirmation of values, or verification of values. Jessup asserts that value-judgments—and here I think he is referring to value-judgments in senses (2) and (4) distinguished above —are verified or confirmed through *agreement* with other value-judgments. The agreement may be between the judgments of the same person (in the personal order) or it may be between judgments of different persons (in the social order). Thus, if I see a thing yellow and you see it as yellow, my judgment is confirmed; so if I find it tastes good now and also next week, or if you also find that it tastes good, the value-judgment is confirmed. There is, he says, a "social dimension" of values on which confirmation of this type is based. He admits that the individual may be right and the group wrong, but says that, even so, eventual coming to agreement is presupposed. "Two 'here-now' facts, either of sensation or of felt value, are in their degree evidence—positive if in agreement, negative if in disagreement—evidence of something in the object or in the subject upon which they are directed or from which they derive."

Now there is no doubt that in some way or in some sense the individual feels that his value-judgments are confirmed when he agrees with himself or when other people agree with him. He has, as he may say, more confidence in his own judgment. But what is the interpretation of this fact? There is one type of case which need give us no trouble, namely, when evaluation depends, as it so often does in part, upon a causal chain of facts. If, for example, I judge that Henry Wallace's trip to Europe, with the speeches he made there, was wrong, because I think it tended in the direction of strengthening the forces for war, and I find that you agree with me, for the same factual reason, then my judgment is confirmed because the factual proposition upon which it partly depended is confirmed, like any other such proposition, by agreement with another person. Of course the entire judgment is not a pure factual judgment, but is, as a whole, a value-judgment, consisting of two parts, one volitional, "I hate war," and another propositional, "Wallace's activities tend towards war."

But let us consider a judgment of value that does not depend upon a causal proposition: "Picasso's painting *The Tomato Plant* is beautiful." Here again my judgment is in some way confirmed if you, or at least if certain people, agree with me. Now in this case it seems clear to me that confirmation means that the value that I attach to the picture is some-how strengthened by agreement, and that it would be diminished by disagreement. In other words, confirmation brings intensification, dis-confirmation brings diminution of intensity of satisfaction. But this phenomenon does not prove that value has some sort of objectivity in the sense that it is an entity, but only that, as Jessup says, values have a social dimension, in the specific sense that we want to share our values, and when we fail the intensity of our satisfaction is qualified. We want to escape, here as elsewhere, from the loneliness of our individuality, and the whole impact of our being upon the world is magnified through agreement.

Clearly, then, the situation is not the same as when a judgment of fact is confirmed by agreement with someone else's judgment. For, although the same desire to escape from loneliness operates here too, another factor enters, namely, that the agreement of another person means additional evidence gathered by that person and made available to me. We must therefore carefully distinguish between these two factors in confirmation of judgments of fact by agreement—intensifica-tion of the value of believing through sharing of belief, on the one hand, and provision of additional evidence supplied by a fellow investigator or knower, on the other hand.

The second matter with regard to which I am not sure whether I agree with Jessup or not concerns the distinction between fact and value. Prima facie I am willing to stand by such statements of his as these: "To know fact and to take an interest in it, is not the same thing. Truth as verifiable belief about fact is a wider experience than value as felt satisfaction in fact." "A description of an object never strictly denotes value."[3] ". . . 'good' predicated of something is neither a summary description of it nor an addition to the description of it."[4] Yet, while from these statements it does seem to follow that the quota-tion from Dewey[5] is true as it stands: "The significance of being, though not its existence, is the emotion it stirs, the thought it sustains," it does not follow (to rewrite the quotation) that being is not the stirring of emotion, the sustaining of thought. In other words, the recognition of the validity of the distinction between judgments of facts and judg-ments of value does not prejudice the issue between naturalism or

[3] P. 133.   [4] Pp. 133–134.
[5] *Intelligence in the Modern World*, ed. by J. Ratner, New York, 1939, p. 248.

materialism and idealism. And the reason why it does not is that every judgment of value in senses (2) and (4) is for somebody. Let me explain further. It is fair to hold that every moment of a human being's experience is, on the whole, either a satisfaction or a frustration—a value or a disvalue. Yet if there is a human being who is my enemy, and his satisfaction is caused by some injury inflicted on me, I shall not make the judgment "His injury of me is good," for that would be equivalent to my saying "His injury of me is good for me," which would be nonsense. Now, then, if one holds, as I do, that existence consists of centers of feeling—of satisfactions and frustrations—there would be a sense in which value and reality would be co-extensive, yet the distinction between the descriptive value-judgment, "There is a satisfaction or value of a certain kind there" and the judgment of value, "That satisfaction is good (a satisfaction for me, or for us)" would still hold. What I miss now and then in Jessup's treatment is a recognition of what I call the centricity of the judgment of value. Yet, on the other hand, he does seem at times to recognize this, for does he not himself affirm "the value attitude has no shadow of meaning if it is isolated from that which it is from"?

II

I make the following comments upon Morris's paper with diffidence owing to the fact that I have not read his *Signs, Language and Behavior,* to which he often refers for elucidation of his ideas, and I fear that I shall not have time for it before the deadline set for all of our contributions in this inquiry.

First, I note with gratified interest Morris's careful qualification of the behavioral point of view, to which he feels himself committed. He expresses his willingness to use the results of introspection, though with caution. But if he goes thus far, why not farther? Why not use art and literature? Isn't it really *unempirical,* not to say foolish, to deny ourselves any available information that might conceivably help us to solve the problems of men? Why, when we are dealing with substances capable of communication, should we not study them with the aid of their free communications, instead of confining ourselves to the methods alone available for the study of non-communicating substances such as metals and rats? Surely Morris did not discover his "paths of life" this way, but from the reflections of philosophers and religious teachers as freely communicated to us in their writings. Man will never submit to experimentation as a rat will, and whatever is discovered about men through experiment must be interpreted in terms of the experimenter's self-knowledge of striving, frustration, suffering or happiness, in order to possess any significance for the theory or control of valuations.

With regard to all of Morris's criticisms of Dewey's position, I am in full accord. The differences between him and me seem to be so much mere matters of language that I feel sure we could easily come to agreement. Against the view of values as being wholly situational, he states with full lucidity the fact that the individual has certain enduring preferences with respect to which other preferences are evaluated—these I call the "matrix self"—preferences which carry through from one situation to another, and justify, in a manner, the old distinction between means and ends. From this follows a fact of prime importance, which has, nevertheless, been neglected (if I remember correctly) by every other participant in this symposium, namely, that situational preferences may be harmful, in the sense of frustrating the enduring needs and choices of the individual. Why have we paid so little heed to this fact of evil, I wonder?

It is, moreover, significant of Morris's largeness of view that in the course of the discussion of this matter he writes (with an implied criticism of some of our colleagues)

for we must distinguish between the motivations of an organism and the mere continual survival of the organism. Survival is not necessarily the dominant drive of an organism, and in relation to an actual drive objects and actions may be valued which do not in fact permit the continued existence of the organism.

We must, I should say, find a place in value theory for heroism and suicide, both of which lead us, in my opinion, and I believe also in Morris's, beyond a purely biological to a social and perhaps supersocial approach. In some ways, suicide and heroism are the most significant facts of experience.

Of Morris's discussion of the relation between scientific and value expressions, I write with special diffidence because of my ignorance of his book. Judging by the few pages devoted to this topic in his symposium paper, my attitude toward his views is a mixture of assent and dissent. On the side of assent, I should suppose that his distinction between designative and appraisive signs covers in part the distinction which I draw between volitional and descriptive expressions. Yet I cannot fully agree with him when he declares that if "good," ordinarily an appraisive sign, refers to the need-reducing properties of an object, it is wholly a designative sign. I suppose that what he is asserting is something like the following: if I say "water is good," meaning merely that water quenches thirst, I am making a statement no different in kind from "water boils at 100 degrees centigrade." But I think, on the contrary, that this would be true only if by "thirst" I meant a pure mechanical process, but usually "thirst" includes a felt want as well. Hence when I say "water quenches thirst" I am expressing a desire of my own or of someone with whom I can sympathize, and my language is not purely descriptive, but is partly volitional. Or, in Morris's terminology, if I use the word "good" in the expression "water is good because it quenches thirst," "good" is partly an appraisive and not solely a denotative sign. On a pure behavioral or mechanistic theory, all appraisive signs become pure designative signs. For to be high up in a series of perferences can then mean no more than that, as a matter of statistics, most organisms, or a single organism most of the time or on most occasions, have been moved by a sign in such a way as to appropriate the object signified by the sign, and therefore will probably be so moved in the future. "Left wing" behaviorists are, therefore, consistent in denying the difference between volitional and descriptive expressions (or between appraisive and designative signs).

As for Morris's statement that, despite the distinction between appraisive and designative signs, valuation may be scientific, I feel that either I have not fully understood him or that he is not quite clear in his own mind with regard to some of the subtle points involved. But perhaps this is again a subject that would be clarified for me if I had read his book. If by a scientific valuation he means one, as he says, "made after careful scrutiny, the utilization of reliable knowledge, the consideration of consequences," then, of course, it may be scientific. But even so, the basic difference between evaluation and science remains—that the one is an expression of a wish, the other of a fact. It is indeed true that a wish may be modified by knowledge of the consequences that would ensue if action upon it took place—it may even be abandoned—and the more scientific this knowledge is, in the sense defined above, the better; but the expression of the wish as so modified, or of the resolution to abandon the wish for the sake of some other wish, is not a scientific, but a volitional expression. And no amount of scientific knowledge can *create* a wish. This fact is ignored by some of those who hope to save the world through science, who seem to forget that what counts is the bearing of science upon volition. The same scientific knowledge, including knowledge of one's own and other people's desires, may drive one man to suicide, another to murder, a third to saintly effort. It is so often taken for granted that scientific knowledge will be used by a benevolent will, as if there had been no scientifically trained Nazi sadists.

Finally, I wish to consider the important problem of the sense in which volitional expressions may be confirmed. Morris says "confirmation is . . . desirable and proper with regard to appraisive signs no less than to designative signs." The assertion "the table is good" is confirmed "by observation of whether one does or does not accord a preferential place to the object when one acts with respect to it in the situation in which it is appraised." Let us now consider the case of the table with some care. I think we can assume that the expression "the table is good" is meant either as general, that is to say, as an hypothesis with unlimited validity for anyone, or else as referring to a single person. If the former, it may be rephrased as "If someone wants something upon which to place things securely, this table is that sort of object, and will satisfy his wish." Then surely, if someone does in fact want something upon which to place things and finds the table to be that sort of thing and that his wish is satisfied by using it, there is confirmation of the expression, although since it is general, no proof of its truth. The expression is confirmed much as any hypothesis is confirmed by a single case. If, on the other hand, the expression refers to one person, being equivalent to "the table is good for *K*" then if *K* finds the table the kind of thing that does satisfy his wish to have something upon which to place things, the statement is again confirmed and confirmation is equivalent to truth. And in both cases, confirmation appears to be of the same kind as confirmation of empirical descriptive statements. Yet I am not sure that it is quite the same, after all, and for the reason given in the discussion of "water is good because it quenches thirst." For just as when I say "water is good," and so forth, I am expressing my own interest in water, so when I say "the table is good," I am expressing my own interest in the table, and if anyone, be he *K* or someone else, also finds it good, then there is confirmation in another sense than that of verification, namely, in the sense which Stevenson has called "agreement in attitude."

That confirmation of appraisive signs (or volitional expressions) has this second meaning can be shown by examining a case where the appraisive sign signifies not a means object, such as a table, but an end object, such as a work of art. Suppose I say, "The Brahms First Symphony is beautiful." Now one might, to be sure, try to interpret this as saying "If anyone hears the Brahms First, he will enjoy it," when, if someone does hear it and enjoy it, the expression will be confirmed, though not proved; or if, alternatively, it is interpreted as saying "*K* will enjoy the symphony if he hears it," and *K* does hear the symphony and enjoy it, the expression would be proved true. But neither of these statements is what I mean when I say "The Brahms First Symphony is beautiful." What I do mean is something like the following: "The Brahms First gives imaginative satisfaction to my desires in an orderly fashion, and I want it to give satisfaction to yours, so that we may share this experience." That I am not saying that it is beautiful because it *will* satisfy you or someone else if you hear it is shown by the fact that I shall still say that it is beautiful even if you do not take satisfaction in it when you hear it. In other words, it is not like a scientific hypothesis which can be refuted by a single counter-instance or like a prediction regarding an individual, which may likewise be refuted. On the other hand, if you do take satisfaction in it, you will confirm my expression in the sense of agreeing with me, and if you do not like the symphony, you will be refuting my expression in the sense of not agreeing with me and not supporting me in my desire to share my satisfaction with you. The situation is the same as when, fighting for a cause, you fight on the same side with me, who want and need your help in my endeavor, whereas if you take the other side, you are disagreeing with me and opposing and frustrating my will. The situation is again analogous to—I should venture to say that it is metaphysically the same as—when I pull in one direction and you pull with me, as contrasted with the case where you pull in the opposite direction, against me. Here I submit, is another meaning for confirmation, different from, though not incompatible with, the meaning of verification. In the one case we have to do with volitional expressions that are parts of interested acts; in the other, with disinterested statements of facts.

Naturally I do not deny that experiment may, when interpreted by men of culture and rich personal experience, yield knowledge of human values. Morris's investigations will perhaps show us how much may thus be achieved.

III

I note with pleasure a broad agreement among some members of this symposium on the general nature of value, or at least with regard to the field where it is to be found. Thus Aiken, Rice, Jessup, Pepper and myself (and perhaps also, in part, Lepley), are agreed that value, and its negative, reside in the facts of desire, satisfaction, and frustration. I think Garnett could be included if he were to admit that what he calls "activity" is to be identified generically with appetition. There are, of course, differences of opinion concerning other aspects of the general theory of value among the members of this group. Thus, for example, Pepper and I are at odds over the nature of statements of value, and Aiken thinks my concept of value "too voluntaristic," meaning, I suspect, that I do not sufficiently recognize the part played by "reason" in standard value, or that I stress desire rather than joy (Rice's beautiful word). In my rejoinder to Pepper I have endeavored to meet his criticisms. I wish I had space, but unfortunately do not, to consider Aiken's criticisms. I can only say, as I like to put it metaphorically, that desire is hidden in the heart of joy, and joy, and often anguish, in the heart of desire; and that reason can never be the master, but no more (although that is much) than the seeing-eye dog of desire.

Those of us who agree on fundamentals should recognize, however, that most of the more subtle and complex problems of value, such as are involved in the conflicts of value and the methods of resolving them, are not solved by a generic definition. Some of these problems I have touched on in Sections III and IV of my essay.[6] With regard to these matters also there is room for much disagreement. Moreover, even though, as I believe, the categories of value can be made intelligible and accurate on the basis of given experience alone, some way to translate them into the language of behavioralists like Morris should

6 See pp. 233 ff.

be found. For to every value in oneself there corresponds a visual or auditory behavior pattern in the experience of another. And, to call attention to another important matter, we must accept the challenge of Lepley and show how, granting the continuity of man and nature, the concept of value can be applicable to sub- (and also super?) human realities. How I for my part believe this can be done by following the Leibnizian path, I have explained in brief in my rejoinder to Lepley. And last, we should not ignore, as I fear we all have, the views of those who hold to a religious, supernaturalistic concept of value.

Both Geiger and Pepper think my concept of value leads to an overstressing of the place of force in human affairs. But let me say at once that I am a man of peace. During the crisis with Hitler I was one who hoped against hope that some arrangement could be worked out to avoid war. When war came, I disapproved of the unconditional surrender policy (only God is unconditional), and I still disapprove, despite Mr. Stimson's apology, of the ruthless use of force represented in areal bombing, and especially in the dropping of *two* atomic bombs, thus cruelly wiping out fair cities and whole populations, when the war was virtually won, and, incidentally, destroying forever our own security. In the mounting crisis with Stalinate Russia, I am again in favor of all means that might lead to a peaceful *détente.* But, on the other hand, I cannot close my eyes to the strain of tragedy in life itself and in all of nature, for which the centricity of values is partly responsible, whereby the good of one center may not be the same as that of another. The relation of the beast of prey to its victim is a flagrant example. The relations of individual men and of societies to one another are not exempt from this tragic conflict, on elementary and on higher planes. In the end, if all methods of persuasion and compromise fail, it may again become necessary to fight for the continued existence of our way of life. And this itself is a paradox—I mean that a civilization, whose religion is that of love, should be compelled to take up the sword. The study of such paradoxes is the desperately, increasingly urgent need of our "time of troubles."

There is just one contribution to this symposium to which I have to confess a feeling of hostility—that of Ayres. I should be faithless if I failed to express my resentment over what he says regarding the claims of artists and art lovers. If he had put up even the slightest show of argument I should have been obliged to answer it. But it is so easy to say the word "humbug" (his own word) that I shall myself refrain from using it.

REJOINDER BY JESSUP

Parker's first point of criticism notes my "inclusive use of the term 'value-judgment,'" and a consequent, at least apparent, indeterminateness in terminology, which he invites me to clear up. What he seems to miss, he says, "is the emphatic recognition of a judgment of value more immediate than evaluative, operational value-judgment. . . ."

Parker himself lists four "discriminable types of statement" relevant to value discussion: (1) Descriptive judgment simple. (2) Primary or simple statement or expression *of* value. (3) Descriptive value-judgment. (4) Operational value-judgment or evaluation. I am in agreement with this classification and believe that I have observed it in my essay, though with some differences in phrasing. I clarify my usage in relation to Parker's as follows:

1. Parker's first type of statement is not a value-judgment at all. It is a factual judgment.

2. His "expression *of* value" is, as he rightly supposes, my "value predication." It is meant to denote an act "more immediate than evaluative, operational judgment." However, I do not in my essay intend to subsume this act under the inclusive term "judgment of value." It is the act of *valuing*, or as a statement, it is an expression of valuing. I think there is no disagreement except in Parker's use and my non-use of the term "value-judgment" to cover valuing.

3. Parker is right in saying that my descriptive value-judgment is the same as what he calls judgment *about* value.

4. We are agreed also on the meaning of operational value-judgment or evaluation.

Concerning, then, "all these distinctions" which Parker is not sure that I recognize as discriminable types of statements relevant to value, I observe: That there are only three types of value statements mentioned, namely, (2), (3), and (4). Of these, only (3) and (4) are value-judgments, and they are in my essay clearly distinguished from each other. (2) is a value expression, or a value fact, ultimately the referent of value-judgment but not itself a judgment.

Parker's second point of comment concerns my account of verification of value-judgment by the method of agreement. Parker holds, and

I agree, that a felt value may be and normally is strengthened or diminished in intensity as it is or is not shared by others—on the principle that we normally "desire to escape from loneliness," or, as I say, that our values commonly have social dimension. However, he holds further, such sharing or agreement in matters of value does not constitute verification in the sense in which verification is meant in factual matters. In the latter, a second observation in agreement with a first is "additional evidence" for belief in the first. In matters of value, agreement is not additional evidence; it "does not prove that value has some sort of objectivity in the sense that it is an entity. . . ."

As an example of a judgment of value which is not verifiable in the established sense of being supportable by evidence in the way of agreements Parker offers the statement, "Picasso's *Tomato Plant* is beautiful." His position, I understand, is that if the judgment expresses the fact that I once feel aesthetic satisfaction in the painting it is then and therefore beautiful and no further experiences of aesthetic satisfaction, my own or others, are evidence for the proposition.

This, I think, is correct; but it does not quite touch the question of verifiability of value. The statement "X is beautiful" may express two kinds of judgment. It may be (1), as it is in Parker's comments, a reporting judgment, that is, an historical judgment, meaning "I now feel or I once felt aesthetic satisfaction in X;" or it may be (2) a generalizing judgment to the effect that the object X in view of evidence has continuing or stable possibilities of evoking aesthetic satisfactions. In the second sense it is verifiable, and it is so in terms of agreements (the evidence in view) and because norms have been set up. The norms are social satisfaction, recurrent satisfactions, and correlations or integrations with other satisfactions. These norms are, however, themselves felt values, and hence proving a value does not mean that it is made into some sort of bogus entity independent of feeling.

Evaluation, the generalizing judgment of value, is not constituted by a simple or insulated act of valuing. It includes, aside from factual matters to which it ordinarily refers, (a) a given felt value, that which is judged, and (b) a second, larger or more comprehensive felt value, in reference to which the first is judged. A comparison of values is involved. The first may be, for example, a simple desire for or enjoyment of a good-tasting food (one which I like to indulge in); the second, my health (which I want to maintain); my family budget (which I try to keep balanced); my family itself (which I want to provide for), and so on and so forth, to considerations conceivably as wide as the world and as long as time.

In brief, any given felt value may be seen to have consequences, and the consequences, experienced or forseen, evoke a further feeling or valuing such that the given felt value may be rejected. Felt value does, accordingly, have "a kind of objectivity" and can therefore be verified. And this verification is a matter of agreement. If a second or third or nth experience of the felt value in question occurs or can be predicted, then it is verified. Multiplying and varying the circumstances of its occurrence strengthens the verification. But if in multiplied and varied experience it does not recur, then it is unverified. It remains historically an occurrent value but becomes dimensionally questionable or unacceptable, that is, in terms of revised or enlarged feeling.

As for Parker's final comment, I do not intend to raise or prejudice the issue between materialism and idealism. In maintaining the distinction between fact and value, I merely insist that whatever the larger framework or theory within which value is to be discussed, there must be some discrimination between the cognitively real and the value real, between true and good. Parker himself makes the distinction within his idealistic framework. He holds that every real is in a sense a value or a disvalue for someone, and then observes that "Yet if there is a human being who is my enemy, and his satisfaction is caused by some injury inflicted on me, I shall not make the judgment 'His injury of me is good,' for that would be equivalent to my saying 'His injury of me is good for me,' which would be nonsense."

I think this observation supports my point. The correct way of speaking of such a case is to say that my enemy's injury of me is real for him and real for me but that it is good for him and bad for me. The distinction does emphasize the "centricity" of value and also the nature of value as a further determination within the real.

REJOINDER BY MORRIS

Parker's comments give me an occasion to clarify my argument for a "behavioral" approach in axiology.

The behavioral approach which is suggested is entirely *methodological*. As such it involves no choice of a psychology, neither "behaviorism" nor any other. It merely suggests that a good place for axi-

ologists to begin is the study of preferential behavior; it does not say
that this is necessarily the place for them to end. And it is a good
place to begin only if we can get, in this way, an initial set of terms
which cause less dispute as to their applicability than do such terms
as "value," "good," "felt satisfaction," "joy," "satisfaction of a need,"
"wish," and the like. No claim is made that such terms are meaningless; the problem is merely which terms are the best foundations for
a science of axiology. The slow but steady orientation of psychologists
around a behavioral methodology may give us a clue as to how axiologists might proceed with profit.

This approach does not prohibit us from using "art and literature,"
or the verbal reports which we or others make. For we can study—as
in the reported experiments we do study—preferential behavior to
works of art and literature. There need be nothing artificial in such
experimentation; the data are gathered by allowing persons to choose
among works of art and literature. The question then is to find what
persons make what selections or rejections under what conditions.

And if we can find the relation of verbal behaviors which contain
such terms as "good," "value," "joy," to the preferential behavior of
those persons who produce such signs, then such words may be employed to give us data about preferential behavior which is too subtle
or too complex to be directly observed. Such communications are in
fact indispensable; the problem is merely the methodological one as
to how the reliability of such communication is to be controlled. The
question, I repeat, is where to begin. We know where we want to end:
the maximum possible understanding of actual persons' valuings and
evaluations in all their complexity.

The issue can be illustrated by turning to Parker's analysis of appraisive signs. Elsewhere he has written that "every value statement
expresses a wish or satisfaction and an invitation to a hearer to share
in it." So he states in his present comments that in calling Brahms' First
Symphony "beautiful" he means that "The Brahms First gives imaginative satisfaction to my desires in an orderly fashion, and I want it to give
satisfaction to yours, so that we may share this experience." The appraisive term thus is said to involve a volitional factor which differenti-
ates it from purely descriptive terms.

I do not deny that this may be a translation of the term "beautiful"
or that appraisive terms may contain a wish for shared satisfaction.

The methodological problem is how we can know whether this is so or not. And here I can see no alternative but the slow and laborious construction of a behaviorally oriented semiotic in which we can find operational criteria for deciding whether a given sign is or is not appraisive. Without this we will only continue to talk to one another. For instance, the two parts of Parker's translation of what he means by saying the Brahms First is beautiful seem to me to be *non*-appraisive (but designative) in signification—the first designates that the work gives him imaginative satisfaction, the second designates his wish that others share his satisfaction. And I would find it strange to call a sign appraisive which is analyzable into a compound of designative signs. Similarly, when I try to analyze what I mean by calling something good it seems to me that in many cases I am not wishing someone to share my satisfaction. I do not find that all significations of wishes are appraisive or that all appraisive signs involve wishes.

I shall not repeat how I have attempted to differentiate appraisive signs from designative signs in terms of their effect upon preferential behavior. For my immediate point is rather to insist that until we develop a theory of signs which gives us operational criteria for distinguishing one kind of sign from another, and for controlling our verbal reports about our own meanings, we can make no significant advances in the analysis of evaluations. Only then can we increase agreement as ˙ᴉ the similarities and differences between evaluations and statements, nd the similarities and differences in their manner of confirmation. The .nost I would claim for my own attempt to approach valuings and evaluations in terms of preferential behavior is that it indicates a methodologically sound way to advance towards agreement in axiology.

I have concentrated on only a few items in Parker's analysis. For the large area of agreement which he has indicated I am grateful. And he can be assured—though he does not need this assurance—that investigations of the sort I am championing will always need to be interpreted and supplemented and corrected by sensitive and discerning persons. My problem is merely whether we cannot find ways to increase the area of common agreement among such persons. I see no way to do this except by following the hard road which science has in other domains found it necessary to traverse.

❧ CRITICISMS BY PEPPER

P<small>ARKER</small>, along with some other contemporary writers on value, affirms that statements of value are not statements of fact and consequently are not verifiable. It follows that a "theory" of value composed of statements of value is not a cognitive hypothesis that can be regarded as true or false or probable. This view, to those of us who regard a theory of value as a cognitive hypothesis responsible to factual confirmation, is a very serious and quite unnecessary error.

Such minor differences as I have with Parker's many observant statements about value in his excellent paper are so overshadowed by this one major difference that I shall confine my comments entirely to this one subject. First I shall inquire into the facts of the situation, trying to make out just what entities Parker is denoting by "statements of value" which are neither true nor false. Second, I shall consider his view that ethics and theory of value are themselves such "statements of value" neither true nor false, and point out that this is an arbitrary, unnecessary, and unusual definition of the subject matter of these studies. Third, I shall point out that such a view, besides being unnecessary and false, is exceedingly dangerous in its practical action. And lastly, I shall demonstrate that the view is entirely definitional, and logically empty of material significance, and consequently a source of deception because it is offered as a guide to action as if it had some cognitive bearing. In short, I seek to show that the idea is a nest of confusions.

1. First, then, let us take a look at the facts. The crux of Parker's argument consists in his declaration that "statements of value" are "expressions" of desire, wish, command, and the like, and that they are not statements of fact. He distinguishes between (a) "I love you" uttered by a lover and (b) "He loves her" uttered by a bystander who overhears the lover's words. The one, he says, is a "statement of value," the other a mere statement or verbal expression about value, a mere "statement of fact."

Parker correctly points out that (a) and (b) are quite different things, and that (a) cannot successfully be reduced to (b). For (a) includes "the lover's love, a warmth contained as in an envelope of words, a force there trying to kindle a like love in the beloved." Quite correctly he insists that in (b) "love is absent, and only a cold, conceptual description, a knowledge about the other's love is there."

Note that this distinction between (a) and (b) is a cognitive distinction, a matter of observation, and verifiable. I should agree with Parker that it is a true distinction. A fact of actual valuing is intrinsic to (a) which is not intrinsic to (b). (b) is a statement about (a). (b) is true or false depending on whether (a) actually is in fact this act of valuing which (b) affirms it is. (a) is the value act itself. The lover's "I love you" is a loving act, an act of the lover's wanting, and for Parker human desires are human values. Being an act of value in fact, the lover's act is, of course, not true or false, for a fact simply occurs and is neither true nor false. But the bystander's statement about the act, of course, is true or false.

There would be nothing, so far, to object to except Parker's dubious employment of the term "statement of value" applied to the lover's act. In common speech we do say regarding a lover's verbal expression of his desire that he made a "declaration" or "statement" of his love. Also when a lover expresses a desire for marriage, we say he made a "proposition." But these are colloquial uses of the terms, obviously quite different from their customary logical uses. Would it not be wise in a technical discussion, such as this one on theory of value where the issue focuses in this very technical term, to be particularly scrupulous in the use of the term? Would it not be wiser to restrict the term "statement" to its customary logical use as a sentence that is true or false or probable? Why take any chances with the fallacy of equivocation?

For this same reason should not Parker be particularly careful in this discussion with the term "expression"? We speak of an "expression of value" and an "expression of fact." So employed, "expression" is open to the same ambiguity as "statement" similarly employed. A hug, or a kiss, or a bouquet of flowers, or "I love you" are all expressions of a lover's love, all acts, facts, neither true nor false. These are expressions of value. But one of them happens to be a verbal expression, and for that reason very easily confused with the quite different type of verbal expression, "He loves her." Would not it be wise to restrict the term "expression" in discourse about the present issue to "emotional expression," and again take no chances with the fallacy of equivocation?

I do believe there would be little inducement to espouse Parker's position if we could completely do away with the ambiguities of these terms, "statement" and "expression."

There is another circumstance in the facts of the situation which increases the insidiousness of these ambiguities. Just now I mentioned a number of alternative emotional expressions of a lover's love. The verbal expression "I love you" was just one of these. The fact that a single drive may have a number of expressions of it, leads to a correct factual discrimination of a drive from its expressions. If this drive is then equated with the value, the expressions of the value have a relation to the value somewhat analogous to the relation of a descriptive statement with the facts it describes. The expressions of a drive signify the drive, just as a descriptive sentence signifies the fact described. But, of course, the expression of a drive is not a description of it, not true or false as a descriptive statement would be. The possibilities of ambiguity are thus increased by the factual relations themselves, since the relation between a drive and its emotional expressions resembles the relation between a fact and its description. Moreover, if the emotional expression happens to be a verbal one like a lover's "I love you," verbally communicating emotion much as a descriptive sentence verbally communicates the truth about the facts it describes, the possibilities of ambiguity increase yet more.

Therefore, let us look for an example of valuing other than the lover's loving, some example that is free from the complications of verbal communication. Consider the thirsty geologist described in my paper. His activity in seeking and finding water to satisfy his thirst did not involve any communication. His thoughts may have gone on in words but they need not have. To remove verbal elements entirely, we could substitute a thirsty rat in a maze if we wished. But I think we shall find it easier to understand the facts of the situation in terms of the man.

Now, clearly the geologist had an impulse of thirst. The geologist was thirsting as Parker's lover was loving. The thirst impulse was a steady drive distinguishable from a lot of other things the geologist did in connection with his drive. Also Parker's lover unquestionably did many other things in connection with his loving besides uttering, "I love you." Now what in the geologists's valuing activities corresponded to the lover's "I love you"? For on Parker's view it would seem that there should be a "statement of value" for the geologist's desire. Otherwise, here is a value that goes without a "statement of it." (That is, it would be one that could not enter into a theory of value.)

Let us spread out the important sorts of things that occurred in the course of the geologist's appetitive activities. First, there emerged the impulse which consisted introspectively of a specific feeling and could be physiologically described as a pattern of conditions arising from the dehydration of the body. Second, there were some innate readinesses to take care of this need such as tendencies to swallow and a general restlessness leading to activities to find a satisfaction for this need. Third, in this geologist there arose at once the idea of water, an anticipatory set of references as to the suitable terminal goal object that would bring satisfaction to this need. Fourth, there arose ideas of a number of subordinate goal objects which the geologist anticipated would lead him to water. Fifth, there were a succession of overt acts in commerce with the succession of anticipated goal objects until the geologist finally got his water. Sixth, and finally, there was the consummatory act of drinking the water and its accompanying feeling of satisfaction.

These were the essential elements in the course of the geologist's appetitive activity. Where among these acts is Parker's "statement of value"? Of course, the whole preceding paragraph consists of "statements about value" in Parker's terminology, but these are not what Parker thinks we are concerned with in value theory.

Taking Parker's alternative phrase, "expression of value," one could say in a very broad sense of the term "expression" that every one of the six types of activities listed above was an "expression" of the geologist's thirsting. But what is it to say this other than that all of these were factual occurrences involved in the geologist's desire to satisfy his thirst? Moreover, there is no evidence in Parker's article that he would select any of these as a "statement of value."

On the evidence of his article, Parker would look for some symbolic expression, preferably verbal, corresponding to the "I love you" of his lover, uttered here by the geologist. If the geologist in the course of his appetitions had uttered, "Gosh! I'm thirsty," or "I wish I had a drink," or "How dry I am!" or "Heaven help me," or just "Hell!" Parker would have found in one of these the "statement of value" he wanted. But notice how relatively irrelevant these expressions are to the geologist's activity, and consequently to any theory of value. True, the same thing cannot quite be said of the lover's "I love you." That is why I suggested the example of the geologist, so that these verbal expressions of value could be seen in their purity where they are not serving other value functions besides being just expressions of value. The lover's "I love you" was of course really effective as an instrumental subordinate act in achieving the goal of the beloved's reciprocated love. But does Parker regard every instrumental act of an appetition as a "statement of value"? If he does, the geologist's walk down the slope, his digging of the hole, his drinking of the water were all also "statements of value." But why, then, not continue and add the other facts involved in the appetition as well? Why not regard the impulse of thirst itself as a "statement of value," and the consummatory act and the final satisfaction also? Then "statement of value" is equivalent to any fact of value. Then why have two terms for the same thing, especially when one of them, "statement," is so suggestive of "proposition" rather than of "fact"?

Parker evidently does not intend to equate "statement of value" with "fact of value." He apparently intends to equate it with only a restricted class of facts of value. This class comprises apparently any verbal expression charged with a drive such as a lover's "I love you" or a thirsty man's, "Gosh, I'm thirsty," together with a few non-verbal acts somewhat similar in origin such as a piece of music or a painting.

No one surely would deny the existence of this class of facts. But why should Parker make such an issue out of them? It is a very heterogeneous, hit-or-miss group of facts so far as their relevancy to total value activities go. Some intense and extensive desires may be entirely without them. All animal desires are, so far as we know. Many human desires are without them. The geologist may not have verbalized at all. In a large proportion of value activities verbal or similar "expressions" of value are of no consequence whatever in the structure of the act or even for purposes of casual communication. What if the geologist did make some remarks to himself in the desert? Only where such "expressions" are stimuli to influence other people in the furtherance of one's desire, or, as in some types of aesthetic creation, are stimuli for the consummation of one's desire, are they value facts worthy of any particular consideration.

So I offer Parker and others who hold that "statements of value" should be distinguished from "statements of fact" the following dilemma: Their "statements of value" are identical either with "facts of value" or with a restricted class of "facts of value." If the first, then it is confusing not to call them the facts they are, and to imply by calling these facts "statements" that descriptive statements about them are irrelevant, useless, or (perhaps) impossible. If the second, then the restriction of "statements of value" to a class only of value facts when followed by the further restriction of the study of value to "statements of value" as above defined results in a falsification of the facts of value. It means that all those value facts which are not within the class of facts defined by these writers as "statements of value" are arbitrarily excluded from study. The thirsty geologist's activities, for instance, would be excluded from Parker's studies (if Parker were held to consistency), unless the geologist obliged by verbalizing his thirst. Even then (in strict consistency) it would seem as if the geologist's verbalizing act were all that would enter into Parker's theory of value. For the thirst itself and all the other acts, not being "statements of value" cannot enter the sphere of value theory.

In short, the view that "statements of value" are not descriptive statements like those of any empirical study, can be given either a broad or a narrow interpretation. On the broad interpretation, "statements of value" are indistinguishable from facts of value, which produces an unnecessary and quite inexcusable confusion of terms. On the narrow interpretation, "statements of value" are but one class of value facts. This restriction is also confusing, but when accompanied by a further restriction to the effect that theory of value is limited to this class of facts only, the result is a falsification of the evidence. Parker apparently accepts the second interpretation. This forces us to consider what he does with ethics and theory of value.

2. The full seriousness of his view comes to light only when Parker definitely asserts that ethics and law and theory of value are concerned solely with "statements of value," as he defines these, and not with statements about value. "Both legal and ethical expressions," he writes, "seem . . . impersonal, in which regard they simulate cognitive expressions. But this impersonality is actually a sham, and both types can be shown to be of the nature of wishes and commands." To those of us who have thought that ethics and theory of value were bodies of knowledge, conceptions of what truly were good and bad, Parker's assertion that such notions are a sham, would come as something of

a shock had we not already got more or less used to such ideas along with certain other oddities that have emerged in our time. Parker can make out a better case as regards law, though even there he is not fully justified. A code of law is, of course, a command. But is jurisprudence a command? Let me therefore express the issue between us clearly by asserting that according to my definition of these subjects, ethical statements and statements in theory of value are cognitive statements and that all expressions masquerading as ethical statements which are not cognitive are a sham.

How does Parker undertake to defend his extraordinary definition of ethics? He might say that he just prefers to define ethics as a body of non-cognitive verbal expressions. If that were his defense, there would be no issue for none would be raised. He would simply be expressing a queer preference, a non-cognitive fact. "I want ethics to mean so-and-so, and that is a fact about me," he would be saying, and that is all. But he does not stop with that. He wants all the rest of us to have the same preference he has.

He accordingly undertakes to persuade us. His persuasions run along three lines. His first line is that ethical expressions are like legal expressions. They are commands, or, at least, wishes. This is the point at issue and may be simply denied. Only as regards *authoritarian* ethics would I agree with Parker. But authoritarian doctrines are dogmatic on principle and merely raise the point at issue on a wider scale. For the issue is as to whether ethics truly is authoritarian.

The second line is that the books of the traditional moralists were not intended as statements of fact, but as expressions of moral ideals— that is, of the writer's wishes. This is an issue of fact about the intentions of men like Spinoza, Locke, Hume, Butler, Reid, Mill, Sidgwick, and others. The evidence of these writers' intentions, however, judged by their writings appears strongly against Parker. These writers seem to be trying to make true statements.

The third line is that whatever these men's intentions, the results were nevertheless simply expressions of wishes. This is also a factual issue. But Parker would find it hard to argue behind an author's expressed intentions after declaring, as he does, that "Expressions of desires, taken as wholes, are not propositions at all—but volitional expressions; *for their intention, by which their status is determined,* is not to express anything true or false." [1] If intention establishes the status, and most classical moralists show they intend to state propositions about the good and the bad, Parker is constrained to accept their intentions. Moreover, I do not know how one would distinguish a proposition from a verbal expression of desire anyway except by the form or by the intention. If the form cannot be trusted (for "I love you" certainly has the form of a proposition), then one must trust to the intention.

But it may be argued: Should we not here also follow Parker's intention and not his literal words? Is not it true that an ethical system is an expression of a man's character or of the culture of his time, however strong his intention to set down true statements? In answer I should say, "Certainly, but is this anything unusual about cognitive statements? All writings are human and subject to bias. What is logic and scientific method but statements of means by which cognition seeks to avoid bias? Ethics is a difficult subject in which to make true statements free of bias. Admitted, but the statements are nonetheless cognitive statements, and every effort can be made to free them of bias."

Parker's arbitrary definition of ethics as "expression of desire" is the more arbitrary for him in that he expressly admits that for every "expression" or "statement of value" a corresponding "statement about value" can be given. He admits freely that there are cognitive statements about values. Obviously anyone interested could collect these statements and systematize them, and such a system would be what I and many others define as ethics. Parker cannot consistently deny that an ethics or theory of value so defined may exist. In fact, of course, it does. Possibly Parker thinks such a system of statements would be anthropology. But the facts anthropology systematizes are those things which groups of men approve as objects of value. The facts studied in theory of value are the valuings themselves.

3. This brings us to our third point; that since Parker's position is untenable, it is pertinent to indicate that the view is socially dangerous. The unpalatableness of a view is never an argument against its truth. But if a view is quite probably false and belief in it can be injurious, then it is important to note its dangerousness so as not to give it the support of authority carelessly.

[1] Italics mine.

If Parker's view of ethics were right, ethical and social aims would not be open to cognitive inquiry. His attitude discredits all ethical theories which by intention are concerned with verifiable statements about values. This is serious because it leads people to think there is no use trying to find out any facts about values. It gives encouragement to a growing belief that men and nature are quite different; that though men have learned to control nature, men can never learn to control themselves. It encourages men to think that any talk about values is just so much camouflaged propaganda. Trained experts in the subject tell them that indeed this is the *truth* of the matter. Yet ironically this very view denies that experts in the subject are possible at all since "statements of value do not express anything true or false." We may try to persuade people to accept our prejudices. We may even use reason to support our persuasion. But if reason fails, should we be surprised if men, persuaded that ethics is the expression of desire, resort *easily* to force, social pressure, the concentration camp, and the purge?

What we need most of all today is not to give way to our prejudices but to understand them with the intent that we may control them. The control, no doubt, is in the end by force. But there is a great difference between an intelligent, cognitively well-grounded, application of force and an unintelligent application. Does not Parker see that in discrediting the cognitive study of values, he is encouraging and hastening the unintelligent application of force?

4. Finally, let me point out that from a purely methodological point of view, this whole issue is simply a matter of definition. Formally, it might be said that Parker has framed his doctrine in such a way that it is irrefutable. For if his doctrine is established by nominal or volitional definition, then the consequences he draws are simply the analytical consequences of his definitions. But the irrefutability of his doctrine is then bought at a price. The price is that the doctrine shall be cognitively meaningless. For if the doctrine is established by volitional definition which is neither true nor false then it merely expresses Parker's volitions, and is neither true nor false.

Now, I do not know whether Parker's definitions of "statement of value," "ethics," "law," and "theory of value" are intended by him to be volitional definitions, or are supposed to be definitions of matters of fact and responsible to the facts. This is another one of the confusions of his doctrine. But it must be very clear by now that Parker cannot maintain his doctrine unless he can maintain his definitions. *If* he can define "statement of value" as some sort of "expression" relevant to value and neither true nor false, and *if* he can define "ethics," "law," and "theory of value" as consisting themselves of such "expressions," then all the consequences of his doctrine follow. But we have shown that the facts of desire and satisfaction to which Parker makes many empirical references do not (to speak conservatively) require us to accept the definitions he frames. It is only Parker, then, who requires us to accept his definitions. That is, Parker virtually says, "If you want to understand what I mean by 'statement of value,' 'ethics' and so on, you must accept the definitions I give to these terms." That is, Parker wills that these terms be given these meanings whatever the facts may be. That is, Parker's definitions of these terms are volitional and nominal, and have no reference to truth or falsity.

But if Parker's definitions are volitional, then, as I have pointed out, the doctrine that is deduced from them is empty of empirical significance. It is irrefutable, but at the expense of being cognitively meaningless.

Actually, I get the impression that Parker's exposition vibrates irresponsibly, as so much other work in theory of value does today, between deductions from nominal definitions and references to fact picked to fit the definitions. It is actually a definitional doctrine throughout, but it is given an empirical aroma by abundant references to empirical material. The method is the new way of the a priori, and is a modern adaptation of the ontological argument.

To avoid this sort of thing, I urgently suggest that we banish the nominal or volitional definition from empirical inquiry. Let us keep it for the use for which alone it is adapted—namely, to give names to things. It is fitted for giving a name to Carlo, names to the two sides in a game of charades, a name or short symbol to substitute for a longer expression. It is not suited for defining the characteristics of classes of natural objects such as animals, plants, or chemical substances. It is liable to be a source of inconvenience and misunderstanding in demarcating fields of empirical study. It is actually a fallacy and a way of distorting the facts when used to demarcate the facts of value.

The reason a nominal or volitional definition is so disturbing to empirical inquiry in the value field is that the making of such a definition in this field is itself an evaluative act. For the definition constitutes the criterion for judging what is or is not a value and determines those facts which are relevant to practical evaluative decisions.

If, then, this evaluative criterion is not fully responsible to the facts relevant to such evaluations, if it is not constructed in conformity with the facts rather than according to the wishes of a writer, it will inevitably be irresponsible and merely reflect the bias of the writer.

The sort of definitions appropriate to the study of value are those that I have called descriptive definitions.[2] These are definitions which not only give a name to a field of observation, but also stipulate that the name shall refer to a description of the field as nearly true to the facts as available observation can make it. The act of giving a name to a body of empirical material is, in other words, at the same time bound up with the act of truly describing the material. The definition is thus responsible to a careful and truthful report of the facts defined. Such definitions are, moreover, adaptable to improvements in the reports. The personal bias of the observer is thus rendered subservient to the nature of the facts. A descriptive definition is by stipulation as empirically objective as the reports on which it is based.

Returning finally to Parker's definitions, we see that descriptions of appetitive acts like loving and being athirst will not justify the evaluative function Parker gives to what he calls "statements of value." For having defined the latter as non-cognitive, and then having defined ethics and theory of value as of the same nature it follows that ethics and theory of value are also non-cognitive. He thereby makes a negative evaluation of theories of value which purport to be descriptive and true to empirical fact. Since by definition these theories are excluded from consideration, it is useless for exponents of such theories to refer to facts. By definition, empirical considerations are irrelevant to "statements of value." In short, by volitional definition Parker has negatively evaluated theories of value which do not meet with his volition. What is important for us to notice in this procedure is that in consequence he excuses us from paying any cognitive attention to his ideas. He has simply uttered an elaborate "Ouch!" to our conception of theory of value as an empirical hypothesis intended to be true.

[2] "The Descriptive Definition," *The Journal of Philosophy*, XLIII (1946), 29–36.

REJOINDER BY PARKER

I think I can make this rejoinder very brief, but hope that in so doing I will not create the impression that my brevity is due to a lack of appreciation of the importance of the issues raised. The issues seem to me to be of transcendent importance, yet I have always felt that with regard to the first and the last things of philosophy there comes a point where too many words uttered or written by either party to a controversy rather obscure than illumine. I will number the points to which I wish to make reply, although this is my numbering, not Pepper's.

1. I wonder how I gave the impression that what I call value statements or expressions are the sole material or data of value theory? I have reread my paper carefully, but do not find any assertion there to that effect. At all events, if there is such an assertion, I retract it, for I do not believe it. Desires and satisfactions and frustrations seem to me to be data of value theory, just as they do to Pepper. His delightfully written story of the geologist going in search of water is well worth the study of any theorist in our field, whether the man said, "Gosh, I'm thirsty" or not. As a fact, I wrote Pepper a rather long letter about it.

2. Nevertheless I do believe that value expressions are of special interest to value theory because expression, as language, is the most important means by which values are shared and so become social. The great attention given to value expressions by philosophers, beginning with Kant, in their relation, say, to scientific expressions, which might appear to be a prejudice, is thus justified. Then there is a specific form of value expression, namely art, in which I have personally been long and deeply interested, and to which perhaps I attach an exaggerated importance. But Pepper is also an aesthetician, so he ought to bear with me in this weakness, if it be such. And whether one draws one's illustrations of the language of value from poetry or the discourse of lovers, or from the speeches of Churchill, Bevin, Molotov or Truman, or from those given in the U.N. Assembly, some of which I heard while in New York this past year, or from John L. Lewis's discussions with the mine operators, the results are the same—there remains a fundamental difference between lyrical and practical expressions of value,

on the one hand, and scientific expressions, including expressions about values, on the other hand, because the former are acts, deeds, forces overflowing into words or other media for the purpose of sharing, or effecting certain results, while the latter are commentaries on, or descriptions of, acts, deeds or forces, whether of man or of nature or of God.

3. I find no place in my essay where I say that value *theory* does not consist of propositions that are true or false, or probable. Surely all that part of value theory that consists of descriptive definitions (to use Pepper's admirable phrase) of value, analyses of desire and satisfaction and their dimensions, is of this sort. But when philosophers of value advocate certain ways of life, then we no longer have value *theory* but what I call volitional expression, a sort of ethical poetry, which is not true or false or probable, but may be fine and noble.[3] Nevertheless, as philosopher, I must regret that these expressions are often supported by extraordinarily specious arguments. Value theory has usually been a mélange of poetry and prose, as I put it in the article referred to above; but it need not be—one can meticulously separate the one from the other, as one honestly and competently should.

4. But let me try to locate and then discuss the prime matter at issue between Pepper and myself, putting my view a little differently perhaps from the way I have expressed it in my essay.

Pepper admits that desires and satisfactions are not true or false, but are facts. He also admits that certain as I call them expressions or statements of these are not true or false, since they are phases of acts of volition, not of cognition. We both agree that these acts, whether accompanied by verbal expression or not, can be described. But where he thinks we disagree is in this: he believes that ethics or theory of value can somehow give us conceptions—as he says—of what truly is good or bad, while I do not. Ethics and theory of value, according to his view, are "bodies of knowledge"—knowledge of good and evil. Obviously everything hinges on the interpretation of the key phrase, knowledge of "what *truly is* good or bad." Now if he only means adequate or true general descriptions of desire, satisfaction, and frustration, there is no dispute between us. It is one of the important parts of value theory to offer this. But I take it that Pepper means more

[3] See my article in *Ethics*, LVI (1946), 193–207.

than this. He means that ethics and theory of value can tell us what is universally good and bad, concretely good and bad for all men. This implies that he is using the term "good" not in the most generic sense as desire and satisfaction, and the term "evil" not in the most generic sense as desire and frustration, but "good" in the sense of a selection or preference as between desires and satisfactions, and "evil" as a failure to make such a selection or preference—and validly for all men. Theory of value can tell us—not merely recommend to us—that not only will we all have more satisfaction on the whole, be happier, if our desires when appeased are more intense, numerous, and harmonious, but *which* desires should be encouraged and *which* discouraged.

On the contrary, I do not think that ethics and theory of value can tell us, in a general way, which desires are better, and for the reason that the good is always *for someone,* for an individual, and preference, yes, preferability is also for someone, for an individual. In order to know what is someone's good, you must enter imaginatively into his life, experiencing the pull of his desires, making his yours, and then, by a reflexive act of self-knowledge which is also knowledge of another, you can tell him what to prefer and what not to prefer. But only to a limited extent, even so. For preference is a creative act, and the scope of imaginative union with another's life is limited. By art and education I can, to be sure, become a factor in the creation of a preference, yet a residuum of indeterminism always remains. Hence, I repeat, there is no concrete, universal good or bad, only individual good and bad. Such statements as "Love is better than ambition"; "Freedom (in the Anglo-Saxon sense) is better than security"; "It is better to have loved and lost than never to have loved at all"; "It is better to love than to be loved" are not propositions like Newton's Law of Gravitation or Boyle's Law of Gases, supposed to hold universally, but volitional expressions, expressions of preferences of individuals or like-minded groups of individuals—the poetry of action. No one can *prove* them valid for another. But one can try to create them in another by means of art and education.

So then I say that books of ethics are partly systematizations of such volitional expressions as are willed by the writer and other members of his group—as jurisprudence is a systematization of legal volitional expressions—and partly descriptions, the record, or echo of, such expressions of other men and groups in the past; for example, E. A.

Westermarck's *The Origin and Development of Moral Ideas*.[4] Usually these parts are mixed in a curious mélange. Books on value are apt to be the same kind of thing—for instance, R. B. Perry's chief work. Philosophers think their own ethical principles are rational or empirical propositions, but really they are deeds expressed in words, forces working toward goals. For example, "The good of each man is equal to the like good of another"; "The good of the many is greater than that of the few"; "The greatest happiness of the greatest number"; "The all-benevolent will."

5. Pepper thinks my views are socially dangerous. Well, I think his are, and for this reason: if you believe you can demonstrate the validity of your own ideals to the semi-oriental despots who threaten freedom everywhere, including our own in America, you will leave our defenses weak (see Eisenhower's Report to the Senate Committee on Military Affairs). If our civilization goes under, it may easily be the work of some of our well-intentioned liberals and rationalists, who are committing the second *trahison des clercs*. Philosophically, their error stems from not recognizing that what is preferable for one may not be preferable for another, and that there are limits therefore to mutual understanding and cooperation, leaving superior force as the ultimate, if regrettable resource.

FURTHER COMMENT BY PEPPER

Parker's rejoinder clarifies a good many points. I am glad he admits the "descriptive definition." That eliminates the use of the "volitional definition" as an instrument of defense which has to be broken down before we can come to an issue of fact. We agree to abide by the evidence in this issue whichever way the evidence falls.

I did think Parker intended the subject matter—or better the verbal phrases which make up the body of a book on ethics or theory of value —to be what he calls "expressions of value" rather than statements about value. I was relying on the quotations I gave in my Section 2, and the contexts from which these quotations were taken. They struck me as explicit statements descriptive of these studies. In fact, so far as our main issue goes, it seems to me Section 4 of his rejoinder rather confirms than denies my allegation. When he says "books on ethics are partly systematizations of such volitional expressions as are willed by the writer

[4] London, 1912.

. . . and partly descriptions, the record, or echo of, such expressions of other men and groups in the past," is he not saying that the whole content of these books consists of "expressions of value"?

Admitted that there is a legimate truth reference between the "descriptions of such expressions" and the "expressions" themselves, the net result of a book on ethics or on theory of value, in Parker's view, is still not a set of propositions about the facts and laws of conation, affection, and so forth and the ways of attaining more or less of them, but "really they are deeds expressed in words, forces working toward goals." Does he not also add that such a book can be said to be true only of the desires and goals of the individual "since the good is always for an individual"? The book, in short, is really a "deed," the deed of the man who wrote it, and is not to be considered applicable to, or true of, any other man.

Of course, I do not think Parker's own books on value are solely or mainly this sort of thing. They appear to me to contain a great deal about what is "concretely good and bad for all men." That is why I prize them. I recognize also that a book of his is his deed, and I enjoy the evidences of his individual personality that flow through it. But I value the book as a contribution to our knowledge of values because of the width of experience it reflects, because it is so largely true (I believe) for all men.

❧ CRITICISMS BY RICE

I

HAHN'S ESSAY does not profess to reconcile and unify the diverse current approaches to value, but rather to refine a single mode of dealing with the problem, namely, that imposed by a contextualist metaphysics. This turns out to be a restatement and defense of some of the leading ideas of Dewey's, though perhaps with a relaxation of several of the latter's *partis pris*. The advantage of Hahn's restatement consists in his use of the vocabulary of E. C. Tolman's "purposive behaviorism," a psychological terminology more systematic than that which Dewey himself has customarily employed in presenting his theory of value, and more lucid than that which is being offered to us over the joint signatures of Dewey and A. F. Bentley.[1] Since Tolman's terms seem well suited to give precise expression to a contextualist psychology, with the turn that Dewey has given it, one may hope that Hahn will carry this undertaking further than his brief essay in this volume has permitted. We shall then be able to escape some of the linguistic bewilderments that assail the student of Dewey's own writings on value, and to judge more adequately the merits and the shortcomings of both contextualist metaphysics and its allied psychology when applied to our problem.

Initially, one may express certain hesitations of a general character. Hahn has chosen to restrict himself to the categories and "postulations" of contextualism, in pretty much the form in which they were stated by Pepper in *World Hypotheses*. These assumptions will, then, seem adequate only to those who are satisfied with the contextualist world hypothesis—unless, indeed, Hahn can show us that they are fitted comprehensively to interpret the facts and solve the problems with which value theory has to deal. Hahn calls upon the other participants in this inquiry to state their own metaphysical biases. Mine will have to be put briefly and dogmatically, since there are limits to the

[1] See their series of articles begun in *The Journal of Philosophy*, Vol. XLII (1945).

extent to which this symposium can expand into metaphysical controversy. I agree with Pepper that contextualism, as developed hitherto, is only one of four or more large ways of looking at the world, and taken by itself it seems to me to offer a metaphysical lens that is especially distorting. I disagree with Pepper, however, in his conclusion that his analysis has shown each of his four world hypotheses to be based on a "root metaphor" which is irreducibly distinct from those underlying the other systems, so that there exists no ground for the mutual translatability of the four world views, no foothold for genuine mutual criticism and correction, and no hope for a selective synthesis of what is valid in their respective insights.

From my own paper, it is apparent that I tend to take as fundamental the categories of what Pepper has called "mechanism," more particularly mechanism of the "consolidated" variety, and one which takes account of the fact of emergence. This bias is not, I believe, merely a matter of temperamental congeniality, but it springs from my detailed attempt to understand the world. Contemporary mechanism retains the traditional categories of the determination of all events by law, and of a "substance" or continuant which obeys a conservation principle. "Causal" determination may be either "molar" or meroscopic in various domains, and we now treat the continuant as the "space-time continuum" or the "electromagnetic field"; its constant is mass-energy. The basic notion of the "field," after winning triumphs in physics, biology, and neurology, is now invading psychology and the value studies, but has not yet received a thoroughgoing philosophical exposition. The category of the field, it seems to me, offers the possibility of absorbing within a deterministic view of the world the organicist notion of "purpose" and the contexualist emphasis on "function." These would be interpreted by mechanism, not as isolated or ultimate phenomena, but as referring to special—though highly important—cases of emergent field-determination, whose "molar" character is dependent on the complicated internal configurations of living organisms in interaction with their environing regions. Contextualism has a lively sense for the flavor of the immediate, and, as Pepper points out, a tendency to follow its strands off into the environmental "context," in a vagrant and miscellaneous fashion which overemphasizes the uniqueness of particular contexts and ignores the recurrent and typical features of configurations which enable them to be subsumed under scientific laws.

Hence, it may be suggested, springs contextualism's keen perception of the involvement of values with the manifold modes of conation and reflection, its inability to settle on any one of them as central to the fact of value,[2] and its consequent failure hitherto to give us any kind of systematic set of definitions and postulates for value theory in such a way as to render it genuinely "scientific."

Another but related ground of initial hesitation over Hahn's choice of assumptions arises from his devotion to a single psychologist. Most philosophers who try, humbly but critically, to learn something from the current psychological work are forced to adopt, provisionally and for lack of anything better, an eclectic attitude. The contemporary psychological schools seem to exhibit the same one-sidedness and partisanship as the philosophical schools themselves. This is particularly true—and admitted by psychologists of my acquaintance—in those branches of psychology that have potentially most relevance to theory of value, namely, the studies of motivation, learning, and feeling. Tolman's "purposive" treatment of the reinforcement of motives—which makes it a direct function of expectation and interest—has gained general respect for exploring *an* important factor in these phenomena. But the more mechanistic treatments of the problem, such as the Holt-Guthrie conception of learning by performance, on the one hand, and, on the other, the perhaps more widely accepted theories, such as those of Thorndike and Hull, which make learning a function of "effect" (satisfaction, reward or need-reduction), seem to have been at least as fruitful. As I have suggested in my preceding essay, the consensus of psychologists who are attempting to bring these approaches into some kind of unified theory seems to be that what is needed now is not a disproportionate emphasis on a single set of such factors, but rather a comprehensive framework which will display their more precise individual roles and their interrelationships. This situation supports what I have said above about the one-sidedness of each of the four world hypotheses in their usual partisan presentations— Hahn is to be praised for his insistence on the close relationship of metaphysical outlooks both to psychological systems and to theories of value.

[2] Cf., for example, Dewey's vacillation between a maintenance theory of value, which makes valuing essentially an effort to preserve something in existence, and a remedial theory, which makes valuing an effort to remedy a "lack" and restore harmony to a troubled situation.

Although Tolman's emphasis on purpose and function has been a necessary corrective to those "mechanical" or atomistic behaviorisms which overlooked the molar directional tendencies of the organism, it has been criticized for taking drives and goal-sets as ultimate and irreducible phenomena. For example, Hull's system, which he also calls a "molar behaviorism" (a term which he prefers to "purposive behaviorism"), makes a much more sustained effort to go into the detailed operation of drives, in accordance with the principle which Kant laid down in the *Critique of Judgment,* that the biological sciences must assume as a working hypothesis that *every purpose or function is itself a mechanism*—that teleology and mechanistic determination are not incompatible but complementary notions. It is largely, I believe, the ignoring of this Kantian principle that has made pragmatism, together with its affiliated psychologies, seem for all its contributions a half-hearted version of naturalism and has given rise to the charge that pragmatism has been obsessed by the "dominance of the foreground" to the neglect of the background of causal law.[3]

There are many aspects of value phenomena, as of other human activities, which can be treated more effectively in terms of mechanism than in terms of purpose. The extreme teleologist assumes that joy or pleasure always results from the accomplishment of a purpose. A particularly striking exception to this rule-of-thumb is furnished by the presence of intensely pleasurable phases in the course of certain ailments, such as tuberculosis, epilepsy, and some types of migraine. Such phenomena lend themselves more readily to explanation in terms of physiological mechanisms than in terms of goal-sets. The presence of joyful and ecstatic states in these diseases supplies a partial compensation which must be taken into account in comparing the value of the condition of illness with that of health—Dostoievsky and Thomas Mann, among others, have had much to say on this point. Here is an obvious, if somewhat peripheral, case where the occurrence of value does not depend either on purpose or on "evaluation"; but there are many commoner instances to be drawn from non-pathological evidence.

To apply these considerations to some of Hahn's own more specific treatments of valuation. He offers three value concepts, each of which

---

[3] Although instrumentalism always refers to explanation in terms of "conditions *and* consequences," in practice it frequently emphasizes consequences to the neglect of conditions.

is analyzed, though not formally defined, in terms of the behavioral act as described by Tolman: immediate value, instrumental value, and standard value. His immediate value corresponds to what earlier in this volume I have called "imputed" value. We assign value, initially and provisionally, to those objects and situations which present themselves as goals, with a minimum of reflection. Their tentative value-character is recognized (Hahn would also say, more debatably, *constituted*) by their relation to "prizing," which—and here Hahn's use of the term seems considerably wider than Dewey's—consists in our expectation that they will satisfy a drive or a demand. We then cast about for means to achieve such goals, and instrumental value is imputed to those things which will serve this function (though Hahn also admits a broader use of "instrumental," to include the conditions of results other than those sought through human or organic agency). The difference between these more provisional forms of value and standard value depends on the amount of warranted reflective knowledge that goes into the testing of tentatively chosen ends and means. The actual and stable demands of the situation are discovered by a thoroughgoing "examination of conditions and consequences."

This analysis of valuation is unexceptionable so far as it goes, and for the special types of value situation which Hahn has in mind; I should not wish to be taken as upholding any position which is incompatible with what it affirms. The issues that mainly divide the contributors to this symposium arise in the effort to pursue the analysis further, and center about two additional questions: (1) Though any sustained process of *valuation* must include the elements just mentioned, is the *occurrence of value* always constituted by them? and (2) What is the nature of this "examination of conditions and consequences" which establishes standard value?

Hahn seems to hold, in disagreement with Dewey, that the occurrence of value is not always dependent on evaluation proper, though he does hold it to be dependent on prizing. For him, however, the difference between mere prizing and evaluative appraisal is one of degree. Since prizing is always concerned with means in some measure, prizing at its minimum level implies not the complete absence of reflection but simply the presence of "relatively little reflection." The amount of reflection required is very small indeed: apparently it may consist merely of "some reference, anticipatory or retrospective."

Now I do not see that Hahn has established, or could establish, his thesis that this reference, at its minimum level, always includes a concern with utilitanda, much less a reflective one. It seems to me that there are many cases of unexpected enjoyment and unforeseen distress where such anticipatory reference as is immediately involved consists merely in an impulse to prolong the enjoyment or to get rid of the distress, where its sources are not yet known and means have not yet been suggested. It may take some time for us to diagnose the situation even tentatively; and appraisal in Dewey's sense of thoroughgoing empirical testing is certainly an elaborate process which supervenes upon the mere recognition that the immediate experience or situation is good or bad in itself. This recognition is not canceled by later reflection on the instrumental values of the situation, though these may outweigh the intrinsic values in our judgment on the situation as a whole, and lead to its modification.

Whether it is possible, as Hahn assumes, to have "enjoyment of qualities without some reference, anticipatory or retrospective" is a difficult psychological problem on which I have no assured convictions. There is probably some sense and some degree in which we can "live in the present" rather than in the past and the future, though whether the sense is literal and the degree absolute is not a question I am prepared to answer. But I believe it is possible to go even further than Hahn in acknowledging some measure of "purposive" (directional or vectorial) character in any considerable span of experience, and still take exception to his conclusions. He is, of course, quite right in saying that mere enjoyment is not always, and perhaps never, sufficient for us to assign, in general and on the whole, positive standard value—which includes both intrinsic and instrumental elements—to the occasion, for the enjoyment may constitute a distraction to our main purposes, and thus be outweighed by the instrumental values concerned. Disagreement could arise only over the issue whether *enjoyment or hedonic tone in some cases can be the ground of prizing.* An affective theory of intrinsic value asserts that it can, that enjoyment is, to use Hahn's language, precisely that "mark" which renders the experience "prizeworthy" in itself and worth sustaining for itself. The instrumentalist view, on the other hand, seems to hold that the only marks that can render an experience *prizeworthy* are "objective" means-relationships in the situation which lead to further prizing. This reveals, I believe, the focal point in the dispute between conative and affective theories. Conative theories refuse to go beneath the *fact* of prizing and to search out the rational *ground* of prizing—except with regard to conditions instrumental to further acts of prizing. Affective theories, on the other hand, urge that the prizing is not ultimate and self-justifying, not a mere matter of "buy more land to raise more corn to grow more hogs to buy more land . . . ," but that where an experience, or some element of it, is prized, on other grounds than its consequences, analysis discloses the presence of positive affective tone in such an experience. The issue cannot, I believe, be threshed out until conative theories face the question whether the prizing of a thing for its own sake is something self-sufficient and unanalyzable or something that seizes upon certain elements in the experience rather than others.

If the enjoyment is the mark which renders the experience prizeworthy in itself, then we are justified in equating the intrinsic value-quality with the enjoyment, and in holding that the occurrence of the value is epistemically—and often temporally—prior to the prizing. The prizing may supervene so instantaneously upon the occurrence of the enjoyment that the two are existentially inseparable; yet the prizing is not a prior condition of the enjoyment and not constitutive of it. The enjoyment, furthermore, is not always a by-product of a specific antecedent purpose. It is sometimes a matter of luck. Hence the need for a certain irony—which need not be so extreme as to paralyze effort —about human purposes and their fruitfulness in value.

On the second question, then—and it is the crucial one—an incompatibility between Hahn's position and those who hold an affective theory of intrinsic value exists only if he would deny that the feeling quality of an act, or kind of act, were among the "conditions and consequences" relevant to the establishment of standards. Doubt arises from his following Dewey in his use of this phrase, for the affective quality of an experience would ordinarily be called neither a "condition" nor a "consequence" of the experience, but rather a constituent of it. Dewey has made it quite clear [4] that he holds the affective quality to be unsuited to serve as part of the evidence for a reflective judgment of valuation. Although Hahn takes the usual instrumentalist sideswipe at those theories which define value "in terms of inaccessible areas of feelings, ones which make no difference in what we observe" (does

[4] In our controversy in *The Journal of Philosophy,* Vol. XL (1943).

any contributor to this symposium hold such a theory?) he seems to go beyond Dewey in admitting—in principle—"introspections concerning values" into his tolerant behaviorism, and in acknowledging (though only in a footnote) that "as molar behaviorists it does not seem to me that we are excluded from noting the felt quality of the experience involved." His paper does not make clear to me whether this "noting" of the felt quality of the experience can be relevant to "considerations of the nature and amount of value afforded by a given end." If it is relevant, then there are grounds for *rapprochement* between Hahn's view and the one I have been trying to outline.

It follows that the issue hinges on the criteria by which we should judge the "nature and amount of value afforded by a given end" and particularly on whether the "demands of the situation" include the requirement that some phases of the process should be affectively rewarding, or at least free from the stigmata of suffering. Thus, to use Hahn's example, we can demand not merely that the ball game should go on, and that it should not overexcite the children so as to interfere with future needs such as eating and sleeping, but also—in some cases—that their game should be more enjoyable than alternative games. Ordinarily, we do not press this latter demand in the case of children's play, since we assume in general that any kind of absorbing play is rewarding. But there may be exceptions even here; and certainly in the case of adult vocations as well as recreations it is an ever-present demand. There are, indeed, situations in which the "demands" may seem to be exhausted by considerations of instrumentalities alone—for example, the demands that a housewife get her dishes washed, that a professor grade his papers with fairness and dispatch, and that a platoon of soldiers take a given objective. But even here there may be a "hard" way and a less hard way, so that we must not rule out foresight of felt qualities entirely. And there are many other situations—the choice of a way of spending a vacation, the decision whether to put Prokofieff or Delius on the phonograph, the student's selection of a career, an employer's consideration of working conditions for his employees—where empirically founded anticipation of felt qualities for those involved may be at least as important in determining standard value as "objective" knowledge of the efficiency of instruments in quieting the drives that are operating. The demand for a life that is affectively rewarding, and as free as possible from suffering which is not required for the ultimate enrichment of someone's experience, is a general "end" so ubiquitous that I do not believe our man in the street will take seriously any delimitation of the value facts which ignores it or underemphasizes it. There is certainly no "separation" of ends from means involved in the view that I am suggesting. Although the general end can be abstracted and symbolized for purposes of analysis, this does not imply that it can be planned in detail without attention to means; and its specific content is intimately dependent on the nature and availability of the means. The instrumentalists have been so busy warning us against a failure to take account of the means that they have told us little about those intrinsic characters of the total means-end continuum which would justify the life process as a whole.

II

From our essays, it is evident that Garnett and I are largely in agreement in our objections to purely conative theories, though it is likely that we would invoke diverging reasons if we went very far into the metaphysical backgrounds of our respective views. We agree further that value theory cannot dispense with the notion of intrinsic value, that feeling tone is an indispensable ingredient in it, and that self-observation of feeling can be conducted in such a way as to be in accordance with the empirical method.

Our difference is that Garnett has a double standard of intrinsic value, while I have proposed a single standard. He holds that the term has reference "to *both* form and quality, to both the *direction* of the striving and the *tone* of the feeling"; I take the "quality" alone to be constitutive of intrinsic value, and treat the "form" as auxiliary or contributory.

Garnett's objection to a purely affective theory of intrinsic value is one that has appealed to many of that theory's critics from Plato on, and therefore must be given weight. We would not consider a passive state of the most intense pleasure, even if prolonged without change for a lifetime, to be the best possible life. Garnett does not present this argument in precisely Plato's form, namely, that we should recognize a life containing both wisdom and pleasure as intrinsically better than a life of pleasure without wisdom, presumably because he sees that the values of wisdom are so largely instrumental that the case so presented would be far from clear-cut. Garnett's argument is, rather, that we would gladly exchange such a passive life of even the most intense pleasure "for a little variety, for an opportunity for genuine activity." So, he holds, while hedonic tone is a necessary and sufficient mark of the bare *presence* of intrinsic value, judgments of comparative intrinsic value must include conative criteria, and more specifically the tendency to promote "growth" or "frustration." This is particularly true in the case of intrinsic *ethical* values, where the criterion is the "development of personality."

Now I would not deny that activity, variety, complexity, growth and development of personality are important considerations in judging the positive value of a life pattern as a whole. The issue is rather whether we should treat them as direct criteria of intrinsic value, or rather as conditions of intrinsic value which are stably and reliably, though not invariably, such—and hence as instrumental or extrinsic in a strict analysis.

If we can find a single standard of intrinsic value that is adequate, the theoretical advantages will be considerable. Garnett's "formal" components include a large and miscellaneous list of characteristics, which may conflict with each other and with affective tone. They are heterogeneous and incommensurable, so that I fear we shall be forced to appeal to "intuition" whenever we encounter difficulties in comparing and assessing them. Before we expose ourselves to the hazards of intuitionism, we should explore thoroughly the possibilities of a single standard as an alternative to a double—or, as it turns out, a multiple—one.

Can we, then, take "quality" as, in general, instrumental to "form" or form as instrumental to quality? It is obvious that we do not always consider the more active, the more complex, or the more varied life as more worthwhile in itself: arguments can be invoked against such proposed standards of intrinsic value similar to those which Garnett has brought against hedonic tone, and I believe more convincingly. So far as intrinsic worth is concerned, it seems to me that we do commonly judge variety, complexity, and so forth, by their fruits in affective tone rather than vice versa. These properties can be perplexing, distracting, destructive, and consequently painful. When this is the case, we seek to make experience more uniform and simpler, unless instrumental factors are urgent. Similarly, at the ethical level, we treat "growth" and "development of personality" either as instruments of adaptation, or as contributory to a richer quality of experience, or as a combination of the two. Unless these terms can be so analyzed, they seem so vague as to be unilluminating: there is no commoner mysticism today than the mysticism which takes "growth" and "personality" as ultimates.

Perhaps Garnett would reply that I am analyzing experience too atomistically, that while variety, complexity, and so on, are not intrinsically good in isolation, when they go to make up the organic unity or Gestalt of an experience that is *also* hedonically positive, they heighten the total intrinsic value of the experience independently of their effect on hedonic tone. In order to establish this view, it would have to be shown that these formal properties can be introduced or enhanced to increase intrinsic value without making the affective tone more intense, more choice, more ecstatic. I am unable to conceive what might be meant by such a statement, and it seems to me clearly contradictory of my own observation. It is, I believe, a commonplace of aesthetic analysis that when any of these properties are modified, even in slight degree, the total "feeling" of the work of art changes radically. Affective tone—as indeed both direct inspection and the study of its presumed neural counterpart suggest—is itself a global phenomenon, a field-effect, a resultant of complex and diverse factors. According to the view I am suggesting, it is precisely in their conjoint effect on feeling quality that these "formal" elements bear fruit in intrinsic value.

Plausibility is lent to Garnett's view by this further consideration: that such characteristics as complexity and variety seem to be properties constitutive of, and hence "intrinsic" to the experience in its immediacy, whereas other admittedly instrumental properties are extrinsic to it in a literal sense, as falling outside it. But I believe that we are not required to take all the properties of the experience that are "intrinsic" to it in this sense as constitutive of its intrinsic *value*. If this were the case, the value aspect of the experience could never be distinguished from its other constitutive properties, and valuational analysis would be forestalled. Such properties may be immediately contributory to the value, and existentially inseparable from it—as indeed affective tone is in most cases inseparable from a sensory, imaginal or ideational content—without being its very stuff and its direct mark. From similar considerations, C. I. Lewis [5] has chosen to divide "extrinsic" value into two types, "instrumental" value, comprising those properties which fall outside the immediate experience in question, and "inherent" value, a term devised to designate those properties directly present in the experience which contribute to the intrinsic value without being constitutive of it.

In reply to Garnett it may be urged, finally, that the crucial imaginative experiment on which he bases his case against a purely affective definition of intrinsic value refers to a fictitious notion of pleasure, and not to the pleasure or joy that we know as a natural quality of real activities. The affective quality with which we are acquainted is not a passive disembodied state which can be prolonged indefinitely without change but requires for its genesis and maintenance precisely such conditions as variety and growth—though it cannot be defined as a simple function of any one or any combination of these. It is no disparagement of such conditions to call them extrinsic or contributory in value. In any case, Garnett has performed a service in calling our attention to them, whether he has provided a usable standard of intrinsic value or not.

On this point, I might add that the views I have offered about the nature of affective quality are very tentative. I believe that nobody knows very much about the subject, and this is not surprising in view of the scanty attention that it has received as a consequence of the recent dominance of conative theories. But I do not see how value theory can advance just now unless it explores such hypotheses as I have tried to indicate.

REJOINDER BY GARNETT

Rice presents an able critique of my paper from the Hedonistic standpoint. He insists that it is the quality alone of an immediate experience that makes it good, not form and quality together. Since we both agree that positive form and positive quality (and negative form and negative quality) tend to go together the difference might seem to be unimportant. But this, I think, is not the case.

Two well-known objections to Hedonism are (1) the difficulties of the "hedonistic calculus," and (2) the tendency of Hedonistic judgment to evaluate intensity of sensory pleasure as a greater good than

[5] In his *An Analysis of Knowledge and Valuation*, La Salle, Ill., 1947, ch. xii.

less intense pleasure of our higher mental activities. The recognition that *what* is good is *mental activity*, and that its goodness consists in its having the dual character of being positive in both form and quality, overcomes these difficulties. It means that we judge the intrinsic (not instrumental) value of any period of mental activity (sensing, perceiving, thinking, willing, and so forth) not by trying to sum its pleasure-pain content, but by trying to sum the amount of positive mental activity (minus negative) in the period, which is much more feasible. In such a scale the relatively passive sensory enjoyments rate low compared with thought, imagination, aesthetic creativity, and appreciation. And this seems to be more in accord with the general verdict of enlightened common sense. It was to remedy this second defect in Hedonism that J. S. Mill sought to distinguish between higher and lower pleasures as differing in quality. But the difference he was really evaluating (so far as it was an intrinsic good) was that of the greater amount of positive mental activity involved in what he called the pleasures of finer quality.

Rice's chief objection to my analysis is a vagueness he finds in the notion of "positive form." I have used a number of adjectives, such as "creative," "constructive," "appetitive," to point to the sort of mental activities that are positive. Some of these adjectives refer both to the instrumental as well as the intrinsic character of the activity, which, for the sake of clarity, is unfortunate but unavoidable. The common formal character of all the mental activity which I am claiming is, ipso facto, "good" is that it is *positive;* that is, it is a striving *for* or *towards* the goal directly, not merely avoiding obstacles or frustrations or fruitlessly seeking an outlet. Such activity is, at every level, pleasantly toned and is commonly pronounced good. It is pronounced instrumentally good (in most instances) because it tends to produce further intrinsic good. But it is pronounced good in itself also, both for the pleasure accompanying it and for the kind, or form, of activity it is.

Perhaps a clinching consideration concerning the common sense referent of the term "intrinsic good" may be found in our views of the relative value of animal and human pleasure. If the man in the street is asked which has the greatest intrinsic value, five minutes of pleasant activity in the life of a human being or five minutes of equally pleasant activity in the life of a dog, I think he will have no hesitation in placing the greater value on that of the human being. Here the pleasure is, by hypothesis, equal. What differs is the level, or degree, of mental activity involved in five minutes of life of man and dog. And it is this difference, I think, that accounts for the view that there is more value in the one than in the other.

REJOINDER BY HAHN

Certain of the issues between Rice's mechanistic naturalism and my contextualism, as developed in his acute analysis and searching comments on my paper, would require far more extended treatment than I can give them here, but I should like to comment briefly on a few points. Though apparently in agreement with me concerning the crucial relevance of metaphysics for psychological systems and theories of value, Rice is troubled somewhat by my devotion to a single metaphysics, contextualism, and a single psychology, the more especially since he places a far lower estimate on the value of at least the former than I do. On the basis of my previous study of contextualism, the view seems to me to have definite advantages over alternative views in theory of perception; and I should like to develop it more fully to see what it has to offer in theory of value. I incline to think that the strengths and the weaknesses of a metaphysics will come out most clearly if we push its interpretation of the relevant facts as far as it will go before concerning ourselves very much with possibly needed supplementation by other views.

With reference to the psychological side of the question, moreover, in view of the admittedly partisan character of the psychologies which have potentially most relevance to theory of value, I prefer working initially from one which fits with my metaphysics; and Tolman's psychology, with certain exceptions, seems to me both to fit in with and to use contextualistic assumptions (though Pepper has made use of this psychology to formulate, in his *Digest of Purposive Values,* a mechanistic theory of value). Since Rice agrees that "Tolman's terms seem well suited to give precise expression to a contextualist psychology," perhaps it is well for a contextualist to continue along these lines and leave other fruitful developments in psychology to the advocates of other views. In pursuing this line of explanation, I might add, the contextualist need not emphasize consequences to the neglect of conditions, for both, and not merely the latter, have a place on his view.

Rice questions my insistence upon the presence of a cognitive reference, an element of reflection in even immediate value; but I shall forego comment on this point to consider briefly another question he regards as more crucial—namely, that of whether the felt quality of an experience can be relevant to considerations of the nature and amount of value afforded by a given end. The felt quality of an experience, or a type of experience, seems to me to be thus relevant, to afford a ground for prizing. I should even grant that in some cases hedonic tone or continued affording of such hedonic tone, might be a ground for prizing, though I doubt that we are justified in holding that "where an experience, or some element of it, is prized on other grounds than its consequences, analysis discloses the presence of positive affective tone in such an experience." An experience may be prized for its vivid, enhanced quality rather than the pleasure afforded; and though this is another point on which further psychological studies are needed, there is evidence to indicate that some of our most interesting experiences lack positive affective tone—as witness, our interest in tragedy.

Though as a contextualist I am skeptical of those experiences which are alleged to look neither backward nor forward but rather to find their whole nature in a self-contained now, I do have some concern for what Rice calls the intrinsic characters of the means-end continuum which would in a sense justify the life processes as a whole; and I think that such contextualistic works as Dewey's *Art as Experience,* Edman's *Arts and the Man,* and Pepper's *Aesthetic Quality,* in their account of vivid, enhanced quality, treat of these characters of experience.

Biological selectivity, 193
Bio-social continuum, 103
Bliss, E. L., 275n
Body, human: wisdom of, 193, 354
Bosanquet, Bernard, 202
Brogan, A. P., 202, 206, 339, 356, 362, 402, 403; theory of value and logic of value-judgments, 191 f.; quoted, 207
Bronk, D., 279n

Cannon, W. B., 278n
Carings-for, identified with valuings, 67; misapprehension of meaning, 71; as *de facto* valuings have a motor aspect, 74; conditions of, 152; attitude taken toward an object, 154; may vary independently of knowing, 147, 303, 309; *see also* Prizing
Carnap, 31
Carr, H. A., 285n
Cartesian dualism, *see* Dualism
Castell, A., 179n
Certainty, quest for, 49
Central nervous field, hedonic tone a function of stresses in, 278
Cherishings, as *de facto* valuings have a motor aspect, 74
Choices, are objects of choice mutually exclusive, 45; demand that philosophy pay attention to social, economic, and political backgrounds of human interests and, 95; values are products of, 96; what excludes them from science, 99; can objective and scientific reports be made about? 100; is realm of choice non-instrumental? 100; is realm meaningful? 101; process of free inquiry as a determiner and criterion of, 102; "end-means" motif, 105; where criterion for, must be found, 107; free intelligent inquiry of supreme consideration in area of, 111; final determiners, 178; necessity of intelligent inquiry as to results, 315
Civil liberties, desertion of, 109
Coercion, physical and emotional, 50
Cognition, relationship between interest and, 34; in behavior, 117, 298; and valuation, 131, 248, 351, 372; function of, 255; functional interdependence of attitude, belief, and, 298; interpenetration of will and, 350
Cognitive statements, 237, 447; and volitional aims, 31, 33, 360

Cohen, Felix, 191
Cohen, Morris, 419
Coleridge, definition of philosophy, 395
Common sense realism, 400, 404, 408
Communication concerning values, search for referents in cases of successful, 78 ff.
Comparative theory of value, 161, 162, 202, 402
Compromise, conflict resolved by, 241 f.
Conation, 377, 378; conative activity, 39; 117 ff. *passim;* source in drive, 250; relations between affection and, in re behavior tensions, 257; sufficient condition for existence of values, 260; manifold ways in which related to affective element in value, 280; are also cognitions (*q.v.*), 351
Conative theories, treatment of striving and feeling, 265-71; appeal to the scientifically minded, 266; classification, 266-71, 405, 406; all types stress motor phases of effort, 272; many make no distinction between intrinsic and extrinsic value, 282; constructed to account for moral and socio-moral values, 309; refuse to search out rational ground of prizing, 462
Conative value, 250 ff., 293, 373; actual object of, 251 ff., 259, 374; potential objects, 252 ff., 259, 373; does not entail judgment, 255; positive wanting in appetitions, negative wanting in aversions, 258, 373; affective values acquire evaluative priority over, 258
Concepts, echoes of primary experiences, 236
Conceptual tools most potent tools, 104
Conditional objects, 253
Conduct, split between intelligence and, 110
Conflict-situation, characteristic background for all inquiry, 106; adjustment through compromise, substitution, and integration, 241
Conjunction, conditioning by, 285
Consciousness, is anything instrumentally good that has no affect upon? 81 ff.
Consistency of values in social pattern, 43-49
Consummatory act, 443; pleasure in, 249 ff., 256 ff., 372
Consummatory quality, Dewey's notion of, 284

309 f.; Lepley, 167, 170-76, 347; Mitchell, 190-210, 348; Morris, 214, 418; Parker, 228-33; Pepper, 260, 377-80; Rice, 289, 460-67
—*Question III*, re logical or scientific status of appraisal, evaluation, as judgment or proposition: discussion by Aiken, 24-31, 360 f.; Ayres, 48 f.; Dewey, 73-77; Geiger, 96-111 *passim;* Hahn, 123; Jessup, 139-43, 352-54, 435; Lee, 163-65; Lepley, 167, 176-83; Mitchell, 208; Morris, 215-19; Parker, 233-41, 396-99, 425-31, 451-54; Pepper, 260, 379, 440-50, 454; Rice, 289
—*Question IV*, whether scientific method is applicable in valuation: discussion by Aiken, 31-36; Ayres, 52-63, 419-21; Dewey, 76-77; Garnett, 88, 89, 318; Geiger, 98-111 *passim,* 326-28; Hahn, 123; Jessup, 126-46 *passim,* 435 f.; Lee, 165; Lepley, 167, 183-89; Morris, 211-22, 415 f., 421; Parker, 241-44, 431-33; Pepper, 260; Rice, 261-88 *passim,* 290
—*Question V*, whether values and valuation should be treated on an individual psychological basis or in socio-cultural context: discussion by Ayres, 44 ff., 302-7; Dewey, 77; Geiger, 97-111 *passim,* 330; Hahn, 123, 124; Jessup, 127 ff.; Lee, 165, 166; Lepley, 167, 169; Parker, 231, 241-44 *passim;* Rice, 290
Digest of Purposive Values (Pepper), 422, 469
Direct apprehension, importance derives from myth, magic, and mores, 305
Direct experience, 160, 303
Disagreement, 143, 185-86
Diseases, pleasurable phases, 459
Disposition and its active arousal, distinction between, 17
Dispositions or attitudes, 6; *see also* Attitudes
Dostoievsky, 459
Drive, in structure of appetition, 247 ff.; conative value ascribed to potential object is the intensity of, 252; absolute end, 254, 372; relation between quiescence-pattern and, 255, 295; every, has a pain threshold, 256; organisms primarily motivated by, 257; refers ultimately to its satisfaction, 369; object actually charged with, 374; oper-

ates through nervous system, 411; expressions of a drive signify the drive, 442
Dualism, between morals and technology, 109; Cartesian mind-body, 148, 149, 203, 339, 340, 346, 400, 401, 405
Dunbar, H. F, 278*n*

Economy, value, 43
Ecstasy, 54
Edel, Abraham, 102
Effect, Law of, 285 f.
Eisenhower, General, 454
Electromagnetic field, 457
Emergence, theory of, 158; social process characterized by, 204; mechanism which takes account of fact of, 457
Emerging values, term, 208
Emerson, Alfred E., 55, 57; quoted, 52
Emotion, emotive theory, 31*n*, 54, 298, 300, 304; resurgence of emotionalism, 49-54; why any importance is attached to emotional judgments, 56; plays big part in life, 58; James-Lange theory, 273, 275; in behavior, 298; importance derives from myth, magic, and mores, 305
Empirical method, 262 ff., 326; need to extend conception of, 413; *see also* Dewey's questions (*Question IV*)
Empiricism, defined, 262
Ends, 69, 70, 194; as fulfillment, 39; final end, 106; satisfaction of the consummation, 195; absolute, 254, 272; relative, 254, 272; *see also* Means and ends
Ends-in-view, 33, 106; ostensible or trial, and real values, 36; provisional objectives for desire, 38; function, 40
Energy, conservation of, 272
Enjoyment, meaning, 6; biological roots: behavioral correlates and conditions, 17; capacity for innocent, 47; mere fact of, not enough to constitute value, 122; data of value includes, 126; satisfaction of consummation of the end experienced as, 195; connection between prizing and, 259; prizeworthy in itself, 461
Enlightenment, race between superstition and, 55
En-valuation, 140
Environment, 104; adjustment between internal and external, 194

476

486

INDEX

Value (*Continued*)
bility of distinguishing several senses of the term, 36, 173-74; ostensible or trial, and real, 36, 39, 367; futility of a purely conative definition, 39; of a means and as a means, 41; general mutuality, 45; matter of degree, 48; determinants, 55; is there any such thing as, which is not the value of some particular thing, event, or situation? 60, 154, 226, 281n; search for referents in cases of successful communication concerning, 78 ff.; criterion of degrees of, in instrumental things and processes, 83; relation of obligation and, 84; brought within scope of scientific investigation, 89; and inquiry, 93-111; is issue of, a matter for technical philosophy? 94; discussion singularly inoperative, 94; definitions not fundamental, 95; nonbehavioral conception of, 98; natural history of, still to be written, 98; processes must be regarded as non-scientific, 101; final, 105; only genuine problems in field of, 113; pre-discussional agreement required, 125; inspectional definition, 130; a post-factual discrimination, 131; putative quality or property, 156, 162, 402; typical standard, 160; distinction between potential object of, and object of potential value, 162; when not a necessary condition for the existence of values, 167, 175 f.; unexperienced, 174; untested and tested, 174; when valuation is a necessary condition for existence of, 175-76, 337; generated by new and changing conditions, 188; point of emergence, 194; facts that distinguish it from inorganic, and from elementary organic forms, 195; direct, 195 ff.; belongs in nature and art, 203; possibility of developing a general relational, melioristic theory as alternative to two-value systems, 203; object of, 204, 252; relation between satisfaction and standard value, 228; appraised from point of view of competing interests, 229; which is intrinsically end, 250; precondition of, 266; correct and incorrect estimates, 267; search for an affective definition of a primary sense of, 280; clarity re nature of, 297, 299; indi-

vidually determined, 303, 309; is felt and achieved, 307; instrumentalists unable to distinguish pseudo-value, 315, 319; as unmodifiable bias-fact, 323; comparison of concepts of life and, 324; viewed as differing only in degree from evaluation, 345; need for achieving through experimental procedures, 347; neither substantive, nor adjectival, but relational, 356, 364; acceptance or rejection of, 359; affective and motor theories, 359; distinction between trial and real, 368, 376; has social dimension, 426, 427, 436; *see also* Dewey's questions
Value-centric predicament, 244
Value data, the beginning of discussion of value, 125; how field found, 126
Value-decisions, put outside area of intelligence, 100; test of, 107; must rest on knowledge, 107
Value economy, 43
Value-expressions, definitions likely to be implicitly persuasive, 18; scientific use of, 18; intended as descriptions, 35
Value-facts, are they bias-facts? 11, 97, 241; belong in behavioral field, 64; different areas of, cited as significant ones, 112; clearer and more certain than metaphyiscal theory, 113; are also descriptive-facts, 131; term, 206; *see also* Facts
Value-feelings, 127, 135
Value field, 64-77, 424; observational and probable, 127 ff.; Dewey's restriction of, 214, 312
Value-judgments, as contrary-to-fact conditionals, 17; scientific use of, 18; as genuine judgments, 22; affective-conative and cognitive factors, 29; denied cognitive status, 31; are they different from other judgments and propositions? 123, 350; may reject, censure, or approve feeling and will, 127; nature of evidence which can verify, 139; descriptive and operational, 139, 425; depend upon facts of dimensionality and interconnectedness of values, 141; two kinds, 160; most fruitful source of error, 163; amenable to investigation by scientific method, 165; relation between judgments of fact and, 183, 216, 427; all instrumental values involve, 255; Brogan's calculus fits structure of, 402;